THE GUARDIAN
YEAR, 2004

THE GUARDIAN YEAR, 2004

Edited by Martin Woollacott

Introduction by Nicholas Hytner

Atlantic Books
London

First published in 2004 by Atlantic Books, on behalf of Guardian Newspapers Ltd.
Atlantic Books is an imprint of Grove Atlantic Ltd.

10 9 8 7 6 5 4 3 2 1

A CIP record for this book is available from the British Library.

ISBN 1 84354 051 7

Printed in Great Britain by MPG Books Ltd, Bodmin, Cornwall
Design by Helen Ewing

Grove Atlantic Ltd
Ormond House
26–27 Boswell Street
London WC1N 3JZ

CONTENTS

INTRODUCTION
Nicholas Hytner

It is axiomatic these days that the press is another branch of the entertainment industry, but during the last twelve months it has often seemed that the theatre has been muscling in on territory more commonly occupied by the press. At the National Theatre, the Iraq war has unavoidably taken centre stage; the subject not just of a powerful new play by David Hare, but also, it turned out, of plays by Shakespeare and Euripides.

The players, said Hamlet, are the abstract and brief chroniclers of the time. Determined to chronicle our times with journalistic immediacy, I asked David Hare to write *Stuff Happens* in six months – an almost unimaginably luxurious deadline for a journalist, but barely enough time for a playwright to synthesize the events of two years and create for them a theatrical structure. Reading this collection, however, I am struck by the reassuring gulf between our trades. *Stuff Happens* is a history play, Shakespearean in form; and in staging it I often found myself repeating what I'd done a year earlier with *Henry V*. In intention, it does to those who reported the war what Shakespeare does to Holinshed (which is not to suggest that Hare is as good as Shakespeare, though maybe James Meek and Ghaith Abdul-Ahad could give Holinshed a run for his money). The theatre invites its audience into a conspiracy. Suspend your disbelief and we'll take you into the White House, and discover together what we feel about its inhabitants. Piece out our imperfections with your thoughts. Think, when we talk of horses, that you see them. Imagine this man is George Bush.

The playwright's art, and the actor's, is to conceal the fact that art generates the illusion of reality and provokes the white heat of emotion and debate. Maybe this book's apparent spontaneity springs from an art that is every bit as rigorous, yet from its first page it often seems to give an unmediated account of the events described and the arguments they provoke. Read in retrospect, yesterday's journalism loses nothing of its urgency. Elena Lappin was locked in a glass-fronted cell 20 miles from Los Angeles Airport on 3 May because she didn't have the right visa. She wrote about it a month later with a terrifying rawness. The degeneration of the American body politic that it seems to represent shows no sign of slowing down.

There are pieces here that are powerful precisely because history has moved on. Angelique Cristafis reports from a Madrid that still thinks it has been bombed by Eta. Max Hastings calls for his Tory friends to ditch the turnip who leads their party. It's hard even to remember the turnip's name now, but almost poignant to experience directly the distress of one of the dispossessed voters he was supposed to represent. It would be nice to think that it won't be too long before history has dispatched Peter Mandelson and Alastair Campbell the same way as IDS, but meanwhile Simon Hoggart's lethal sketch of their Channel 5 gig can't do any harm to history's prospects.

It is beguiling to read Hoggart skewer Mandelson in the same book as Martin Kettle lays into 'culture of contempt towards politicians (and thus of democracy) ... that is too prevalent in British journalism'. Kettle was one of the few commentators who defended the Hutton report, alarmed more by the media's 'avoidable failure to be fair, the want of explanation and the persistent desire for melodrama'. Another gulf opens here between his world and mine. The theatre has never been much concerned with fairness, often at its most vigorous when sceptical of authority and generally weakest when required to show respect. Much art aspires to the state that requires no explanation, which provides the sort of insight that eludes rational elucidation, though a brilliant interview with Andras Schiff, again by Martin Kettle, offers a fascinating stab at explaining how Bach's Goldberg Variations work. It is good, too, to be reminded how much of the *Guardian* has been driven, over the years, by writers with a genuinely informed passion for music.

Chris McGreal and Linda Grant are juxtaposed to much deadlier effect than Hoggart and Kettle. 'They killed my son a few months ago,' says a Palestinian mother to McGreal. 'Here is my son under a granite stone,' says an Israeli father to Grant. As raw and immediate as anything in the collection, these reports could nevertheless have been written last year or the year before or during many of the years before that and probably for years to come. Jonathan Freedland exposes the grotesque hypocrisy of Sharon's 'disengagement' from Gaza with the restrained clarity that distinguishes everything he writes. Having spent six months staging the build-up to the Iraq war, nothing left me angrier than Bush's cynical bullshit about the road map, abandoned with Tony Blair's full support barely a year after it was published, 'the one promise he extracted for his dogged fidelity in Iraq trampled on so publicly'.

Blair is keen for us to move on, though he hasn't been clear yet what he wants us to move on to. He could do a lot worse than to embrace Jackie Ashley's programme, a salutary and eloquent rebuke to anyone who runs any kind of business or institution. This book, meanwhile, ranges wide, preserves the furies and the graces of the last twelve months and seems to propose that it is only by dwelling on what just happened that we can move on with any sense of purpose.

Nicholas Hytner
September 2004

EDITOR'S PREFACE
Martin Woollacott

When Alastair Hetherington, then foreign editor, came to speak to Manchester Grammar School sixth-formers in the mid-fifties, he brought with him a wobbly pile of different kinds of paper and, by way of introducing the boys to the nature of his profession, sorted them out on the table in front of him. Here was Reuters, here the Press Association, there Associated Press. If memory serves, one was pink, one green, one white. Here was telex copy, with big holes at the edges, sent from far away; this was dictated copy, phoned in from nearer but still distant places, like Leeds or Hull; these were typed stories by reporters, the carbons and flimsies floating off into the audience as he plonked them down; these were cyclo-styled versions of the same stories, with scribbles and markings all over them. Then there were column pulls and page proofs, and finally, like a magician producing his rabbit, Hetherington laid a *Manchester Guardian* first edition on top of all the heaps he had already put on the table. It was a way of showing us how a paper was created and how diverse were its sources and processes. Hetherington's talk also reinforced schoolboy pride in our city, of which his paper, like our school, like the Hallé Orchestra, like Manchester University and Manchester United (or Manchester City, according to tribal allegiance), were all equally ornaments.

The *Guardian* now, if far from absolutely paperless, definitively becomes paper only at the end of its production cycle and has a growing constituency of on-line readers. And, of course, it is no longer primarily a Manchester publication. Hetherington, a Scot, himself presided over the move to London, part of that continuing accretion of power and influence to an already powerful capital, which the British deplore but have been unable to restrain. It is difficult now to recall how strongly Mancunians, and those from the other cities and towns which make up the Greater Manchester conurbation, felt about the paper. It was both valued and feared, and experienced as a firm moral hand on Manchester's shoulder. In that wonderful play, *Hobson's Choice*, this ambivalence is expressed for me in the passage in which Hobson, told that his drunken accident might reach the pages of the *Salford Reporter*, replies, '*Salford Reporter*! When ruin and disaster overtake a man of my position and importance, it'll be in the *Manchester Guardian* for all the world to read!'

A number of writers of these prefaces have, over the years, asked whether something Mancunian lingers on, and the answer remains that the *Guardian*, although in London, is not entirely of London. It maintains a certain distance. In Alastair Hetherington's decision to oppose the Suez intervention there was an element of provincial (and Caledonian) doubt about the wisdom and probity of those who decide our affairs in the capital. We may flatter ourselves that we continue doubtful. But there is a further, and dominant, *Guardian* characteristic that connects us with the Manchester past.

There is, at a usually subliminal level, a conversation between a newspaper and its readers which defines both. If the *New York Times*, for instance, says to its readers, 'You know', and *Le Monde* says, 'You understand', the *Guardian* whispers 'You care'. Or, as Julie Burchill put it in her last column for the paper, *Guardian* readers 'Care About Stuff'. An emphasis on superior information, on intellectual grasp, or on moral concern does not, of course, rule out the other qualities. But it cements an agreement with the reader on what should generally be uppermost. Different though they were, writers like Hugo Young, Paul Webster, Norman Shrapnel, Alastair Cooke, Paul Foot and Harry Griffin, to mention only those we have lost during the period covered by this book, were all parties to that contract with the reader.

The span covered is from 1 September 2003 to 31 August 2004. One piece, on the school siege in Beslan, was written a little later but included as we went to press because of the importance of that terrible incident. Selecting the articles has been hard, because there is so much that is outstanding and interesting, yet so much that has to be left out. *Guardian* reporting is getting longer and longer and, whether that is good or bad in itself, it makes choice even more difficult. My thanks to those colleagues who offered unselfish recommendations of other people's copy as well as to those whose eloquent arguments for the inclusion of their own pieces helped me make the decisions. I am also very grateful to Richard Nellson, head of the paper's research department, and to James Bisset, Lucy Moffatt, Joanne Kennedy and Tom Clare, all of that department, who patiently dug out hundreds of pieces from the archive. Ben Mudge helped organize the material electronically. Gina Cross, of the *Guardian* Graphics Department, chased down the cartoons and illustrations, while Roger Tooth, the *Guardian* Pictures Editor, gathered the photographs together. Finally, Lisa Darnell provided vital encouragement and guidance.

Martin Woollacott
September 2004

SURVIVING

5 June 2004

ELENA LAPPIN

Welcome to LA

Somewhere in central Los Angeles, about 20 miles from LAX airport, there is a nondescript building housing a detention facility for foreigners who have violated US immigration and customs laws. I was driven there around 11 p.m. on 3 May, my hands painfully handcuffed behind my back as I sat crammed inside a security van in one of several small, locked cages. I saw glimpses of night-time urban LA through the metal bars as we drove, and shadowy figures of armed security officers when we arrived, two of whom took me inside. The handcuffs came off just before I was locked in a cell behind a thick glass wall and a heavy door. No bed, no chair, only two steel benches about a foot wide. There was a toilet in full view of anyone passing by, and of the video camera watching my every move. No pillow or blanket. A permanent fluorescent light and a television in one corner of the ceiling. It stayed on all night, tuned into a shopping channel.

After ten minutes in the hot, barely breathable air, I panicked. I don't suffer from claustrophobia, but this enclosure triggered it. There was no guard in sight and no way of calling for help. I banged on the door and the glass wall. A male security officer finally approached and gave the newly arrived detainee a disinterested look. Our shouting voices were barely audible through the thick door. 'What do you want?' he yelled. I said I didn't feel well. He walked away.

I forced myself to calm down. I forced myself to use that toilet. I figured out a way of sleeping on the bench, on my side, for five minutes at a time, until the pain became unbearable, then resting in a sitting position and sleeping for another five minutes. I told myself it was for only one night.

As it turned out, I was to spend twenty-six hours in detention. My crime: I had flown in earlier that day to research an innocuous freelance assignment for the *Guardian*, but did not have a journalist's visa.

Since September 11 2001, any traveller to the US is treated as a potential security risk. The Patriot Act, introduced forty-five days after 9/11, contains a chapter on Protecting the Border, with a detailed section on Enhanced Immigration Provision, in which the paragraph on Visa Security and Integrity follows the sections relating to protection against terrorism. In this spirit, the immigration and naturalization service has been placed, since March 2003, under the jurisdiction of the new department of Homeland Security. One of its innovations was to revive a law that had been dormant since 1952, requiring journalists to apply for a special visa, known as the I-visa, when visiting the US for professional reasons. Somewhere along the way, in the process of trying to develop a foolproof system of protecting itself against genuine threats, the US has lost the ability to distinguish between friend and foe. The price this powerful country is paying for living in fear is civil liberty.

None of this had been on my mind the night before, when I boarded my United Airlines flight from Heathrow. Sitting next to an intriguingly silent young man who could have been a porn star or a well-camouflaged air marshal, I spent most of the eleven-hour flight daydreaming about the city where he so clearly belonged and that I had never visited. My America had always been the east coast: as tourist, resident, journalist and novelist, I had never ventured much past the New York–Boston–Washington triangle. But I was glad that this brief assignment was taking me to sun-kissed LA, and I was ready to succumb to its laid-back charm.

The queue for passport control was short. I presented my British passport and the green visa waiver form I had signed on the plane. The immigration official began by asking the usual questions about where I was staying and why I was travelling to the US. It brought back memories of another trip there to write a series of articles about post-9/11 America for the German weekly *Die Zeit*. I had written about commuters who preferred the safety of train travel to flying, and about a wounded New York that had become a city of survivors. I had seen a traumatized, no longer cockily immortal America in a profound state of mourning. But it had seemed to me that its newly acknowledged vulnerability was becoming its strength: stunned by an act of war on its own soil, Americans had been shocked into a sudden hunger for information about the world beyond their borders.

'I'm here to do some interviews,' I said.

'With whom?' He wrote down the names, asked what the article was about and who had commissioned it. 'So you're a journalist,' he said, accusingly, and for the first time I sensed that, in his eyes, this was not a good thing to be. 'I have to refer this to my supervisor,' he said ominously, and asked me to move to a separate, enclosed area, where I was to be 'processed'. Other travellers came, waited and went; I was beginning to feel my jetlag and some impatience. I asked how long I'd have to wait, but received no reply. Finally, an officer said, noncommittally, 'It seems that we will probably have to deport you.'

I'm not sure, but I think I laughed. Deport? Me? 'Why?' I asked, incredulously.

'You came here as a journalist, and you don't have a journalist's visa.'

I had never heard of it. He swiftly produced the visa waiver (I-94W) I had signed on the plane, and pointed to what it said in tiny print: in addition to not being a drug smuggler, a Nazi or any other sort of criminal, I had inadvertently declared that I was not entering the US as a representative of foreign media ('You may not accept unauthorized employment or attend school or represent the foreign information media during your visit under this program').

My protestations that I had not noticed this caveat, nor been alerted to it, that I had travelled to the US on many occasions, both for work and pleasure, that I had, in fact, lived there as a permanent resident and that my husband was a US citizen, as was my New York-born daughter, all fell on deaf ears. He grinned. 'You don't care, do you?' I said, with controlled anger. Then I backtracked, and assumed a begging, apologetic mode. In response, he told me I would have to be 'interviewed', and that a decision would then be taken by yet another superior. This sounded hopeful.

Finally, after much scurrying around by officers, I was invited into an office and asked if I needed anything before we began. I requested a glass of water, which the interrogating officer brought me himself. He was a gentle, intelligent interrogator: the interview lasted several hours and consisted of a complete appraisal of my life, past and present, personal and professional. He needed information as diverse as my parents' names, the fee I would be paid for the article I was working on, what it was about, exactly, and, again, the names of people I was coming to interview. My biography was a confusing issue – I was born in one country, had lived in many others – who was I, exactly? For US immigration, my British passport was not enough of an identity.

The officer said, pointedly, 'You are Russian, yet you claim to be British', an accusation based on the fact that I was born in Moscow (though I never lived there). Your governor, went my mental reply, is Austrian, yet he claims to be American. After about three hours, during which I tried hard to fight jetlag and stay alert, we had produced several pages that were supposed to provide the invisible person in charge with enough material to say yes or no to my request to be allowed entry. My interrogator asked one last obligatory question: 'Do you understand?'

'Yes, I understand,' I sighed, and signed the form.

The instant faxed response was an official, final refusal to enter the US for not having the appropriate visa. I'd have to go back to London to apply for it.

At this moment, the absurd but almost friendly banter between these men and myself underwent a sudden transformation. Their tone hardened as they said that their 'rules' demanded that they now search my luggage. Before I could approach to observe them doing this, the officer who had originally referred me to his supervisor was unzipping my suitcase and rummaging inside. For the first time, I raised my voice: 'How dare you touch my private things?'

'How dare you treat an American officer with disrespect?' he shouted back, indignantly. 'Believe me, we have treated you with much more respect than other people. You should go to places like Iran, you'd see a big difference.'

The irony is that it is only 'countries like Iran' (for example, Cuba, North Korea, Saudi Arabia, Zimbabwe) that have a visa requirement for journalists. It is unheard of in open societies and in spite of now being enforced in the US is still so obscure that most journalists are not familiar with it. Thirteen foreign journalists were detained and deported from the US last year, twelve of them from LAX.

After my luggage search, the officer took some mugshots of me, then proceeded to fingerprint me. In the middle of this, my husband rang from London; he had somehow managed to locate my whereabouts, and I was allowed briefly to wipe the ink off my hands to take the call. Hearing his voice was a reminder of the real world from which I was beginning to feel cut off.

Three female officers arrived to do a body search. As they slipped on rubber gloves, I blenched: what were they going to do, and could I resist? They were armed, they claimed to have the law on their side. I was an anonymous foreigner who had committed a felony, and 'those were the rules'. So I was groped, unpleasantly, though not as intimately as I had feared. Then came the next shock: two bulky, uniformed and armed security men handcuffed me, which they explained was the 'rule when transporting detainees through the airport'. I was marched between the two giants through an empty terminal to a detention room, where I sat in the company of two other detainees (we were not allowed to communicate) and eight sleepy guards, all men.

I would have been happy to spend the night watching TV with them, as they agreed to switch the channel from local news (highlight: a bear was loose in an affluent LA neighbourhood) to sitcoms and soaps. Their job was indescribably boring, they were overstaffed with nothing to do, and so making sure I didn't extract a pen or my mobile phone from my luggage must have seemed a welcome break. I listened to their star-struck stories about actors they had recently seen at LAX. We laughed in the same places during *Seinfeld*, an eerie experience. I was beginning to think I could manage this: the trip was a write-off, of course, but I could easily survive a night and a day of this kind of discomfort before flying back. But then I was taken to the detention cell in downtown LA, where the discomfort became something worse.

Though my experience was far removed from the images of real torture and abuse at Abu Ghraib prison in Iraq, it was also, as one American friend put it, 'conceptually related', at distant ends of the same continuum and dictated by a disregard for the humanity of those deemed 'in the wrong'. American bloggers and journalists would later see my experience as reflecting the current malaise in the country. Dennis Roddy wrote in the *Pittsburgh Post-Gazette*: 'Our enemies are now more important to us than our friends ... Much of the obsession with homeland security seems to turn on the idea of the world infecting the US.'

On a more practical level, this obsession, when practised with such extreme lack of intelligence (in both senses of the word), as in the case of my detention, must be misdirecting valuable money and manpower into fighting journalism rather than terrorism. Ordinary Americans, rather than the powers that be, are certainly able to make that distinction. According to an editor at the *LA Times*, there has been a 'tremendous' response from readers to the reporting on my case, and I have received many emails expressing outrage and embarrassment. The novelist Jonathan Franzen wrote, 'On behalf of the non-thuggish American majority, my sincere apologies.'

These would have been comforting thoughts the following morning when I was driven back (in handcuffs, of course) to the communal detention room at LAX, and spent hours waiting, without food, while the guards munched enormous breakfasts and slurped hot morning drinks (detainees are not allowed tea or coffee). I incurred the wrath of the boss when I insisted on edible food. 'I'm in charge in here. Do you know who you are? Do you know where you are? This isn't a hotel,' he screamed.

'Why are you yelling?' I asked. 'I'm just asking for some decent food. I'll pay for it myself.'

A Burger King fishburger never tasted so good. And it occurred to me that a hotel or transit lounge would have been a better place to keep travellers waiting to return home.

As documented by Reporters Without Borders and by the American Society of Newspaper Editors (ASNE) in letters to Colin Powell and Tom Ridge, cases such as mine are part of a systemic policy of harassing media representatives from twenty-seven friendly countries whose citizens – not journalists! – can travel to the US without a visa, for ninety days. According to ASNE, this policy 'could lead to a degradation of the atmosphere of mutual trust that has traditionally been extended to professional journalists in these nations' and it has requested that the state department put pressure on customs and immigration to 'repair the injustice that has been visited upon our colleagues'. Someone must have listened, because the press office at the department of Homeland Security recently issued a memo announcing that, although the I-visa is still needed (and I've just received mine), new guidelines now give the 'Port Directors leeway when it comes to allowing journalists to enter the US who are clearly no threat to our security'. Well, fine, but doesn't that imply some journalists are a threat?

Maybe we are. During my surreal interlude at LAX, I told the officer taking my fingerprints that I would be writing about it all. 'No doubt,' he snorted. 'And anything you'll write won't be the truth.'

22 November 2003

IAN JACK

In my father's shed

My mother outlived my father by more than twenty years and died in 2002. In all those years, and in the many months since my mother's death, two outlying provinces of the household remained undisturbed: the garden shed and the coal shed, both arranged and ruled by my father in his role as gardener, repairer of domestic goods, coal-drawer, shoe-mender and, long ago, hen-keeper to the family and toy-maker to his children. The coal shed occupies the hollow space beneath the outside stair. It last kept coal in 1979, when the local authority installed central heating and 'modernized' every flat in the street, chucking out a lot of fine old panelled doors and 1920s tiled fireplaces while they were at it. The garden shed dates from the mid-1930s, when my parents got their first flat with a bathroom and a garden. That wasn't this flat, the flat they lived in ultimately, but one far away in Lancashire. When we moved, the shed came with us, taken apart in Bolton and re-erected in Fife, where it has stood for the past fifty years, though recently rather shakily and leakily.

It was the condition of the garden shed that made me decide last month to sort its contents and transfer those worth keeping to the coal shed, while we decided what to do with the flat. But first we would need to sort and discard the contents of the coal shed, to make room. Both places were crowded with things. My father wasn't a man who easily threw them away. Sometimes I felt like one of his heroes, Howard Carter, whose discovery of Tutankamen's tomb had thrilled my father as a young man. A Carter, in this instance, who not only rescued Tutankhamun for history but miraculously remembered how he had been when alive.

'There's a funny thing right at the back like a barrel with two bulges,' my wife said when we'd cleared a path through the coal shed. I went to look. Not one barrel, but two, stacked one above the other. They were metal but surprisingly light. Zinc was the material. The date 1930 was stamped on their bottoms. Each had a small oblong shelf protruding from a part of the rim. Dolly-tubs! I remembered how a brick of red soap would lie on this small shelf when not actually in my mother's hand as she scrubbed clothes on a Monday. But why two dolly-tubs? I tried to reconstruct the process. One filled with hot water for washing, the other with cold for rinsing; a pole to press down and stir the clothes, its wood furred below a certain level due to its frequent immersion; a washboard to scrub with; a mangle to squeeze; on dry days clothes poles to stretch the rope on the drying green; on wet days a clothes horse suspended from the ceiling on pulleys.

But why the name dolly-tub? Why did that whitening powder come in a packet labelled Dolly Blue? Because, according to my later consultation of the *Shorter Oxford*, from about 1790 dolly became a pet name for a child's doll and was then further applied to 'contrivances fancied to resemble a doll', hence (dialect) 'a wooden appliance with two arms, and legs or feet, used to stir clothes in wash tub, called a d.-tub'.

I told my brother about our find. He remembered wash days with a shudder in his voice: 'All that steam and the smell of damp cloth, and the food not being quite up to scratch on Mondays because Mum had no time – a couple of boiled potatoes and a bit of bacon, that kind of thing.' I remembered that, too, but also the light-green cabbage that came on the same plate: a combination that preceded the (then, to me) tastier era of tinned spaghetti and which I'd happily now sit down to, any time.

We dug further around the coal shed and discovered evidence of its original purpose: a sack, the fragments of a small shovel. Coal had landed here once a week with a thud and then a dull rattle as it escaped its hundredweight sack, upended by the men who brought it down the path from the Co-op coal lorry, men who wore leather vests with steel studs on the back. Had they really shouted, 'Small c-o-a-l and brickettes' in the street? I guess they must have done, because that's what my parents sang whenever they heard Mario Lanza or David Whitfield on the radio, their voices being judged to be about as good as the coalman's.

The coal then came up two flights of stairs in buckets, carried by my father and sometimes by me. I don't want to bring Orwell into this, to add grandeur to the ordinary, but his passage in *The Road to Wigan Pier* about the essentialness of coal to the comfort of British life – to the nancy-boy poets, and so on – remained absolutely true long after he wrote it. Without coal – and coal in the kitchen cupboard, not at some distant power station – no heat. Without heat, no hot water. Without hot water, far less frequent washing of the person, armpits and groins, and none at all of clothes. The first noise I heard every morning as I drowsed in bed was the scraping of the grate and the curling of newspaper, the scratch of a match. Without coal we would have been cold and dirty. Even with it, I am sorry to say, baths were weekly. When the wind got up, we would hear the quick clatter of the whirler on the chimney pot, which was meant to promote the up-draught and which, for some reason (the *Shorter Oxford* is no help here), we called a 'granny'. On the streets, many women far younger than grannies had legs mottled in pink and red through the habit of pushing up their skirts and warming themselves by the fire. We called this 'fire tartan'. All this, you might say, was part of the departed culture of coal, and the coal shed.

The garden shed was even fuller. Some items stood out: my mother's heavy cast-iron griddle for scone-making, an antique blowtorch, the cobbler's last on which my father had re-soled the family's shoes, the vice that had once gripped the wood that became my lovely model yacht, as well as the wooden railway engine made from factory leftovers. We passed through layers of biscuit, toffee and tobacco tins (Huntley and Palmer, Sharp's – 'The Word for Toffee' – Bulwark, Walnut Plug), which contained neatly categorized screws, nails, tacks, bolts, hammers and files. Eventually we got down to my father's three toolboxes – he had been a fitter all his life – which were locked and had to be crowbarred open to reveal many spanners, many chisels, many bolts, and spirit levels and steel rulers.

We took most of the stuff to the dump, though I kept a dolly-tub with the idea that it might be a plant-plot. Recycling is the thing. A man showed us the various skips: this one for household refuse, this one for metal, this one for wood. In they went – the last, the griddle, the files, the chisels, the tobacco tins – with banging finality. It took several trips. I thought: how strong my parents must have been, how physically strong and skilful, to have used so many things to make and maintain so many things, including us.

17 September 2003

LOUISA YOUNG

That rainbow again

So there I was, sitting in Johnny Cash's front room in Hendersonville, Tennessee, about ten or twelve years ago. He'd been with journalists most of the day and I was the last. A couple, I knew from chatting to them, were hacks with less than no interest in country music. I was worse – I was a fan.

He's looking a little tired, and a little fed up, in a polite way. The room is dim, lots of furniture, glass-fronted cabinets full of June's crystal and cut-glass collection.

'So,' I say, 'are you still the Man in Black? Can you tell me why?'

He goes into the stock answer: quoting the song lyrics, about wearing black for the poor and the beaten down. But I know all that – I'm wondering if that's still how he feels, thirty years later. 'I mean, are you still doing it?' I ask. 'For the same reasons?'

'Now?' he says gently. There's a wry look in his eye. 'Now more than ever ...'

We get to talking about the evils of the world. I mention a song he recorded: 'Here Comes That Rainbow Again', by Kris Kristofferson. It's a small drama. A pair of Okie kids, a waitress and some truckers are in a roadside café. The kids ask, 'How much are the candies?'

'How much have you got?' the waitress replies.

'We've only a penny between us.'

'Them's two for a penny,' she lies.

A trucker notices. 'Them candies ain't two for a penny,' he says.

'So what's it to you?' she replies. Then when the truckers leave, she calls, 'Hey, you left too much money!'

'So what's it to you?' they reply.

It sounds hokey – but it's not, not the way Cash sang it, and certainly not in its first incarnation; the song is based on an intensely touching scene from Steinbeck's *The Grapes of Wrath*. I mention this.

'You know that book?' he says, his face lighting up.

'I love that book,' I say. 'And you know that book!' Why am I surprised that Johnny Cash has read Steinbeck?

'Know that book?' he says. 'I was that book.' He smiles at me. It's kind of like being smiled at by Monument Valley, or the Hoover Dam. He pronounces it 'Grapesawrath', like 'Rose of Sharon' is pronounced Rosasharn.

'You like that song?' he says, and he pulls over his guitar.

What, really? He tunes up. I can't quite believe my fortune here. He starts to play, and he sings that song. In his front room. That pure, deep, thundery, reverberating voice, just across from me on the other sofa.

'All that was part of my childhood,' he says, when it's over. Then he tells me about the flood when he was a kid, that leads to 'Five Feet High and Rising'. 'You like that song?' Yes I do. He sings it for me.

'What else, now,' he says. 'You like "Man in Black", don't ya?'

Well yes, I do. And 'I Walk the Line', and 'The Tennessee Flat-top Box', and 'The Long Black Veil', and 'Ring of Fire', and 'The Ballad of Ira Hayes', and 'John Henry', and some I'd never heard before.

So, we were there all afternoon, in that shadowy room, and it was one of the finest afternoons I've ever spent, and definitely the worst interview I've ever done. We hardly talked. This is how he's choosing to communicate, I realized. By singing. Which from a singer is not unreasonable – in fact, it's possibly more right, more true, than answering interview questions. Also – I turned the tape recorder off. Why? A one-on-one personal Johnny Cash concert on the sofa and you turned the tape off? Why? Answer: because I knew this was not something which could be repeated. Couldn't be, shouldn't be.

He did say one thing I remember: 'You have to be what you are. Whatever you are, you gotta be it.'

And I came out realizing that I didn't want to be a journalist any more.

Although it was journalism that had given me this extraordinary day, I didn't want to be the person oohing and ahhing on paper about Kris Kristofferson, John Steinbeck and Johnny Cash. I wanted to be the person writing and making the stuff that makes the other people ooh and ahh. Cash loving Kristofferson's song; Kristofferson loving the way he sang it; both of them loving Steinbeck's book. I wanted to be one of them. Yeah, I know. But I might as well admit it.

Somebody took a photo with my camera of Johnny Cash and me standing grinning outside his house, squinting against the low spring sun. He's in black, I'm in green. He has his arm round my waist. He picked me a daffodil from his front garden, gave me a kiss, and then I went home, to give up journalism, bit by bit, and start trying to be what I was: someone who wanted to create.

I had the daffodil on my desk while I wrote my first book. I still have it – a little dried-up papery ghost of a thing, reminding me that that's what integrity means: being what you are.

Johnny Cash died on 12 September 2003 at the age of seventy-one.

20 October 2003

EMILIA DI GIROLAMO

Marked for life

In October 1985, I attended a pop concert against my parents' wishes. By the end of the night I had been gang raped in circumstances similar to those alleged by the seventeen-year-old girl accusing several men, including Premiership footballers, of raping her at the Grosvenor House hotel. The men who raped me weren't celebrities and they weren't even rich. In reality they were nobodies. But to me, a fourteen-year-old girl, only 4ft 11in tall, with very limited experience of the world, they were glamour personified.

The men, who were about six years older than me, were in a pop band, playing village halls and occasional support slots to bigger bands. They talked about a world I knew nothing of, a glamorous world of recording studios and record contracts. Their faces pouted out of photographs in the local paper. They were local celebrities. They were a gang with catchphrases I didn't understand, mostly referring to sex acts, and little hand signals that my best friend and I emulated and giggled over in the playground at lunchtime.

That night, I watched them on the stage high above me and when they smiled at me, pointed me out and waved, I felt grown-up and glamorous, and important. I had been seeing one of them, Liam, for three weeks, and had met Phil and Simon once or twice. Liam asked me to arrange to stay out the night of the concert. He suggested I lie to my parents and say I was at a girlfriend's house, so we could 'spend the whole night together'. I would have done anything he asked because I had fallen in love with this man who spoke of grown-up things, who said, 'I can't believe you're only fourteen, you look so much older' – though the photos I gaze at now tell me that I didn't. He also told me that he couldn't believe I was a virgin when I first met him. Couldn't believe his luck, more like.

So I arranged my alibi and went to the concert. I wasn't plied with champagne but with cheap vodka. I didn't drink much of it and certainly wasn't drunk. I was never a teenage drinker. After the concert, the men were on a high, enjoying the attention of their groupies. I waited while they circulated for half an hour and then they came over to me. Liam asked if I had made the arrangement to stay out. I said yes and he shuffled me out of the door quickly, followed by the others.

Liam asked if I would like to stay at Simon's house where we would 'all be together' or go back to the fourth member of the band's bedsit. (He was also a model and actor and was having a party.) I didn't understand the hidden meaning. I thought he wanted us to spend the night alone together at Simon's, so this was what I chose. This is what, he later told me, he took as my consent. Asking me where I wanted to stay was taken as consent to group sex.

The year before, our county had been terrorized by a rapist known as the Fox. Malcolm Fairley broke into houses during the night and raped women at gunpoint in front of their husbands. My father, desperate to protect his family, would stay up all night after barricading the windows. He was determined no rapist would get near us.

I felt safe, with my father watching over me. That was what I thought rape was, a man climbing through your window in the night. I never thought it would happen at a local music festival, the first I had ever attended, after days of begging and pleading with my parents. I didn't think Liam would spend three weeks getting to know me, before passing me on to his friends.

I was taken to a small modern house. There was a black leather sofa, black ash veneer furniture and Athena pictures of semi-naked women. It was a 1980s bachelor pad, I suppose, though I had never been in one before. I still had a Pierrot duvet cover. The men said they were tired and that we should go to bed. I followed them up the stairs, led by Liam. When we reached the room I looked around, confused. I asked Liam where we would sleep. He said, 'We'll all squeeze in together.'

As the other men got into bed I asked Liam if we could sleep downstairs, but Phil was growing impatient and told us to hurry up because he wanted to sleep, and Liam jumped at his command, hurrying me along. I left my shirt and underwear on and got into bed next to the man I had trusted, feeling embarrassed, knowing that I wouldn't sleep a wink.

The light went out and Liam started touching me. I whispered, no, said it wasn't right with his friends there, and asked again to go downstairs. But he wasn't even listening. He had sex with me. I won't say this was rape, though it was statutory rape because of my age, but I was uncomfortable and uncooperative, hating every second of it. I thought that if I just let him do it, it would be over and I would be able to wait out the long hours until it was safe to go home without arousing my parents' suspicions. But then the light was on and Phil said, 'Can we join in?' And Liam said, 'Be my guest.' None of them asked me.

I won't torture the reader or myself with the details of what they did to me. Suffice to say, I was the victim of a 'ramming' – one of their catchphrases. I was raped by Simon and Phil in turn, each with the 'assistance' of the other. To this day I can still feel the chill metal of Phil's nipple-rings pressing against my flesh as I was torn apart in every sense. I often wake from nightmares where I am having the breath squashed out of me, a huge weight pushing down on me and the smell of his aftershave in my nose.

In Nicholas Meikle's words, like the seventeen-year-old girl, I 'stayed for breakfast', though I didn't eat a thing. I watched them stuff their mouths with fried-egg sandwiches and waited for them to drive me home. I couldn't call my parents or go home early, or they would know I had lied and, like many teenagers, I was scared. So I waited and they drove me home. I ran a hot bath and began a ritual that would last for years, scrubbing my flesh in an attempt to get clean. Friends frequently joke about how obsessive-compulsive I am when it comes to cleaning but the truth of this obsession lies in that night.

I have lived with the shame and consequences of their actions for the past eighteen years. The emotional repercussions have been enormous. Soon after the attack I attempted suicide but I never told a soul my secret. The men, however, bragged about the 'three's up' as they put it. It wasn't seen as rape, though. It was seen as me being a slag, a willing participant in group sex, even though I was a child with no experience of men like them, and almost no experience of sex. I have suffered from clinical depression, panic attacks, nightmares and many symptoms of post-traumatic stress disorder ever since. The physical consequences of that night scarred me, too, and the physical damage I sustained during the attack has had serious health implications for me ever since.

I have dealt with my disgusting secret without therapy or help of any kind, other than the endless support of my husband and family. But now, everywhere I turn, I am faced with the story of a teenage girl who says she was gang raped by a group of men who had wooed her with their celebrity. It is in every paper, on the radio and the television. It isn't hearing about it through the media that causes my anger, but rather the comments and opinions of others who question what she was doing drinking in those sorts of bars, pursuing those sorts of men, going back to hotel rooms with strangers, and in their judgement of her behaviour, I feel judged – though they know nothing of what happened to me.

Teenage girls will always be impressed by older men, particularly those who promise a world of glamour and glitz that is far away from their experience. For some girls it might be a Premiership footballer but for others it will just be the lad in her class who everyone fancies, or the singer in a local rock band.

I applaud the seventeen-year-old's ability to tell her parents and go to the police. Much of my anger is at myself for my inability to do these things. At the age of fourteen, I could only see that it was my fault. I lied to my parents, I agreed to go to the house, I didn't know how to stop the men raping me and so how could I face my family with that amount of shame? I didn't report the rape until many years later, and even then I decided in the end that I couldn't go through with it. I had moved away and wanted to forget it had ever happened.

At a book signing, in my hometown, sixteen years on, Liam turned up. I had him ejected. Some months later, Phil turned up at a friend's party just a few minutes from my home. He said hello as if we were old friends. Furious, I confronted him with the truth.

'The thing is, Emilia,' he said, 'we really liked you. We thought of you as one of the gang.'

But I was never part of their gang. Their gang was about subjecting schoolgirls to humiliating, degrading sexual acts. What these footballers are accused of is nothing new. The frightening part is that this has always happened. It happens in small towns and cities up and down the country, on council estates and in middle-class suburbs. It happens to nice girls and girls who get drunk, in bars and clubs, and it will go on happening until this issue is tackled head on.

I don't think Phil or Simon believed at the time that they were committing rape. They viewed this type of sex as 'normal'. Liam later told me he thought I was participating. 'You never said anything,' he said. When confronted with the victim's perspective they are forced to consider their actions in an entirely different light. I asked Phil to imagine his fourteen-year-old daughter subjected to an identical situation to mine. Would this be rape? I wanted him to consider me as a person, a child rather than a piece of meat. 'Looking at that scenario [the rape],' he said, 'I can paint it blacker in my head than probably you can...' I don't think so, but I do believe that he is now aware that rape isn't just grabbing a woman in a dark alleyway at knifepoint.

Young men need to be taught that it isn't rape only when a girl screams and shouts and kicks. There are different types of power and sometimes a woman doesn't even need to be held down. I didn't shout or scream or kick. I lay with my eyes shut tight, crying silently while Phil held Simon by the hips and pushed him into me, brutally, shouting, 'Ram, ram, ram' and laughing. Afterwards, he asked me if I had come.

8 December 2003

PETER PRESTON

Ends

It is inevitable, inescapable, either brutal or banal. It lurks at the back of our minds awaiting its moment. Anyone for death today? The grim reaper never knocks twice.

And yet, in a way, that's precisely what happened to me. I had two fathers, and they both died. One went suddenly in the night. He was young and fit, and an ambulance, screaming alarm, took him away. We three small children never saw him again. The other father, the friend who stepped into his shoes, died last week, more than half a century later. There was nothing sudden here, just a slow, gallant slide into darkness.

You can go for decades barely thinking about death itself, thinking only of *Six Feet Under* and Ethiopia and French pensioners expiring as the temperature tops a hundred. A passing show. I saw no more of it for years after my first father died, and then found it again on the smoking battlefields of the Punjab and the flooded fields of East Bengal, where human bodies and cows, both bloated, both stinking, lay face up in the mud.

That was vicious death, delivered by force of arms or force of nature. But mostly, these days, it seems more random than that. There's the house in the village I lived in where Jacqueline, the six-year-old with short, blonde hair, set fire to her bedroom and perished in a trice, leaving only a soot-stained window behind. There's the hospice where Jo, the golden girl from the next village, was finally defeated by MS, unable to speak, only pleading in her eyes. There, still etched on the memory, is Peter Niesewand, the bravest *Guardian* reporter of them all and handsome as a Greek god, turned cruelly to dust. There's the three-hour delay on the train to Manchester after a child played cowardy custard on the line, and lost.

The pace, of course, quickens as life winds on. There are the hospitals and nursing homes and offices where mothers and in-laws died, all of them, as it happens, in a moment. 'I shall die this week,' my mother-in-law announced to the world one morning, and by that evening she was gone. But my second father went more gradually, more gingerly.

First, five years ago, his legs began to betray him. He would fall and fall again. Parkinson's? That was the eventual diagnosis. He couldn't cope and there was no means of coping with him at home. He needed nursing care and accepted the need uncomplaining, immured in a kindly place. Where was the man who had rowed and charged up and down rugby pitches as player, then referee? Even been the county over-seventies golf champion. He was here, in his chair. Where was the big, bellowing man who'd borne the weight of building a business on his shoulders? Here, sitting by the window, watching the lorries he would never load again pass by. There was nothing remotely exceptional here, you see. It was an everyday tale of decline and fall. But yet I think I learned more from it than from any other death.

He was a good, kind man. He had friends and family popping in to see him all the time, and a wonderful second wife always on hand. He was loved. And we sat by the bedside last weekend and said the things you say when a ninety-two-year-old body, cough-wracked by pneumonia, swilling in morphine, finally gives up the ghost: 'it'll be a mercy really'; 'he wouldn't want to go on like this.'

And, well, that was right enough, in its leaden way. But what did he think, lying there in shallow, chest-rattling sleep, hand sometimes twitching, eyes sometimes opening for a second at the sound of a new voice? Perhaps, I hope, he felt the togetherness in the room, the way those who came and went supported each other because they could sense the impending loss. And beyond that, perhaps, he felt a sense of completeness.

I've always, over those fifty-plus years, reckoned I knew what dying would be like, because after my first father died I hovered for a week between life and death myself, drifting in and out of consciousness. They thought that, probably, I'd had it; and I remember vividly, in its dreams and images, what dying seemed to be like.

Now, perhaps again, Father Two was drifting himself, remembering, hearing voices. A sort of peace and shutting down. And because he was old and frail, because there was no chance or wish for recovery, there was also a line drawn firmly.

Death came twenty-four hours after the doctors had said it would come. He never took instructions literally. The stream of visitors had stopped for a few moments; he was alone and he slipped away. When I came back, too late, the body was laid on the bed with a Bible and a rose and the business of certificates and funerals was under way.

He'd wanted a cardboard coffin and the barest of crematorium farewells. Come later and have a good party. Be happy, not sad. Remember him for what he was. Which is easy to do because, in his simplicity and warmth, the memories thrive. But where was death at the last, and its sting-a-ling-a-ling?

It arrived as a beneficence, as a natural state accepted without fear or remonstration. It had an essential symmetry.

Where sudden death cuts short, here was the full story, beginning and end, and the gathering of those who wanted to salute and tell each other about him. The life had been there, in the gasping for breath, and then, almost tangibly, it departed. Does that life, the life independent of body, go on once the great chill descends? Probably not, but certainties fray when the things you know come full circle. And somehow, this week, I can't bring myself to care much about top-up fees.

ARGUING

16 September 2003

HUGO YOUNG

In abject thrall

Secret intelligence, we have certainly learned, is not a science. For some people this is a grave disillusionment. Brought up on fictionalized versions of an impenetrable world, they perhaps imagined it had access to super-secret stuff that quite transcended the vague banalities they could read in the press. It came from deep within, couched with an exactitude the rest of us were not meant to know about. New prime ministers, first entering this secret world, have attested to their fascination and, in the beginning, their ready credulity. I suspect that Tony Blair was one of these.

I'm prepared to believe that he published September's dossier of claims against Saddam Hussein for good reasons. He wanted to admit the voters to some of the secret intelligence. The trouble is that it had lost its magic. He deprived it of such precision as it ever had. From being the ice-cold product of cautious analysts, it became political. Mr Blair became his own chief intelligence analyst. And his attitude became the opposite of cool. It was meant to serve a wholly political purpose.

On the one hand, we now know that senior intelligence people were categorically advising in February that their assessment pointed towards more terrorism not less if we went to war in Iraq. Blair simply rejected it. On the other hand, when remonstrating with sceptics in private he pleads the mind-blowing evidence that crosses his desk from many intelligence people at home and abroad as if it were raw gospel truth. If you could only see it, he says. If you knew what I do, you would never dream of challenging the need to go to war to stop weapons of mass destruction falling into the hands of terrorists.

Intelligence, in other words, has become a flexible friend, a political instrument. Its chief agent, John Scarlett, moreover, has become a crony of Number 10 rather than a distant and detached truth-teller. Among the many corruptions this war has brought about, we can therefore say, is the degradation of what was once advertised, and globally agreed, to be a jewel in the Whitehall apparatus.

This happened for a prior reason, which is not new but deserves frequent repetition. The intelligence, culminating in the dossier, had to fit a prior decision. This has been the great over-arching fact about the war that Blair will never admit but cannot convincingly deny. He was committed to war months before he said he was. Of course, he wanted it buttered up. He wanted a UN sanction. He fought might and main to push Bush in that direction. But he was prepared to go to war without it.

He needed this skewed intelligence to make the case, and he didn't really mind what he had to say to get it. He had made his commitment to Bush, stating among other extraordinary things that it was Britain's national task to prevent the US being isolated. But he was also in thrall to the mystic chords of history. He could not contemplate breaking free of ties and rituals that began with Churchill, and that both Downing Street and the Ministry of Defence – the Foreign Office is somewhat wiser – have cultivated, out of fear and expectation, for decades.

He was driven by something else, to which none of his predecessors, not even Margaret Thatcher, has succumbed. Without exception they all kept their eye on the British ball. They could all make a kind of case for a profitable connection between the hard British national interest and occasional benefits from the special relationship. For Blair, in his Bush-Iraq mode, this has been a lot more theoretical: the theory of pre-emptive intervention in a third country's affairs, for moral purposes, at the instigation of the power whose hyperdom he cannot resist.

What does this mean? That we have ceased to be a sovereign nation. There's been a tremendous amount of talk about sovereignty in recent years. It became, and remains, the keynote issue at the heart of our European debate. Something to do with sovereignty was clearly operative in the Swedes' decisive rejection of the euro: more, many observers suspect, than the minutiae of economic policy – important, in the Swedish case, though those were. What it means to be an independent nation is a question that touches the wellsprings of a people's being. Yet it is one that our leader, as regards this war, has simply disguised from his people, egged on by sufficient numbers of North American papers and journalists who seem to be wholly delighted at the prospect of surrendering it.

I do not believe this obtuseness can last for ever. If there is one virtue in the unfinished history of the Iraq war, it is that the British may finally wake up to what the special relationship is doing to their existence. Do I have to qualify that with assertions of my decades of affection for America, my sense that very many Americans detest this war as much as I do, even my optimism that if George Bush can be forced from office a certain sanity will return to the world? Probably it has to be said. Meanwhile, though, Mr Blair has to live with a bond he has willingly created, from which Jack Straw, we now learn, thanks to John Kampfner's revelatory research, apparently made a hopeless attempt to save him at the eleventh hour.

The episode tells you once again that this is Blair's war and, except for Bush, hardly anybody else's. There are two ways to see him.

The first is as the great deceiver. Driven by his own juices, compelled by moral imperatives obliterating pragmatism, forced by those compulsions to avoid levelling with his people, in the grip of a high belief in the need for the intervention of good guys against bad guys in this new world where the enemy is to be found everywhere and nowhere. Throttled by a history he refuses to relinquish. This could yet, in certain circumstances, be the end of him, if our one-man intelligence chief is found to have twisted truth, for whatever good motive, too far.

There is another person emerging from this mist, though. This is a great tragic figure. Tony Blair had such potential. He was a strong leader, a visionary in his way, a figure surpassing all around him at home and on the continent. His rhetorical power was unsurpassed, as was the readiness of people to listen to him. He had their trust. He brought credibility back to the political art.

It is now vanishing, though not before our open eyes. All this seems to be happening below the radar screen of opinion polls. The country carries on at least as semi-normal. Our boys are out there dying in a futile war, to which there is no apparent end, certainly not one that we control. The leader goes about his business, awaiting without too much trepidation, we may suppose, a suitably ambiguous Hutton report. Yet something big is happening. This concerns not merely him and whether he survives, but our country and what becomes of it in abject thrall to Bush and his gang.

Hugo Young died on 23 September 2003 at the age of sixty-four. This is the last piece he wrote for the Guardian.

25 September 2003

SEUMAS MILNE

The meaning of freedom

'Is this what they mean by freedom?' asked Zaidan Khalaf Mohammed on Tuesday after the US 82nd Airborne Division had killed his brother and two other family members in Sichir, central Iraq, in an air and ground assault on their one-storey home. The Americans had come, he said, 'like terrorists', while US forces claimed they had only attacked when they came under fire. No evidence was offered and none found.

These killings are after all merely the latest in a string of bloody 'mistakes' by US occupation forces, including the repeated shooting of demonstrators, murderous attacks on carloads of civilians at roadblocks and this month's massacre of members of the US-controlled Iraqi police force. In most countries, any of these incidents would have provoked a national or even an international outcry. But in occupied Iraq, US officials feel under no pressure to offer more than the most desultory explanation for the destruction of expendable Iraqi lives.

Six months after the launch of the invasion, it has become ever clearer that the war was not only a crime of aggression, but a gigantic political blunder for those who ordered it and who are only now beginning to grasp the scale of the political price they may have to pay. While George Bush has squandered his post-9/11 popularity, raising the spectre of electoral defeat next year as American revulsion grows at the cost in blood and dollars, Tony Blair's leadership has been irreversibly undermined by the deception and subterfuge used to cajole Britain into a war it didn't, and once again doesn't, support. Every key calculation the pair made – from the response of the UN to the number of troops needed and the likely level of popular support and resistance in Iraq – has proven faulty.

Whatever the formal outcome of the Hutton inquiry and the displacement activity of the government's row with the BBC over an early-morning radio broadcast, it has unquestionably confirmed that Alastair Campbell and other Downing Street officials did strain every nerve to create the false impression of a chemical and biological weapons threat from Iraq, a threat that it is increasingly obvious did not exist. Even more damagingly, the inquiry has revealed Blair's reckless dismissal of the February warning by the Joint Intelligence Committee that an attack on Iraq would increase the threat of terrorism.

Combined with the failure to find any weapons, the admission by the former chief UN weapons inspector Hans Blix that he now believes Iraq long ago destroyed them, and the discrediting of a litany of propaganda ploys (links with al-Qaida, the forged Niger uranium documents, the 45-minute weapons launch claim), Hutton has helped to strip the last vestige of possible legal cover from the aggression and shift opinion against the war.

So has the chaos and resistance on the ground in Iraq, where guerrilla attacks on US soldiers are running at a dozen a day and US casualties are now over 300 dead and 1,500 wounded. Latest estimates of Iraqi civilian war deaths are close to 10,000, while in the security vacuum hundreds more are now being killed every week, a point driven home by yesterday's bomb attacks in Baghdad and Mosul. In Baghdad alone, there has been a 25-fold increase in gun-related killings since the invasion, from twenty to more than five hundred last month. Paul Bremer, the head of the US occupation authority, insists 'there is enormous gratitude for what we have done', and the dwindling band of cheerleaders for war have seized on contradictory and questionable Baghdad opinion surveys conducted by Western pollsters to back the claim.

But it is not the story told by US Defense Department officials, who last week conceded that hostility to the occupation and support for armed resistance were growing and spreading well beyond Iraq's Sunni heartlands. Hence George Bush's humiliating return to the UN this week. But any attempt to prettify US-led colonial rule in Iraq in the colours of the UN (already the target of armed attacks) is no more likely to work than the League of Nations mandate Britain secured in Iraq in the 1920s. As then, the US and Britain insist in true colonial style that Iraqis 'are not ready' to rule themselves, and the hostility to President Chirac's demand for an early transfer of sovereignty confirms that the US will willingly hand over power only once it is confident of controlling the political outcome.

The real meaning of US promises of freedom and democracy was spelled out this week by two decisions of the US-appointed, and increasingly discredited, Iraqi governing council. The first was to put the entire economy, except oil, up for sale to foreign capital, combined with a sweeping free-market shock therapy programme, pre-empting the decisions of any elected Iraqi government. The second was to impose restrictions on the Arabic satellite TV stations al-Jazeera and al-Arabiya for their reports on the resistance to the occupation.

The reality is that the occupation offers no route to democracy, which in Iraq is unlikely to favour US interests. What is needed is a political decision to end the occupation, a timetable for early withdrawal and the temporary replacement of the invading armies with an acceptable security force, perhaps provided by the Arab League, while free elections are held for a constituent assembly under UN auspices.

But none of that is likely to happen unless the US, the UK and their allies find the burden of occupation greater than that of withdrawal. Unpalatable though it may be, it is the Iraqi resistance that has transformed the balance of power over Iraq in the past six months, as it has frustrated US efforts to impose its will on the country and the US public has begun to grasp the price of military rule over another people. By demonstrating the potential costs of pre-emptive invasion, the resistance has also reduced the threat of US attacks against other potential targets, such as Iran, North Korea, Syria and Cuba.

Bush, Blair and the newly cowed BBC absurdly describe those defending their own country as 'terrorists' – as all colonialist and occupation forces have done – and accuse them of being 'Saddam loyalists'. In fact, the evidence suggests a much more varied political make-up, but if Bush and Blair have managed to achieve a partial rehabilitation of Ba'athism in Iraq they have only themselves to blame.

There is now a popular majority in Britain against the war and the occupation. Blair has repeatedly emphasized his personal judgement in the decision to join Bush's war – and that judgement has been shown to be fatally flawed. Iraq has become the crucible of global politics and the testbed for the US drive to global domination. It is in the interests of the security of us all that there is now a political reckoning at home and in the US for that aggression.

15 January 2004

DEREK BROWN

Zero, just to begin with ...

It is pretty universally acknowledged that an informed world view is not a prerequisite for success in daytime television. Even so, Robert Kilroy-Silk's anti-Arab diatribe is not only offensive and stupid; it also speaks of a startling degree of ignorance. 'We owe Arabs nothing,' he wrote. 'Apart from oil, which was discovered, is produced and is paid for by the West, what do they contribute?' Arabs, according to the sage of the sob story, are 'suicide bombers, limb amputators, women repressors'.

It is slightly ironic that, at the time this balderdash was printed in the *Sunday Express*, Mr Kilroy-Silk was topping up his studio tan in a Spanish beach resort. Had he been in the mood for a slightly more demanding cultural shift, he could have gone to the south of that country, to Granada in the province of Andalucia, where he could have seen some of the most beautiful architecture in Europe. Arab architecture. Planned, built and exquisitely decorated by the ancestors of the people Mr Kilroy-Silk apparently thinks so inferior.

It is not only in Spain that Arab architecture has left a European mark. The pointed arch, so eagerly adopted by medieval builders and known today as gothic, was an idea copied from the East, and brought to the West by the early Crusaders. And while those religiously crazed bigots were burning and slaughtering in the Holy Land, Arab poets, mathematicians, astronomers, philosophers and scientists were advancing human civilization to unprecedented peaks of sophistication.

The Abbasid caliphate of Baghdad, which flourished for half a millennium from about AD 750, was arguably the most dazzling of regimes the world had seen up to that date. Arab scholars picked up from where the Greek ancients had stopped centuries earlier, and extended human understanding in virtually every field. As every schoolboy knows, the mathematical concept of zero was discovered by Arabs, when northern Europeans were still wearing horns on their helmets. In fact, as a *Guardian* reader pointed out this week, every schoolboy is probably wrong: the zero idea almost certainly came from India, but, crucially, it was first written down by an Arab.

Writing is a key part of the Arab nation's bequest to the world. Paper was introduced from China before the end of the first Christian millennium, freeing Arab writers from the costly straitjacket of parchment and papyrus, some three to four hundred years before paper reached Western Europe. The result was a torrent of poetry and prose, philosophy and scholarship, learning and entertainment. This was the era of *The Thousand and One Nights* and of vast public libraries. There were astronomical observatories, pharmaceutical laboratories and medical schools. And most of these were flourishing before England's King Alfred was born.

Mr Kilroy-Silk might argue that these are spent glories, and that the modern Arab culture is debased. He would be compounding his ignorance to do so. More poetry than prose is published in Arabic today. The visual arts are vibrant. Music, both popular and traditional, is flourishing. Calligraphy, that most elegant of arts, continues to fascinate users of the flowing Arabic scripts. Arab cuisine – Lebanese mainly, but increasingly Egyptian and other North African – is being belatedly discovered in the West.

For sure, the Arab world has more than its share of despotic rulers and religious bigots. But to lump everyone together under Mr Kilroy-Silk's puerile labels is not only false, but plain daft. Cultures and their values are not only measured by historical achievement, but also in terms of day-to-day living.

I lived in the Holy Land for nearly four years as the *Guardian* correspondent. I was greeted and treated by virtually every Arab I met with the greatest courtesy and grace, even in the most trying and sometimes downright tragic circumstances. Sometimes I would poke a little fun at close friends by making up absurdly flowery compliments in the local style – my best invention was 'May the womb of your favourite she-camel never wither!' – and invariably they would giggle helplessly. Indeed, the Arab propensity for laughter and friendship is one of my fondest memories of those times.

The Arab people have been traduced enough in the Western world and – let's be honest – the Western media. It is perhaps time we poured our collective bile over a more deserving target. Cheap, mindless, voyeuristic, shallow, nasty, lobotomized daytime telly, to take a random example.

18 August 2004

POLLY TOYNBEE

What's the rationalist to do?

Last month, the website of an organization called the Islamic Human Rights Commission made me the 'winner' of their 'Most Islamophobic media personality' award. It has caused me a bombardment of emails of both extreme pro- and anti-Islamic poison, each one more luridly threatening than the last. The occasional note of reason from moderate Islamic groups is so weak it hardly makes itself heard. I had challenged the legitimacy of the idea of Islamophobia and warned of the danger to free speech of trying to make criticism of a religion a crime akin to racism. I pointed out yet again that theocracy is lethal. Wherever religion controls politics it drives out tolerance and basic human rights. The history of Christianity has been the perfect exemplar, a force for repression whenever it holds any political sway. It only turns peace-loving when it is powerless.

People led by some unalterable revealed voice of God cannot be tolerant of the godless. At present it is Islamic states that head the danger list – though the dread power of southern Baptists in US politics endangers world peace, as do extreme Jewish sects holding power in Israel. Women are always the main victims, since extreme religions express their identities through male priestly supremacy and disgust of women.

To give a flavour of the Islamic Human Rights Commission awards, Nick Griffin of the BNP won the most Islamophobic British politician award, Jacques Chirac and Ariel Sharon shared the international Islamophobic politician award, and Islamophobe of the year was George Bush. That's the company I found myself in.

When Griffin was interviewed on *Newsnight* after he was filmed saying disgusting things about Muslims, bizarrely accusing Islam of encouraging the rape of non-Muslim girls, he quoted my name in general support. So these days criticizing any aspect of Islam risks landing you down among the worst racists. Other voices claim you for their cause. There is a particularly virulent swirl of extreme Hindu emails spreading fear and loathing of Muslims. But it's not all one-sided. A dangerous stream of Muslim anti-semitic venom also billows out on to the airways, inciting maximum hatred against Jews and sometimes Christians.

The government wants to make incitement to religious hatred a crime, caving in to a vociferous Muslim campaign, although it is unlikely to make a spit of difference to these rabid religious enmities. (If the government really wants to foster religious harmony, it should abolish all religious schools, not build more.) To reassure outraged rationalists, ministers say that only a couple of people a year are expected to be prosecuted under it. So, why bother? That will inflame the religious even more as they refer case after case, expecting the law to protect their right not to be offended by mockery or criticism. They want religion placed in a realm beyond ordinary argument – and it is beginning to happen.

Fear of offending the religious is gathering ground on all sides. It is getting harder to argue against the *hijab* and the Koran's edict that a woman's place is one step behind. It is beginning to be racist for teachers or social workers to object to autocratic patriarchy and submission of women within many Muslim communities. Islamic ideas that find the very notion of democracy incompatible with faith are beginning to be taken seriously by those who should defend liberal democracy.

Of course most Muslims are not extremists. They speak of the peacefulness of their faith – as most religious people do. But they still too rarely speak out against terror when they should be combating their own extremists and being seen to do it. Moderate groups protest often against arrests of Muslim terror suspects, while the Muslim Council of Britain has sent out just one tepid call to mosques to cooperate with the police. Moderates excuse, rather than refute, the many ferocious verses calling for the blood of infidels in their holy book, verses that justify terror. Both the Koran and the Bible ought to be banned under the new law, since both are full of God's incitements to smite unbelievers.

It is bizarre how the left has espoused the extreme Islamist cause: as 'my enemy's enemy', Muslims are the best America-haters around. The hard left relishes terrorism: a fondness for explosions and the smell of martyrs' blood excites their revolutionary zeal, without sharing a jot of religious belief.

More alarming is the softening of the brain of liberals and progressives. They increasingly find it easier to go with the flow that wants to mollify Muslim sentiment, for fear of joining the anti-immigration thugs who want to drive them from the land.

The liberal dilemma over Islam is not unlike the prevarications of some over communism in the cold war. To attack the atrocities of the reds put you in bed with the anti-socialist Thatcher/Reagan red-baiters. What would George Orwell write about Islam now? He would probably ignore what others said about the company he kept, shrug off those claiming him for their own ends and plough his own furrow, speaking out against both the danger of religious fanaticism and the Muslim-hating racists – the polite ones in *The Times* immigration panic articles or those with steel-toed boots on the streets of northern towns.

There is a coherent non-Islamophobic position and Turkey holds the key. Here is a democratic Islamic society, where the radical secularizing reforms of Kemal Ataturk make it a model for states needing to escape a theocratic past. It is progressing fast to meet human rights and economic criteria for joining the EU and should be welcomed with open arms, as a symbolic embrace for moderate secular Islam. Giscard d'Estaing's claim that the EU is 'Christendo' was sheer racism, the same deranged clash-of-civilizations thinking that led to the disastrous Iraq war.

Expecting a terrorist attack on Britain soon, this week the Muslim Council of Britain and chief police officers are preparing a booklet for Muslim households, warning them to prepare for a backlash. If these grim events happen, it will be more important than ever to keep a rational perspective on both the Muslim community and its back-lashers. Fellow-travelling with terrorism, either within the Muslim community, or by the left and woolly-minded progressives, will not serve.

It will be more important than ever to stand like Voltaire, ready to defend Muslims, their right to be here and to practise their beliefs, against the growing swamped-by-aliens talk. But if we want to stop the right demonizing Islam, it would be wise to be more outspoken against its deformed branch that fosters terror. Muslims must also accept the right of others to criticize religions without smearing any critic as a racist.

1 April 2004

LEADER

Towards a British Islam

Several details about the eight young men arrested in raids across the Home Counties this week stir much thought. They are all British-born. They do not live in areas of high deprivation, but in places like Crawley, Ilford and Slough. Some have young families. None fits the conventional profile of Islamist terrorists as alienated, isolated immigrants. If this is suburban Islamism, it poses difficult questions about Britain's record in integrating the Muslim community and in fostering a secure, strong sense of a British Islamic identity.

There are many in the Muslim community whose warnings, through the early 1990s, of a radicalized generation fell on deaf ears. They would argue that Britain has not so much failed to integrate Muslims, as failed even to try. As they saw the traditional authority structures of their community undermined in the urban West, they saw the dangers of a disorientated youth, vulnerable both to drugs and Islamism. Organizations like the Muslim Council of Britain at the interface of state and Islam struggled to establish and maintain their credibility with both. The state's apparatus of multi-culturalism, with its emphasis on ethnicity rather than religious identity, served Muslim needs ill, they claimed. They would point to a catalogue of neglect towards the Muslim community, evident in high unemployment and high educational underachievement, particularly among Pakistani and Bangladeshi males. They argue that the response to setting up Muslim schools was too slow, and that boys' vital religious instruction in mosques on Saturdays has remained in the cultural clutches of religious authorities back in Pakistan or Bangladesh. The resources were inadequate to promote a vibrant Islam of which these British youngsters could be proud.

The crucial ingredient which radicalizes this kind of community disaffection into some individuals undertaking acts of extreme violence is the international context. It began with the slow international response in Bosnia, but now spans the globe from Chechnya and Palestine to France where the sisters cannot wear the *hijab*. The perception everywhere is that the proud, expansionary faith of Islam is under attack. That makes a faith in which the *ummah* (international community of believers) is central and, when combined with modern mass communications, quite literally explosive. Worryingly, this international context – in particular the war on Iraq – is now sapping the will of the British Muslim community to integrate, as a recent *Guardian*–ICM poll found.

Britain faces a pressing task of mapping an effective strategy of engagement with Islam, one that spans both the global and local contexts. It is about when and why we embark on wars with Muslim nations, but it is also about the kinds of schools and estates which are built and the methods used by police against Muslims. This may take the British state into new territory – funding the training of imams, supporting mosques which run Arabic and scripture classes – and it is vital to listen to those who have been closest to the development of the Islamist threat over the last two decades. This includes a fundamental re-examination of our understanding of integration that does not simply entail minorities conforming to a British prescription; it challenges secular liberalism to offer more than polite distaste.

It is helpful, given the current sense of fear, to bear in mind a useful precedent. In 1795, in the midst of war with France, Britain began to fund the Catholic Maynooth seminary in Ireland to stop students going to France to be trained. The example may seem arcane, but at the time it was contrary to all the principles of a Protestant state. National emergency dictated that piece of British pragmatism – and it may do so again.

19 March 2004

MARTIN WOOLLACOTT

Why are we in the Middle East?

Why are we in the Middle East? This is the real question that the Madrid bombs pose for Europe and the United States, and for the nations of that region themselves. The struggle in which we are all caught up is, ultimately, neither about Iraq nor about terrorism narrowly defined.

The intra-Western quarrel over Iraq and the growing fear of terrorism tend to obscure the fact that those almost certainly responsible for last week's assault on the Spanish people are not just against American intervention in Iraq but against all kinds of Western action and influence in their region. They even go beyond that to deny that the Muslim and Western worlds impinge upon one another naturally, are shaped by some common traditions and are subject to the same forces. It is, indeed, the reality of converging societies and cultures against which they are in revolt, aiming at a separation as brutal as it is unrealistic.

The new Spanish prime minister has called the occupation of Iraq a fiasco. Maybe it is, maybe it isn't. But that is in the end a tactical issue, concerning the best forms of Western action in the Middle East, and the best choices for Middle Easterners themselves.

It is also yesterday's issue, for the Iraq intervention can now only be modified, not undone. To make policy in order to win points in an argument that is essentially over is irresponsible, whichever side of the argument is sustained, whether by American Republicans in Washington or Spanish Socialists in Madrid. We have to return to the fundamental fact that the intention of al-Qaida and its allies and associates, the driving aim of this ideology, is not only to get Western forces out of Iraq, but to get the West in all its manifestations out of the whole region. Not just its soldiers, but its businessmen, clerics, scholars, teachers and aid workers. And not just Westerners, but those Arabs who have allegedly become Westerners in their hearts.

It is the contention of al-Qaida and its allies, or at least it is the illusion that guides these groups, that Western support for Arab regimes and for Israel, and the insidious Western cultural influence that goes along with that support, are the two great obstacles standing in the way of a purification and renewal of the Muslim world. Once the West has been cowed into a retreat, then the real war for power and religious dominance in the Middle East can begin.

Given the complex realities of the societies they imagine they will at some point control, and the utter inadequacy of their own resources – other than for destructive purposes – their ambitions are certainly doomed to fail. But on the way to that failure they can clearly do grave damage to both civilizations.

It has to be said that 'Why are we in the Middle East?' is nevertheless a legitimate question, as it has been ever since Napoleon landed on Egyptian shores in 1798. The same mixture of motives evident then – to liberate, to modernize, to learn and understand, but also to bend to our purposes and to exploit – is still visible today. It may be possible to say that exploitation is a less prominent element today than it was in the past. That depends on how the oil industry, Western economic activities and advocacy of free markets, on the one hand, and Western political relations with the sclerotic regimes that rule much of the Middle East, on the other, are perceived. But a simple theory of dependency and control is not convincing. Middle Eastern regimes appear to be simultaneously dependent and autonomous, cooperative and cantankerous, open to advice and heedless of it; or, in other words, not too different from other nations the world over.

Still, could 'we', however defined, just go, as the al-Qaida types wish? Would that be better for us, in terms of protecting ourselves from terrorist attacks, and might the outcome in the Middle East be better if we could somehow leave them to fight out their internal quarrels on their own? Merely to put the question shows how unreal is the notion of departure. We can't leave because of oil, because of Israel, because of the possible further spread of weapons of mass destruction and, not least, because of the way in which Europe and the Middle East affect one another economically, socially and culturally.

Above all, this is a zone in demographic upheaval as its youthful population races ahead of local capacities to socialize, educate and employ. This is a phenomenon that rocks Iran as much as Egypt, that exacerbates the conflict between Israelis and Palestinians, and that unavoidably overflows the region, as it exports both its best and its worst, its able and hard-working migrants as well as its angry extremists.

Yet the very diaspora that makes Europe and America vulnerable to attacks is also a resource in preventing attacks. Who can doubt that the specialists, agents and translators tracking the terrorists are already being drawn from the ranks of that diaspora, and more will be in the future? This is only one of hundreds of connections, benign and malign, that tie us together. There is no escaping the embrace in which Europe, America and the Middle East are locked.

Given this embrace, one thing that is not going to happen, it can be predicted, is that outside attempts to influence the Middle East will cease. Another is that such attempts, although they may be better judged, will always be risky and have unpredictable consequences. The American right-wingers who urged intervention in Iraq on the Bush administration had the idea that a transformation of the region could spring from a single dramatic act. A year later it is clear that, while the theory may still ultimately prove to hold some truth, it could be a long time before we find out. Preventing Iraq from becoming a disaster rather than generalizing its success across the region, while simultaneously defending, and not always successfully, against terror attacks, are the problems of the day.

In times of such upheaval, separation has its attractions, as does isolation. The Middle East seethes with notions about how the West is undermining, destroying and ruling from behind. In Europe, a dual anti-semitism, directed at both Jews and Muslims, can be traced to the same cause. So can a certain kind of anti-Americanism, distinct from measured criticism of American policy, which seeks to trace every problem and danger back to Washington.

As Spain demonstrates, it may be that in future the Western leaders who will have to deal with the consequences of the Iraq intervention will not be those who led it. But deal with it they must, as well as take other decisions that may prove equally hazardous, if the pernicious idea is to be defeated that the West and the Islamic world have separate futures linked only by hostility.

17 February 2004

DAVID AARONOVITCH

Was I wrong about Iraq?

A year ago last weekend up to a million anti-war marchers took to the streets of London, and I couldn't be one of them. With the exception of those who now offer their support to the murderous armed 'resistance' in Iraq, the many thousands who protested against the war are – unlike me – uncontaminated by any responsibility for the bad things that have happened since. And right now, that is quite an enviable situation to be in. Kind colleagues, thoughtful colleagues smile gently at me and wonder aloud when I will say those three little words that they are so confident they will never have to utter – 'I was wrong.'

Well, was I? Haven't the failure to uncover even a single anthrax shell, and the car bombs going off every few days around Baghdad combined to show that people like me got it wrong? Forget all the oil and imperialism stuff, weren't we mistaken on our own terms? I'll attempt to show where I have got to on all this, and to be as honest as I can. There are plenty of debating points that could be made but – for once – let's not make 'em.

From the outset of the Iraq debate I was a WMD agnostic. I knew that security sources, leaking regularly to sections of the press, argued that the regime had maintained biological and chemical weaponry since finally admitting – in 1995 – what it had for so long denied. But I wasn't convinced. I am a journalist, not a prime minister, and I don't have to base any part of my judgements on the tales of spooks. It seemed unlikely to me that Saddam Hussein would ever dare openly to use such weapons, if he had them, as he had earlier done against the Kurds and the Iranians. Unlikely, but also not impossible. And Saddam's failure to comply with UN resolutions (and, my God, he certainly failed to comply, beginning with resolution 687 and ending with 1,442) had also locked us into a cycle of sanctions and suffering that seemed unstoppable. This cycle was then, as much as events in Palestine, poisoning the air of the Middle East. Sanctions plus Saddam – in effect, Western policy after 1991 – was a killer.

Even so, for most of 2002, as the war drums grew ever louder, I dithered about the best way out. In the early autumn I wrote: 'I am with Al Gore in his attack on the astonishing way in which the hawks of the Bush administration, led by Dick Cheney, have squandered the goodwill of the post-September 11 world.' I continued: 'They have created the clear impression that they do not care whether the inspectors go back in, or even whether every dot and comma of every UN resolution is adhered to. Their objective is exemplary regime change, and that's that.'

I too wanted Saddam gone, but I was looking for some nice, multilateral, centre-left way of accomplishing it. In that context I found little to help me in the famous September dossier, which I wrote about in the week of its publication. The 45-minute claim, now legendarily supposed to be the 'central' justification for war, passed me by altogether. I argued that the proper response to what I called a 'restrained' document was a new UN resolution, 'renewing and updating the tasks of the inspectors, and setting a deadline for Iraqi compliance'. Such a resolution was passed. The inspectors went back in; Saddam still didn't fully comply. I began to hope that he wouldn't, and wondered whether some folk – including the French government – actually cared whether he did or not.

Last week my colleague, Jonathan Freedland, dealt with what he called the 'comedy' of George Bush's search for why the quest for WMD has turned up nothing. 'And to think,' he wrote '[Bush] could have known all the facts without firing a single shot – if only he had let Hans Blix and his team of UN inspectors finish their work.' But I now realize that there would not have been such a moment. Blix would never have been sure, and the US and UK intelligence services, as Hutton showed, would always have believed – and told their political masters – that something remained. Saddam's history, and the world after September 11, meant that such a comforting certainty couldn't be ours.

But, as Polly Toynbee recalled recently, I have to deal with what I said on this page as the heavy bit of the military campaign ended last April. The key sentence was: 'If nothing is eventually found, I – as a supporter of the war – will never believe another thing I am told by our government or that of the US, ever again. And more to the point, neither will anyone else. Those weapons had better be there somewhere.' According to that, my rattle should be well out of the pram by now.

I deserve to be reminded of such a bombastic bit of posing. Even so, the bit about 'anyone else' is clearly true. The government has lost a great deal of trust precisely because the weapons haven't been found, and because the Gilliganesque charge that Number 10 somehow lied about their presence, has stuck. The trouble is that – partly as a result of the Hutton inquiry (the evidence, not the report) – I don't believe the government did lie. As the MoD intelligence dissident Brian Jones wrote to the *Independent* last week: 'I cast no doubt on Mr Blair's integrity. He evidently believed that Iraq possessed a significant stockpile of chemical or biological weapons and expected them to be recovered during or soon after the invasion ... such a discovery would have enhanced, rather than undermined, "the global fight against weapons proliferation".'

Perhaps I might allay disappointment by blaming Blair et al for being too credulous, or too willing to adopt the precautionary principle, in order perhaps to maintain solidarity with the Americans. But I invite open-minded readers to consider this: had there been a dossier released detailing WMD proliferation in, say, Libya, and blaming rogue Islamicist scientists from, say, Pakistan, I would have been just as (or more) sceptical than I was over Iraq. Yet last week Mohammed El Baradei, head of the International Atomic Energy Agency, said that Abdul Qadeer Khan, who has admitted trading nuclear information and equipment with countries including Libya, was 'the tip of an iceberg for us'. What now seems extraordinary is that Iraq may not have been part of the submerged mass. Perhaps Butler will tell us why our government thought otherwise.

So much for WMD. For 'liberal interventionists', however, the Iraq issue had another, more significant dimension. Wasn't war, in the end, the only way of bringing down the tyranny of Saddam, and wouldn't that war end in an Iraq – and a Middle East – that was safer and freer than before? On this, above all, was I wrong?

16 April 2004

JONATHAN FREEDLAND

Sharon's folly

Most observers of the conflict between Israelis and Palestinians threw away their rose-coloured spectacles long ago. But if they were to put on a pair now, they would be stunned by what they see. Ariel Sharon, godfather of Greater Israel, travelling to Washington to win America's blessing for a surrender of territory he fought so hard to keep. Hard-man Sharon, still renowned for his 1982 surge into Lebanon, now preaching pull-out from Gaza. No wonder President Bush embraced Sharon's gesture, hailing it as 'historic and courageous'.

But take off the rose-coloured glasses and what do you see? Yes, the Israeli prime minister proposes 'disengagement' from Gaza, but that is only half the picture. The other half is a promise to keep hold of large chunks of the West Bank, those which now house more than 200,000 Jewish settlers. Sharon sees this as a quid pro quo: Israel gives up Gaza and in return gets to keep choice cuts from the West Bank, not for the time being or until a final peace deal but, as Sharon puts it, 'for all eternity'.

It is a mark of his achievement that Sharon has persuaded the United States to bless this move. By packaging it as a withdrawal and a painful concession, he has won what few thought possible: US backing for the long-held dream of Sharon and the Zionist right – a permanent Israeli grip on crucial segments of the West Bank.

That's why Sharon looked fit to burst with pride at the White House podium on Wednesday. From his point of view, he had just shaken hands on a great deal. Gaza is a burden rather than an asset, a wretched place seething with poverty and violence, and of scant historic resonance for Jews. Giving it up is painful only to the most zealous of Israeli nationalists.

In return he has won a reversal of decades of US policy: no longer does Washington regard settlements as illegal and 'obstacles to peace' but instead sees them as 'new realities on the ground' to be recognized. By keeping them under Israeli rule, what's left of the West Bank will be sliced into a Swiss cheese that can never be the 'viable' Palestinian state Bush still promises, thereby preventing the two-state solution which is surely the best hope for both peoples. As if that were not enough, Bush threw in a bonus, explicitly echoing the Israeli position that any return of Palestinian refugees will have to be to the future Palestinian state, not Israel.

Defenders of the Bush–Sharon move say that this is not quite as dramatic as it seems. Even the doves behind last year's Geneva accords acknowledged that the final borders between Israel and Palestine would not be precisely on 1967 lines, and recognized that most refugees would not return to Israel.

But this is different. The five settlement blocs Sharon has in mind amount to a much larger sweep of territory than earlier peace plans envisaged. Nor did Bush suggest that Israel offer any of its own pre-1967 territory in a compensatory land swap, as Geneva advocates. Besides, there is a world of difference between two sides negotiating a compromise – à la Geneva or the Clinton plan of 2000 – and one side, backed by the world's sole superpower, deciding the final dispensation without so much as talking to the other party.

This is a break not only from Bush's own road map – which called for a negotiated rather than imposed settlement – but also from thirty-seven years of US policy, under both Democratic and Republican administrations. It confirms the extent to which Bush's is the aberrant presidency, a period future historians will marvel at as a rupture from all that had gone before. The abandonment of even the attempt to appear to be an honest broker in the Middle East, along with the doctrines of pre-emptive war and unilateralism, are departures from the post-1945 US consensus with no precedent.

It has a kind of logic: Bush knows that supporting Sharon will please his predominantly conservative Christian, pro-Israel constituency, and a foreign policy achievement can only help in an election year marred by bad news from Iraq. Harder to fathom is why Tony Blair should go along with such a shift. He persuaded a reluctant parliamentary Labour party to vote for war on Iraq last year with the promise that he would push Bush to act on Israel and Palestine. His reward was the much-delayed publication of the road map, which was hardly a great triumph, merely a set of toothless guidelines and a hoped-for timetable. Now even that is in shreds, and yet Blair smiles and takes it, welcoming Bush's green light to Sharon as a positive 'opportunity'.

It's beginning to look humiliating for Blair – the one promise he extracted for his dogged fidelity in Iraq trampled on so publicly. You would think now would be the moment for Blair to show some daylight between himself and Bush, if only for his own self-respect. Will that happen today in Washington? Don't bet on it.

22 May 2004

KATHARINE VINER

War and pornography

I received some horrific photographs by email yesterday. Purporting to be from Iraq, they depicted the sexual abuse of women by US servicemen. On some, *chadors* were hitched up over the women's heads. On others, the women were naked while they were raped by groups of men. It is impossible to tell whether the photographs are real – those images we know have been seen by American senators – or faked. They make you sick to your stomach. And they look strangely familiar – like the XXX films in hotel rooms, like those 'Live Rape!' emails sent to internet users, like porn.

If the photographs are genuine, they are the visual evidence of the sexual abuse of Iraqi women – abuse we already know is common, with or without these grotesque images. We know that such images exist, because a US government report confirmed it. And we know that Iraqi women are being raped throughout the country, because both Amal Kadham Swadi, the Iraqi lawyer, and the US's own internal inquiry say that abuse is systemic and widespread. We also know this because all wars feature the abuse of women as a by-product, or as a weapon: the First World War; the Second World War; Bosnia; Bangladesh; and Vietnam – where the gang rape and murder of a peasant woman by US soldiers was photographed in stages by one if its participants. The ancient Greeks considered rape socially acceptable; the Crusaders raped their way to Constantinople; and the English invaders raped Scottish women on Culloden Moor.

But even if the pictures are mocked up, it makes you wonder where the images came from. Some woman, somewhere, had to be raped, or make it look as though she were being raped. The poses, the large numbers of men to one woman, the violence – they have all the hallmarks of contemporary porn. Indeed, there is suspicion that the photos are part of a gruesome new trend – the manufacture of films showing the rape of women dressed as Iraqis by men dressed as US servicemen.

There's a difference, of course, between the making of pornography for money and the photographing of pornographic poses as war trophies: the consent of the woman involved. But to the consumer of these images, there's no way of knowing if there's been consent or not. They look the same.

Modern porn has become increasingly savage. 'You're seeing more of these videos of women getting dragged on their faces, and spit on, and having their heads dunked in the toilet,' says even pro-porn campaigner Nina Hartley. At the same time, the multibillion-dollar porn film industry, bigger than Hollywood, is widely seen as acceptable; just this week, *EastEnders* actor Nigel Harman told *Heat* magazine: 'I have always wanted to make porn; I think the industry is very underrated.' It is aggressively mainstream.

Nevertheless, right now the American pornography industry is in shock. Not only has the military stolen its thunder, with ritual sexual humiliations of its own performed for the camera, but also three performers have tested positively for HIV, which means that no porn films will be made for sixty days, until all actors are tested. So, in an intriguing quirk of timing, while the making of porn itself is halted, pornography is still being generated – by US soldiers.

Lara Roxx is eighteen, and arrived in California's San Fernando Valley, the capital of the US porn industry, only days before she contracted HIV. She had moved down from Canada with the aim of making quick money. She was infected while being penetrated anally by two men, simultaneously, neither of whom was wearing a condom. This act is the vogue in pornography today: condoms are rarely used, and the double penetration of a single orifice, whatever the physical consequences or limitations, is seen as hot.

Porn directors are devastated by the news of Roxx's infection. David Brett, CEO of Passion Pictures, told the industry's website, AVN: 'I would be mortified if anyone got sick in connection with one of my projects. I have to sleep at night … I would never earn my living at the expense of some other human being's health and safety.' So now there is some discussion of compulsory condoms. But there is no discussion of how 'healthy' and 'safe' it is to brutalize teenagers in the name of entertainment.

Roxx's interview with AVN itself shows the fluidity of 'consent' in these matters: 'I told [my manager] I wasn't interested in anal at all, and I was a little freaky about the no-condom thing, too,' she said. On arriving at the film shoot, she was pressured into performing the 'double anal' scene by the director, Marc Anthony. She says: 'So I get there and Marc Anthony tells me it's a DA, which stands for double anal. And I'm like, "What? I've never done a double anal." And he was like, "Well, that's what we need. It's either that or nothing." And that's how they do it … I think that sucks, because he knew double anal was dangerous.' Later, she says, she was in pain and could not sit down.

It is hard not to see links between the culturally unacceptable behaviour of the soldiers in Abu Ghraib and the culturally accepted actions of what happens in porn. Of course there is a gulf between them, and it is insulting to suggest that all porn actors are in the same situation as Iraqis, confined and brutalized in terrifying conditions. And yet, the images in both are the same. The pornographic culture has clearly influenced the soldiers; at the very least, in their exhibitionism, their enthusiasm to photograph their handiwork. And to the abusers in Abu Ghraib, or to the punters in pornography, the victims don't have feelings. Both point to just how degraded sex has become in Western culture. Porn hasn't even pretended to show loving sex for decades; in films and TV most sex is violent, joyless. The Abu Ghraib torturers are merely acting out their culture: the sexual humiliation of the weak. So Charles Graner and his colleagues can humiliate Iraqi prisoners because the prisoners are dirt; they can humiliate women, forcing them to bare their bodies and raping them, because that way they can show their power.

The annihilation of Lynndie England, while her superior Graner, clearly in control and already with a history of violence against women, was left alone, fits this story too. They are both repulsive, torturers; but she has been vilified for her involvement, while his is passed off with a shrug. Some women in the military – if they are not themselves being raped by male soldiers (in February, US soldiers were accused of raping more than 112 colleagues in Iraq and Afghanistan) – seem to have to prove that they are one of the guys by sexually humiliating the only people less important than they are: Iraqi prisoners, of whatever sex. It's a chilling lesson, that women can be sexual sadists just as well as men. Just give them the right conditions – and someone weaker to kick. It's proof that sexual aggression is not really about sex or gender, but about power: the powerful humiliating the powerless.

The real images of sexual abuse of Iraqi women, if they are ever released, will at once appear on pornographic websites. They will be used for sexual gratification. People are already joking that England (though not Graner) can have a nice little future career for herself in porn. Of course we are horrified by these images. But we should be horrified too by their familiarity, and how much they tell us about our own societies.

1 July 2004

JACKIE ASHLEY

Equality

Looking for a better theme than 'choice' on which to fight the election? How about 'equality'? No, I'm not joking. Nor am I calling for a return to the dinosaur years of taxing the rich till their pips squeaked. The new equality has a different meaning. A word that was once a core Labour value, and was then dropped in embarrassment by the modernizers (who thought 'fairness' was nicer) is returning to the centre of New Labour thinking. In the haze of the third way and triangulation, nobody predicted this, but there are good, hard-nosed reasons for it.

Last October, the government announced that it was merging the three equality commissions – on race, disability and gender – into a new mega-organization, the Commission for Equality and Human Rights. Its white paper in May promised a 'step change in how we promote, enforce and deliver equality'. At a time when the cabinet's alpha-males get all the media attention, it is worth recording that campaigners say little of this would have happened without the personal commitment of Patricia Hewitt and Jacqui Smith.

Now equality is less about tax and more about giving women, minority ethnic groups, disabled people and gay people rights and muscle in the labour market. It is still about money and power – 70 per cent of people in ethnic minorities live in Britain's most deprived urban areas and the yawning pay gap between men and women has been unchanged for a generation – but it is less about class.

This reflects the changing nation and its frankly selfish needs. Britain, like other European countries, will thrive or wither depending on how well it exploits the whole labour force. Ethnic minorities still only make up 8 per cent of the population – 4.5 million adults – but they will account for over half the growth in the working age population in the next ten years. Yet they hold the lowliest jobs.

In two years' time, something highly significant will happen to Britain that has never happened before in our history: there will be more older working people (those aged fifty-five to sixty-four) than young people (aged sixteen to twenty-four). 'Equality' will be vital to sustaining not just the NHS, but also private profits, all our pensions and the tax base.

Even more strikingly, we have more than twice as many disabled adults in Britain as people from ethnic minorities: recent figures from the Department of Work and Pensions show there are now 10 million disabled people. Politicians are beginning to realize that disablement rights mean more than being kind to people in wheelchairs. Helping the disabled contribute to the economy, using carrots and sticks for employers, has become essential.

And even their numbers are dwarfed by huge numbers of women in the working population, who are still earning a lot less than men. The pay gap remains at a staggering 40 per cent. Given the fast-changing demography, any economy that discriminates against women is going to lose out, and quickly. Pay, women's lower pensions, the need for universal childcare and help for carers are all on the agenda for Labour's women's policy forum next weekend.

Equality issues are certain to feature in the agonized internal debate about what, seven years in, a Labour government is really for. It is time to accept that society has changed, that the old model where he worked and she kept house has largely gone, and the workplace needs to adapt. But we should be frank: the new equality agenda is politically dangerous.

It may seem a bland working-motherhood-and-apple-pie thing in the trendy commissions and policy hothouses of central London, but across most of this country, it raises hackles, suspicion and derision, including among traditional Labour voters, reading their brutally prejudiced and traditional daily rags. The far-right message is that this is a publicly funded system of feminist, gay and migrant back-scratching, at the expense of white working-class men – political correctness gone mad. It's a message that is widely accepted. The jibes work.

Anyone with a teenage son needs no lessons on the casual homophobia in British schools, nor the raw racism of the streets. Yet Britain has seen nothing like the aggressive positive discrimination of US colleges and public institutions, which have tried so hard and succeeded so well in growing a generation of black leaders and role models. (Greg Dyke was torn apart by media critics for calling the BBC 'hideously white'. Of course he was wrong – if you count the cleaning staff, there are lots of black people working there, but that is exactly the point.) Some spheres are making progress, slowly – one black newscaster here, one black comedian there, one black cabinet minister (all right, two) and so on. But neither the public nor the private sector, which has been making efforts too, has seen a real transformation.

Similarly, we are way behind other European countries in the number and visibility of women at the top of institutions, particularly in the private sector, where a handful of endlessly cited media women have to stand in for their missing sisters across the City and business. There's, er ... Marjorie Scardino and, er ... Sly Bailey and, er ... The male hierarchies of British companies and public institutions are still pursuing a work ethic and culture which excludes people with children, or other caring responsibilities, and above all women, unless they agree to mimic the lives of family-free males.

On disability, gender and race, there is a lot to do and there is a ready and waiting opposition to all of it. A surprising amount of the anti-European feeling in the country resolves down to small-business resentment against 'regulation' – and those regulations surprisingly often boil down to issues of equality and discrimination. The interleaving of asylum, immigration and anti-EU politics is now well understood and infects housing estates and suburban avenues across the country. And to cap it all, there are truly tricky issues about religious equality and the survival of our prized liberal secular culture, which have the potential for a cultural civil war on the left.

Equality in its new meaning is not going to be much easier for New Labour to sell than 'old equality' was for old Labour twenty-five years ago. This is why the new commission, when it finally launches, must make much of the hard-edged case for equality as a founding principle for our economic success in the decades ahead, as well as the social justice case.

We are all going to die, but we all hope to grow old first. That means we all need people to keep earning to fund our pensions, to be there to care for us, to keep our streets safe and our cities clean. And that in turn means we need a workforce that uses all its talent. People in Number 10, I hear, are still struggling for 'big ideas' for the election. Here's one, right in front of their noses.

2 December 2003

GEORGE MONBIOT

Bottom of the barrel

The oil industry is buzzing. On Thursday, the government approved the development of the biggest deposit discovered in British territory for at least ten years. Everywhere we are told that this is a 'huge' find, which dispels the idea that North Sea oil is in terminal decline. You begin to recognize how serious the human predicament has become when you discover that this 'huge' new field will supply the world with oil for five and a quarter days.

Every generation has its taboo, and ours is this: that the resource upon which our lives have been built is running out. We don't talk about it because we cannot imagine it. This is a civilization in denial.

Oil itself won't disappear, but extracting what remains is becoming ever more difficult and expensive. The discovery of new reserves peaked in the 1960s. Every year we use four times as much oil as we find. All the big strikes appear to have been made long ago: the 400 million barrels in the new North Sea field would have been considered piffling in the 1970s. Our future supplies depend on the discovery of small new deposits and the better exploitation of big old ones. No one with expertise in the field is in any doubt that the global production of oil will peak before long.

The only question is how long. The most optimistic projections are the ones produced by the US Department of Energy, which claims that this will not take place until 2037. But the US Energy Information Agency has admitted that the government's figures have been fudged: it has based its projections for oil supply on the projections for oil demand, perhaps in order not to sow panic in the financial markets.

Other analysts are less sanguine. The petroleum geologist Colin Campbell calculates that global extraction will peak before 2010. In August, the geophysicist Kenneth Deffeyes told *New Scientist* that he was '99 per cent confident' that the date of maximum global production will be 2004. Even if the optimists are correct, we will be scraping the oil barrel within the lifetimes of most of those who are middle-aged today.

The supply of oil will decline, but global demand will not. Today we will burn 76 million barrels; by 2020 we will be using 112 million barrels a day, after which projected demand accelerates. If supply declines and demand grows, we soon encounter something with which the people of the advanced industrial economies are unfamiliar: shortage. The price of oil will go through the roof.

As the price rises, the sectors that are now almost wholly dependent on crude oil – principally transport and farming – will be forced to contract. Given that climate change caused by burning oil is cooking the planet, this might appear to be a good thing. The problem is that our lives have become hard-wired to the oil economy. Our sprawling suburbs are impossible to service without cars. High oil prices mean high food prices: much of the world's growing population will go hungry. These problems will be exacerbated by the direct connection between the price of oil and the rate of unemployment. The last five recessions in the US were all preceded by a rise in the oil price.

Oil, of course, is not the only fuel on which vehicles can run. There are plenty of possible substitutes, but none of them is likely to be anywhere near as cheap as crude is today. Petroleum can be extracted from tar sands and oil shale, but in most cases the process uses almost as much energy as it liberates, while creating great mountains and lakes of toxic waste. Natural gas is a better option, but switching from oil to gas propulsion would require a vast and staggeringly expensive new fuel infrastructure. Gas, of course, is subject to the same constraints as oil: at current rates of use, the world has about fifty years' supply, but if gas were to take the place of oil its life would be much shorter.

Vehicles could be run from fuel cells powered by hydrogen, which is produced by the electrolysis of water. But the electricity that produces the hydrogen has to come from somewhere. To fill all the cars in the US would require four times the current capacity of the national grid. Coal burning is filthy; nuclear energy is expensive and lethal. Running the world's cars from wind or solar power would require a greater investment than any civilization has ever made before. New studies suggest that leaking hydrogen could damage the ozone layer and exacerbate global warming.

Turning crops into diesel or methanol is just about viable in terms of recoverable energy, but it means using the land on which food is now grown for fuel. My rough calculations suggest that running the United Kingdom's cars on rapeseed oil would require an area of arable fields the size of England.

There is one possible solution which no one writing about the impending oil crisis seems to have noticed: a technique with which the British and Australian governments are currently experimenting, called underground coal gasification. This is a fancy term for setting light to coal seams which are too deep or too expensive to mine, and catching the gas which emerges. It's a hideous prospect, as it means that several trillion tonnes of carbon that was otherwise impossible to exploit becomes available, with the likely result that global warming will eliminate life on Earth.

We seem, in other words, to be in trouble. Either we lay hands on every available source of fossil fuel, in which case we fry the planet and civilization collapses, or we run out, and civilization collapses.

The only rational response to both the impending end of the oil age and the menace of global warming is to redesign our cities, our farming and our lives. But this cannot happen without massive political pressure, and our problem is that no one ever rioted for austerity. People tend to take to the streets because they want to consume more, not less. Given a choice between a new set of matching tableware and the survival of humanity, I suspect that most people would choose the tableware.

In view of all this, the notion that the war with Iraq had nothing to do with oil is simply preposterous. The US attacked Iraq (which appears to have had no weapons of mass destruction and was not threatening other nations) rather than North Korea (which is actively developing a nuclear weapons programme and boasting of its intentions to blow everyone else to kingdom come) because Iraq had something it wanted. In one respect alone, Bush and Blair have been making plans for the day when oil production peaks, by seeking to secure the reserves of other nations.

I refuse to believe that there is not a better means of averting disaster than this. I refuse to believe that human beings are collectively incapable of making rational decisions. But I am beginning to wonder what the basis of my belief might be.

IRAQ

JAMES MEEK

Something happened

Something happened in Baghdad yesterday, but what exactly? What we know is that somewhere in Saddam Hussein's sprawling former cantonment on the banks of the Tigris, behind silver miles of new razor wire, behind high concrete barriers stronger than most medieval fortifications, behind sandbags, five security checks, US armoured vehicles, US armoured soldiers, special forces of various countries and private security guards, behind secrecy and a fear of killing so intense that none save a handful of people knew it had happened until after it was over, an American bureaucrat handed a piece of paper to an Iraqi judge, jumped on a helicopter and left the country.

Paul Bremer's departure and the handover of a limited form of sovereignty to an unelected Iraqi government was to be the end of military occupation and the beginning of independence.

From London and Washington it may look that way and Iraqis, too, seem eager to believe that yesterday was the beginning of the end of chaos and fear. But the Bremer who waved from the steps of his departing C-130 did not only leave sovereignty, in the form of a terse two-paragraph letter, with the Iraqis. He left 160,000 foreign troops, a broken economy and a land beset by ruthless, reckless armed bands.

The first thing reporters saw as they came into the sunshine from the banal auditorium where the newly sworn-in Iraqi government hailed the new era was two US Apache helicopter gunships, pirouetting low in the furnace sky.

The journey out of the fortified cantonment, previously known as the Green Zone, now renamed the International Zone, still winds through ramparts and fortifications, past jumpy US soldiers threatening to confiscate mobile phones. In the streets beyond, menacing signs in English and Arabic still hang beneath US watchtowers: 'Keep Away, Deadly Force Authorized'; 'Tactical Military Vehicles ONLY'; 'Do Not Enter Or You Will Be Shot'.

The handover was held in a single-storey former Saddam-era guesthouse in the Zone which has been given to the new prime minister, Ayad Allawi. Fear of the bombers gave the occasion all the pomp of an office leaving do. It lasted only twenty minutes.

Mr Allawi's residence and a similar building for the president, Sheikh Ghazi Ajil al-Yawar, look out on pleasant lawned gardens studded with pools and orange trees. It is a delightful setting from which to reinvent independent Iraq, except Mr Allawi and Mr Yawar are sandwiched by the enormous weight of American enthusiasm, there to make sure they get the independence thing right.

On one side, the huge new US embassy. On the other side, Saddam Hussein's lavish principal former palace or, as it is known since yesterday, the annex to the

US embassy. Mr Yawar had hoped to be waking up in that palace this morning but was told the Americans needed it too badly; in that sense, as in so many others, today will be just another day in the Zone.

The first many people knew of yesterday's events was an Iraqi flag billowing in the hairdryer-hot breeze from the Zone's tallest building. Inside the Zone, logos of the now defunct Coalition Provisional Authority that Mr Bremer headed, emblems which had started to look permanent, disappeared.

There was a curious ceremony in the Zone's convention centre, which, apart from the odd Saddamish mural, could be a convention centre anywhere, intended to mark the handover of military authority from the coalition to the Iraqi military. A column of US cavalrymen, dressed in the blue shirts, kerchiefs, gauntlets and black broad-brimmed hats of the Custer era, marched out across the industrial carpeting, bearing their departing standards. It was as if they were leaving. But they were not, any more than Mr Bremer's departure is America leaving.

It was hard to get away from the reality of the beleaguered, hunkered-down US military behemoth. Before the ceremony a pleasant, anxious, motherly Virginian woman began to chat. She'd only just arrived for a six-month tour. She was a Pentagon civilian, but they had put her in camouflage fatigues. They had not given her a gun. She had never used one before. She was worried she might find herself under attack and unable to help her comrades out. She lives next to the US military cemetery at Arlington. 'They're doing twenty-six funerals a day,' she said. 'People go jogging there, but they show respect.'

There were other, more transient visitors in the Zone. There was Gregg Andrew, a Pentagon contractor who described himself as an 'advance man', hired to choreograph the handover so it would look decent on TV. He said of the ceremonies: 'There is a pageantry involved.' Yet there was not. The swearing-in of the president, prime minister and government could not have been more simple. The principals sat on an auditorium stage adorned by nothing more than eighteen Iraqi flags, and swore plain oaths under God to Iraq, democracy and the people with their hands on a big red Koran. It was appropriate to the occasion. The advent of what is supposed to be the opposite of dictatorship looked suitably modest.

Just before the swearing-in began, the Iraqi leadership waved to the people watching. As they did, they looked like middle-aged people look when the restraining bar locks into place on an extreme funfair ride about to lurch into the air. For despite the constraints the US and Britain will keep on them, they have power and responsibility, and they know that in trying to invent a new narrative for Iraq, they are only doing what their Arab and Kurd predecessors did in learning the strange art of politics under the Ottomans and the British, likewise times of violence, revolt, occupation and compromise.

We will have to wait for Mr Bremer's memoirs to know what he thought, looking down, as his Chinook banked over the parched date groves, yellow cubescape and sluggish brown river of summer Baghdad for the last time.

Yet between the disastrous spell of looting that began the US occupation, the disbanding of the army and police which enabled crime to flourish, the failure to rebuild the country, the continued presence of a vast US force and the uncertainty surrounding future elections, the creation of a transitional government seems a thin achievement, particularly when that government is showing authoritarian tendencies.

But an Iraqi government, any Iraqi government, seems to many like the overdue fulfilment of what they wanted from the Americans all along, which was to painlessly extract Saddam and his family from their lives, like a bad tooth, and immediately vanish. Instead, the dentist moved in.

25 June 2004

GHAITH ABDUL-AHAD

'You had the machine gun yesterday'

By the time I arrive in Kerbala, in the last week in May, the clashes between Moqtada al-Sadr's Shia militia and the Americans have been going on for weeks. Apart from the scores of Shia militiamen running around the streets with RPGs on their shoulders, the streets are empty. The police have evaporated, leaving only their burned-out cars from previous skirmishes with rebel fighters.

We park our car on the outskirts of the shrine area. Normally, thousands of devout Shia pilgrims from Iran, Afghanistan and central Asia would be bustling around on buses, taxis and donkey carts, but today there are no buses, no donkeys and certainly no pilgrims.

The main street leading to the shrine is terrifyingly empty, with shattered windows and piles of garbage everywhere. As we start along the street, militiamen from the Badr brigade, one of the main Shia factions, demand our press passes. They are all dressed alike – in flip-flops, black T-shirts and pyjama pants – and all are carrying AK-47s. 'I'm sorry,' says one ugly militiaman. 'You are not allowed in. We have instructions not to allow journalists to take pictures of the shrine because this will compromise the safety of the shrine.' As if the hundreds of Americans and militiamen shooting at each other just metres from the shrine are not compromising its safety. We ask him to check. After a few minutes of creaking noises from the radio, he comes back with a big grin: no journalists allowed.

It takes us a little while to figure out the game that we will have to play for the next three days. The Shia factions, we work out, are very keen not to allow journalists to go into the centre of the city and report the activities of the other Shia factions – they are not yet fighting each other, but they don't like each other much. After all, it's a family issue, and we Iraqis don't like foreigners to mess with our affairs. So we do a big loop and sneak through the alleys, telling the guards at every checkpoint that we are not here for the fighting but have an appointment with Ayatollah X, Y or Z.

We finally come out of one alley to find ourselves face to face with three gunmen, their heads wrapped in keffiyehs, and Kalashnikovs and RPGs in their hands (this is now considered the new Iraqi dress code, or the 'muj style'). They are the Mahdi army, a militia led by Moqtada al-Sadr, which, according to the

US army, includes highly trained former Iraqi military officers. I manage to convince one of them to take us to their HQ. He puts his AK on his shoulder, points at the end of the street – 'Snipers; run very fast' – and we sprint across the street.

He leads us through a maze of alleyways which make up part of the old covered souks of Kerbala, the shops heavily barricaded with steel bars, the streets piled with weeks-old rubbish, fighters sitting in groups of three to five, smoking. Every once in a while someone shouts, 'Americans, Americans!', one or two move into a sniping position, shout at each other and then come and sit down again. They look tired, hungry and bored, fiddling with their RPGs and rifles.

Finally, we arrive at the HQ, 50 metres from the shrine and a street corner where most of the fighting has taken place in the past few days. They take us to the 'sheikh' for permission, a young guy in his early thirties with a big bushy beard who is the local Mahdi commander. I spend the next two days with these men on a clutch of street corners from where they take occasional pot shots at the Americans.

This is the front-line elite, a bunch of badly equipped men with rusted AKs and decade-old RPG rockets. When we first arrive they are brewing tea, piles of RPG rockets stacked on the walls two feet away from the fire.

'So how long you have been here?' I ask one of them.

'Three weeks now.' He says he is here because he wants to defend the shrine of Imam Ali. 'I'm unemployed and have nothing else to do.' He is seventeen.

Others start to gather around us. 'Don't talk to them.' 'No, do talk to them, they must know what's happening.' 'Are you Americans?' 'Are you spies?' 'Who sent you here?' 'Take my picture.' 'No, take my picture with an RPG.' 'No, don't let them photograph the RPGs – they'll sell the pictures to the Americans.'

Suddenly, there are some explosions, and three of them run towards the corner. We hear heavy machine-gun fire and I see American APCs firing at a building in the street.

'Where's the machine gun?'

'I don't know! You had it yesterday!'

'No, you had it!'

'No, no, it's there with Ali.'

'Where's Ali?'

'He went home.'

'So where is the machine gun?'

'With Ali.'

So they decide to fire RPGs without machine-gun cover. They hop into the street, fire off a grenade and hop back. All the while we are squeezed behind the corner. All I can think is that I have to stay alive otherwise my girlfriend will kill me.

They can't see what they are shooting at but shout 'Allahu-Akbar' all the same, and everyone starts giving numbers of how many Americans they have killed. Then another man shows up, shortish and in his forties, and while everyone is ducking or hiding behind columns, he strolls about as if he is in the park. Another fighter loads an RPG for him and the guy turns with the thing on his shoulder as if looking for the direction he should shoot in. Someone shouts,

'Push him into the street before he fires it at us!' Another fighter grabs him around his waist and pushes him to the corner where he stands, bullets whizzing around him, takes his time, and – boom! – fires his RPG. He stands there until someone grips his trousers and pulls him in. His eyes are not even blinking at the sounds around him. They give him another one and he spins again and everyone hits the ground. Someone shouts, 'He can't hear you; go and show him!' The deaf mute is getting support fire from a kid who shoots off a few rounds, then jumps back to fix his AK, which is falling apart. 'If you take a picture of me fixing this, I will kill you.'

We wait for the fire to subside and run across the street to the other side, the same dark alleys in which the same bored fighters are sitting doing nothing but chewing over the same old conspiracy theories. The walls and the ground are varnished with fresh blood. In the market a couple of shops are on fire from earlier fighting. A man is hiding behind a pile of empty banana boxes with his eight-year-old son.

That is when we catch sight of a small boy with a stunned look on his face. He says his name is Amjad and he is eleven years old.

'How long you have been here?'

'Ten days. Since my brother was killed. There, at the end of that street.'

'And why are you here?'

'To become a martyr like my brother.'

I ask him why he wants to die.

'We should all die for the sake of our leader!' shouts one of the militiamen who have gathered around us.

On the last day, while I am trying to leave this crazy place, we are chased by an overheated young muj (from mujahideen, which means simply a religious fighter – since the Shia started fighting the Americans, they too have been happy to call themselves muj). He demands that we give him all our films. 'You are foreigners working with the Americans!' We tell him it's not true. He click-clicks his AK, and points it at us: 'I said, give me the films or I will shoot!'

'No, leave them alone,' someone calls out. 'They have been with us for the last two days; the sheikh knows about them.'

Shaking, we leave, and head to the shrine to see if there are any pilgrims there. As we are sitting on the pavement, three men with AKs come over and tell us we are under arrest. I wish I had taped the previous conversation.

They take us to the shrine of Imam Abbas, and into a marble-clad room filled with big, ugly guys with thick beards and an arsenal of automatic weapons. These men are from the Shrine Protection Force, a militia loyal to the grand Shia Ayatollah Ali al-Sistani, and so loosely allied with the Americans.

'It is all because of journalists that all this is happening,' says a guy dressed in black, sitting behind a big wooden table. He says that the Mahdi are manipulating the media. 'They are thugs and assassins, they have paralysed the holy city of Kerbala, they have desecrated the shrines and shoot from behind them, trying to provoke a response.

'But, *alhamdulillah* [thank God], the Americans are very wise and respect the shrines. Our brothers, the Americans, are taking very good care of this thing, but as far as the Shias around the world and in Iraq are concerned, they hear that the Americans are fighting "close to the shrines", and that Shias are being killed. They see the smoke on your films so they come en masse to fight and they are immediately brainwashed by Moqtada and his thugs.'

If that's the case, I ask, why doesn't the Ayatollah come out publicly and denounce those people, and show his support for these 'brothers'?

'Are you crazy? It's *haram* [forbidden by Islamic law] to support an infidel, even when he is right, against a brother Muslim.'

'So what is your strategy?'

'We will pray for Allah to stop this.'

I decide that Allah has a few other things to solve in Iraq first.

In any case, once they discover that we are photographers and not video cameramen, the detention comes to an end pretty quickly. And I decide to stop chasing bullets and RPGs and find somewhere calm. So I resolve to head to Falluja – after all, the Americans have managed to install peace over there, haven't they?

Falluja is very calm by the time I arrive. I have been there once before, in April during the 'great battle', as they now call it up there. Back then it was like *Apocalypse Now*, with muj running in the streets and American marines firing at any house they suspected had 'enemies' inside. Falluja is a peaceful town now; shops are open and cars are in the streets, and Iraqi security forces are everywhere: ICDC (the US-trained civil defence corps), policemen, traffic police and the new Falluja brigade, known as the 'brigade of the heroes' by the locals. You can even say that things are normal.

After a devastating military campaign that left more than 800 Iraqis dead, the US liberators established the Falluja brigade out of the former military, some of whom had been fighting the Americans but are now on their payroll. Falluja is now like a déjà vu from the good old times of Saddam; there are so many former Iraqi military in khaki uniforms, big moustaches and bellies that I am scared someone will come up and ask me for my military ID card.

But, as with everything in the new Iraq, the picture is blurred, and no one in Falluja can figure out what the new arrangement actually means. For some Fallujans, it meant that their people would get paid again and they would be in charge of their own security without being seen as collaborators. For the Americans it meant the new force would work with them to enforce law and order in the city, helping to build a new Iraq. But for other Fallujans, he who works with Americans is seen as the enemy of God. Which means that we now have Falluja versus Falluja in the biggest stand-off of the year: who really controls Falluja?

The city is now like a loose federation of Sunni mosques and mujahideen-run fiefdoms. These have become the only successfully functioning 'civil society' institutions, although the only form of civil society they are interested in is a 1,400-year-old model. So they raid houses where sinners are believed to be drinking alcohol, and insist on forcing their own version of the *hijab*. If you have a record shop in Falluja, it had better be selling the latest version of Koranic chanting; Britney Spears could get you flogged.

A bunch of Falluja kids, just finishing their exams, are hanging around their school when two muj trucks surround them and pick up all the kids who don't have a 'decent' haircut. They will be taken to get their heads shaved. (Bear in mind that we are talking about Falluja, which is already one of the most conservative towns in Iraq. There aren't too many funky haircuts here to begin with.)

As I arrive at the main entrance to the city, two shaking Iraqi ICDC are handing flyers to Fallujans driving into the city. The leaflets are designed to advise how to file a complaint for compensation, and to reassure them about what the Americans are up to: 'The marines came here originally to help the people of Falluja, and they will work together to defeat the enemies of the Iraqi people.'

I head towards one of the mosques where people are going to get aid and charity donations. A guy in his forties approaches me with the famous welcoming smile of the Fallujans, a look of, 'What the fuck are you doing here?' I tell him that I'm a journalist and would like to meet the Sheikh.

'How did you manage to get in? Didn't they stop you at the checkpoint?'

Thinking he is talking about the marines' checkpoint, I say, 'No, everything was fine.'

'Did they see your camera?' I tell him I was hiding it.

'This Abu Tahrir, I don't know what kind of mujahideen cell he is running! I told him that every car should be thoroughly searched and all journalists should be brought here!'

I am ushered inside where, surrounded by three muj fighters, the new mayor of Falluja gives me his geopolitical analysis of the American plot to control the world by occupying Falluja: 'You know, we were all very happy when the Americans came, we thought our country would be better with their help, but Allah the Mighty wasn't pleased,' he tells me. The Americans started making mistakes, he explains, and now, 'It's all Allah's plot to stop the believers from dealing with infidel foreigners.' He opens his drawer and pulls out two sheets of paper: the demands and the strategies of the resistance. One details an American-Shia plot to kill the Sunni clerics, technocrats and former army officers: 'Be careful, oh brothers, because the Americans and their traitor allies, the Kurds and the Shias, are planning to come after your leaders.' The other is a letter sent by the joint committee for the Iraqi resistance to Lakhdar Ibrahimi, the UN envoy working to form a new government. Its demands can be summarized as a request to hand Iraq to a bunch of wacko Sunni army generals.

The meeting is interrupted many times, once when a small kid comes into the room and everyone stands to shake his hand. 'He is our best sniper here. He has killed three Americans; he wants to call the Americans out for a sniping competition.'

One of the local muj cell leaders, Abu Tahrir ('father of liberation'), is complaining how part of the muj corps has deserted and joined the Americans. He is in his late thirties, overweight and a bit grim; a typical former *mukhabarat* officer who mixes bits of the Koran with chunks of nationalist and Ba'athist ranting. Ten minutes later, another muj comes into the room complaining that different muj groups haven't shown up to take their positions. The mayor makes a few phone calls using his mobile phone – 'We have cell phones now, you know' – before returning to his thesis of where the American invasion went wrong: 'The Iraqi army has been staging coups and counter-coups from 1958 to

1968; it was the army who managed to get everything under control, instead of those stooges on the governing council. The Americans should have counted on the real Iraqis …' And so on, until the muj who brought me in comes back and says: 'You have to leave now. The commanders of the mujahideen cells are going to have a big meeting in Falluja in fifteen minutes, and soon there will be muj checkpoints everywhere.' As we leave the mosque, he waves to a passing police car and orders them to follow, so that we drive out of Falluja escorted by both the muj and the police.

Sadr City is an easy job for a journalist: all you have to do is cruise around looking for trouble. It is a Soweto kind of slum: rubbish-filled streets, ponds of sewage and thousands of unemployed kids.

It is Saturday, and we are driving through the streets for the second time in the day. It is late afternoon when we see a bunch of kids directing the traffic away. By now we are able to sniff trouble from miles away, but I tell my driver to head to that street. Makeshift barricades are laid in the middle of the road, made of stones, tyres and chunks of car metal. Someone's house has even been dismantled for the barricade.

'Don't go, there are Americans down the street,' shouts one of the kids, so we duck into a side road. The battlefield is an empty plot of land by a mosque, surrounded by alleyways.

In one of them, a dozen teenagers, three or four of them wearing Arsenal T-shirts and flip-flops, are emptying a car boot of a mortar tube and a sackful of shells. I am allowed to stay and take pictures, but with the usual proviso: 'If we discover that you are working for the Americans, we will kill you.'

The target is a police station and three Humvees parked in front. Masked like a Western cowboy, the shooter, or the 'expert' as they call him, takes measure of the angle and shouts to another fighter, 'Give me one!' The other guy produces what looks like a rusted, 2-ft shell. The fighters here are also Mahdi, and the fighting in Sadr City often feels like one big carnival. All the kids are by now doing their cheering chant: 'Ali wiyak, Ali!' 'Ali with you, Ali!' If I were an American soldier, I would be expecting a flying shell every time I hear kids cheering in Sadr City. After all, this is the only fun they get, shooting at the sitting ducks. The expert tosses the shell into the barrel, and a big explosion follows. 'Right a bit!' shouts one of the kids at the end of the street. 'It fell on a house!' The second one falls much too far to the left. 'It fell on another house, move to the right a little bit!' The third one falls something like 10 metres away from us, but doesn't explode. The fourth lands by the Americans, and detonates. 'Ten dead, I saw it with my own eyes!' shouts another kid. The fifth doesn't leave the tube, and he has to upend the tube and shake it.

In all, the firefight lasts for an hour, and after a couple more rounds and a few more civilian houses destroyed, the fighters jump into their car and drive away.

Then the RPG session starts, kids aiming at the Americans and hitting whatever target they fancy. As one prepares to fire his RPG, the rusted rocket doesn't launch.

'Come, you can use mine,' says a man who is standing by, watching.

Helpfully, he goes to his nearby home and returns with his RPG, as if he were lending a neighbour his Hoover.

Then: 'They are coming, they are coming!' Everyone starts to run, the fifty or so kids who have gathered to watch the game, breaking into a sprint. We jump into the first open door, where a man pulls us inside and closes the door.

The house is nothing but two rooms and an open courtyard, home to two families with countless tiny kids. 'So they shoot and run, and soon the Americans will come and start breaking into the houses and firing at us,' says the man.

Within a few minutes we hear a Humvee pull up by the door, and – boom! boom! boom! – they start firing what sounds like a heavy machine gun. Everyone jumps to the ground, and Ali is asked once again to show his mercy upon us. 'This has been our life for the past few weeks; we don't know when we will be killed and who will kill us,' says the father. After a while the Humvees go, and we hear the sound of the kids in the streets again. Everything back to normal.

That evening, after another session of shooting and counter-shooting, we are sitting with the fighters by the office of Moqtada al-Sadr. We are prepared for a long night waiting for American mortar shells. I think to myself, here we go, another dozen houses gone.

A young muj extends his hand and says, 'Do you want a beer?'

I am stunned, and what remains of my religious belief rapidly evaporates. But the beer is good and I sit all night with the great religious fighters, drinking beer and waiting for the shells that never come.

11 May 2004

HAIFA ZANGANA

Abu Ghraib

Earlier this year, I met Adnan al-Obaidy in Baghdad. A dignified man in his seventies, he had just been released from Abu Ghraib prison where he had been detained for six months. Surrounded by his wife and three children, he greeted visitors carrying trays of *baklava*.

In a rare moment of silence, I asked, 'Were you tortured?'

The polite smile deserted his face. 'No,' he said. With a strange emptiness in his eyes, he looked sideways.

In the 1970s, during my parents' first visit to see me in Abu Ghraib prison, my mother hugged me and whispered in a quavering voice. 'Have they treated you badly?'

'No,' I said and, like Adnan, I looked sideways.

How can you talk about your humiliation, your weakness, letting yourself and others down, your reduction to an animal sleeping with urine and faeces? Can you explain how your mind loses its grip on nerves and muscles, how fear grows inside you like weed? Silence becomes your refuge while carrying your shame and guilt for being alive. Thirty years on I still wake at 2 a.m. every morning. That is the time they used to lead me out of my cell for interrogation. How long will it take Iraqi prisoners under occupation to overcome their sense of humiliation and talk about their ordeal?

The Red Cross estimates there are 10,000 to 15,000 prisoners. No figures are available for the number of women. According to the *New York Times*, 'Iraq has a new generation of missing men.' Torture has been practised in Iraqi prisons since day one of the occupation. The country's own human rights organizations reported its use as early as last June. But the occupation forces have chosen not to see Iraqis as humans. Faced with the anger of Iraqi people, members of the US-appointed 'governing council' finally echoed the condemnation by the coalition provisional authority of the 'incidents'. Nevertheless, they rushed to remind the world that 'these incidents are not as bad as what used to occur under Saddam'.

Indeed, we were imprisoned and tortured, and many of our loved ones were executed. But let us make this clear: Saddam's regime has never been our role model for a new Iraq. Nor has it been a yardstick to measure our aspirations for justice, freedom and democracy. Iraqis did not struggle for decades to replace one torturer with another. By embracing the occupiers' policy in every aspect, the governing council shares responsibility for its outcome. Iraqis are outraged that no high-ranking officials in the previous regime have been put on trial. They also resent the fact that the governing council refuses to admit that, like Saddam's regime, the occupying forces have absolute power with no accountability.

Torture has left a deep scar on our collective memory, and death is no stranger. We wanted to put an end to both. But occupation has resulted in more than 10,000 civilian deaths. This is the humiliation of a nation. Torture as an instrument of submission is a vital part of continuing occupation.

It is not enough to condemn torture and demand an inquiry. The occupation forces still seek to justify their crimes by blaming a few individuals. An apology is acceptable only when it genuinely marks an end to unacceptable practices. That is not the case. Last week occupation forces in Tikrit handed over four dead prisoners to their families, tortured and riddled with bullets.

We are a proud people, welcoming to guests but unforgiving of those who tread with heavy boots across our privacy, integrity and history. Saddam's regime managed to oppress us, but only because he was supported by the West for decades and we were then weakened by thirteen years of sanctions. This is not going to happen again.

5 May 2004

JONATHAN STEELE

Right at the wrong time

By any measure Amer al-Saadi ought to feel vindicated. The dapper, British-educated scientist who was the Iraqi government's main link to the United Nations inspectors before the US invasion repeatedly insisted that Iraq had destroyed its weapons of mass destruction years earlier. David Kay, the American inspector who headed the Iraq Survey Group and was sure he would find such weapons when he went to Iraq after the war, now accepts Dr Saadi was right. So does Hans Blix, the chief UN inspector, who up to a month before the war still thought Iraq might have had WMD.

Yet, astonishingly, Dr Saadi does not know of their change of mind or of the political fallout their views have caused in Western countries. He is like a lottery winner who is the last person to be told he has hit the jackpot. Held in solitary confinement in an American prison at Baghdad's international airport, Dr Saadi is denied the right to read newspapers, listen to the radio, or watch television.

'In the monthly one-page letters I am allowed to send him through the Red Cross I cannot mention any of this news. I can only talk about family issues,' says his wife, Helma, as she sits in the couple's home, less than half a mile from US headquarters in Baghdad.

Barely three days after the statue of Saddam Hussein was pulled down by US troops in central Baghdad, Dr Saadi approached the Americans and became the first senior Iraqi to hand himself in. It was the last time his wife saw him. He was sure he would soon be released, Mrs Saadi says. He was a scientist who had never been part of Saddam's terror apparatus, or even a member of the Ba'ath party.

CIA interrogators have repeatedly interviewed him. Had there been any WMD to discover, Dr Saadi would have had an obvious incentive to reveal their location once the regime had collapsed. But from the reports of the Iraq Survey Group it can only be assumed that he has maintained his line that they were eliminated long ago.

Dr Saadi is described officially by the Americans as an 'enemy prisoner of war'. This allows them to detain him indefinitely without access to a lawyer or visiting rights from his family until George Bush declares the war to be over. Whether he is still held out of spite or to hide Washington's embarrassment is not clear. He has already been in custody for more than a year.

His CIA interrogators have finished their work and apparently feel awkward about his continued detention: 'My handlers have appealed to higher authorities for my release but it seems it's political and God doesn't meddle in politics,' Dr Saadi wrote in one letter.

'It would speak well for them if they admitted they were mistaken. They would look human,' Mrs Saadi says. German by birth, she and her husband have always conversed in English. They were married in Wandsworth register office in south London forty years ago last October, when he was studying chemistry at Battersea College of Technology. The prison letters she shares with the *Guardian* reflect the tenderness of a long and successful partnership. Despite the censorship they resonate with affection and occasional whimsical flashes of humour, as well as periods of depression. 'Leave the brooding to me. I have time enough. Be constructive,' he urged her in one letter.

By a second cruel stroke of fate, she was in the UN headquarters last August, seeking help for her husband, when a suicide bomber blew it up. Twenty-two people died, including the woman she was talking to when the upper floor caved in. Mrs Saadi was unconscious for forty-eight hours and awoke in a US military hospital.

3 December 2003 Students protest about fees outside the House of Commons. Student with a sticker on her face saying grants not fees. (Martin Argles)

12 March 2004 Schools minister Stephen Twigg on a visit to Grange Park primary school. (Martin Argles)

24 June 2004 Darius Vassell sinks to his knees after missing the crucial penalty during the England v Portugal quarterfinal shootout. (Dan Chung)

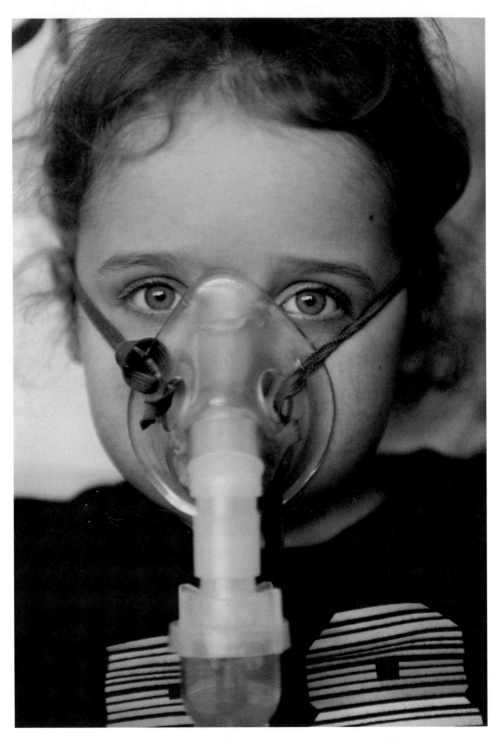

2 April 2004 Four-year-old asthma sufferer Georgia Conely, from Flitwick.
(Sean Smith)

The couple's children have lived most of their lives in Germany. 'We didn't want them to develop under the regime. He never saw his children grow up. It breaks my heart,' Mrs Saadi says. She spent twenty years bringing them up in Hamburg and making only short visits to Baghdad. Dr Saadi was not allowed to go abroad except on official business. The regime urged him to divorce her but he refused.

In prison under US custody he is not even allowed pen and paper, except to compose his one-page Red Cross letter. He does crosswords by filling in the blanks in his head. His wife sent him a computerized chess set but was not allowed to provide replacement batteries when the first ones ran out. He has been teaching himself German. 'If it were not for impressing the grandchildren, I wouldn't bother,' he wrote last year. Last month he joked about Paul Bremer, the top US official in Iraq. 'Bremer, I found out from the German lessons I am giving myself, is a man from Bremen! Yet another German!' Dr Saadi is kept in his cell all day except for an hour of exercise in a supervised area. His wife was able to send him running shoes. In October he wrote that his conditions had slightly improved: 'The awfully sagging bed has now a wooden board, and a plastic chair is provided instead of the back-breaking sitting on the floor on the very low bed which rolls you towards the centre with your bottom nearly touching the floor.'

With a British PhD in physical chemistry Dr Saadi is essentially a rocket scientist. Now sixty-six, he was awarded a scholarship from the defence ministry under the Iraqi monarchy to study in Britain, which meant he had to commit himself to work for the military later. During the war with Iran, when Saddam's Iraq was being armed and helped by the West, he organized a team of scientists who developed a ground-to-ground missile with a range of 400 miles, capable of reaching Tehran. This prompted the Iranian regime to agree to a peace deal. In 1994 he retired with the rank of lieutenant general but was appointed the next year as a scientific adviser to the presidency. He regularly met the UN weapons inspectors and when they resumed their work in November 2002 he was the government's main liaison man. He became a well-known figure on TV, wearing a suit rather than uniform, and speaking fluent English at press conferences. His wife insists he was never close to Saddam and last met him in 1995.

In his presentation to the Security Council in February last year the US secretary of state, Colin Powell, attacked Dr Saadi. He described his job as being 'not to cooperate, it is to deceive; not to disarm, but to undermine the inspectors; not to support them, but to frustrate them and to make sure they learn nothing'. Dr Saadi rejected the charges and hit back, describing Mr Powell's speech as a 'typical American show, full of stunts and special effects'. Mr Powell admitted recently that key parts of his presentation were wrong.

Dr Saadi's younger brother, Radwan, has worked in Iraq's oil ministry for thirty years and was reinstated by the US as head of its finance department. He tries to be hopeful: 'The Americans are taking it case by case. There are various agencies who all have to approve anyone's release. Some detainees were released very early who were closer to the regime than Amer. It's like dealing with a black hole.'

Dr Saadi is number thirty-two on Washington's most wanted list, and the seven of diamonds on the notorious deck of cards. Ironically, he now spends a lot of time with cards, playing Patience in his lonely cell.

24 August 2004

LUKE HARDING

Own goal

On Sunday evening Karim al-Zuheiri was watching Iraq's footballers play Australia at the Olympics. There had been no power for weeks in Najaf's old city where he lives, and so – ignoring the shellfire from the nearby Imam Ali shrine – Mr Zuheiri hooked up his television to a car battery.

He and four friends were on the pavement watching the first half when they heard several shots. 'We realized an American sniper was shooting at us,' Mr Zuheiri said yesterday. 'We ran inside like gazelles. By the grace of God we got the TV set back on in time to see Iraq score. With the goal we forgot some of our sadness and pain.'

For the past three weeks the dusty alleyway where Mr Zuheiri lives has been transformed into a war zone. The road is 500 metres south of Najaf's golden-domed shrine, where the rebel Shia cleric Moqtada al-Sadr's militia have been holding out against the US army. To get to the shrine you have to go past Mr Zuheiri's terraced corner house, across a shot-up boulevard and through a dense network of small lanes. From there it is a sprint left to the shrine's gateway, opposite Najaf's souk. 'If you walk twenty metres beyond my house you are at the frontline,' Mr Zuheiri said.

In the past two days US tanks have advanced further towards the shrine than ever before, encircling the south and east of the complex. They already control the west, and have been pulverising the Wadi al-Salam cemetery to the north. Last night, smoke rose above the old city within a mile of the shrine. Shrapnel fell in the courtyard of the gold-domed mosque, whose outer walls have already been damaged.

Given their superiority, Mr Zuheiri said yesterday he could not understand why the US military had not yet finished the job. 'It took them nine or ten days to invade Iraq and get rid of Saddam Hussein,' he said. 'Why can't they get rid of Moqtada?'

But with the battle for Najaf entering a stage of bloody attrition, life for the civilians caught in the middle has become intolerable.

Five days ago, a US tank pulled up outside the house of Yassir al-Abayechi, one of Mr Zuheiri's neighbours, whose home is now on the wrong side of the frontline.

'The tank suddenly appeared,' said Mr Abayechi, a 22-year-old student. 'The American soldier in it started shouting, "Go, go." I understand a few words of English so I grabbed my stuff and ran. I took my mother, sister and brother. We haven't been back.' Mr Abayechi was bitterly critical of all sides. 'If I step out of my house I get killed in a mortar attack. If I criticize the Mahdi army they will kill me. If I attack the interim government they will kill me. And if I attack the Americans they will kill me as well.'

He said that Saddam had arrested and executed his father and uncle in 1985, but that life under his regime was preferable to the current situation: 'Under Saddam we were living in a big prison, but there was security. Now they claim we have democracy, but what is the point of that if we don't have security?' he asked.

At least fifty-two civilians have been killed and 223 wounded in Najaf since Mr Sadr launched his latest uprising. Mr Zuheiri said an old woman living a few doors away had been one of the victims. 'An American sniper shot her in the chest and stomach,' he said. 'It was impossible to get her to hospital. She died. We, the people of Najaf, are the victims of all this.'

Civilians in Najaf's old city have had no water or electricity since the fighting began. They have had no ration cards for two months, and are running out of food. While we were sitting in Mr Zuheiri's sweltering front room, a group of Mahdi army fighters knocked on the door, demanding to know who we were. Several minutes later an American tank rumbled past. When someone is killed, residents say it is not always easy to know who to blame. The night bombings by US jets are terrifying, they say. 'We didn't sleep,' said Mr Zuheiri, who teaches at the local primary school.

Soon after midnight yesterday a US warplane pounded the city again. Artillery exchanges continued until the fighting eased at 8 a.m. By lunchtime the mortars had started again, crashing into Najaf's cemetery. 'We don't want a bloodbath in the holy city,' said one of Mr Zuheiri's relatives, Sabar al-Zuheiri. 'We call on the Islamic world to intervene.'

And what about the Olympics? Could Iraq's football team surprise the world and win the gold medal after its 1–0 victory over Australia?

'I don't think so,' Mr Zuheiri said.

FRONTS

CHRIS McGREAL

Rafah's ordeal

The moment al-Brazil plunged into darkness, Amjad Alweda knew what was coming. He grabbed his wife and three young children and bundled them down a pitch-black stairwell to a room at the back of their small block of flats. And then he stopped and listened.

'The sound of the tanks echoes along the streets around here so it seems they are coming from every direction at once and you never know which way to run,' says the 32-year-old Palestinian man.

Minutes later an engine roared and tons of steel – he didn't wait to discover whether it was a tank or a bulldozer – came crashing into the front of Alweda's computer shop. He squeezed his children through a back window and told them to run as the clanking monster tore at his livelihood.

'The soldiers were calling over the megaphones for everybody to leave their houses but there was no chance for people to get out before they started shooting from the tanks. It was completely dark and there were bullets flying around,' he says. 'Usually, we try and stay in the house when the fighting starts but we knew the army had been everywhere else so it must be our turn.'

For two weeks now, the Israeli army has been grinding its way through Rafah refugee camp in the southern tip of the Gaza Strip. 'Operation Root Canal' is ostensibly aimed at destroying some of the dozens of tunnels the military says are used for smuggling weapons under the border with Egypt. As about sixty-five tanks, armoured vehicles and mammoth armour-plated bulldozers rolled into Rafah, the Israeli army said it had intelligence that surface-to-air missiles were being hauled through the tunnels. But there was no sign of them as dozens of Palestinians attempted to exact some kind of price for the attack with pistols, AK-47s and homemade hand grenades. By the time the Israelis withdrew to the fringes of the camp where the tanks and bulldozers are perpetually at work, eighteen Palestinians were dead, including three children under fifteen years old, and more than 120 were wounded.

Just three tunnels were found, and no weapons. But in the process, the military crushed or rocketed nearly 200 homes, throwing about 1,700 people on to the street. The army claimed it never happened, that just ten homes were wrecked, and then sent back the bulldozers to grind the evidence that the houses ever existed into the dirt.

The raid was one of the largest of the past three years of intifada, rivalling the notorious levelling of the heart of Jenin refugee camp last year in the scale of destruction, if not loss of life. Yet there was barely a peep of protest from Britain or other European countries over the attack, and President George Bush defended the Israeli assault as a necessary part of the war on terrorism.

There is no such thing as a quiet night in Rafah. The shooting usually begins around dusk, punching the darkness with rapid machine-gun fire and tracer bullets for minutes at a time. Most of the Palestinian fire is aimed at the concrete pillboxes and lookout posts planted every 50 metres between the edge of Rafah and the Egyptian border where Israel retains control of a narrow strip of land along the frontier known as the Philadelphi road. The border is a tangle of wire, broken buildings and mud, bearing a resemblance to a First World War battlefield. Not far beyond are the Egyptian lookout towers, a tantalizing reminder to Rafah's 145,000 residents that there is a world outside the occupation. Palestinian bullets rarely reach their intended target. Israeli fire is more effective. The results can be seen peppered over the front of the houses that face the border, and in the death statistics.

Palestinians in Rafah have killed three soldiers and one Jewish settler during the intifada. The Israelis have killed about 280 people in Rafah over the past three years, accounting for about one in nine Palestinian deaths during the uprising and making the refugee camp and neighbouring small town one of the most dangerous places in the occupied territories. One in five of the dead are children or teenagers.

The Israeli military has designated Rafah a war zone. In doing so, the military exempts itself from many of its own restraints and provides a ready justification for the 'collateral damage' of civilian deaths. The government's view is summed up by a declaration signed by several cabinet ministers at an international summit in Jerusalem earlier this month that states 'the war on radical Islam is a righteous cause. The state of Israel is, symbolically and operationally, on the frontline of the battle to defend civilization.'

The latest battle was fought in al-Brazil, a civilian neighbourhood of Rafah refugee camp. The tanks moved in after dark, and the bulldozers tore down power lines. Among those fleeing as the tanks blasted away at Palestinian fighters was Naja Abu Neima, a 55-year-old grandmother. When she returned three days later, there was nothing left of her home. Today she is camped on an island of broken bricks and concrete under a makeshift shelter with a carpet on top and twisted metal sheeting against two sides.

'This tent represents all that is left of my house. All of our furniture, clothes, fridge, everything is destroyed,' she says. 'They killed my son a few months ago, and now they have destroyed my house. The Israelis claim we are terrorists. What do you see with your own eyes?'

Most of the casualties ended up at Rafah's only hospital. The director, Dr Ali Mousa, is resigned to the parade of corpses but he was unprepared for those of a couple of young children. 'Their bodies arrived here without any heads. Can you imagine how two children – twelve and fifteen years old – come to be without heads? They were hit by a tank shell. What could they have done to tanks?' he says. 'This is the worst attack of the past three years because they closed Rafah from all sides. The attacks on the refugee camps on the border are taking more and more time. It used to be they came in for a few hours at a time, but now it's for days.'

Dr Mousa faced a daily battle to get the wounded out of the battle zone and to move the serious casualties on to better facilities elsewhere in the Gaza Strip. One of his medics was shot in the chest as he helped move a man with a gunshot wound to his head. 'Many people tell us about pregnant women trying to get to hospital by moving from house to house, trying not to get shot,' he says.

After smashing in the front of Alweda's store, the army decided that his home, two floors above the shop, would make a good sniper's nest. The flat has a view across the open ground in front of the buildings and up each of the approaching side streets. The snipers broke up the floor tiles in the hallway and packed the fragments into sandbags. The military also destroyed much of the furniture and Alweda's small computer store where dozens of machines lay among the rubble. 'I work as a teacher in a refugee school. We are not highly paid. I earn $630 [£370] a month. It cost me $5,000 to set up my shop,' he says.

The soldiers stayed in al-Brazil three days and demolished a couple of dozen homes without finding any tunnels. Their final victim of the raid was fifteen-year-old Shadi Abu Elwan who went to help a friend recover furniture from under the rubble.

'There was gunfire and Shadi's friends found him lying on the floor bleeding from his head,' says the dead boy's distraught father, Nabil Abu Elwan. 'His head was completely broken by a bullet. He lived for a few minutes more, but then he died. When his friends looked they saw a tank parked close by, on the same side where the Palestinian homes were destroyed. My son was no threat to the tank, he was just helping his friends. I believe the Israeli soldiers in the tank like to kill people because they don't think of the Palestinians as people, they think of us as animals. Even the women and children are animals to them. It's sport, hunting. What can one boy do to them in their tanks? What threat was he?'

The army's claim that tunnels exist is not in doubt. Some of those uncovered are quite sophisticated, with wooden panelling, lighting and even phone lines linking the two ends. The tunnelling began back in the early 1980s under the domination of two Bedouin families who made a small fortune charging fixed fees to smuggle people, cigarettes, drugs and alcohol into Rafah. Even today, a packet of cigarettes is noticeably cheaper in Rafah than in Gaza city. But the military says their main use of the tunnels today is to shift weapons. 'This operation is the inevitable cost that the people of Rafah are paying for the tunnel industry. The trouble is that when no one else is practising law and order, we have to do it ourselves,' says an army spokeswoman, Major Sharon Feingold.

The newly homeless in Rafah question what the destruction of their houses has to do with unearthing the tunnels. 'Any house used to shoot at the [Israeli] force immediately lost its immunity and was destroyed,' says Feingold. 'This was partly the reason for so many houses being destroyed. There was a lot of resistance at the beginning of the operation.'

When Israeli troops go in to Rafah, they rarely have an easy time of it. 'Our main duty is to block any attack using all kinds of local made weapons we have,' says one of the fighters in the camp, who goes by the nom de guerre of Abu Abed. 'There is no balance between the force we have and the occupation army. We know our simple weapons can't affect their forces, but we want them to know there is a price to pay when they come.' Abu Abed waves a pistol and one of his comrades fiddles with the pin on a hand grenade until he is asked to stop. 'I think this resistance is one of the reasons the Israelis don't try and reoccupy all of Gaza like they have done with Jenin and Nablus and those other places,' he says.

But 'the resistance' is not always welcome. Few want to talk about it, although Alweda was unusually frank: 'Sometimes we kick the resisters out of our areas. We don't want to get stuck in the crossfire,' he says.

Abu Abed admits as much: 'We face lots of trouble with the Palestinian civilian population and it happened several times that we clashed with them because they don't want us. When we face a problem, we call our leaders and they usually order us to withdraw.'

For the governor of Rafah, Majid Ghal, the claims about tunnels and resistance are all nonsense. He says the demolitions are yet another grab for Palestinian land. 'What they are doing is to carve out a buffer zone between Rafah and the border. The Israelis have always said they do not want Palestine to control its borders or to have borders with other countries. They are trying to drive people out,' he says.

The army denies any such motive. But a clue to Israeli intent can be found in comments made on Israel radio a year ago by the then head of the military's southern command, which has responsibility for Gaza. Colonel Yom Tov Samya said house demolition was a policy and an end in itself, not a by-product of a search for tunnels: 'The IDF [Israeli Defence Force] has to knock down all the houses along a strip of three to four hundred metres. It doesn't matter what the future settlement will be, this will be the border with Egypt,' he said. 'Arafat has to be punished, and after every terrorist attack another two or three rows or houses on the Palestinian side of the border have to be knocked down ... This is a long-term policy. We simply have to take a very extreme step. It is doable and I am happy it is being done, but it's being carried out in doses that are too small, I regret to say. It has to be done in one big operation.'

Last Tuesday, nine young Rafah men in ill-fitting, rented shiny black suits had other ideas. All were to be married later that day, and all came from families whose homes were bulldozed a few days earlier. But first there was a bus tour under a banner with mangled English spelling but a clear enough sentiment: 'Wedding among destuton despit the pans'.

The nine grooms placed flowers stuck in makeshift vases fashioned from discarded Israeli shell casings on the remnants of their homes. 'It's to send a message to our enemies that we will go back to our homes,' says Younees Abu Jazaar, a fresh-faced twenty-year-old who married a cousin. 'We feel the pain but life can't stop. We are kind of happy to be getting married but kind of sad because we no longer have homes. But why should we allow them to wreck everything for us?'

Next stop was Gaza International Airport, a monument to Yasser Arafat's vanity, but also a source of some pride to the residents of neighbouring Rafah. The Israelis put the airport out of business at the beginning of the intifada by bulldozing craters into the runway, but the staff still turn up for work.

The bridegrooms posed beneath posters of 'martyrs' – suicide bombers, fighters and innocent Palestinian civilians killed – before moving on to the arrivals hall for photographs next to the luggage carousel.

'We are very proud of our airport,' says Abu Jazaar. 'Look at how beautiful it is. This is our hope, that all life can be as beautiful as this airport. Except the runway. Right now our life is like the runway.'

A few hours later, the nine were married in Rafah stadium where most of their parents are once again living in tents, half a century after their families were driven to Gaza by Israeli independence.

17 April 2004

AVI SHLAIM

Earth and stones

The literature on the Palestine question is usually so wrapped up in partisanship and polemics as to obscure, or at least to relegate to a secondary plane, the human and emotional side of the problem. It is therefore particularly pleasing to come across a writer who dwells not on politics but on the less familiar aspects of the Palestinian predicament. Mourid Barghouti is a prominent Palestinian poet who writes with great sensitivity and insight about his own experience of exile. But while writing in an autobiographical vein, he throws a great deal of light on the condition of his people.

I Saw Ramallah is an intensely lyrical account of the poet's return to his hometown on the West Bank from protracted exile abroad. It had an enthusiastic reception in the Arab world when it was first published in 1997. Ahdaf Soueif, the Egyptian novelist and critic, translated the book into English. Edward Said wrote a foreword, rating it as 'one of the finest existential accounts of Palestinian displacement that we now have'. So a great deal of literary talent went into the making of this English edition.

Having himself made a similar trip to Jerusalem (after an absence of forty-five years), Said knew well the mixture of emotions – happiness, of course, regret, sorrow, surprise, anger, among others – that accompanies such a return. The great novelty and power of Barghouti's book, as Said notes, is that it painstakingly chronicles the whirlwind of sensations and thoughts that tend to overwhelm the visitor on such occasions. Palestine, after all, is no ordinary place. Every Palestinian today is in the unusual position, in Said's words, of 'knowing that there was once a Palestine and yet seeing that place with a new name, people and identity that deny Palestine altogether. A "return" to Palestine is therefore an unusual, not to say urgently fraught, occurrence.'

Barghouti left his hometown in 1966, when he was twenty-two years old, to return to university in Cairo. Then came the Six-Day War and he was denied entry into Palestine. It was not until thirty years later that he was allowed to return home following the conclusion of the ill-fated Oslo accord between the PLO and Israel. The narrative begins with Barghouti crossing from Jordan into the West Bank over a rickety wooden bridge that stretches over a dried-up river. Behind him is the world; ahead of him is his world. But at the point of entry, he is assailed by self-doubt. What is he? A refugee? A citizen? A guest? He does not know. The land ahead of him could be defined in so many different ways: his homeland; the West Bank and Gaza; the Occupied Territories; Judea and Samaria; the Autonomous Government; Israel; Palestine. Last time he was there, everything was clear. Now everything is ambiguous and vague.

The one thing that was not vague was the Israeli soldier in charge of the crossing, wearing a yarmulke and carrying a gun. In the gun Barghouti saw his personal history, the history of his estrangement: 'His gun took from us the land of the poem and left us with the poem of the land. In his hand he holds earth, and in our hands we hold a mirage.' Again and again, the poet confronts the harsh reality: 'The others are still the masters of the place.'

Settlements built by Israel in the occupied territories in the aftermath of the Six-Day War drive home the message and disfigure the landscape. Yet these settlements are clearly there to stay: 'These are not children's fortresses of Lego or Meccano. These are Israel itself; Israel the idea and the ideology and the geography and the trick and the excuse. It is the place that is ours and that they have made theirs ... The settlements are the Palestinian diaspora itself.'

The joys of return and reunion with the homeland thus intermingle with a pervasive and insurmountable feeling of loss. 'The Occupation,' writes Barghouti, 'has created generations of us that have to adore an unknown beloved: distant, difficult, surrounded by guards, by walls, by nuclear missiles, by sheer terror. The long Occupation has succeeded in changing us from children of Palestine to children of the idea of Palestine.' He believes that it is in the interest of an occupation, any occupation, that the homeland should be transformed in the memory of its people into a bouquet of symbols. Merely symbols. Israel evidently succeeded in this respect for even in the aftermath of Oslo, the Palestinians acquired only the symbols without the substance of sovereignty and statehood.

Ramallah, the city of Barghouti's childhood, had changed beyond recognition. From a sleepy suburb of Jerusalem it was transformed into a bustling centre of Palestinian urban life. 'She has gone her own way,' Barghouti observes, 'sometimes as her people willed, and more often as her enemies willed. She has suffered and she has endured. Is she waiting to rest her head on your shoulder or is it you who seeks refuge in her strength?' It was a characteristically confused encounter but one that made it clear to the author that the events of 1967 had made him permanently homeless. As he himself discovered the hard way: 'It is enough for a person to go through the first experience of uprooting, to become uprooted for ever.'

Much of this beautifully written and evocative book is a lamentation on the conditions of exile. In the course of his enforced exile, Barghouti moved from Cairo to Baghdad to Beirut to Budapest to Amman and to Cairo again. It was impossible to hold on to a particular location. If his will clashed with the will of the 'masters of the place', it was always his will that was exposed to breaking. Mild criticism of President Anwar Sadat's visit to Jerusalem led to Barghouti's expulsion from Egypt. For seventeen years he and his wife Radwa Ashour were forced to live apart from each other, he as the PLO representative in Budapest, she and their son Tamim in Cairo, where she is a professor of English at Ain Shams University. Before Tamim was born, their friends used to joke that

Mourid and Radwa had decided to postpone having children until the Middle East problem had been solved.

Considering the pain and the heartaches he had to endure in exile, Barghouti writes about the Israelis with relative restraint, more in sorrow than in anger. Occasionally, however, his anger bubbles up to the surface, anger with the Zionists for taking over his country and anger directed at his own people for failing to put up more effective resistance. Professional politics has little appeal for him because, by his own admission, he reacts to the world with feelings and intuition. But politics inevitably enter into his narrative because they have come to dominate the life of the Palestinians 'since the Zionist project started knocking on the glass of our windows with its sharp nails and then on the doors, which it kicked down to enter all the rooms of the house and throw us out into the desert'.

The one trait of the Zionist movement that infuriates Barghouti above all others is its tendency to arrogate to itself the status of victim in this protracted struggle for Palestine. One example of this tendency was Itzhak Rabin's speech at the signing ceremony of the Oslo accord in the White House garden, in which he presented Israel as the victim of war and violence. On hearing Rabin's words, Barghouti felt a sharp pang of pain. He knew that the Palestinians had been defeated again: Rabin took everything, even the story of their death.

3 December 2003

LINDA GRANT

The day my son died

'Me, Yosi Mendelevich, I was considered to be a very protective father. But there was a hole in my plan: I let my son take buses. I'm going to show you everything that happened on the last day of my son Yuval's life, which was 5 March 2003, when he was thirteen and a half years old, so you will understand the banality of the atrocity.

'At 6.45 a.m. I woke him up. He hugged me and said, "Give me some strength for the morning", so I hugged him strongly. He got up, he washed his face, brushed his teeth, ate Coco Pops and milk for breakfast, and put a cheese sandwich into his schoolbag for his lunch.

'While he was waking up, his murderer, Mohammed Kawasma, was travelling back from Hebron, where he had gone to pick up the bomb, through Abu Dis where they are now building the fence, but there was no fence there then and no one stopped him at the checkpoint. Around 11 a.m., when Yuval was finishing maths, the murderer was arriving here in Haifa. He decided to wait until 2 p.m. when all the kids from school were going home and the buses were more crowded. At 2.05 p.m., Yuval got on the number thirty-seven bus here, at the stop by his school, sat down in the fifth row from the back, on the right, directly behind the murderer, and at 2.07 p.m. the bus started moving.

'After driving 300 metres, Yuval rang his mother to let her know he was on his way home. After this traffic light, at 2.10 p.m., Yuval rang me. He told me he was a little late because his art teacher had asked him to stay on after school to make a paper lion for Purim. I told him a joke; he laughed, he said, "Daddy, I love you," and at that moment, 2.14 p.m. and 32 seconds, according to the time his watch stopped, the murderer activated the detonator of the belt carrying 17lbs of explosives, along with hundreds of small metal balls designed to worsen the impact. The bomb was made by a master of such diabolic devices in Hebron, Ali Alan, who has now been killed by Israeli security forces.

'When the phone went dead, I thought it was only a disturbance in the cellular system and I didn't get suspicious. Then I got a call from a friend who said, "How is Yuval?" I said, "Why?" He said, "You heard there was a suicide bomb in Moriah Avenue?" I was shivering, a cold sweat was on my skin. I drove down the street and saw the bus. The other bodies were on the road in body bags but Yuval was still there, under a blanket, too burnt to be identified. His left arm with the stopped watch was blown off his body and was hanging out of the window on the other side of the bus. The air smelled of scorched flesh and I thought of Yuval's great-grandparents who were wiped from the earth in Poland in 1941. That was their holocaust; this is his. Moriah, by the way, is the name of the mountain where God tested Abraham to sacrifice his son Isaac, but no one called from the sky to save my boy.

'Now I want to show you the wall here behind the bus stop, where the blood of our children was spilled. Seventeen people were massacred that day – a Druze, a Muslim Arab, a girl of the Bahai faith. Exactly two weeks before Yuval was murdered he participated in a co-existence project in an Arab village. This was bi-national Haifa. My barber, our butcher, our grocer are all Arab. Seven thousand people came to our house in the days of mourning, but no Arabs came. That is a devastating issue for me. Meanwhile, in Abu Dis, the family of Mohammed Kawasma were holding three days of celebration. He was not a refugee; his house was not demolished. He was a computer student in the Islamic Polytechnic of Hebron. Nothing brought him to that deed but religious ideology.

'This is our house. This is Yuval's room. He loved Harry Potter and *Lord of the Rings*. Here is his Nintendo, his dartboard, his clothes, his trainers; here is the paper lion he stayed behind at school to make. Did you see this sticker on his door? It says "A whole generation wants peace" but he changed it to "A whole Yuval wants peace".

'I am an engineer, not a humanities person. However deep I go into language, I have no words to describe the agony. Some major part of myself is a black hole. Now we are at the cemetery. Here is his grave in the section that the municipality set aside for the victims of terror. It is filling up quite quickly. Here is my son under a granite stone, the dates of his life: 10.9.1989–5.3.2003.'

This piece was based on a lengthy interview with Mr Mendelevich by Linda Grant.

27 November 2003

HELENA SMITH

Back to Bingol

Of all the graves dug into the windswept bluff overlooking Bingol, that of Gokhan Elaltuntas is by far the smallest. When, under armed guard, relatives buried the suicide bomber in the middle of the night they had only to lower his casket into a tiny gash in the earth. Now the man who drove his 'car of death' into a synagogue in Istanbul lies under a mound of red clay no bigger than a short Turkish rug. 'They couldn't do otherwise because he came with no head or arms or legs,' said Harkan Turk Ilmas, a policeman who watched over the ceremony. 'It was just his torso that they managed to retrieve.' Across the sullen mountain town, in a roadside grave, lies his comrade Mesut Cabuk, who died almost simultaneously in a second synagogue attack. When no one was looking, his family buried him, too.

That was last Tuesday. Two days later Azad Ekinci and Feridan Ugurlu followed suit, driving their 'cars of death' into the British consulate and HSBC bank, also in Istanbul. The first attack, it seems, had given them their cue. Within hours of the first explosions they were driving out of Bingol. Passing military checkpoints, they took the 500-mile route to Turkey's great commercial capital and the heart of their mission: their country's worst ever terrorist attack.

These two men – so good, so calm, say friends – were no strangers to hardship. From early on they had known suffering, first as ethnic Kurds who inhabited the heavily militarized badlands of Turkey, then as Muslim fundamentalists. Ekinci, who would ram his explosive-laden truck into the British consulate, saw his father, Idris, shot dead by Turkish nationalists when he was two.

'Idris was a good man who led a workers' union at Bingol's town hall, but Turkish nationalists shot him because he was a prominent member of the PKK [the outlawed Kurdish rebel group],' said Ridvan Kizgin, who heads the local Turkish Human Rights Foundation. 'I think his death played a role in making Azad the sort of person he became.'

For the rest of his childhood and much of his adult life, Ekinci was kept indoors by a protective mother – until he met Mesut, who had a taste for Jean-Paul Sartre and the Islamist guerrilla group Hizbullah. With no work and little else to do, the pair soon became inseparable.

'They were so tight, one couldn't go without the other to the toilet,' said Adul Ali Benghizou, a middle-aged man who said he knew the two well. 'Ekinci was a bit isolated, but when he met Mesut he changed. Mesut was obsessed with existentialism and Jean-Paul Sartre. Personally, I think he had psychological problems, but he had a great influence on Azad.'

Although Ekinci had displayed no particular affection for political Islam, he began patronizing the plethora of mosques and Koranic schools in Bingol.

Through the charismatic sheikhs who lead underground religious sects, known as *tarikats*, the pair soon became infused with a militant Islam that took them to Bosnia, Afghanistan and Chechnya. In Bingol, with its population of 60,000, many believe it was the sheikhs who first schooled the bombers in the fundamentals of hate. The four Turkish Kurds reportedly spent years criss-crossing into Iran, Syria, Pakistan and the Gulf states to train in the art of wiring explosives. In Istanbul, the experts on militant Islam say the trips were almost certainly funded by the business-endowed foundations that support the sects.

But the bombers could have come from anywhere in Turkey's remote south-east, where most residents barely scratch a living from the land. 'When you have no work and no hope of a job you get angry, and then you look elsewhere for things to do,' said Mr Benghizou, a former Istanbul journalist who returned to Bingol to look after his mother. 'A lot of young people here are so desperate they become nihilists. The only thing Bingol offers them is heroin smuggling from Iran. With nothing to lose, they become open to the spirit of al-Qaida. When they go to Pakistan they can make money to send back to their families. It's the same with Hizbullah. Once you're in Hizbullah, I hear, they make sure to look after you and your family.'

Until 1999, when Kurdish separatists declared a unilateral ceasefire in their fight to create an independent state in the south of Turkey, successive governments in Ankara gave support to Islamic radicals in the region. For more than two decades Hizbullah received arms and money from Turkish security forces to crush rebels in the PKK. As a Hizbullah stronghold, some of the most brutal fighting took place around Bingol.

'They were tolerated on the basis that the enemy of my enemy is my friend,' said Ersin Kalaycioglu, a political scientist at Istanbul's Sabachi University. 'But when Hizbullah stopped being of use to the government it clamped down on them with a vengeance. According to police databases, it had around 20,000 members, but only 4,000 were caught. So the question is, what happens to the rest?'

Mr Kizgin, the human rights worker, says the answer is obvious. 'When the dirty war was over, Hizbullah began looking to radical Islamic groups for support. Unfortunately, it's a repeat of the same story that we saw with the Americans and the Taliban. The Turkish state created Hizbullah and now it is paying the price.'

In this climate the movements of Ekinci and his comrades went unchecked. Although there was clear evidence that 1,000 Turks had gone abroad as religious warrior volunteers, their missions appear to have been dismissed by the Turkish security forces. Western intelligence services now think the Turkish jihadis acted as intermediaries between local groups such as Hizbullah and networked links to al-Qaida.

The Istanbul bombings plunged Bingol into a strange mourning. The revelation that all four suicide bombers came from the town has shamed locals, who want nothing to do with terrorists. The mountain-rimmed town, famed for honey and nuts, had barely recovered from an earthquake that killed 167 in May. But as Ankara turns its military might against terrorism, the residents of

Bingol will have to live with the fear that the security forces who have now swamped the town will make their lives even harder.

'The whole of Bingol is very upset,' said the town's deputy governor, Fikret Zaman. 'Even the relatives of the four bombers are very upset. Not at their deaths so much, but that they brought this terrible shame to Bingol. We Turks are not Islamic fundamentalists. We are very proud that we have the Muslim world's only secular state.'

But Bingol is also in denial. The suicide bombers were not an isolated group. They were a product of a system that appears to nurture religious-inspired hate – as well as the country's failure to address the problem of its 12 million ethnic Kurds. Few believe that this is the end of the flow of suicide bombers from these areas.

'All the ingredients are in place for several more to come along,' said Mr Kizgin. 'Turkey has to give us Kurds better basic rights. It has to give us our dignity and a better education. We have to be able to use our own language, have our own names ...'

That would be one of the better steps authorities could take to ensuring that no more oddly sized graves overlook the wild, windswept bluffs of Bingol.

Three more alleged accomplices in the Istanbul bombings were arrested, two of them women, on charges of belonging to and aiding an illegal organization. Around thirty accomplices have since been arrested and charged with complicity in the bombings but the masterminds are still at large. They are rumoured to have sought refuge in Iran.

13 March 2004

ANGELIQUE CHRISAFIS

Madrid mourns

No one was sure whether it was over. Bob Dylan's 'Knocking on Heaven's Door' and U2's 'Sunday Bloody Sunday' hummed from radios, in between tearful speeches from DJs.

On screens in empty bars, newscasters were carefully listing the distinguishing features of corpses which hadn't been claimed – woman in her thirties; height: 5 feet. Children left uncollected at kindergarten were presumed to have gone to relatives to sit by the phone.

In the streets, Spanish flags with black ribbons clung to every available façade, lamppost, cashpoint, street-sweeping machine in Madrid. But there was a reticence before the grieving and demonstrations began. A fear that there could possibly be more to come: another blast, another explosion. Because, as one tax inspector said as he entered a terrifyingly empty tapas bar, 'We're in some kind of suspended nightmare. We still don't know what the hell is going on here. Why? Someone, please, tell me why.'

Then, slowly, thousands began to congregate in squares, unfurling banners begging 'We don't want to die' and 'Death to Eta', 'Peace not terrorism'. As the thousands multiplied into a million, and then two, Madrid knew it was witnessing the biggest mass-protest in Spanish history.

At first, the worst thing was the silence. The loudest, most raucous city in Europe – famous for its working class, which never draws breath and is always there with an opinion – was suddenly mute. 'There are no words to describe this,' was the answer from the cleaners at the station, the Italian woman in furs at the bus-stop. Language had failed everyone. The city had been up all night trying to make sense of it in darkened living rooms. People looked drawn, gaunt, scowling, afraid. 'I've never seen us look like this,' said an insurance inspector. 'So tense, so goddam furious, looking left to right, hunching over and walking straight ahead.'

By 7 p.m., over 2 million people were marching on the centre of Madrid – a canopy of umbrellas trying to reclaim the streets from an unknown enemy. 'Madrid is weeping,' they chanted. The infirm stood still and let the crowds sweep past them. They marched for hours, but opinions were gradually polarizing.

An architect with a Spanish flag brushed off Eta's denial of the attack. 'Of course it was Eta,' she spat. She would vote for prime minister José María Aznar on Sunday.

A civil servant from Madrid would spoil his vote. 'Al-Qaida did this but it doesn't suit our pro-war government to tell us until the elections are over.'

The three days of mourning was launched at noon with ten minutes' synchronized silence as taxi drivers climbed out of cabs and workers went outside. People stood side by side on Madrid's avenues, but there was not yet the frenzied embracing and outpouring they might have expected. It was a city almost pre-grief. They were still gripped by fury, rage and, something they remembered from lesser Eta bomb blasts over the last twenty years, a horrific tension. Society was winded. And when the silence took hold and the scented candles in the street caused people to pause to reflect, their ears tuned into the sirens which still droned through the city.

Those who had run from another bomb scare on a rail line into Atocha yesterday morning were still shaking. Many had left the trains wrapped in black ribbons to walk into town to lay their candles.

At the Puerta del Sol square in front of the regional government headquarters, thousands of students gathered with placards: 'The tears of 200 people'; 'No to terrorism'; 'What are you going to do with power when you are dead?'; 'We're Spanish. Is it a crime?'

As the drizzle began, they sat down on the pavement punctuating the silence with a steady chant: 'No Eta no, Eta no, Eta no, Eta no' or 'Eta, you sons of a bitch'.

Fourteen-year-olds had painted black ribbons on their faces, or large CND signs. They handed out stickers saying 'No to terrorism'. One, whose brother's best friend had been killed in the first explosion, had 'peace' tattooed in ink on her forehead. She didn't cry but her eyebrows were raised in a silent grimace. 'I'm scared. I'm terrified. We were ushered out of the underground this morning in another bomb scare. I don't know what to do.' She and her friends believed that Islamist militants had carried out the killings, and that there was a script of some sort from September 11 that they could now follow – if they could remember what people did in New York, they would be OK. Better to huddle in this square and promote peace than go home to face the TV images.

They had started by gathering under flags. It was beyond their imagination that this act of 'animal barbarism' could have begun at home. 'It must be related to September 11. It must be,' said a sixteen-year-old. 'The scale of it, the simultaneous attacks. It had to be them. Nobody in Spain could do that to other Spaniards, surely?'

The pensioners, for the most part, felt different. Their brows were knitted. They felt sick to the stomach. They said they remembered an era of fascism when horrors were committed by Spaniard against Spaniard; they mentioned the not-so-distant civil war.

'Why now? Why, when everyone has liberty, everyone has everything they want in Spain?' asked a 55-year-old grandmother in an empty department store. She had survived an Eta bomb attempt many years earlier herself.

Gloria Alcaine, another grandmother from Burgos, said, 'This has killed the Spanish soul, numbed us. It has ripped the heart right out of Spain. People are crying in their homes; that has never happened before. They have killed all of us, all of us.'

At Atocha's makeshift memorial were shrines with candles, flowers and Virgin Marys; on pavements and concourses sat those who would have been on the trains that day and who had now come into the city centre to march: the cleaner who had overslept; the hotel worker who had had a day off and who was now resolved to vote fascist; the Ecuadorian cleaner who woke up to the bomb blast outside her home facing Atocha and heard the police ringing every doorbell in her building telling people to keep their windows closed, and whose eleven-year-old daughter turned wild with fear and had to be held down until the panic subsided. 'They were workers, immigrants who minded their own business. Not politicians, but the strivers, the underclass.'

Some refused to blame Aznar, as the election banners hung useless behind giant sheets with black ribbons. 'It's not his fault,' said a retired telecoms worker. But others were afraid that if Eta wasn't responsible, how on earth had their country, with a population 90 per cent opposed to war in Iraq prompted this scale of murder against them? One man hinted Mr Aznar could have reaped what he had sown. 'Aznar, the dead thank you,' said the message on a wall at Atocha as the marchers gathered.

On the walls of the back streets were the faintest remnants of Catalan graffiti, which sat uneasily under the skin of everyone marching against yesterday: 'Aznar, war criminal'; 'Aznar resign'; 'No war, no occupation.'

'We don't know who the hell did this. There is no rhyme or reason for it. Don't ask anyone for an explanation,' said one newspaper vendor, like many, unable to have a conversation about it yet. 'Until an explanation is given, we just feel sick, sick, sick and afraid.'

10 March 2004

SERGEI GLAZYEV AND VITALY BAKHRUSHIN

Letters to President Putin

For centuries, Russian peasants with grievances took letters to the tsar, hoping for his help. In the run-up to Sunday's presidential election, the tradition has seen a revival, with the Kremlin receiving 11,000 pleas each week for Vladimir Putin's personal attention. Here is a selection.

A private letter from the parents of a conscript killed in the first Chechen war, 19 February 2004.

Good afternoon, Vladimir Vladimirovich,

I, Yuri Tsepukh, and my wife, Nadezhda, are the family of Sergeant Vladimir Tsepukh, who died in Chechnya. Our son was called to the Army service in June 1994 and he went to Chechnya as a volunteer in February 1995. On 18 April, as their unit returned from Chechnya, his column was ambushed. Both officers were killed and our son took command of the unit, ordering their retreat. After they exhausted their munitions, they fought with knives and finally he died.

Two days later, for a ransom, Chechen fighters gave the corpse of my son back to the unit. Our son was decorated with the Order 'For Bravery' and during the next year we have been paid everything normally given in such cases – about 10,0000 rubles [£190]. The only thing we cannot understand is why the families of [the sailors who died on the submarine the] *Kursk* were paid several hundred thousand rubles.

Before my son's death I worked as a tractor driver, and my wife was working too. But after my son's death everything became a mess: my wife spent about a year in different hospitals, both of us dropped our work, and she still has serious health problems. Our local hospital was closed and without money it is senseless to go to the [larger] regional hospital where you have to pay for all medical care.

My wife is paid 1,196 rubles pension for our son, and my salary now is 500 rubles. Do you think a person can live on such money and find their health improves?

We also have a daughter; she is now twenty-three. She graduated from the Teacher's Institute, then she went to Moscow. It wasn't bad at first. She had a job at a school and [highly sought after] registration to live in Moscow. Then she got acquainted with a man, they married and had a daughter. But her relations with her mother-in-law are bad, and she refuses to [provide the necessary documents] for my daughter to be registered in her flat. It's no use for my daughter to go back to our village; there is no work for her here.

That is why we have to address you. Vladimir Vladimirovich, we would like to ask you to provide our daughter with a room in a communal flat. For me and for my wife you are the only hope, because if our son was alive my life would be completely different and I would never think about addressing you. You have so many things to take care and to think of.

An open letter from the Society for the Victims of the Terrorist Act Nord Ost theatre siege last October, in which 129 people died after lethal gas was deployed to end a standoff with forty Chechen gunmen and suicide bombers. It was written on 6 February 2004, the day a suicide bomber killed forty-one commuters on a packed Moscow metro train.

Vladimir Vladimirovich!

Several hours ago another act of terrorism happened again in the Russian capital. Again in Moscow people are stirred into searching for their relatives in the hospitals and morgues. How many more tears will fall this time? The government of Russia and of Moscow have not learned the bitter lessons of the tragedy at Dubrovka theatre ... Clearly you are not personally interested in how a cell of over forty people can penetrate Moscow incognito and assemble there such a large quantity of arms and explosives?

After Nord Ost in Moscow there were again explosions on Tverskaya Street, at the Tushino Aerodrome [rock concert] and at the Hotel National. In the days before the election, we wretchedly and loudly ask you: aren't you the active guarantor of our security and our human rights? Are we able to believe your words, your pre-electoral campaign, and be sure that in Russia, in the country where we live, the president will do everything to ensure that people can live peace fully, have a right to simple, human happiness and do not need a supply of black clothes for one funeral after another? Today, we are no longer asking but rather demanding that you guarantee our right to life and security.

From families of Chechens who have disappeared after being arrested, 14 January 2004.

Dear Mr President,

Endless despair makes us – close relatives of people who have disappeared after their arrest by Russian law enforcement – address you. We make our call to you as the guarantor of the constitution of the Russian federation. We have addressed you several times before individually and in collective letters but probably they didn't reach you. If they had reached you, we would have seen positive work towards solving one of the hugest problems in Chechnya: the disappearances that go on without end here.

Over a period of four years, unknown armed people in camouflage have kidnapped 255 persons. One hundred and ninety-seven of them have disappeared, thirty-nine were returned to their villages bearing signs of torture, and in eighteen cases corpses were found bearing signs of a violent death. One can say that this data is not the whole truth, because there are many more victims and this happens on a very small territory with only thirteen villages, so you can understand how enormous our tragedy and pain is.

In most of the cases the kidnappings were carried out with the help of military equipment such as APCs [armoured personnel carriers] and military cars. The kidnappers used this equipment to travel to the scene of the crime and back again through the checkpoints of the federal forces. In some cases we found it possible to pass the numbers of the equipment and cars the criminals used to the prosecutor's office. Some of these cars were later found on the territory of the military command's office or in police headquarters. These facts make it evident that, in most cases, these crimes were committed by representatives of federal law enforcement.

30 August 2004

THOMAS DE WAAL

Lucky charm

Eight years ago in Grozny, at the end of the first war in Chechnya, I met a man who called himself a sharia judge. He was an ex-footballer turned rebel fighter, one of the men who had come down from the mountains and thrown the Russians out. The twenty-something judge's grasp of Islam seemed about as poor as mine as he chatted flirtatiously with my female colleague and smoked incessantly. His 'sharia court' had done virtually nothing.

The ex-footballer embodied all the confusions of a conflict that is still not properly understood. On the surface an Islamic radical, he was a Chechen nationalist who had picked up Islam like a lucky charm amid the ruins left behind by the Russian army.

Things have changed in Chechnya since then. I thought of the sharia judge last week on hearing of the plane explosions in Russia, which were probably the work of Islamic Chechen extremists or their allies. During the past two years, terrorism associated with Chechnya has killed several hundred Russian and Chechen civilians. Five years ago, when Moscow launched an 'anti-terrorist operation' to recapture Chechnya, there was no real terrorism there. Now, thanks mainly to Moscow's policies, it is becoming a real threat.

From a distance, the war in Chechnya has acquired a dark aura of inevitability: an implacable Islamic warrior people fighting an invading Russian army. But the Chechens are far from being Afghans. They are a small mountain people with a history of resistance to the Russian state, but also of pragmatic accommodation with it. Most speak Russian much better than they do Chechen, and almost all have relatives working in the rest of Russia.

Moreover, most Chechens I know are viscerally opposed to the Islamic fundamentalism that has slowly been infiltrating their republic during the past ten years. If they are Muslim, they are Sufis practising a form of local Islam that is all but incomprehensible to Arab incomers. For years, the Chechens sent away these interlopers with curses when they were told to stop visiting their local shrines or to start veiling their women. The Arab zealots have kept on coming, though in much smaller numbers than the Russians claim. There are ties with the Middle East that didn't exist before. And there are Chechens whose lives have been so broken by bombings, abductions and 'filtration camps' that they are ready to be suicide bombers.

The tragedy of Chechnya is that most Chechens are fed up with the zealots, but have nowhere else to turn. They would almost certainly give up the hope of independence for a peaceful existence in the Russian state – if only the Russians would guarantee them basic rights.

A villager in Paul Mitchell's recent film on Chechnya for BBC4 says of Moscow's second military intervention in 1999: 'If the Russians had been just a little civilized and decent to the ordinary working man, then the people would have welcomed them with open arms. But so many innocent people have been tortured and killed. Everybody knows that hundreds of people just disappear. Where are they?'

Now, Chechens are governed by two vicious and criminal armed groups. Russian soldiers earn money from extra pay and black market oil trading, and have every incentive to stay, treating the Chechen population as a target for extortion and intimidation. The second group, the Kadyrovtsy, are Chechens loyal to 27-year-old Ramzan Kadyrov, son of the late pro-Moscow Chechen leader Akhmad Kadyrov, who uses thousands of armed men to maintain his economic and political power. His Balkan equivalents ended up in the courts of The Hague.

These venal agents of violence make Moscow's 'war on terror' unwinnable. Corruption is so rife that in June the rebels were able to bribe their way past a dozen checkpoints and attack police stations in the neighbouring republic of Ingushetia, 100 miles from the 'combat zone'. Yesterday, the Kadyrovtsy's man was elected president of Chechnya in a rigged poll. Alu Alkhanov had no real opposition and not many votes.

The official Russian position is more or less as follows: Chechnya is a front in the international war on terror and our policies there deserve unreserved Western support; however, it is a domestic political issue and no international organizations can be involved. The situation is getting back to normal; but it is still too dangerous for journalists or human rights workers to be given free access.

The Western position is equally short-sighted. It is to mildly condemn human rights abuses, express sympathy for Russia's problem with terrorism, pray that the extremists do not attack a Western target next, and hope that Chechnya will go away.

It will not. The extremists have nothing to lose. Almost everything has been tried except a broad-based political process not manipulated by Moscow, and a genuine international presence by the UN or the Organization for Security and Cooperation in Europe to monitor what is going on. This darkest corner of Europe desperately needs some light.

13 September 2004

NICK PATON WALSH

Three days in Beslan

At first it seemed as if someone had made an embarrassing mistake. The presidential aide to the North Caucusus, Vladimir Yakovlev, said on Russian news wires that an entire school had been kidnapped. This was so hard to believe that it was a while before the rush to head south began.

Beslan airport was promptly closed, and we opted to use a local stringer and a proper package for Thursday's paper. *The Times* and *Independent* headed straight for Beslan and got there at about 11 p.m., or 8 p.m. London time. I landed about fourteen hours later at the same Mineralniye Vodi airport, two hours north of Beslan. At the airport, a gruff policeman dragged me into a cramped office where they made it clear they were looking for a German reporter and al-Jazeera.

They let us go after photocopying our documents. Two hours later, we crossed into Northern Ossetia easily. Others were less lucky – Anna Politkovskaya, a reporter known for her bold coverage of Chechnya, and a Georgian TV crew say they were drugged, presumably by the authorities.

But once we were in Beslan, federal control evaporated. Before the siege began, a cordon was maintained by local police and some federal troops, blocking all vantage points on to the school. The gunmen had been taking pot shots and blew up a car that came too close on Thursday.

For the next two days, a tense group of about two hundred journalists milled around the Palace of Culture, a cinema where officials gave press conferences. The information came out in dribs and drabs, not much of it credible. Mobile phone coverage was patchy, many people switching to the local network or satphones.

Until Friday morning – the final day of the siege – official spokesmen had left the total of hostages at 354 – perhaps a quarter of the final total. It was a tacit admission that casualty figures would be high. During one such announcement, the crowd jeered the official, unable to tolerate the falsehoods any more.

There was little for relatives to do other than talk anxiously to the media. Many were hard to talk to: the Caucasus mentality is strictly private in grief. Some were angered by the intrusion.

I ended up staying with a local family. It was Thursday night, and I had a low battery on my laptop and an imminent deadline. I knocked on a random door and the grandmother let me use their electric socket. The son, Gior, aged thirteen, was edgy. His mother was inside the school, as was his sister, aged seven (they are both safe now). He had been expelled from the school recently for bullying. They offered me their couch.

The mother and father were local law enforcement officials. My host, who insisted on getting me very drunk the night after the siege and his wife's release, used his status to get me access and introduce me to families who would otherwise have kept mum. At one point, my host was discussing the siege in his kitchen with two friends. I interrupted to correct him over the timing of the first explosion in the school. He looked at me and grinned. 'You see. He wrote it all down,' he told his friends. He saw the press as the only chance of hearing the truth about what happened at Beslan.

On Friday, at 1.05 p.m., I was near the local administration building when a huge blast shook the floor. Then another; then gunfire. Both blasts and gunfire kept getting nearer. 'It' had clearly started. The living bodies of children, covered in someone else's blood and their own grime, were carried out via the gaps between the buildings. One policeman said there had been an explosion, that no gunmen had died and hostages had. I approached a normally charming senior Kremlin press aide to ask in Russian if the siege had officially started. He looked at me, furious, and panicked. 'Be gone!' he screamed, pointing the way out.

Thirty minutes later I moved round to where the school meets the railway line. There stood two Russian tanks and one uptight *spetznaz* soldier. While he insisted I leave, the local militia goons, sweaty men in tracksuits carrying hunting rifles, asked if I wanted to hang out with them. I was soon dragged away.

At the Palace of Culture, the cordon that once held us back had disappeared. The small paths down from the school had become a shuttle service for stretchers. Those carrying casualties were greeted with little bar cameras, a few emergency workers, sequestered cars, and some anxious locals. Three days in, the press had managed to get there from London, but the Russian government had not managed to create a proper triage system.

It was a mess. Bodies were dumped on the grass verge. Some journalists tried to do live broadcasts, while others ducked behind walls. I noticed a column of local men heading up one path towards the school itself and followed. A series of garages provided some cover just to the left of the school courtyard. Here I met the *Telegraph*, the *Baltimore Sun* and a Sky News cameraman.

Locals were everywhere – be they militia or anxious parents. Throughout the siege, Western television – CNN, BBC, Sky – carried live footage. But Russian state TV – and even local TV – used live and pre-recorded shots that they played in hourly bulletins. The people of Beslan had to go to the site of the siege to follow what was happening.

Anarchy ruled. The federal government sent in their finest special forces to fight, but did not use their plentiful conscripts to erect a protective cordon for their operation. Half an hour after the Dubrovka theatre siege in Moscow two years ago, I had to barge authoritatively through a line of tired conscripts to reach the front of the theatre to see the triage. I was also detained as I tried to leave the siege site.

Here, ninety minutes into the siege, there was no line to cross and only your judgement held you back. It was possible to walk through one garage, whose back wall had been punctured to provide an escape route for hostages, and see the school's yard. I walked round to the front of the school where the fighting was most intense and hid behind a wall, ducking low behind a crowd of large, tall men, gaping as if they were at a football match. One stray round caused the gaggle to step back. But then some, a few in tracksuits, a few in smocks, strolled in a column down one wall that linked the garages to the gym, the site massacre.

The siege was ongoing, but had apparently moved to the back of the s_____.

Few stray rounds were hitting the courtyard now. I feared access to the scene would be impossible later, so I headed towards the gym.

Seen from the gym door, the floor contained nothing recognizable except roof material and some black mulch. It had clearly been completely destroyed. I crossed over to the other side of the courtyard, and moved down to the other side of the gym where a Russian cameraman and photographer joined local militia and *spetznaz*. More bodies were being brought out of the window. Inside, the walls were blown plasterless.

At 4.30 p.m., the stream of corpses coming from the school was still endless.

The gunfire and blasts were constant. My desk insisted that I start writing at 5.00 p.m. The gunfire continued, but I left and interviewed my host's wife, who had a detailed grasp of events inside the gym.

I had seen enough.

AMERICA

3 November 2003

JULIAN BORGER

Poverty jam

The free food is handed out at nine o'clock, but the queue starts forming hours earlier. By dawn, there is a line of cars stretching half a mile back. In Logan, it is what passes for rush hour – a traffic jam driven by poverty and hunger.

The cars come out of the Ohio hills in all shapes and sizes, from the old jalopies of the chronically poor, to the newer, sleeker models of the new members of the club, who only months ago considered themselves middle class, before jobs and their retirement funds evaporated.

Dan Larkin is sitting in his middle-of-the-range pick-up truck. Since the glassware company he worked for closed its doors this time last year, he has found it hard to pay his bills. His unemployment benefits ran out six months ago and his groceries bill is the only part of his budget that has some give. He and his wife sometimes skip meals or eat less to make sure their six-year-old daughter has enough.

'I would have a real problem putting food on the table if it wasn't for this,' Mr Larkin said, his car inching towards Logan's church-run food pantry. As the queue rolled forward, he reflected on the ironies of being a citizen of the world's sole superpower. 'They're sending eighty-seven billion dollars to the second richest oil nation in the world but can't afford to feed their own here in the States.'

George Bush's America is the wealthiest and most powerful nation the world has ever known, but at home it is being gnawed away from the inside by persistent and rising poverty. The 3 million Americans who have lost their jobs since Mr Bush took office in January 2001 have yet to find new work in a largely jobless recovery, and they are finding that the safety net they assumed was beneath them has long since unravelled. There is not much left to stop them falling.

Last year alone, another 1.7 million Americans slipped below the poverty line, bringing the total to 34.6 million, one in eight of the population. Over 13 million of them are children. In fact, the US has the worst child poverty rate and the worst life expectancy of all the world's industrialized countries, and the plight of its poor is worsening.

The ranks of the hungry are increasing in step. About 31 million Americans were deemed to be 'food insecure' (they literally did not know where their next meal was coming from). Of those, more than 9 million were categorized by the US Department of Agriculture as experiencing real hunger, defined by them as an 'uneasy or painful sensation caused by lack of food due to lack of resources to obtain food'. That was two years ago, before the recession really began to bite. Partial surveys suggest the problem has deepened considerably since then. In twenty-five major cities the need for emergency food rose an average of 19 per cent last year. Another indicator is the demand for food stamps, the government aid programme of last resort. The number of Americans on stamps has risen from 17 million to 22 million since Mr Bush took office.

In Ohio, hunger is an epidemic. Since George Bush won Ohio in the 2000 presidential elections, the state has lost one in six of its manufacturing jobs. Two million of the state's 11 million population resorted to food charities last year, an increase of more than 18 per cent from 2001. In Logan, over 500 families regularly turn out twice monthly at the food pantry run by the Smith Chapel United Methodist Church.

'In all our history starting in the mid-eighties we've never seen these numbers,' said Dannie Devol, who runs the pantry. The food comes from a regional food bank, which is stocked by a mix of private donations and food bought from local farmers by the government.

Fresh vegetables, cans of meat and tuna, and boxes of cereal are stacked in the car park and as the line of cars breaks into two queues to edge past the pallets, volunteers inspect identity cards (customers have to show they live in the county and are in need) before loading rations of food into the backs of the vehicles. It is an efficient and peculiarly American solution to hunger – a drive-through soup kitchen.

Those without cars hitch rides with neighbours. Mothers come with their children in the back of trucks. Karin Chriss brought one of her three children in a ten-year-old Chevrolet van. 'If they stopped this I'd be hurt food-wise. I'm cutting down the amount we eat as it is,' she said. Her husband is a truck driver but does not earn enough to pay the bills. The people in Washington, she feels, 'need to come down and see how many people are in these lines'.

Not many Washington politicians do. There was a time when fighting this kind of poverty was at the core of American politics: Franklin Roosevelt made it his life's work; Lyndon Johnson declared a war on poverty with his Great Society programmes in the 1960s. There are more Americans living in poverty now than there were in 1965, but neither party has much to say about it. The Bush Republicans see it as a matter for 'faith-based charities', the status quo before Roosevelt's New Deal in the 1930s. The trouble is that hard times are drying up donations at the very time private charities are being asked to take on most of the burden. Democrats, meanwhile, are anxious not to appear as class warriors, and most of the Democratic presidential contenders in this election portray themselves as champions of the middle class, for good reason. Americans who see themselves as middle class are much more likely to vote than those who know they are poor.

Mrs Chriss thinks all parties should be abolished. Angela Cooper, also queuing with a young child, complains that families like hers have been forgotten. But then again, she has relatives posted in Iraq and feels she ought to 'support our troops' by voting for the president.

'There's resentment down deep but people don't know what to do with it. A lot of people turn inward, rather than outward. You think it would be ripe for an outcry. But it's not, it's all kind of dulled,' said Bob Garbo, who runs a regional food distribution centre in this corner of Ohio. 'There's a feeling you can't do much about it, that politicians are all bad. Voting rates are down, and politicians are taking advantage of that. Here, only 20 per cent turn out to vote in some counties.'

It is hardly surprising the very poor feel they have no one to turn to. A string of local factories have closed in the past two years to relocate to Mexico, a delayed consequence of the North American Free Trade Agreement established by Bill Clinton in 1994. And two years later, it was Clinton, in cooperation with a staunchly Republican Congress, who dismantled much of the welfare system built in the New Deal and the Great Society. Clinton's welfare reform set a time limit on how long the poor and unemployed could draw social security payments. It helped force people back into work with the encouragement of an array of federally funded job training programmes.

It worked well while the economy was booming, cutting the number on welfare from 12 million to 5 million in a few years. But now there are no jobs. Those who went to work under welfare reform are among the first to be fired, and often find that welfare is no longer available to them. Some have used up their lifetime maximum. Some have accumulated too many assets to qualify, such as a car or a house that they do not want to sell for fear of falling yet further into destitution. Others have had difficulty dealing with the welfare system's more demanding requirements. A few in the line at Logan said they were struggling without success to extract vital documents from former employers, who have either gone bankrupt or gone abroad.

So, while poverty rates have been rising in the past few years, the number of Americans on welfare has been steadily declining. Another impact of the 1996 welfare reform was that the unemployed were obliged to take service jobs at the minimum wage (now $5.15 per hour) without benefits such as paid holidays or health insurance. On paper they were part of the success of the welfare-to-work project, but the jobs stocking supermarket shelves or cleaning offices usually left them worse off, especially if someone in the family fell sick. In Ohio, according to Lisa Hamler-Podolski, more than 40 per cent of the people in the food lines are the working poor.

The harsh impact of welfare reform was initially mitigated by the nineties boom and Clinton-era social programmes to support the working poor and retrain the unemployed. Those programmes are now disappearing under an administration that fundamentally does not believe government should have a direct role in alleviating poverty.

Melissa Pardue, a specialist on poverty at the market-oriented Heritage Foundation, reflects the beliefs of many in the administration when she argues welfare reform has not gone far enough. 'The impact of the recession would have been far greater without welfare reform,' she said. 'The people who continue to be affected are not working. People who choose not to get a job are not going to see more income. It's all the more reason to give greater incentives to looking for work.'

The government still distributes food stamps, but they are worth on average only about $160 (£100) a month, not enough to buy food for a family with no other income. Furthermore, more than 10 million 'food insecure' Americans, at risk from hunger, do not apply for them. Often they are unaware they are eligible. Welfare reform pushed them out of a system that they have lost contact with.

A study this year by Washington-based think tank the Urban Institute found that 63 per cent of this forgotten category sometimes or often run out of food each month. All these factors explain why, although the current slump in America has not been as deep as the last major recession a decade ago, the food lines this time are longer. They also explain why hunger remains a largely invisible problem. The Americans in the food lines often do not show up in the statistics and usually do not turn up for elections.

'Hunger is a hidden thing,' said Lynn Brantley, who runs a food bank in Washington, where the very poor live within sight of Congress. 'It's something we don't really want to look at. We don't want to admit it.'

17 January 2004

SUZANNE GOLDENBERG

Dean's army

Carol Haas's entry into American politics began on the cold dawn of an Ohio morning, with the last of her run of midnight nursing shifts. She got off work and into a waiting car, riding ten hours across the rolling plains of the Midwest before she got a chance to sleep – hungry, on a bunk bed, surrounded by eleven male strangers, in a cabin with no indoor plumbing – at a girl scout camp 20 miles from town.

Ms Haas, a 55-year-old nurse, is beaming. She is kneeling on a floor, stuffing envelopes for Howard Dean in the run-up to the first popular challenge of the eight contenders for the Democratic presidential nomination, which takes place in Iowa on Monday. She is going to spend three days on envelope duty – or knocking on the doors of strangers asking them to come out to vote Dean – before going straight back to her job in Akron, Ohio. She can barely contain her admiration for Mr Dean. 'He brought the power to the people,' she says.

In the Des Moines headquarters of Mr Dean, Ms Haas's single-minded devotion to him is hardly exceptional. For months now, his supporters have been gathering their forces – connecting over the internet and in 'meet-ups', the monthly gatherings where supporters write letters and pass on strategy suggestions to paid campaign staff. This weekend, if all goes well, that energy will be channelled into what Dean organizers are calling the 'Perfect Storm'.

Other developments in Iowa could bring Mr Dean's political momentum to a stop. Two opinion polls this week put him in a dead heat in a four-way contest against the Missouri congressman and virtual native son, Dick Gephardt, and Senators John Kerry and John Edwards whose campaigns have experienced last-minute surges in support. After weeks in the doldrums, Mr Kerry is drawing huge crowds. Mr Kerry, a war hero, has his own ground troops drawn from Vietnam vets, and Mr Gephardt has the industrial unions, who have pulled up in large black trucks and matching jackets.

But Mr Dean has the 'storm chasers', some 2,500 volunteers who are expected to converge on Iowa at the weekend. Organizers say there has been nothing like it since the heady activist days of the 1960s and 1970s, and that the resulting force field of energy, hope and commitment is going to tip the balance in favour of Mr Dean in Monday's caucuses. None of Mr Dean's opponents can match the scale of his volunteer brigades in their orange knit hats, or the sense of commitment and urgency.

'I have come to believe that this is the most important election of my lifetime,' says Jerry Cayford, aged forty-six, from Maryland. 'We are either going to go some place to be a country I don't want to live in or something I admire.'

Mr Dean's opponents also cannot compete with the sense of ownership among the volunteers. In most campaigns, volunteers are directed to the nearest phone bank or pile of envelopes and are told to keep to a script. Campaign Dean is an entirely freewheeling operation. Volunteers turn up to make motivational videos, or punch in computer coding, and the centrepiece of their pitch to voters is the 'personal story'.

'The most effective strategy is honest dialogue,' says Ken Saguin, who helped devise the volunteer strategy. 'The content of the story is secondary. We would rather have them just communicate sincerely why they are backing Dean rather than rehashing what is put in their mouths by a paid political professional.'

The faithful have been straggling in all week from across the country in a mass migration. Many are from the last reliable strongholds of liberalism in the US, with large contingents from Seattle and the San Francisco area, New York and Washington DC. But there is a sizeable group from President George Bush's home state of Texas, a smattering from Mississippi and the south, and the heartlanders such as Ms Haas from Ohio, Illinois and the states adjoining Iowa.

On local television, an attack advert paid for by a Republican supporter has an elderly couple running down the Dean volunteers as alien sophisticates: a left-wing, latte-swilling, Volvo-driving, Hollywood-loving freak show. But in the Perfect Storm headquarters, the Dean supporters look a lot less exotic. Although Dean strategists say his strength derives from his ability to recruit brand new voters into the political process, the majority of the volunteers seem to be in their thirties, forties or fifties. The college students are there as well, along with the newly graduated, but this is overwhelmingly a mid-career, professional crowd. They see themselves as reformers – the vanguard of a revolt against what they say is the sheer blandness of American public life, the carefully processed statements from air-brushed politicians, and the politeness of the Democratic establishment.

Mr Dean, they say, has passion. 'I really admired the fact that he staked out some real positions on some controversial issues quite unblinkingly – no waffling,' says Chris Finnie. Over the years, Ms Finnie, aged fifty-three, has voted Republican and Democrat, but never with much enthusiasm. 'For thirty years, I walked into a voting booth, I held my nose, and I voted for the guy most likely to beat the most offensive candidate,' she says.

That passion has resonated with Democrats, who have grown frustrated with the centrist strategy of the party political establishment. They are itching for a Democratic leader to take on Mr Bush directly – not only on the war with Iraq, but on all issues.

'Moderation is not working any more, and it doesn't seem as if any of the other candidates realize that,' says Eric Elliott, a newly unemployed dotcommer from California who spent three days on the road to get here. Many of the volunteers are motivated by anger – although anger is a word that annoys Dean supporters because they say it makes them sound irrational. But it is not entirely clear why they are angry. There is the conservative Christian ascendancy, the swelling deficit under President Bush, the tax cuts for the rich, and Al Gore's failure to become president despite winning the popular vote in the 2000 election. Several of the volunteers barely mention the Iraq war as their reason for backing Mr Dean – although he is viewed as the anti-war candidate. Instead, theirs is a more generalized discontent. It found an outlet in Mr Dean and it transformed the former Vermont governor from an outsider – dismissed by the US media and pollsters – into a contender.

Last month, Mr Dean achieved a commanding lead in fundraising and in the opinion polls. But some of his supporters in Iowa detect worrying signs of change in him. Is he softening his punches? Is he going to turn into a centrist? 'I think he got reined in,' says Helena Johnson, aged twenty-five, from Washington DC.

Part of Mr Dean's intermittent displays of caution are self-preservation. He has come under constant attack from his opponents and under relentless scrutiny from the press, which exposed the dangers of his frank speaking style. Now, with two of Mr Dean's opponents – Mr Kerry and Mr Edwards – moving upwards, the plain talker has grown circumspect. All of this makes the storm chasers nervous. It also makes their mission much more crucial to Mr Dean's success.

Traditionally, turnout is low at the Iowa caucuses. Instead of swiftly casting a vote, participants must give up an evening, and make their choice in public. In the 2000 Democratic primaries, only 60,000 Iowans bothered to attend local caucuses. Mr Dean's strategists are counting on bringing out twice that number – 125,000 caucus-goers – but they need the volunteers to do that. By the time they arrive in Iowa, most of the Perfect Storm people have spent months thinking about Howard Dean. They have gone to meetings and written letters. They may have spoken to his campaign manager in a conference call. The only thing left was to get to Iowa and tell their personal stories.

Andrew Homan's personal story goes like this. He is twenty-three and works two part-time jobs in a small town in Indiana. It cost him $500 (£278) for a rental car and food, and by the time his lost earnings are taken into account, the trip to Iowa will have cost him two weeks' pay. His colleagues told him he was crazy. After getting lost for an hour in the north-western suburbs of Des Moines the other day, he was deposited in a neighbourhood of comfortable-looking homes. He had to knock on several doors before he found someone at home. And she was a committed Republican.

Mr Homan finds it hard to contain his enthusiasm, and he can't understand others who do not share his views. 'I voted for Gore but at the time I wasn't so opposed to Bush. I thought his father was a decent president,' he says. 'Bush has done so many things wrong on so many levels. I couldn't not get involved.'

24 October 2003

MATTHEW ENGEL

Road to ruin

On the map of the United States, just below halfway down the east coast, you can see a series of islets, in the shape of a hooked nose. These are the Outer Banks, barrier islands – sun-kissed in summer, storm-tossed in winter – that stretch for 100 miles and more, protecting the main coastline of the state of North Carolina. They are built, quite literally, on shifting sands.

Twenty years ago, these were, by all accounts, magical places, hard to reach and discovered only by the adventurous and discerning. They are still fairly magical, at least the seemingly endless stretch of unspoiled beach is. It is the lure of that which causes the traffic jams on the only two bridges every Saturday throughout the summer. The narrow strip of land behind the beach, however, has been built up with enormous holiday homes, costing up to $2m (£1.2m) each. And prices rose by 15 to 20 per cent (25 per cent for those on the ocean front) in 2002 alone, according to one agent.

This is what local agents call 'a very nice market', and last month their area had a week of free worldwide publicity. Hurricane Isabel swept in, washing out much of the islands' only road and picking up motels from their foundations and tossing them, according to one report, 'like cigarette butts'. One island was turned into several islets, with a whole town, Hatteras Village, being cut off from the rest of the US – for ever, if nature has its way.

Residents, journalists reported, were in shock. Many scientists were not. Speaking well before Isabel, Dr Orrin Pilkey, professor emeritus of geology at Duke University in North Carolina, described the Outer Banks property boom to me as 'a form of societal madness'. 'I wouldn't buy a house on the front row of the Outer Banks. Or the second,' agreed Dr Stephen Leatherman, who is such a connoisseur of American coastlines that he is known as Dr Beach.

For the market is not the only thing that has been rising round here. Like other experts, Pilkey expects the Atlantic to inundate the existing beaches 'within two to four generations'. Normally, that would be no problem for the sands, which would simply regroup and re-form further back. Unfortunately, that is no longer possible: the $2m houses are in the way. According to Pilkey, the government will either have to build millions of dollars' worth of seawall, which will destroy the beach anyway, or demolish the houses. 'Coastal scientists from abroad come here and just shake their heads in disbelief,' he says.

The madness of the Outer Banks seems like a symptom of, and a metaphor for, something far broader: the US is in denial about what is, beyond any question, potentially its most dangerous enemy. While millions of words have been written every day for the past two years about the threat from vengeful Islamic terrorists, the threat from a vengeful Nature has been almost wholly ignored. Yet the likelihood of multiple attacks in the future is far more certain.

Earlier this year, just before he was fired as environment minister, Michael

Meacher gave a speech in Newcastle, saying: 'There is a lot wrong with our world. But it is not as bad as people think. It is actually worse.' He listed five threats to the survival of the planet: lack of fresh water; destruction of forest and crop land; global warming; overuse of natural resources; and the continuing rise in the population. What Meacher could not say, or he would have been booted out more quickly, was that the US is a world leader in hastening each of these five crises, bringing its gargantuan appetite to the business of ravaging the planet. American politicians do not talk this way. Even Al Gore, supposedly the most committed environmentalist in world politics, kept quiet about the subject when chasing the presidency in 2000.

Those of us without a degree in climatology can have no sensible opinion on the truth about climate change, except to sense that the weather does seem to have become a little weird lately. Yet in America the subject has become politicized, with right-wing commentators decrying global warming as 'bogus science'. They gloated when it snowed unusually hard in Washington last winter (failing to notice the absence of snow in Alaska). When the dissident 'good news' scientist Bjorn Lomborg spoke to a conservative Washington think tank he was applauded not merely rapturously, but fawningly.

While newspapers report that Kilimanjaro's icecap is melting and Greenland's glaciers are crumbling, the US government has been telling its scientific advisers to do more research before it can consider any action to restrict greenhouse gases; the scientists reported back that they had done all the research. The attitude of the White House to global warming was summed up by the online journalist Mickey Kaus as 'It's not true! It's not true! And we can't do anything about it!' What terrifies all American politicians, deep down, is that it is true and that they could do something about it, but at horrendous cost to American industry and lifestyle. In the meantime, all American consumers have been asked to do is to buy Ben & Jerry's One Sweet Whirled ice cream, ensuring that a portion of Unilever's profits go towards 'global warming initiatives'. Wow!

Potential Democratic candidates for the presidential nomination have been testing environmental issues a little in the past few weeks. Some activists are hopeful that the newly elected Governor Schwarzenegger of California is genuinely interested. But, in truth, despite the Soviet-style politicization of science, serious national debate on the issue ceased years ago.

Of course, nimbyism is alive and well. And, sure, there are localized battles between greens and their corporate enemies: towns in Alabama try to resist corporate poisoning; contests go on to preserve the habitats of everything from the grizzly bear to rare types of fly; Californians hug trees to stop new housing estates. Sometimes the greenies win, though they have been losing with increasing frequency, especially if Washington happens to be involved. These fights, even in agglomeration, are not the real issue. Day after day across America the green agenda is being lost – and then, usually, being buried under concrete.

'We're waging a war on the environment, a very successful one,' says Paul Ehrlich, professor of population studies at Stanford University. 'This nation is devouring itself,' according to Phil Clapp of the National Environmental Trust. These are voices that have almost ceased to be heard in the US. Yet with each passing day, the gap between the US and the rest of the planet widens. To take the figure most often trotted out: Americans contribute a quarter of the world's carbon dioxide emissions. To meet the seemingly modest Kyoto objective of reducing emissions to 7 per cent below their 1990 levels by 2012, they would actually (due to growth) have to cut back by a third. For the Bush White House, this is not even on the horizon, never mind the agenda.

Why has the leader of the free world opted out? The first reason lies deep in the national psyche. The old world developed on the basis of a coalition – uneasy but understood – between humanity and its surroundings. The settlement of the US was based on conquest, not just of the indigenous peoples, but also of the terrain. It appears to be, thus far, one of the great success stories of modern history.

'Remember, this country is built very heavily on the frontier ethic,' says Clapp. 'How America moved west was to exhaust the land and move on. The original settlers, such as the Jefferson family, moved westward because families like theirs planted tobacco in tidewater Virginia and exhausted the soil. My own ancestors did the same in Indiana.'

Americans made crops grow in places that are entirely arid. They built dams – about 250,000 of them. They built great cities, with skyscrapers and symphony orchestras, in places that appeared barely habitable. They shifted rivers, even reversed their flow. 'It's the American belief that with enough hard work and perseverance anything – be it a force of nature, a country or a disease – can be vanquished,' says Clapp. 'It's a country founded on the idea of no limits. The essence of environmentalism is that there are indeed limits. It's one of the reasons environmentalism is a stronger ethic in Europe than in the US.'

There is a second reason: the staggering population growth of the US. It is approaching 300 million, having increased from 200 million in 1970, which was around the time President Nixon set up a commission to consider the issue, the last time any US administration has dared think about it. A million new legal migrants are coming in every year (never mind illegals), and the US Census Bureau projections for 2050, merely half a lifetime away, is 420 million. This is a rate of increase far beyond anything else in the developed world, and not far behind Brazil, India, or indeed Mexico.

This issue is political dynamite, although not for quite the same reasons as in Britain. Almost every political group is split on the issue, including the far right (torn between overt xenophobes such as Pat Buchanan and the free marketeers), the labour movement and the environmentalists. The belief that the US is the best country in the world is a cornerstone of national self-belief, and many Americans still, wholeheartedly, want others to share it. They also want cheap labour to cut the sugar cane, pluck the chickens, pick the oranges, mow the lawns and make the beds.

But the dynamite is most potent among the Hispanic community, the group who will probably decide the destiny of future presidential elections and who do not wish to be told their relatives will not be allowed in or, if illegal, seriously harassed. 'Neither party wants to say we should change immigration policy,' says John Haaga of the independent Population Reference Bureau. 'The phrase being used is "Hispandering".'

Yet extra Americans are not just a problem for the US: they are, in the eyes of many environmentalists, a problem for the world because migrants, in a short span of time, take on American consumption patterns. 'Not only don't we have a population policy,' says Ehrlich, 'we don't have a consumption policy either. We are the most overpopulated country in the world. It's not the number of people. It's their consumption.' Ehrlich may be wrong. It is, though, somewhat surprising that the federal government's 4 million employees do not appear to include anyone charged with even thinking about this issue.

This brings us to the third factor: the Bush administration, the first government in modern history which has systematically disavowed the systems of checks and controls that have governed environmental policy since it burst into Western political consciousness a generation ago. It would be ludicrous to suggest that Bush is responsible for what is happening to the American environment. The crisis is far more deep-seated than that, and the federal government is too far removed from the minutiae of daily life. But the Bushies have perfected a technique of announcing regular edicts (often late on a Friday afternoon) rolling back environmental control, usually while pretending to do the opposite. Morale among civil servants at the Environmental Protection Agency in Washington was already close to rock-bottom even before its moderate leader, Christine Todd Whitman, finally threw in her hand in May. Gossip round town was that she had endured two years of private humiliation at the hands of the White House. Few environmentalists have great hopes for her announced successor, the governor of Utah, Mike Leavitt.

What is really alarming is the intellectual atmosphere in Washington. You can attend seminars debunking scientific eco-orthodoxy almost every week. Early in the year, there was much favourable publicity for a new work, *Global Warming and Other Eco-myths*, produced by the Competitive Enterprise Institute, an organization reputedly funded by multinational corporations. Outside Washington, it can be far nastier. 'I've never threatened anyone in my life,' a conservation activist in Montana complained to the *Guardian*. 'I do know, though, that I have gotten very ugly threats left on my telephone answering machine over the past year, and twice had to scour my sidewalk in front of the building to erase the dead body chalk outlines.'

Out in the west, words such as 'enviro-whackos' are popularized by right-wing radio hosts such as the ex-Watergate conspirator Gordon Liddy, who passes on to his millions of listeners the message that global warming is a lie. 'I commute in a three-quarter-tonne capacity Chevrolet Silverado HD,' he swanked in his latest book. 'Four-wheel drive, off-road equipped, extended curb pick-up truck, powered by a 300hp, overhead valve, turbo supercharged diesel engine with 520lb-feet of torque ... It has lights all over it so everyone can see me coming and get out of the way. If someone in a little government-mandated car hits me, it is all over – for him.' Fuel economy in American vehicles hit a 22-year low in 2002.

In this country, green-minded people can't even trust the good guys. The Nature Conservancy, the US's largest environmental group with a million members – with a role not unlike Britain's National Trust – was the subject of an exhaustive exposé in the *Washington Post* in May, accusing it of sanctioning deals to build 'opulent houses on fragile grasslands' and drilling for gas under the last breeding ground of the Attwater's Prairie Chicken, whose numbers have dwindled to just dozens.

On 22 April 1970 more than 20 million people attended the first-ever Earth Day. In New York, Fifth Avenue was closed to traffic and 100,000 people attended an ecology fair in Central Park. The Republican governor of New York wore a Save the Earth button, and Senator John Tower, another Republican, told an audience of Texan oilmen: 'Recent efforts on the part of the private sector show promise for pollution abatement and control. Such efforts are in our own best interests.'

So what happened next? The problem for the green movement was not what went wrong, but what went right. Ehrlich's book, *The Population Bomb*, said: 'In the 1970s, the world will undergo famines – hundreds of millions of people are going to starve to death in spite of any crash programmes embarked on now.' The famine never came. And after the oil crisis came and went, and Americans began to tire of the gloom-filled, eco-oriented presidency of Jimmy Carter; they turned instead to Ronald Reagan, who proposed simple solutions of tax cuts and deregulation and, lo, the world got more cheerful. With doomsday postponed indefinitely, the politics of the Reagan years have lingered.

Some activists remain bitter about the Clinton White House, which was only patchily interested in green issues. 'It left a bad taste in the mouth of the environmental community,' says Tim Wirth, a former senator and one-time Clinton official. 'They trimmed their sails over and over again. The old House speaker, Tip O'Neill, had a very important political aphorism: "Yer dance with the person who brung yer." They never did.' This bitterness was one of the factors that led to the hefty third-party vote for Ralph Nader in 2000, which proved disastrous for Al Gore, the inhibited environmentalist.

In the three years since then, Bush has danced like a dervish with the folks who brung him. Yet, even now, no one dare say out loud that they are against environmentalism: the political wisdom is that the subject can be a voting issue among the suburban moms, ferrying the kids around to baseball practice in their own Chevrolet Silverados. Instead, the big corporations and their political allies have – brilliantly – manipulated the forces that the eco-warriors themselves unleashed and turned them back on their creators. 'In the eighties they took all the techniques of citizen advocacy groups and professionalized them,' explains Phil Clapp. 'That's when you saw the proliferation of lobbyists in Washington. The environmental community never re-tooled to meet the challenge. They had developed the techniques, but were still doing them in a PTA bake-sale kind of way.'

Thus every new measure passed to favour business interests and ease up on pollution regulations is presented in an eco-friendly, sugar-coated, summer's morning kind of way, such as Clear Skies, the weakening of the Clean Air Act. The House of Representatives has just passed the Healthy Forests Restoration Act, presented by the president as an anti-forest-fire measure. Opponents say it is simply a gift to the timber industry that will make it extremely difficult to stop the felling of old-growth trees. Another technique is to announce, with great fanfare, initiatives that everyone can applaud, such as a recent one for hydrogen-based cars. We can expect more of these as November 2004 draws closer. When they are scaled back, or delayed, or dropped, there is less publicity. It is a habit that runs in the family. Governor Jeb Bush's grand scheme to save the Florida Everglades was much applauded; the delay from 2006 to 2016 was little noticed.

Even now the White House does not win all its battles. In the Senate, where a small group of greenish New England Republicans has a potential blocking veto, there are moves to compromise on the forests bill. The New England Republicans were largely responsible for Bush's inability to push through his plan to allow oil drilling in the Alaskan wildlife reserve. Occasionally, there is good news: some of the small dams that have impeded the life-cycle of Pacific salmon and steelhead trout are being demolished; there are reports of a new alliance between the old enemies, ranchers and greenies, in New Mexico; renewable energy is under discussion. But some of their policies are already having their effect. Carol Browner, Clinton's head of the EPA, claims the Bush administration has set back the campaign to cut industrial pollution in ways that will last for decades.

'This administration has sent a signal to the polluting community: "You can get away with bad habits,"' says Browner. 'State governments in the north-east were much tougher, so the north-eastern power stations upgraded their emissions standards in the nineties whereas the Midwest guys, who are their competitors, didn't. Now they're not enforcing the law. So what they're saying to the companies is: "Don't go early, don't comply with the law first. The rules might change." Even a company that wants to do the right thing has to look at its bottom line. If they get into a situation like this, they think: "We spent one billion dollars to meet the requirements and our competitors didn't. Yeah, great. We're not going to do that again."'

Under Bush, the lack of interest at every level has at last come into balance. The US is equally unconcerned globally, federally, statewide and locally. The environmentalists' macro-gloom has been off-beam before, of course. Perhaps global warming is a myth; perhaps the CEI is right and there will be a blue revolution in water use to complement the green revolution. There is probably just as much chance that the next big surprise will be a thrilling one – the arrival of nuclear cold fusion to solve the energy dilemma, say – as a disaster. Maybe biotechnology, pesticides, natural gas and American ingenuity and optimism will indeed see everything right. It does seem like a curiously reckless gamble for the US to be taking, though, staking the future of the planet on the spin of nature's roulette wheel.

But it is only a bigger version of the bet being taken by the home-buyers of North Carolina. In a country supposedly distrustful of government, the Outer Bankers have remarkable faith in their leaders' ability to see them right. Post-Isabel, a group of residents there wrote a letter demanding government action so they can protect their livelihoods and families 'without the fear of every hurricane or nor'easter cutting us off from the rest of the world'. Quite. Who would imagine that in the twenty-first century the most powerful empire the world has ever known could still be threatened by enemies as pathetically old-fashioned as wind and tide?

Orrin Pilkey thinks it quite possible that sea levels might rise to the point where the Outer Banks will be a minor detail: 'We're not going to be worried about North Carolina. We're going to be worrying about Manhattan.' Still, macro-catastrophe may never happen. The micro-catastrophe, however, already has: the US is an aesthetic disaster area.

If you fly from Washington to Boston, there are now almost no open spaces below. This is increasingly true in a big U covering both coasts and the Sun Belt. In the south-west, the main growth area, bungalows spread for miles over what a decade ago was virgin desert. The population of Arizona increased 40 per cent in the 1990s, that of next-door Nevada 66 per cent. That's, as Natalie Merchant sang, 'the sprawl that keeps crawling its way, 'bout a thousand miles a day', which is not much of an exaggeration.

Every day 5,000 new houses go up in America. Many of these fit the American appetite for size, however small the plot: 'McMansions', as they are known. The very word suburb is now old-hat. The reality of life for many people now is the 'exurb', which can be dozens of miles from the city on which it depends. In places such as California, exurban life is the only affordable option for most young couples and recent migrants.

These communities are rarely gated but often walled, creating a vague illusion of security and ensuring that the residents have to drive to a shop, even if there happens to be one 50 yards away. Naturally, they have to drive everywhere else. In August it was announced that the number of cars in the US (1.9 per household) now actually exceeded the number of drivers (1.75).

In many places – especially those growing the fastest – developers have to deal only with the little councils in the towns they are taking over. There are often minimal requirements to provide any kind of infrastructure, such as sewage or schools, to service these new communities. The rules for building houses in the computer game Sim City are stricter than those that apply in most areas of the Sun Belt. Too late, some parts of the country have concluded that this is untenable. The buzz-phrase is 'smart growth', which means no more than the kind of forethought before building that has been routine in Europe for half a century. Even the Environmental Protection Agency is not above being helpful: its policies for making use of brownfield sites have seen people moving, improbably, back into the centre of cities such as Pittsburgh.

But where it matters, no one is talking strategy. 'In the really fast-growing states, the pace of development is such that they can build huge numbers of houses without anyone considering what it means for the infrastructure,' says Marya Morris of the American Planning Association. In California, more than perhaps any other state, there is a debate. But while people talk, developers act: a city catering for up to 70,000 people will soon arise at the foot of the Tehachapi Mountains. According to the *Los Angeles Times*, it would effectively close the gap between Los Angeles and Bakersfield, theoretically 111 miles away. 'Southern California is coming over the hill,' said one resident.

Americans still have a presumption of infinite space. But I have made a curious and mildly embarrassing discovery. In states such as Maryland and Ohio, the pattern of settlement in supposedly rural areas is such that it can actually be quite difficult to find a discreet spot away from housing to stop the car and have a pee. Amid the wide-open spaces of Texas, it can be worse: the gap between Dallas and Waco is a 100-mile strip mall. The concepts of townscape and landscape seem non-existent: there is land that has been developed and land that hasn't – yet.

And yet. Time and again, around the US, one is struck by the stunning beauty of the landscape, not in the obvious places, but in corners that few Americans will have heard of: amazing rivers such as the Pearl in Louisiana, or the Choptank in Maryland or the Lost in West Virginia; the Chocolate Mountains and the San Diego back country in California; the bits that are left of the Outer Banks ...

And equally one is struck by the sheer horrendousness of what man has done in the century or so since he seriously got to work over here. In the context of ages, the white man is merely a hotel guest in this continent: he has smashed the furniture and smeared excrement on the walls. He appears to be looking forward to his next night's stay with relish.

Of course, there are still huge tracts of untouched and largely unpopulated land: in the Great Plains, where people are leaving, in the mountains, deserts and Arctic tundra. But last spring, in another of Washington's Friday night announcements, the Department of the Interior announced – no, whispered – that it was removing more than 200 million acres that it owned from 'further wilderness study', enabling those areas to be opened for mining, drilling, logging or road-building. That's an area three times the size of Britain. The *New York Times* did write a trenchant editorial; otherwise the response was minimal.

Not long ago I went for a walk in the Vallecito Mountains in California. After a while, I got myself into a position where the contours of the land blotted out everything and, after the noise of a plane had died away, there was no sight or sound at all that was not produced by nature. This lasted about a minute. Then, from somewhere, a motorcycle roared into earshot.

Sure, there are still places in this vast country where it is possible to escape, but they get harder and harder to find except for the fit, the adventurous and those unencumbered by children or jobs. Most Americans don't live that way. And nowhere now is entirely safe from being ravaged, sometimes in ways that prejudice the future of the whole planet. Al-Qaida and the Iraqi bombers have no need to bother. America is destroying itself.

28 June 2004

GARY YOUNGE

Politics gets personal

To find Regal Montrose cinema in Akron, Ohio, just head down the 77 interstate and follow globalization's glowing signs. Using brand names as landmarks, helpful people will guide you past Chilis ('Like no place else') and Steak 'n' Shake ('May I take your order?') and warn you that when you get to Taco Bell ('Think outside the bun') you have gone too far. Eventually you'll find it next to

Staples, the chain stationers, whose slogan, appropriately enough, is 'That was easy'. On these strips of Americana, which serve as both pit stops for the long-distance traveller and shopping centres for local people, you could be anywhere in the country. Only the weather suggests that you are in Akron rather than Anchorage or Arizona.

And so it was on Friday night as hundreds of thousands of people across the country turned up at their local cinema to buy a ticket for Michael Moore's film, *Fahrenheit 9/11* on its opening night, either to find it was sold out or to emerge two hours later with tears in their eyes.

Linda Lejsovka, a 25-year-old supply teacher, walked away from the sold-out sign for the 10.30 p.m. screening saying she'd come back another day. Earlier, Suzanne Aylward came out of the 7.30 p.m. screening vowing 'to get everybody I know' to see the film. Aylward was greeted by canvassers inviting her to a meeting to discuss the film and handing out John Kerry stickers and badges, which she declined. Although she voted Nader last time, she is going to back Kerry in November with reservations. 'People don't love Kerry because they're not sure what he stands for. But I'm going to vote for him because he's not Bush.'

One of the Kerry campaigners overheard and shouted, 'That's not true. Look at his position papers. Listen to what he says.'

Aylward shrugs dismissively and her friend, Bobbie Watson, takes over. 'I'm going to politely ask the people I know and who I trust and who trust me, who usually vote Republican or who haven't made up their minds, to at least consider voting for Kerry this time,' she says. 'I think they'll at least listen to me because they know I'm an open-minded person.'

Welcome to the tone and tenor of the personal interactions that are going to assert the strongest influence on the forthcoming presidential election. In debates with friends, family and neighbours, at times hectoring, at others beseeching, filled with venom and vigour on both sides, such a close race is going to be won one vote at a time.

If Howard Dean's emergence from nowhere to challenge the Democratic establishment was described as 'insurgent' then we are about to see the ground war. The air war of television advertising, mail shots and telemarketing will certainly help. But the millions of dollars already spent by both sides have simply kept them at a stalemate.

Most voters have already made up their minds. Many of those who haven't are going to have to be addressed personally. And it will be the lost art of old-style politicking, of door-to-door canvassing, mall leafleting, and coffee-shop and bar-room conversations that will really make the difference.

With the nation polarized and so much at stake, the downward trend in active participation that has characterized American political culture for the past thirty years is set to be reversed. The percentage of Americans actively engaged in politics has been falling steadily and precipitously since the late 1960s. Indeed the only aspect of political participation that has increased substantially is donating money. From 1964 to 1996, spending on election campaigns rocketed from $35m to $700m – with a sharp increase in individual donations and new records being broken all the time. 'Nationalization and professionalization have redefined the role of citizen activist as, increasingly, a writer of cheques and letters,' wrote political scientists Sidney Verba, Kay Schlozman and Henry Brady. In this process, culture is both the galvanizer and the glue. Crudely speaking it gives people something to talk about – a common reference point around which to organize and mobilize. This is as true on the right as it is on the left.

Initial indications suggest *Fahrenheit 9/11* grossed more than the blockbusters playing on more screens and earned more in one weekend than Moore's Oscar-winning *Bowling for Columbine* – until now the highest-grossing documentary ever – did in the entire time it was running. But its opening was greeted with as much excitement on the left as Mel Gibson's *The Passion of Christ* was by the evangelists who form Bush's most reliable base.

The latest edition in the Left Behind series, a modern-day rendition of the Book of Revelation in which the antichrist is the head of the United Nations, was in reprint before it had even launched. The authors, one of whom was a co-founder of the right-wing Moral Majority, have sold more books than John Grisham. Meanwhile more than 20,000 people volunteered for a Left Behind 'street team', promising to disseminate messages about the books to their family, friends and neighbours.

Those who refer to such gatherings as simply preaching to the choir miss the point. With few people poised to change their mind, this election will largely be about who can assemble the biggest choir. The undecideds are not just those choosing between Kerry and Bush but the soft supporters in both camps who must be hardened up.

Nowhere is this truer than Ohio, the ultimate swing state. On the day that Moore's film opened, Kerry was in Akron for his eighth trip to the state since he secured the nomination. George Bush, who won Ohio narrowly last time, has been there almost twenty times in the past four years and Vice-President Cheney is on his way this week. According to the most recent poll Kerry is ahead by 49 per cent to 43 per cent – free from the margin of error, but only just.

Lejsovka describes Akron, home to 217,000, as a town where 'the school system sucks really badly' and she knows 'tonnes of people who are losing their jobs'. Last month, thanks to the decimation of the town's manufacturing base, they finally ditched its motto 'Akron the rubber capital of the world'. On Thursday, while the town's nurses were striking for better wages and healthcare costs so they could afford to get sick in the very hospitals they work in, hundreds of hopefuls turned up at a job fair for the promise of sixty vacancies.

Debbie Holmes, aged forty-four, who last month lost the second job she'd had in a year, was one of them. She was looking for a 'job I can stay in until I retire', she told the *Akron Beacon Journal*.

Lejsovka says she will definitely vote but not for Bush and is otherwise unsure: 'Kerry seems a little wishy-washy to me.'

Winning over the likes of Lejsovka and Holmes will take persuasion rather than position papers. This will make the election far more volatile and predictions as to its outcome far less reliable. Over the past thirty years, American politics has been increasingly left to the professions. This time it's personal.

EUROPE

IAN TRAYNOR

Germany laid low

Forty-eight years a prison warden, retired and living on a generous state pension, Walter has seldom had it so good. The 64-year-old father of two was born in the Third Reich, his childhood and adolescence spent in the hard times and fevered reconstruction of post-war Germany. He recently retired on a civil servant's pension of €36,000 (£24,000) a year, a figure that would be the envy of many pensioners. 'I mustn't grumble,' he admits.

Then the torrent of complaints begins. Germany is controlled by foreigners, he rants. The EU is a foreign plot to keep the Germans down, bankrolled by German money. All politicians are rogues. He won't vote in the European elections because there's no one worth voting for. 'Ever seen a politician being punished? They're all failures. We're all frustrated because of these politicians,' he says, asking for his surname not to be published.

Margit Kloppe, a pharmacist retiring in three years on a pension of around £12,000 a year, says, 'Look at the numbers of unemployed, look at the numbers of welfare recipients. It's unbelievable. We're all dependent on welfare now.'

Helga Stern, a retired housing administrator on a similar pension, adds that times are indeed hard in Germany – but one must not exaggerate: 'It's the German vice to talk things down all the time. It's the fashion. I blame it on the media.'

To open a German newspaper any day of the week is to brace yourself for the feel-bad factor. 'The government is in office, but not governing,' says the right-wing *Die Welt*. 'Aimless, clueless, helpless, a government of strategic confusion,' says the liberal *Die Zeit*. And a glance through the bestseller list supplies little cheer. The top twenty non-fiction books include: *Can Germany Still Be Saved?*; *Germany – The Decline of a Superstar; Inventing Illness – How We Are Turned Into Patients*; and, top of the list, *The Methuselah Plot*, a treatise on the country's ageing crisis that is bound to encourage angst-ridden sleepless nights. 'An alarming diagnosis of our society calling for a conspiracy against the biological and social terror of the fear of ageing,' reads the blurb on the cover.

Six short years into the rule of Chancellor Gerhard Schroder and his coalition of Social Democrats and Greens, Germany appears to be eagerly embracing what the outgoing president, Johannes Rau, has called a fit of 'collective depression'. In his valedictory homily a fortnight ago Mr Rau upbraided the country for its deep-rooted pessimism, stagnation and paralysis, a condition that seemed to be confirmed in the public mind a few weeks earlier when the mighty national football team was thrashed 5–1 by Romania. 'Have we talked ourselves down to the point that we no longer trust ourselves to get anything right?' Mr Rau asked. 'You get the impression that our future does not mean much to many people.' Germany, he said, has turned into a country of whingers.

In Wiesloch, a prosperous small town of 28,000 near Heidelberg in the south-west, it is difficult to see what all the whingeing is about. Unemployment is half the national rate. SAP, a successful software company, employs 10,000 people nearby. The cars are BMWs and Mercedes, the roads and infrastructure are impeccable. And nationally, says Wolfgang Thierse, the Social Democrat parliamentary speaker, Germans 'are living through a period of almost historic good fortune. When has there ever been such a time in German history? Germany is reunified; Europe is reunified. Germany is one of the most successful countries in the world. Now we have the problems of peace, the problems of success.'

The US magazine *Newsweek*'s ranking at the beginning of the year put Germany second only to the US in terms of diplomatic and economic power. Last year it overtook the US to become the world's top exporter.

'To call Germany the sick man of Europe is absurd,' says Gustav Horn, of the German Economics Research Institute in Berlin. 'Germany has changed a lot, and it will surprise everyone yet.'

Mr Thierse embodies the colossal changes of recent years; he reached his position after growing up in communist East Germany, and working there as a printsetter. He has come to Wiesloch to meet the locals and explain how Germany is now living beyond its means and must tighten its belt, buck up and get fit for a new confident morning.

In an old slaughterhouse tastefully converted into a gastropub, he faces a well-heeled, middle-aged, middle-class audience, articulate and voluble, on a glorious spring evening. The scene is almost idyllic. But the mood is one of polite anger.

'Where are the limits to our pain?' asks one man. The reforms being pursued by the Schroder government have produced 'a deep psychic angst running through the entire society'.

The problems may indeed be ones of success, but they are none the less formidable. Schools and universities are not what they were. Unemployment is at least 4.5 million. The non-wage costs of employing people are crippling. The finance minister recently 'discovered' that his estimates of tax income for the next five years were E61bn too high. The national debt is growing; public investment is shrinking. The economy has been stagnant for three years. A public weaned on a high-quality welfare state will soon see visits to the doctor covered by a quarterly fee of E10. Mr Rau's successor, Horst Kohler, was under no illusions after he was elected as the new president yesterday. 'I can't hide my concerns about our economy,' he said.

Social and welfare reform dominates the national debate, deeply unsettling most Germans, and confronting Mr Schroder with his biggest challenge.

'Everyone's worried that in reforming the welfare state, Schroder will throw out the baby with the bathwater,' says Dieter Augstein, a teacher in Mannheim, an hour up the autobahn from Wiesloch.

Ruprecht Polenz, an opposition Christian Democrat MP, says, 'In Germany it used to be that if there were roadworks on the autobahn, the lane was closed and the problem was fixed promptly. Nowadays they just close the lane, put up signs saying drive at 80kph [50mph], and leave it. It's become like the old East Germany.'

It is ironic that it has fallen to the centre-left to fix the perceived mess, to trim a welfare state that is the Social Democrats' proudest achievement. Helmut Kohl spent sixteen years as a Christian Democratic chancellor preoccupied with German unification, doing little to reform Germany from within and bequeathing the mess to Mr Schroder in 1998. The expert consensus is that Mr Schroder has made an honourable start to a complex challenge. But the welfare cuts are costing him dear. His SPD is trailing at historic lows in the polls and party membership is plummeting. Economists point out that the combination of economic stagnation and austerity in public finances means that Mr Schroder is effectively trying to save, rather than spend, his way out of a recession – something that is almost impossible.

'We're just muddling through,' admits Gerd Weisskirchen, the SPD MP for Wiesloch and an old friend of the chancellor. 'Running up more debt would be a disaster. And neo-liberalism would also be a disaster. We're stuck in the middle.'

The Schroder cabinet and coalition present a cacophony of dissenting views. 'This government is tired of governing,' says Rebekka Gohring, of Berlin's German Council on Foreign Relations.

Pollsters predict a turnout of about 45 per cent in the European elections, a very low figure for Germany. But there will also be important regional votes this year, leading up to next spring's election in the most populous state, North-Rhine Westfalia, a traditional SPD stronghold. 'Schroder's fate will be decided in North-Rhine Westfalia,' says Mr Polenz. Yet Mr Schroder appears more confident than the polls warrant; he remains the man to beat. Mr Polenz acknowledges that predictions of an opposition landslide are misplaced.

Mr Horn predicts that by 2006, when the next general election is due, economic growth may be at 2 per cent. Surveys suggest that at least half the electorate think the opposition would not do a better job than the SPD. But in Wiesloch Mrs Kloppe is less than impressed by what Mr Thierse says: 'We've had fifty-nine years of peace and fifty years of democracy. We're four or five times richer than we used to be. We've had a welfare state since Bismarck. And just look what's happening to it now.'

30 April 2004

MATTHEW ENGEL

Bloemendaal wearies of Europe

If there is a European dream to match the American one – a trail that leads to prosperity from a fetid Eastern Bloc village via a back-breaking migrants' life under a gangmaster – it could easily end here. In dreams, anyway.

Just twenty minutes from Amsterdam Central Station is Bloemendaal. Stout Edwardian villas are guarded by laurel hedges, the magnolias are in bloom, the loudest sound is the birdsong and in the spring sunshine the pavement cafés are alive and welcoming. Occasionally, an uninvited guest arrives by train to look for unlocked doors ('junkie tourism'). But the only real threat to safety is being mown down by an elderly lady on a bike.

Bloemendaal was first built up as a retreat for wealthy Amsterdammers in what the Dutch call the golden age: the great flourish of their power and culture that followed the country's independence from Spain in 1648. But in Bloemendaal the golden age never really ended, and rich lawyers and businessmen from the city still gravitate here to bring up their families. This is one of the most desirable suburbs in Europe. As such, it is one of the centres of the other European dream: the once-fanciful notion that Europe could be one, and that free nations could arrange their affairs better by uniting and thus ensuring that the continent would never again be convulsed by the horrors of war. When that idea took shape in the 1950s, it emerged from the business and political elites, not from the people. But no country adopted it with more idealistic full-heartedness than the Dutch.

When the original six members signed the Treaty of Rome in 1957, it was easy to sit in Britain and cynically observe what was in it for five of them. Belgium and Luxembourg would get fat by hosting the institutions; the French and Germans would get the power; the Italians would get the subsidies. The Dutch appeared to believe in Europe for its own sake.

Their view was not entirely altruistic: a nation of traders sitting on a transport hub was bound to do well out of the new order. And it has. However, something extraordinary is happening, a change that as yet has been little noticed outside the Netherlands, but one which may be as crucial to the history of the next half-century as the drive to unity has been over the last. Tomorrow, the European dream will reach its most climactic moment yet, when the EU expands from fifteen countries to twenty-five.

But the moment when empires reach their zenith is the point from which historians chart their decline. And there are signs that the dream is already dying. Bloemendaal is falling out of love with Europe. The whole of the Netherlands is falling out of love with Europe. And if the Dutch feel that way, then suddenly the whole edifice looks less like a great monument and more like a house of cards.

The trend appears to have four main elements. First, it is the result of the immigration crisis, brought to wider notice when Dutch fears were articulated during the brief, but spectacular, political career of the populist Pim Fortuyn, assassinated in 2002. Second, the Dutch Euro-rapture was modified by the discovery that they became, after German reunification, the biggest net payers to the EU. Though they did get some money back, the ill-feeling still lingers. Third, the euro is unpopular, thanks largely to businessmen (bar and café owners are especially blamed) who used it as an excuse to whack up prices. Fourth, there is a rather British frustration at laws emanating from Brussels, and Dutch inability to influence them.

'The European feeling is not heavy here,' says Arie Goote, one of Bloemendaal's *wethouders*, or deputy mayors. 'It is not in our hearts, you'll see in the elections. It doesn't interest our people. They think the men in Brussels are drinking and eating and not doing serious business.'

The fear of competition from hungry East Europeans is exceptionally powerful in a country famous for its liberal attitude to immigration. 'I know a Dutchman who grows flowers in Eastern Europe,' says Gerrit de Winter, a Bloemendaal flower-seller. 'He says half a Polish worker can do the work of five Dutch people.'

Among Bloemendaal's intellectuals, the Iraq war has created a sense of frustration. 'We can do nothing when war is going on,' says Roos Paris, a housewife who helps in the bookshop. 'We don't have any say. In one way Europe is too big, because we cannot make any representation. In another way it's too small. It doesn't make any difference. Most Dutch people don't know what laws are made in Brussels. And youth is not interested at all.'

And Bloemendaal is a haven, with a handful of migrants, untouched by the massive changes that have affected the rest of the country. Schilderswijk, the working-class area of The Hague, now supposedly contains 225 nationalities. The Dutch are not prominent among them. Reputedly, this is a dangerous area, though this seems to be a Dutch kind of perception. The marauding Moroccan teenagers would probably be regarded as tame elsewhere. Abdul Robbi, a Surinamese tailor who has been there for thirty years, says the place is more pleasant now that the natives have left. 'All the Dutch have dogs,' he says. 'There was shit everywhere.' He thinks the locals were taken by surprise: 'They didn't realize what would happen.' This time, as ten poorer countries arrive to take their cut from the existing fifteen, they realize. 'Europe?' he snorts. 'It's not going to work. Not in a million years.'

It seems as though we might have misunderstood the Dutch. It has been so much regarded as a *Guardian*esque conception of heaven – trams, bicycles, soft drugs, sexual openness, consensual government – that perhaps we have ignored the reality of the Netherlands. One eventually begins to twig that the Dutch willingness to let us ignore their language is not just, as is generally assumed, polite self-effacement and good business. It is a way of maintaining distance. You can come and enjoy yourself, they appear to be telling visitors, but you will never understand us.

'Tolerance isn't acceptance,' says Sam Coleman, the American editor of the Amsterdam magazine *Expats*. 'And when the Dutch are speaking Dutch, they are very different. When they see a tourist walking around the streets smoking a joint, they are shocked and think, "We give them coffee shops for this. How much more do they want from us?" But they will never say anything to outsiders. The key word in Holland is *nuchter*, sobriety. That is the ideal for a Dutch person. Visitors think the Dutch are happy to let you come here and do anything. But they're not.'

That reticence seems to be part of their political problem. The Dutch don't like to shout, which is why Fortuyn, who broke the mould, came as such a revelation. The parliament is wordy, worthy and somnolent. Like the people, its members enjoy discussing issues, but are reluctant to express their true feelings. 'Here everything is conciliatory,' says Mr Coleman. 'It's the same in the homes. People don't shout; you keep quiet. Maybe it's to do with it being a crowded country: you don't want the neighbours to hear.'

And the neighbours don't hear. Rob Boudewijn of the Netherlands Institute of International Relations believes the country is damaged within Europe by its system. 'Countries like Britain and France do well in Brussels because they have centralized coordination, and the governments make firm proposals. We do very badly because we seek consensus. Everybody's involved; everybody's opinion is taken care of. So we reach Brussels with a very vague compromise and no one takes any notice.'

If Europe ignores the Dutch, then the reverse is also starting to be true. Dr Boudewijn expects that the turnout in June's European parliament elections will slump to around 25 per cent. He also quotes a poll showing that a third of those surveyed do not know how many countries are about to join the EU. However, that is not a third of the voters – a third of Dutch members of parliament do not know.

Half a century ago, the memory of Germany's invasion still seared the Netherlands. Now, it is ancient history. So what does the union of the next half-century have to offer the Dutch? They are having difficulty working that one out.

Though the atmosphere for migrants has changed, Mr Coleman does not expect the country to become less welcoming to visitors. 'It's a flat swamp with crappy weather. Tourists come because of the relaxed attitudes. No one wants that to change. But, when you live here, you can feel the atmosphere is different. Holland has become very inward-looking.'

The Dutch may soon have the chance to show whether that is right or not. The country is also likely to hold a referendum on the new EU constitution, especially now that Tony Blair has given in. In the end, they will probably be sensible, mature, consensual and Dutch about it, and ratify whatever is agreed. But political analysts accept that is no certainty.

The Dutch turnout in the June European parliamentary elections was 39 per cent.

26 April 2004

LUDVIK VACULIK

The European sickness

The *Guardian*'s request for an article about the Czech Republic arrived just after I received a document that has an absurd relevance to our entry into the EU. It is a memorandum sent in August 1940 to Adolf Hitler by the then '*Reichsprotektor*' in Bohemia and Moravia, Von Neurath, and his secretary, K.H. Frank. Those gentlemen submitted to the Führer a proposal, fairly specific in certain respects, for the liquidation of Czechs in the 'German space' of Bohemia and Moravia.

The liquidation was to assume three forms: the gradual Germanization of amenable members of the nation; the resettlement of the intractable portion somewhere in the east; and the physical liquidation of the intellectual elite, which might be capable of organizing resistance. The familiar expressions of *Endlosung* ('final solution') and *Sonderbehandlung* ('special measures') are also employed. Well, it didn't happen, and we Czechs are sometimes surprised at the surprise of the Germans that after the war, which they lost, almost the contrary occurred, with the exception of that *Sonderbehandlung*.

That history is being recalled here these days, just prior to our entry into the EU. I was sent the document by a reader of my regular column in *Lidove noviny*, a leading daily paper with an honourable pre-Second World War tradition, who read that in the referendum on the Czech Republic's entry into the EU, I had voted against. In his letter, that reader agrees with me and writes that the age-old German plan for our nation's liquidation is back on the horizon, but will be carried out by different methods.

The creation of the EU and our membership thereof is a historical inevitability: a kind of historical denouement, so far as we are concerned. For three centuries after the Battle of White Mountain in 1620, when an Austrian Catholic army routed the Bohemian Protestants in what turned out to be the first major conflict in the Thirty Years War, we felt threatened by the Germans, who were always expanding eastwards. In the nineteenth century, we were actually protected from German expansionism by Austrian expansionism. (Indeed, it has become fashionable to cite imperial Austria as a precursor, or prototype, of a united Europe.) But only those ignorant of certain important factors can have a romantic view of Austria-Hungary. In every Czech and Moravian village there stands a monument to the fallen, each with a long list of men who died in an Austrian war that we didn't need and didn't want. That is a very sensitive issue these days, with the EU's wars in Kosovo and Iraq.

Following the reawakening of the nations in 1848 with Europe in revolt, we battled with Vienna in favour of an administrative arrangement that would enable Czechs and 'Bohemian Germans' to have equal rights. The Germans continuously thwarted it, even when they became a minority after the creation of Czechoslovakia in 1919. In fact, they are to blame for post-war communism, since they ensured that the Soviets took care of our liberation from Nazism.

But I can see that this reader's letter might have caused me to over-emphasize the German question, though it really is an important issue for the older generation. Without doubt we are by now fated to have the Germans as neighbours and, I ask myself, what historical task should we undertake now that the struggle with the Germans has disappeared from the agenda? Or has it disappeared? The answer depends on whether Europe will be German or Germany European – partly Britain's responsibility, don't you think?

Pre-war Czechoslovakia, as it was created on the basis of the Versailles and Trianon treaties, felt threatened by Hungary. It sought to protect itself by means of the Petite Entente [the Declaration of Benes, between Czechoslovakia, Romania and Yugoslavia in 1920], which didn't help us in the least, and I can't recall any instance when such a treaty of mutual assistance and security has ever worked. Membership of the EU finally promises us that kind of security.

I voted against joining the EU for cautionary and aesthetic reasons. My feeling is that this project has set its sights on being a giant economic enterprise. Its drive for collective security is not motivated by ideals or morals, but is a measure to protect capital now united at last. The underlying principle is the single market. After all, it is remarkable that the idea of a common Europe comes at a moment when we are increasingly governed by people no one has elected. Doesn't it strike you that way in Britain? Now that the owners of everything have found each other and reached an agreement, they kindly take us nations and states into their common basket. They are the ones who will do everything to protect and disseminate an affluent way of life and philosophy, just at the moment when these are beginning to be the target of criticism in various countries. I don't hear the Brussels trumpets calling for a stop to the destruction of the environment and the corruption of people.

In other words, the EU is not advancing human awareness and the development of Europeans but, on the contrary, will prove a major obstacle to them. From now on, whatever thoughtful and responsible people strive for will be that degree more prohibited. The EU's constitution and philosophy are not incorporating the results of social, ecological and spiritual criticism. There is not even scope for the emergence of social or cultural movements that would have a hope of success if created on a smaller territory.

However, there are only a few of us with these fears on every street. The majority of people, particularly the young, and every fool, anticipates that they will be joining precisely the affluence and decadence that I described. Were I to take the liberty of wishing for some task we could assume in place of our contest with the Germans, it would be challenging the sickness that Europe perpetuates and fosters.

Translated by Gerald Turner

25 August 2004

CHRIS HUHNE

Our dirty little secret

The government and the House of Commons may just be edging towards a discovery about our dismal relations with the European Union. If the role of British ministers in making every key EU decision is hidden from the British people by a secretive and ineffective Commons scrutiny system, then it is not surprising that the British feel that the EU is disconnected and bureaucratic. Brussels is 'them' who do things to 'us'. EU law is often presented as alien even by the ministers who agreed it.

The result of such unwholesome practices is that British public opinion is the most Eurosceptic in the EU. Fewer of us think that there are benefits to our membership than other Europeans. More of us think that the EU is undemocratic. More of us want to withdraw than in any other member state. UKIP's rise has given us the largest party committed to exit in any of the twenty-five member states.

The reasons for this festering hostility to the EU lie mainly in Britain, not Brussels. Certainly, the EU does stupid things. But most of the 450 million European citizens are wise enough to know that a set of institutions that delivers peace, prosperity and the power to tackle cross-border problems such as pollution is not going to be perfect. The calculus, comparing the past fifty years with any fifty years of European history, is overwhelmingly positive.

The real problem is that successive British governments have failed to make it clear that no major EU decision is taken without British ministers participating, and generally agreeing. The most sensitive issues – such as tax – require unanimity. Even when issues are agreed by majority, Britain is outvoted less often than any other major member state. We win from majority voting.

But would we know it? British MPs often react like scalded cats when they discover that some EU directive has been agreed by ministers and MEPs, and is all over bar the shouting. Once a minister has signed off a directive in Brussels, and it is approved by the European parliament, the UK is committed to implementing its objectives, usually by means of a statutory instrument which requires no Commons debate. We are then even more surprised when Whitehall implements the directive adding items from its own agenda: so-called 'gold-plating'.

The reason for our ignorance is the woeful inadequacy of the Commons' scrutiny of EU matters. Despite dealing with some twelve directives since 1999, there was not a single occasion on which the scrutiny committee either called me, a Liberal Democrat MEP, to give evidence or sent me its views. The Commons scrutiny committee meets in secret with a procedure that essentially involves sifting the paperwork that spews from the EU commission. Not surprisingly, it is swamped.

Nor is this record compensated by greater activity on the backbenches. In a recent survey of written parliamentary questions, my colleague Chris Davies MEP found that a mere seventy-nine questions out of 40,000 put down during one session concerned British ministers' attitudes in the council of ministers. There were ninety-two council meetings, each attended by a British minister, during that time.

This failure to hold ministers to account has an unintended consequence. Because ministers know that there is no political downside in agreeing EU directives and regulations, they often delegate negotiations to British officials. A Brussels bureaucracy is met by a British one. Issues that should properly be political – because they involve values, and have political consequences – are never lifted to a political level except in the European parliament, where MEPs do not have the same profile as ministers.

The Nordic countries have shown there is a much better way. Another Eurosceptic country, Denmark, pioneered the idea of examining Danish ministers before they went to each council meeting. Ministers are even given a rigid negotiating mandate. Danish scrutiny is high profile, public and unrelenting. As a result, the Danish Folketing – and the Danes – are forewarned and forearmed.

The Danish system has its faults. Danish ministers can be so tied down that other ministers do not find it worthwhile negotiating with them, as they know they have no flexibility beyond their public position. The best model is the Finnish Eduskunta. Its grand committee of senior parliamentarians takes evidence before each ministerial meeting. It allows ministers to interpret a mandate flexibly. It can also, crucially, call for specialist evidence from its select committees. One of the great myths of Brussels is that you need to be a Brussels specialist to understand it. In fact, the core expertise in scrutinizing a law on abattoirs is an understanding of abattoirs, not of Brussels procedures. And such expertise is more likely in a select committee than the foreign affairs committee. EU law is domestic, not a branch of foreign policy.

Will it happen here? Peter Hain, the leader of the House of Commons, shows some signs of rising to the challenge. He – and perhaps the modernization committee that he chairs – is beginning to realize the connection between the lack of Commons scrutiny and Euroscepticism. He has proposed a grand committee, meeting in public. So far, so good. The problem is that he has proposed it meet just twice or four times a year.

By contrast, the Nordic grand committees meet almost weekly, so that they can take evidence from ministers before every EU council. That is the guarantee that they are well informed, and examine the issues before decisions are taken rather than succumb to shock afterwards. If the modernization committee is to do more than genuflect to the need for EU scrutiny, it needs to face the far greater time commitment required of some MPs. Let us hope that it does, for our EU membership may depend on it.

21 April 2004

LEADER

Back-foot battle

Let battle be joined, Tony Blair stirringly declared in the Commons yesterday. It sounded good, but it also rang hollow. It is impossible, seven years into a Labour government, not to hear such words without wishing Mr Blair had said them in 1997. If Labour had taken the battle over Europe to the Conservatives and the right-wing press when its authority was at its greatest and theirs was at its nadir, then victory in the European Union constitution referendum that Mr Blair announced yesterday would seem more attainable. Today, the battle is not being fought on terms set by Labour, some of whose most senior members are themselves hostile to the constitution. It is being fought on terms set by Rupert Murdoch and his emissary Irwin Stelzer, whose ultimatum – call a referendum on Europe or News International will back the Tories – was apparently delivered to Mr Blair during the Easter recess.

Mr Blair said many of the right things in his statement to parliament yesterday. Subject to the expected agreement in June on Britain's so-called 'red lines' on such subjects as taxation, foreign policy, defence, social security, criminal justice and treaty change, the prospective EU constitution is a positive draft, which, Mr Blair correctly said, it is in Britain's interests to sign. It will help the newly enlarged 25-nation European Union to work better, doing away with the rotating six-month presidency, confining the use of the veto to areas where it is truly necessary and blocking the graphically named bureaucratic process known as 'competence creep'. It checks the momentum of federalism, it increases the power of national parliaments, it puts the European Council – controlled by the member states – in the agenda-setting place previously occupied by the commission, and it generally draws the line in places which British governments and British public opinion have long advocated. In a less hysterical political culture than ours, the case would be listened to more carefully than it is.

The Conservative party remains deaf to all this, as Michael Howard made clear yesterday. If his party were serious about Europe, it would see the constitution not as a threat but an opportunity. It would see, in particular, that EU enlargement will create many new possibilities for the anti-federalist approach that the Tories advocate. It would be more open to the new alliances and priorities that the ten new entrants will bring to the table. As a new report by Heather Grabbe for the Centre for European Reform makes clear, these new members will redress some of the imbalances of the old: they will be Atlanticist on defence, hostile to the dominance of the Franco-German axis, supporters of deregulation, opponents of tax harmonization and critics of the EU budget. The constitution, partly drafted to embrace their concerns, offers the forces of reform a rare opportunity. The Tories, fixated on the European threat and on point-scoring, miss all this; Mr Howard opposes any EU constitution under any circumstances, a position which inescapably leads to the suspicion that the Tory party's real goal is to wreck an EU of which it wants no part anyway.

Mr Blair made a good start to a long campaign yesterday. But he has a lot to prove after many false dawns on Europe. He has marched the pro-European forces up the hill and down again too often for them to rally unquestioningly to his standard this time. Perhaps this really is the great defining moment. But Mr Blair has issued his call to arms as a tactical ploy rather than as a clarion call. It may indeed be stand-up-and-be-counted time on Europe at last. Many Labour MPs, though, still prefer to sit on their hands, while other potential allies may have lost heart. There is a huge job to do. But is there the spirit and the drive to do it? That, not Mr Howard, may prove to be Mr Blair's biggest problem in the end.

24 June 2004

TIMOTHY GARTON ASH

The race to come

Suppose a champion athlete like Paula Radcliffe had to run 10km through a swamp before she even got to the starting line. This is Europe's position today.

If, after a bruising thirty months of national debates and referendums, the constitutional treaty finally comes into force at the end of 2006, Europe will only be at the starting line of every race that counts: the 100m sprint to provide a credible alternative to US unilateralism; the 1,000m race to foster reform in the wider Middle East before that region's troubles bring car bombs to all our front doors; the 5,000m to become competitive against the rising economic powers of

Asia; the marathon we must start running now if we are to prevent global warming spiralling out of control.

It's the results of these big races, not the details of voting weights, the number of European commissioners or the apportionment of sovereignty, that will determine whether our children are more free, safe and prosperous in twenty years' time – which, in my book, is the main goal of politics. The European Union is only a means to that end, not an end in itself. The institutional arrangements codified in the constitution are but a means to create those means.

Is there a thinking man or woman alive in Europe who is not depressed by the prospect of spending yet more years of bad-tempered debate on such mind-numbing details? There we shall be, the so-called 'opinion-formers', squabbling over contorted paragraphs and wrestling with tabloid shibboleths. Meanwhile, as the huge abstention rates in the European elections just showed, those whose opinions we are supposed to form have long since switched to another channel, to watch the football – or Paula Radcliffe winning the 5,000m in the European Cup. Who can blame them?

The constitution that emerged from the Brussels summit last weekend is not an inspiring document. It entirely lacks the simplicity, clarity and political poetry of great constitutions. Its preamble, written by Valery Giscard d'Estaing, is an embarrassment, especially when set beside that to the American constitution. The whole thing is too long. It mixes first-order statements about rights and responsibilities with second-order legal arrangements and often-vague policy aspirations. On contentious issues, such as the requirements for qualified majority voting or the size of the European commission, it offers awkward compromises that make the EU more difficult, not easier, to explain to sceptical citizens. But it's the best constitution we've got.

It does not drastically alter the way the European Union works already. It should make some parts of the union function more effectively, despite the enlargement to twenty-five member states. Most of the power stays with the member states, although their representatives can find themselves outvoted on a wider range of issues. With a European foreign minister and a single president of the European council, Europe will have more chance of saying something to which the US might actually listen. These are modest gains; yet for twenty-five and more European states to cooperate so closely is already a triumph.

The problem for those politicians who now have to 'sell' the constitution to their bored or hostile voters is that the case for it depends on unprovable alternatives. What, for example, if we had never had a European Union at all? Radical Eurosceptics, such as the UK Independence party, will claim we could have had a better Europe of sovereign, free, prosperous, closely cooperating democracies: a whole chocolate continent of big and little Switzerlands. To anyone with a milligram of historical nous, this is deeply implausible. For a clear majority of the present members of the EU, the return of freedom after dictatorship and the 'return to Europe' have gone hand in hand. Being in the world's largest trading bloc has made us all richer. But you can never prove what would have happened if the EU had not existed.

Less drastically, what if Britain rejects the constitution in a 2006 referendum?

The answer will depend on who else has done what in the meantime. If the French also give it the thumbs-down, in a referendum that Giscard says President Chirac must have, then the EU probably would go back to the drawing board. If Britain alone rejects it, and perhaps does so a second time after some further, cosmetic changes, then the other twenty-four would almost certainly go ahead on their own. Legally, this could put Britain in the splendidly paradoxical position of being the only remaining member of the current European Union. (There is no procedure under the existing treaties for kicking a member state out; so, in extremis, the others would all have to leave and make a new union, leaving little Johnny Bull as the only soldier marching in step.)

Most likely, however, Britain would be joined in a rejectionist lobby by several other states not belonging to the original, core European community of France, Germany, Italy and Benelux. In that case, some of the core countries, led by France and Germany, would almost certainly try to go ahead on their own, in a self-styled vanguard group. But the rejectionists would not take this lying down. If they included, say, Britain, Poland, Denmark and perhaps two or three more Scandinavian or east European countries, they would have the power to form a countervailing alliance. Europe would split, not unite. Some framework institutions of a European Union would remain, but these might gradually weaken into irrelevance, like the Holy Roman Empire. Real politics would take place elsewhere, and 2004 might then be seen by future historians as a high watermark of European unification – never again to be reached.

These more or less likely alternatives to the full, union-wide acceptance of the constitution have one thing in common: they would all result in Europe being preoccupied for still more years ahead with its own internal arrangements. Another American administration would have come and gone, a couple more Arab states would have plunged into chaos, the Chinese economy would have grown another 15 or 20 per cent, rising carbon dioxide emissions would be further overheating the planet, and we Europeans would still be faffing around like a household of old maids, eternally squabbling about the arrangement of the furniture in their front parlour.

So enough is enough. The furniture and the architecture of this European Union are far from perfect, but they'll do for now. To adapt Churchill's famous remark about democracy: this is the worst possible Europe, apart from all the other Europes that have been tried from time to time. Tomorrow, we need to get out of the front door and face up to the challenges that will determine the fate of our children. Otherwise, in 2024, as our then grown-up children leave their small, highly fortified apartments and drag their way through the boiling heat or the blackened snow; as they dodge the nationalist gangs fighting with immigrants on the other side of the street; as they then queue up for hours to beg a half-time job from the local Chinese employer; so they will turn to us and ask, 'What did you do in the great peace, Daddy?' And what shall we answer?

BRITAIN

16 October 2003

JAMES MEEK

The BNP in Burnley

The short political career of Luke Smith began in May with grand promises to the voters of Lanehead ward in Burnley, and ended in August with his use of a bottle of Stella Artois in a role for which it was not designed.

Smith was one of five British National Party councillors elected to Burnley council in May, giving the racist movement eight councillors with the three that they had won in 2002. It was a result that astonished the country.

Smith's election literature promised to 'roll out' a system of community panels, 'giving local people real control over their area'; to push for a unit to target 'anti-white racism'; to crack down on antisocial tenants; to withdraw funds from the council's translation unit 'which only benefits the minority of the minority'. He said he would bring enthusiasm and energy to his role as a councillor. His slogan: 'Fighting for a fairer Lanehead'.

This was mind-wobbling stuff for a 21-year-old with litres of gel on his hair. But the electorate of Lanehead bought it, to the surprise of the BNP. Smith had only been put up as a candidate at the last moment at the suggestion of his uncle, the shadowy, obsessive Steven Smith, who masterminded the party's leap in Burnley from nowhere to somewhere.

'The candidate who was to have stood dropped out at fairly short notice,' Leonard Starr, leader of the BNP faction on the council, told me, 'and at the last minute the uncle asked Luke to stand, in the expectation he wouldn't get in.'

In the expectation, that is, that an electorate obsessed with the menace of yob culture would not vote into a position of power in their town a 21-year-old football hooligan. Smith had been banned from Burnley FC for fighting. They did elect him, but there was no rolling-out of community panels. There was no pushing, there was no enthusiasm, and no energy. Not on the council, anyway. The only accurate pointer to the programme of the BNP's Smith was the part about the fighting.

The doom of the political meteor that was Smith was a fratricidal brawl at a BNP carnival in a Lancashire field in mid-August. What is beyond dispute is that there was a fight involving Smith and figures more loyal to the national leader of the movement, Nick Griffin. Smith was forced by his party to step down from the council, causing the by-election in Lanehead ward today as the BNP try to keep the seat. They may well fail. Like his nephew, Steven Smith has fallen foul of Griffin, who wants his party to be neat, sober, polite and under his strict control. Yet it was the manic, driven leafleting of Steven Smith and his associate, Simon Bennett, that delivered the Burnley result, and the mega-squawks of media coverage that followed, to Griffin. It is a vicious circle for the BNP leader; without his off-message activists, he cannot succeed, but with them, he cannot control his message.

Even those eight, now seven, BNP councillors in Burnley – the neater, more sober, more polite racists – have failed to make an impact. Despite starting out with almost a fifth of the seats on the council, they have not put forward motions, made speeches, left their mark on debates or tried to worm a mildly BNP-flavoured clause into a council initiative. Compared to the Green party, which has won seven seats on Lancaster council without any of the national publicity attending the BNP's success, the racists in the Burnley council chamber have achieved nothing except to convince many of those who voted for them that it was a wasted vote. That solid BNP bloc is still there, however. And the casual underlying racism, the coolly deliberate drawing of crosses by thousands of people that put them there, more chilling than any riot, remains.

'A small majority are hardened Nazis. The rest are people with genuine concerns expressing them in a racist vote,' said Michael Lavalette, the lone Socialist Alliance councillor in Preston. The Alliance, he explained, was not taking on the BNP at today's Burnley by-election because it feared splitting the non-BNP vote.

Whether the BNP has peaked in Burnley or not, their success in May, coming so soon after rioting which acquired a racial character after it was sparked off by a row about drugs, has forced the town, the region and the national government to confront the system of de facto apartheid that has crept into place, with areas that are almost exclusively Asian and almost exclusively white. The divide is sharpest in the school system. Even though non-whites make up less than 10 per cent of Burnley's population, most schools are either overwhelmingly Asian or overwhelmingly white, reflecting strict geographical admissions criteria.

Lancashire is so disturbed that it is taking the radical step, announced a few days ago, of asking the government for £150m to demolish every one of the eight existing secondary schools in Burnley and build five new ones in their place. 'The two communities are even more polarized now than they were before,' said one Labour councillor, who asked not to be named.

Councillor Starr doesn't like the new schools plan. He believes Asians and whites in Burnley aren't polarized enough. Here is his message of hope: 'I think you've got two communities that have got to somehow learn to live separately.' It's too bad for them that the Socialist Alliance has been so busy stopping the war in Iraq and dodging tear gas in coastal resorts such as Genoa and Seattle that it has been unable to tackle the BNP head on. As any Marxist schoolboy would tell you, the forces of bourgeois neo-liberal global capitalism have Burnley by the throat. Little new comes into Burnley that does not have the logo of some far-off authority on it, whether it is Tesco or the imprimatur of Tony Blair's government. Meanwhile, manufacturing jobs leak away, to be replaced not so much by unemployment as by low-wage employment in call centres and retail. The closure of the Michelin tyre factory with the loss of 1,000 jobs hurt Burnley badly. Everyone has stories about highly skilled workers whose earnings used to be in the £20,000 to £30,000 bracket who are starting again in middle age on £14,000 a year.

Burnley used to be a textile centre. It was the looms that brought thousands of immigrant workers from Bangladesh and Pakistan in the 1960s. A little of the textile work remains. It is not that Burnley doesn't make things any more, it's just that it is hard to know what they are. Heard of Jaguar, Rover, Honda, Nissan, Toyota? Well, they never made cars in Burnley. But those black plastic wands sticking out from steering wheels which you use to signal turns and switch on the wipers, they are made by the Burnley subsidiary of a firm called TRW. Not long ago TRW laid off 450 workers.

When younger people in Burnley give you directions, the landmarks they use are branches. You'll see McDonald's. Turn right at Burger King. Go past the NatWest.

For all the poverty, it is a pretty town when you approach it from Blackburn and Accrington, set in the folds of pale green hills with a cluster of blinding white new wind turbines whacking through the air on a summit looking down. Yet as the M65 motorway peters out and the hills draw closer on either side, you remember Burnley lies almost at the head of a valley. It might seem insane and arrogantly metropolitan to talk about an English town being isolated from mainstream currents of thought in the era of the internet, satellite television and Amazon.com, but there is an awful lot of moor up there.

It is true that Burnley has a crisis of empty private homes, many of them derelict, bought up for a few thousand pounds by absentee landlords waiting for – what? Nobody seems to be sure. There are 4,000 such places, boarded up or ransacked. But anyone going to the town expecting to see the kind of urban grot of graffiti, spilled refuse sacks, abandoned cars and dumped household appliances Londoners are used to would be disappointed. Despite the near-universal popular contempt for the council's Labour administration, which appears to have been in place since the Plantagenets, the town looks clean and cared for.

The post-riot anxiety of the authorities shows in a lurid rash of posters, warnings and acronyms that spot the streetscape. The signage convention of a red circle with a diagonal line through that which is banned has contained many black silhouettes. 'No Mobiles' is a common one. In Burnley, there is a 'No Bottles' sign for an outdoor drinking ban in the town centre. There was also one that I had never seen before: 'A No Kicking Somebody Who is on the Ground While Wearing a Baseball Cap and Shell Suit'. This is the logo of BAND: Burnley Against Night-time Disturbance. There are only a handful of asylum-seekers in the town, despite the popular belief to the contrary, which the BNP plays on, and fewer non-whites than in many other urban areas of Britain. The Asian community is concentrated in the centre, in terraces of cramped two-up two-downs that stand in close ranks in the Stoneyholme and Daneshouse areas on either side of the Leeds and Liverpool Canal.

On my way to see Sher Ali Miah, head of the Bangladesh Welfare Association in Stoneyholme, I bumped into two local guys in their twenties coming down past Asda: Shoka Ali, aged twenty-three, wearing a union flag embroidered on to the entire front of his top, and Naz, aged twenty-seven, in *shalwar kameez* and beard.

'I want to move away,' said Shoka Ali. 'It's not just a black–white thing. Everyone's got attitudes. They want to be Tupac.' He meant Asian on Asian violence. 'So when I bring up my kids I don't want it to be in this environment.'

Naz said, 'Stoneyholme's got one of the lowest crime rates in Burnley but every time something happens armed police are on your doorstep and it's in the papers.'

Shoka Ali added, 'Them bastards are fucking twats, the riot police. Normal bobbies are sound as a pound but they're proper racist bastards, those riot ones. They're arrogant fuckers. If I had a gun I'd shoot them. They come from Manchester. They say, "What do you want, you black bastard, come here, you."'

I asked if he went to watch Burnley FC play. Although the club has made a stand against racist chanting on the terraces (the club has three first-team black players), it seems to be harder to wipe out racist inter-fan violence, and Burnley has few non-white fans who attend.

'What's the point of going to a match and getting your head kicked in?' said Shoka Ali.

Talking to people in Stoneyholme, it sometimes seems that if only the BNP was to abandon anti-Islamicism, its hang-'em-and-flog-'em message would find an echo there. More plausibly, conservative Asians and BNP supporters alike would turn to the Conservatives, if they could be taken seriously again. An obsession with the search for lost discipline haunts the streets of Burnley.

'Nowadays, you can't whack your kids,' said Naz, apropos of nothing. 'You can't even give them a clip on the earhole. I once got a blow with a baseball bat. And it worked.'

Waiting in Ali Miah's two-tone purple parlour, I listened to one of his cousin's daughters and one of his sons talking. They talked to two of the older women of the house in Bengali, and to each other in English. Starr claims that the Burnley dialect spoken by second generation Asians cannot be mistaken for the Burnley dialect spoken by white people, but it sounded northern enough to me.

'Eez a raat saddo,' I heard the girl say of a friend.

I asked if I was pronouncing 'Stoneyholme' right.

'We call it the Stony Bronx actually,' she said.

'It seems quieter than the Bronx.'

'Oh, believe, when it gets later, we see a few actions.'

Ali Miah, who moved to Burnley from Bangladesh in 1972, took me for a walk down by the canal, reminiscing fondly about the English education of his childhood and how much he had benefited from being struck on the hand with a ruler. He is the governor of a local primary school that doesn't have any white pupils. The geographical admission rules mean the sweep only takes in Asian children. When the Bengalis and Pakistanis first moved to Burnley, they were not offered council houses, and had to rent what they could get in the centre of town. White people moved out.

'Who used to own houses here thirty, thirty-five years ago? Our white neighbours. Where are they? Why have they all left us? Where have they disappeared? If you talk about integration, it's a two-way process,' said Miah.

Although they don't produce any research to back it up, the BNP states as fact that when successful, well-off Asians move out of Stoneyholme and into Burnley's more spacious areas, house prices go down.

Miah reckoned it was a self-fulfilling prophecy. 'People say we don't try, but in my view we are over-trying. Asian people buy houses worth three to four hundred thousand pounds. As soon as they move in, the "for sale" signs go up on either side. You can't win.'

I first visited Burnley in July, when the BNP were still basking in the afterglow of their eight-seat block from May. I attended a council committee meeting in the town hall. It was the kind of stupefyingly dull occasion that makes you surprised and grateful that anyone is prepared to put up with playing the underpaid, despised, misunderstood local democracy game. This was a bit different, though. Nothing untoward was said. Yet in the committee were two BNP councillors – Barry Birks and Dave Edwards – who, if they were true to their party's soul, did not believe the chairman of the committee, Rafique Malik, had a right to be there.

Afterwards, sitting in an old carved chair in a town hall sideroom, wearing a grey *shalwar kameez*, Malik, who had been Burnley's first Asian mayor, told me that the groundwork for the BNP's success had been laid, albeit inadvertently, by a renegade Labour politician, Harry Brooks. Brooks broke with Labour, formed a group of independents, and began campaigning against the council's paying for an equal opportunities section and against grants for Asian organizations. It was Brooks, said Malik, who created the mythology that Asian areas got improvement grants because they were Asian, rather than because they were poor.

'That was the silent poisoning of racism. He made it respectable,' Malik continued. 'I think by and large it's a protest vote by the opposition to Labour. They have no confidence in the Tories, they have no confidence in the Liberals or the Independents any more, they think: let's try something new.' Labour, he said, had failed the white poor. 'We have young, white, poor people – at least twenty-five per cent of them can't read or write English properly. And they can't benefit from the affluence the rest of us are benefiting from. That's what is wrong with democracy. Seventy-five per cent are OK. We can ignore twenty-five per cent. But if there is somebody there to exploit them, those twenty-five per cent can play hell with the system. So, as we have support mechanisms for the black poor, we haven't set up any support mechanisms for the white poor.'

When I returned to Burnley this week, the BNP's happy spring had turned into a more doubtful autumn in the wake of the Smith family's break with Griffin. I asked Birks and Starr how they had got on with Malik. Both said they couldn't force him to go back to Pakistan.

'What we are saying is we will offer them the opportunity. Nothing about forcing people. Not at all,' said Birks.

'He's here, isn't he?' said Starr. 'Can't just go up to Rafique Malik and say, "On your bike and go away." It isn't going to work. But I don't doubt there are a lot of people in this country who have no particular joy being here and have a wish to go back to where they came from and as a party we're quite happy to see that happen.'

I asked Starr if his party had put forward any initiatives since their success six months earlier.

'No, we haven't.'

Starr, a 56-year-old who spent fifteen years in the army, works for a bus firm which has grown rich very fast on the back of shuttling rail passengers around engineering works. He offered a chaotic tapestry of the ills of Burnley, most

12 February 2004 The memorial service overlooking Morecambe Bay, where nineteen men and women lost their lives in the cockling tragedy. (Don McPhee)

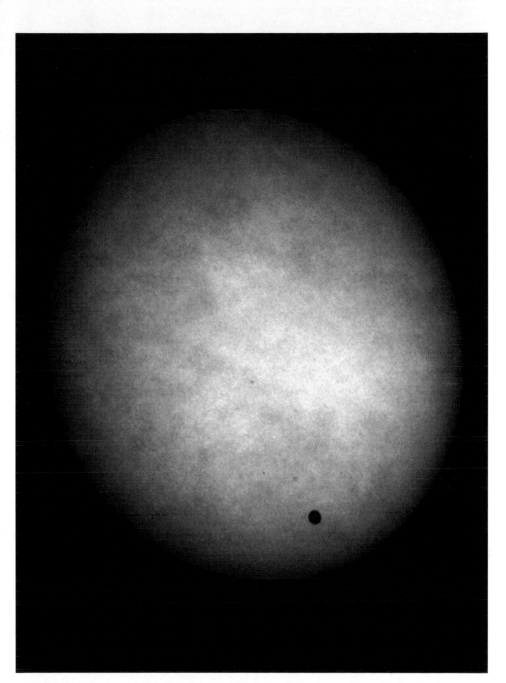

8 June 2004 The transit of Venus viewed from the University of Central Lancashire's Alston Observatory. (Don McPhee)

Opposite *25 April 2004* Aerial view of the City of London. The Swiss Re building, aka The Gherkin. (Dan Chung)

24 March 2004 St Martin-in-the-Fields, Trafalgar Square, London. The church is about to undergo a £34m restoration programme. (Martin Argles)

sourced to the Asian community, from Stoneyholme becoming a virtual no-go area for whites to the fact that Asian lads could chase white women but white lads had no chance with Asian girls. 'They came for economic reasons but finished up with ... monstrous is probably too harsh a word.' He never came up with a word that was just harsh enough. 'This Asian culture doesn't belong here. Don't try to push your culture down our throats, because we don't want it.'

Talking to people in Burnley, hints came through constantly of the closing and corrupting of children's minds by racism. Starr was in a good mood when we left the generic pub where we had met. We were talking about football and he told me a story he thought was about football, but I thought it was about something else. 'My brother said to his son, "Do we hate Pakis?" "Yeah!" "Do we know why?" "No!" "Well, it's the same with Blackburn Rovers."'

In a pub near Lanehead, an aircraft engineer who travels around the world checking other engineers' work told me he had voted BNP before and would vote BNP again because the Asians in Burnley 'were taking the piss'. Yet he wasn't a racist because his eleven-year-old daughter had an Asian godfather, whom she loved. But for some reason, he said, the girl hated other Asians. 'She says we've got to stop them, they're taking over,' said the engineer. 'She goes to a Catholic school. I don't understand where she gets it from.'

Despite Malik's theory, some of the strongest support for the BNP comes from wealthy, white, middle-class areas. I tracked down Steven Smith – 'a recluse!' warned Starr – in the beautiful village of Cliviger, outside Burnley but within the borough. He's an accountant by profession. He lives alone in a tiny cottage with a big Alsatian called Samba. It's dark in his front room. A coal fire burns in the grate and an odd assortment of objects hangs from the low black rafters: a trumpet; boots and shoes; swords; boxing gloves; a warming pan. He never goes to pubs if he can avoid it but his front room looks like one. On the wall hangs one of those full-size, real-weight reproduction *Lord of the Rings* swords made by an American firm called United Cutlery. Smith says it's the one Aragorn used.

Smith cannot take part in elections himself; he is banned because he served six weeks in prison, and six weeks tagged on probation, for electoral fraud – forging signatures on electoral documents. With Simon Bennett, he said, he started the BNP from zero in Burnley in 1999. In six months, they leafleted 35,000 homes in the borough. He did most of the walking. Sitting in a leather armchair by the fire, Smith, who says he reads little, waxed like a prophet on the doom he sees coming. The system is beginning to panic. Britain could be another Balkans. 'The reason they're pulling down these schools in Burnley is the Asians and the whites don't want to live in Burnley together and don't want to go to school together. Should the BNP ever get to power in Britain, I think the climate will be such that probably a great number of ethnic minorities wouldn't want to live here anyway.'

Smith talked and talked. Outside the dark room, the sunshine was blinding, the wind raced in the trees, and it was possible to remember that most people were still not voting for the BNP.

In Lanehead, I knocked on ten doors in a row in an unscientific survey of voter opinion. None of the five voters who answered the door would admit to having voted BNP; all said they would not vote for them this time. One woman, originally from Liverpool, was black. She had two Nigerian grandfathers and two white English grandmothers. Recently she opened the door to a BNP campaigner.

'He opened the door and he just started talking about how decent they were and how things needed to be changed and blah blah,' she said. 'He never mentioned anything about ethnic minorities. I said, "If I'd opened the door and I hadn't been one of the ethnic minorities, what would you have said?" He said, "You're British." I said, "Oh, goody goody."'

The Lanehead ward by-election was won by the Liberal Democrats. The BNP came third, after Labour. The BNP's hold on Burnley was loosened further in February when another of their councillors, a 65-year-old grandmother named Maureen Stowe, resigned, saying she hadn't realized the BNP was a racist party. She later joined Labour. Despite hopes of a breakthrough at local elections in June, the BNP was left afterwards with the same reduced strength on the council – six seats. Nationally, it neither advanced nor retreated. In European elections on the same day, however, 808,200 British adults – more than the population of Leeds – voted for the British National Party.

29 January 2004

JONATHAN FREEDLAND

Snow show

A soft snowfall was swirling outside the high court just before Lord Hutton took his place on the bench. It's a pity it did not last, because a blanket of fresh, white snow would have made the perfect backdrop to what followed: an extraordinary one-man show, a performance which had its audience snorting and occasionally gasping in disbelief. Transferred to the West End, the show could only have one name: *Whitewash*.

For six months the government had been accused of the darkest of crimes: leading the nation to war on a lie and bullying a dedicated public servant to his death. In ninety minutes Lord Hutton crushed those claims entirely. He exonerated Tony Blair, Alastair Campbell, Geoff Hoon, John Scarlett and Kevin Tebbit more completely than any of them can have dreamed. The judge placed a little dollop of pure white snow on the reputation of each of them.

As theatre, the show may have lacked visual splendour: just a modern, Ikea-style blonde wood courtroom with a white-haired judge at its apex, hunched over his text, reading aloud in his gentle Ulster brogue. But what it lacked in set design and costume it more than made up in narrative drive. The Hutton report had no confusing ambiguities or detours. It all thrust in the same, clear direction: the government was right and the BBC was wrong. (Downing Street, which, along with all the parties involved in the Kelly affair had received the report twenty-four hours earlier, must have begun the day with a champagne breakfast. Once Lord Hutton had spoken, officials could barely contain their gratitude. One Labour apparatchik exclaimed: 'Make that man a duke!')

Occasionally, his lordship tantalized with a hint of suspense. He would begin a sentence that seemed destined to hurt the government – only to swerve away with a 'however' or 'nevertheless' that backed the prime minister or his aides. A classic of the form came when the judge assessed whether there had been an 'underhand strategy' to name David Kelly. 'For a time, at the start of the inquiry, it appeared to me that a case of some strength could be made that there was such a strategy,' he began. Perhaps now the drama was about to turn! Perhaps this was to be the second act! But no. He explained that the longer the inquiry proceeded, and the more he heard government witnesses explain themselves, the more his mild scepticism melted away. He concluded 'that there was no such underhand strategy'.

The judge faulted the Ministry of Defence for the way it told Dr Kelly he had been outed. Otherwise, the closest Lord Hutton came to laying a glove on the government was his suggestion that 'the possibility cannot be completely ruled out' that the PM's desire to have a strong dossier on Iraqi weapons of mass destruction had 'subconsciously influenced' John Scarlett and his joint intelligence committee.

Subconsciously! Forget all those memos from Mr Campbell to the intelligence chief asking for multiple changes in wording. There was no pressure to harden the dossier, Lord Hutton decided, just a possible twitch of Mr Scarlett's subconscious – and even that tiny 'possibility' was remote. It was more likely that Mr Scarlett's sole concern had been to reflect accurately the intelligence available.

For the press benches, this was all too much. Several journalists began first to sniff, then to snort and finally to chuckle their derision. Jeremy Paxman, for once barred from asking questions, was shaking his head in bemusement as each new finding in favour of the government came down from the bench. When Mr Scarlett's subconscious was introduced, the room seemed to vibrate with mockery.

Often when judges hand down their judgments, the lesser mortals arrayed below feel compelled to put aside their own biases or expectations and bow to the sheer logic and coherence of the legal argument. Whatever their final conclusions, long, detailed rulings in high-profile cases are often spellbinding essays in tight, rigorous reasoning. Yesterday was not one of those days. Observers who had sat through every hour of the Hutton inquiry, reading and hearing the same evidence as his lordship, were left scratching their heads at his final thinking.

For one thing, Lord Hutton seemed to have turned a deaf ear to crucial facts and testimony. Transcripts of interviews that the BBC *Newsnight* journalist Susan Watts had recorded with Dr Kelly corroborated much of what Gilligan claimed, not least the scientist's statement that the 45-minute claim was 'got out of all proportion'. But Lord Hutton appears to have put those transcripts out of his mind, preferring to assume that Dr Kelly could not have said what Gilligan claimed he had.

Similarly, the judge's belief that there was no 'underhand strategy' to name Dr Kelly glided over Mr Campbell's diary entries in which he confessed his desperation to get the scientist's name out. Lord Hutton concluded there was no leaking, even though newspaper reports from last summer show someone must have been pointing reporters very directly towards Dr Kelly.

He ruled there had been no meddling with the substance of the September dossier, just some beefing up of language, even though one expert witness, Dr Brian Jones, testified that, when it comes to intelligence, wording is substance.

On each element of the case before him, Lord Hutton gave the government the benefit of the doubt, opting for the interpretation that most favoured it, never countenancing the gloss that might benefit the BBC. Perhaps the clearest example was Lord Hutton's very judge-like deconstruction of the 'slang expression' 'sexed-up'. One meaning could be inserting items that are untrue, he said; another could simply be strengthening language. Under the latter definition, Hutton conceded, Gilligan's story would be true. So his lordship decided the other meaning must apply.

The judge also seemed to have a bad case of Wandering Remit Syndrome. The late insertion of the notorious 45-minute claim was within the scope of his inquiry; but whether that claim related to battlefield or strategic weapons was not, even though the reliability of the claim might well turn on precisely that question. Repeatedly, territory that might discomfit the government was declared out of bounds; areas awkward for the BBC were very much in.

The whole performance set you wondering. For this has become a ritual in our national life. If an argument rages on long enough, we soon call for a judge to investigate it for us in the form of a public inquiry. We see and hear the same evidence he does, but still we invest in him some mystical power to reach a conclusive truth we have not seen. And eventually he comes down from the mountain, like the high priest of yore, and delivers his judgment. Yesterday's show shattered that illusion. Suddenly you found yourself seeing through the grandeur and mystique and wondering, who exactly is this man? Why was he chosen for this task? What made him cast this whole, complex dispute so neatly in black and white?

We are not meant to think this way. We are meant to trust and accept the wisdom from on high. But that is becoming harder to do. For Britons remember Lord Denning's conclusions on the Profumo affair in 1963 and his belief that 'people of much eminence' could not possibly have misbehaved. Many remember Widgery's similar whitewash job on the Bloody Sunday case. Or the judge in the Archer trial who believed the 'fragrance' of wife Mary made it unimaginable that Jeffrey would have used a prostitute.

Yesterday was a reminder that these people are human beings like any other. It seems worth remembering that, before he was a law lord, the judge was plain Brian Hutton. That man might just harbour an old-fashioned faith in the benign motives of government and establishment and may, for all we know, take a dim view of journalism.

In a generation's time, the Hutton report may read as risibly as Denning's. Perhaps by then we will have lost our need to ask a single, bewigged man to separate truth from lies in public life. Yesterday such questions were far away, as the government crowed and the BBC bowed its head – and the snow kept on falling.

28 October 2003

MAX HASTINGS

Away with the turnip

For more than a year, I have been imploring my Tory friends to act swiftly and ruthlessly to dispose of Iain Duncan Smith. My motives are selfish. One day, I want to be able to vote Tory again. Like millions of others, I cannot do so while the party is led by a turnip. If the Tories stick with IDS until he has lost a general election, the consequences for them will be catastrophic.

IDS makes Michael Foot resemble Spartacus. He was given the job only because he was not Kenneth Clarke, and because he professed the right-wing enthusiasms prevalent among the very old party members who selected him. His tenure has been disastrous. His recent conference speech was among the worst by any party leader in living memory. Next day some loyalists and – more surprisingly – newspaper pundits claimed that it had been adequate to keep him in his job. Anyone capable of such delusions was in denial about the past, present and future of the Conservative party.

I am among millions of angry former Tory voters, who have watched the party march blindfold over the political precipice since 1997. Those of us who supported Michael Heseltine, Clarke, Douglas Hurd and the old centrist vision of Toryism always feared that after an election defeat the right would seize control. And so they did.

What has happened since 1997 has been dismaying not only because so many of us cannot support the Hague–IDS party, but because it is plain that such leaders, and such policies, can never again hope to win a general election. Not one of IDS's potential successors is capable of leading the Tories to power. But there is a chance that they could lose the next general election with dignity, rather than as an object of ridicule. The new leader's job is to get what's left of the party off the beaches in small boats, so that it may be capable of winning an election in seven or eight years' time.

Consider the candidates. Oliver Letwin is a clever man who could win a poll for the presidency of an Oxbridge college, but is never likely to win a ballot among the British people. David Davis is brighter and nastier than IDS, but punches at about the same weight as, say, Patricia Hewitt – which is not heavy enough to get him to Downing Street. I passionately argued the case for Clarke in 1997, but now it is too late. He despises most Tory MPs, and they hate him. Ken cannot be bothered to take the leadership now unless the party signs an unconditional surrender to his terms, notably on Europe. This it will never do. If Michael Portillo stands, he could be a serious contender. Today it is hard to know what he believes. He is clever and charismatic, but Conservative heavyweights believe that unrevealed aspects of his gay past could still torpedo him. All the indications suggest that he has no taste for exposing his private life to scrutiny. More important, in the eyes of some of us, in office he displayed very poor judgement. He seems too louche to be a credible party leader.

We are left with Michael Howard. I disagree with almost everything Howard stands for, but if I was a Tory MP I would vote for him in a leadership contest. He is an intelligent man of great experience, who can engage Tony Blair in the Commons on something like equal terms. No one expects Howard to win the next election. His task is simply to keep his party in the ring – to enable it to win enough votes to become a contender for power two elections down the track. If he behaves sensibly, he might be capable of doing this. He could afterwards disappear into honourable retirement, making way for the leader of a new generation.

If you are bemused by the notion that any left-of-centre Tory could support such a man as Howard, even as a stopgap, think again about the alternatives. Over recent years, all the old knights of the shire and voices of moderate Conservatism have retired or been winnowed out. Right-wing Stalinism has overtaken the party, of such a kind that anyone who is not 'sound on Europe' – which means loathing everything to do with it – possesses no hope of getting or keeping a parliamentary seat.

Old Bill Deedes observed at a *Daily Telegraph* leader conference back in 1987 that he believed the Conservative party could destroy itself over Europe. At the time, I thought his prophecy extravagant. Yet now we see it close to coming to pass. The old pragmatism, the respect for consensus, which won elections for the Tories generation after generation, has been systematically purged.

The Tories learned utterly the wrong lesson from the experience of Mrs Thatcher. In 1979, amid a national economic and industrial crisis comparable to 1940, she ruthlessly rewrote the rules, not only of the Tory party, but of British life. By 1990, she had achieved remarkable and important things, but the British people were surfeited with her style of government. The Tory right proclaimed in November 1990 that the party was making a huge error by dumping her, that both Conservatives and the country would repent the folly. Not so. No one outside Tunbridge Wells lamented the departure of Thatcher. Just as Winston Churchill was rightly dismissed by the people after performing his historic service to them as a war leader, so there was no room in British politics for Thatcher after she had done her business in the 1980s. Yet since 1997, the Tories have genuflected constantly to 'the Thatcherite legacy'. Both Hague and IDS have offered a sleigh-ride back to the halcyon days of, say, 1983 – a place to which the British people have not the smallest desire to go.

The Tories will never be electable until they can find a leader who can offer the British people a vision of the future, not of the past. Britain is now a social democratic country. Barring a national cataclysm, a visibly right-wing party will not again achieve power here.

Ever since 1997, the party and its media supporters have addressed the political agenda with an iron-clad ideological rectitude, based upon the beliefs that: a) sooner or later, the turn of public opinion will bring the Tories back to power, whatever follies they commit or policies they espouse; and b) even if this proves untrue, it is better to be ideologically virtuous than to trim in mere pursuit of power. Both these propositions are ridiculous.

Politics is meaningless unless a party achieves power. Until the last few years of the twentieth century, the Conservatives always understood that it was necessary to adapt some policies in order to win the chance to implement others.

Most of the above is obvious to millions of British voters, but it has not seemed obvious to the Tories. Their duty is to ditch the turnip, so they can choose the man under whom they will lose the next election. But they should be thinking now, today, about what comes after that – about which man and what policies might fulfil the purpose the Conservative party is supposed to exist for, and return it to power.

21 November 2003

JOAN BAKEWELL

Playing the identity card

I already have an identity card. I have it right here: a folded piece of green card declaring on the cover: National Registration. Inside, a National Registration Office stamp tells me it was issued on 15 July 1950. The date is a bit of a mystery. Neither a significant birthday – eighteen or twenty-one – nor a landmark national crisis. There had been many such documents in the early months of the war and people got used to peremptory orders concerning ration books for food (an allowance of points) and for clothing (a matter of coupons). Everyone had to register with a butcher and a grocer and these became their only authorized suppliers. Faced with war, the population was meekly agreeable to any amount of government regulation.

By 1950, the war had been over for five years yet my identity card has all the harshness of wartime diktats: 'Always carry your identity card. You may be required to produce it on demand by a police officer in uniform or member of HM armed forces in uniform on duty … Any breach of these requirements is an offence punishable by a fine or imprisonment or both.' And within is my identity number: LEXJ 259:3. The three was because I, the firstborn, came after my parents. My father was one, of course. This number had been drummed into me so thoroughly during the war that it has stayed with me more than fifty years later (along with that other vital number, the Co-op 'divi' number. Ours was 929 and without it we couldn't claim our quarterly dividend).

Thus it was in wartime that an entire generation came to accept government regulation on a scale never experienced before or since. What is more, it was welcomed as a great improvement on the shortages of the First World War. So rationing was seen as conspicuous fairness: the rich and poor treated as equals. Even the royal family was included. There was a unanimity then that made us ready to be compliant. We had such a sense of national identity – Britain standing proudly alone against the enemy – that our individual identities, set out in those green cards, were but a part of the greater national identity to which we all belonged.

That isn't the case now. The return of the identity card comes at a time of identity crisis. It is said that we don't really know who we are any more. We are a more fragmented country, more conscious of our differences than aware, as we once were, of what we have in common. What is more, government control of our lives – rather than falling away after the war – has got closer and closer. Identity cards were finally abolished in 1952 after an incident. A police constable stopped a motorist and asked to see his papers there and then by the kerbside. The motorist refused and was charged. But a judge later ruled that police should not demand identity papers as a matter of routine. Will that ruling still stand if David Blunkett has his way?

It isn't surprising that we aren't as compliant as once we were. There was a time when you could build a garden shed, park a car, smack a child, with that confident sense of identity, of being in charge of your own destiny, that has been so consistently whittled away by the world in which we live. I wonder, is the ID card a step too far: too intrusive, too Orwellian, to be acceptable? Or are people once again, as in wartime, so fearful that they will accept its return?

Wartime was an era of actual fear, of a proximate and visible enemy. But now people whose lives are, in fact, less directly threatened than once they were, are being encouraged to see the world as perpetually menacing. The prominence given to crime, so-called scroungers, illegal immigrants, lone stalkers and, above all, the suggestion of ever-present terrorists, wind us up into a state of permanent anxiety. We are convinced that we live in times of unique terror, rather than one of the most peace-loving nations on earth.

Having had an identity card once, I am not much bothered about carrying one again. What worries me is the fact that I am constantly losing things: gloves, rail tickets, scarves. I am sure to lose the new plastic ID. Perhaps it would be better to tattoo the number on my wrist. Oh, no. That has been tried in wartime, too, we discovered. Better not.

10 February 2004

HYWEL WILLIAMS

Welsh twilight

The blitheness of the Welsh is one of their leading characteristics. Not for us the angularities and the asperities of other Celtic traditions. Apart from the odd second-home blaze on a remote hillside, Welsh politics avoids the incendiary option and opts for celebration instead.

The survival, against such overwhelming odds, of a distinctive identity nestling awkwardly by the side of the country that has spawned a global Anglophone culture, has something of the miraculous about it. It all seems a testimony to that native gift for accommodation with the invasive presence, for achieving by stealth and charm what could never have been won by outright battle. Ours is a consensual tradition, and traitor identification is not a popular Welsh sport.

We do, however, make an example of Vortigern (or Gwrtheyrn), who, in the Welsh annals, is fingered as the source of all our woe by yielding his Kentish territories in the fifth century to the German mercenaries he enrolled as allies in his fight against the Picts. It was a done deal, but also a very bad one and Vortigern learned to count the cost. Having first invited those Germanic tribes in, he soon found that they were at his throat, driving him and his Cymry beyond the Severn. The pattern was set: English cultural success is founded on that unyielding mental refusal to assimilate on its own part, while expecting all others to bend the knee.

Some 1,600 years on, the publication of the Office of National Statistics' Focus on Wales shows that Gwrtheyrn's heirs are still around. It took some agitation to get the data, based on the 2001 census, published in this separate Welsh form. But now we can start to count the cost of a millennium-and-a-half's accommodation. We are still – by a surprisingly large majority – proud to be what we are. Some 60 per cent of those living in Wales declare themselves to be Welsh – and Welsh alone. And another 7 per cent call themselves first Welsh and, second, British. But 25 per cent of Wales's inhabitants are now English-born – a statistic which has grown remorselessly over the past twenty-five years.

It is Mid and North Wales that has born the brunt of the invasion. South-east Wales may be the area where industrial decline has been most alarming, reducing every valley to a condition of utterly distressing dereliction. But that is also the region where pride in Welshness is most marked. Go to Conwy in the north – where Edward I's disgusting castle shows the iron fist at its most blatant – and almost half the population are now English-born. Travel further west into the ancient kingdoms of Gwynedd and Deheubarth and the desolation deepens. Farming has already died here.

It is not just a question of milk quotas and uneconomic hill farms: in Carmarthenshire there are now dozens of cash-rich buyers from over the border waiting to pounce on the next farm available in Tywi's broad acres. Often the invader's ambition is to aggregate farms together to form the larger economic unit, with the farmhouse itself sold off as yet another second home.

We may be proud to be Welsh, but we also close our eyes to the fact of Welsh linguistic decay, that *Götterdämmerung* of a whole culture, but one couched in Welsh diminuendo. Listen to our fatuous Welsh cultural establishment, and you might think that a great victory has been won. For the first time in census history there is an apparent advance on previous decline. Over 21 per cent now claim to be Welsh-speaking. But look below the headline, and you will find that only 16 per cent can read and write the language. That other 5 per cent just do pidgin Welsh. This is simply the continuation of a century's story of steady attrition.

To travel across Wales now is to see a country united in deep distress, with a poverty which stabs at the heart. Cardiff, and a mile or two of territory on either side of the M4 spreading into mid-Glamorgan, is the continuation of Thames Valley prosperity. Elsewhere is death.

Some 23 per cent of the Welsh in 2001 claimed to have limiting, long-term illness or disability. Go to the top of the Rhondda Valley now, and look back at that narrow strip of land that created radical Britain, and weep. Because for all that hollow talk of regeneration as one acronymed quango-beast bumps into another in the subsidy-based culture that is Wales today, there is no possibility of rebuilding what has been lost. The winds of winter blow down from the Brecon Beacons to the north and presage the return of nature grassing over where once there was life and work.

Go into small-town Wales and the evidence of sickliness lies on every side. In Milford Haven, in the far west, where once the mighty tankers docked, the elderly gather over chips and beans in tobacco-stained cafés and look out to sea with watery eyes. In any Welsh conurbation, the poverty is there in two forms – thin-poor and fat-poor – both testimonials to a dreadful diet. The effects of a century of free-trading capitalism have been compounded by a half-century of deadbeat municipal socialism.

Gwrtheyrn – returned to his people – would recognize the Welsh phrase for this terrible Welsh state: '*Heb laith, Heb waith, Heb wlad*' – language-less, work-less, land-less.

2 December 2003

MARTIN KETTLE

As the sparks fly

At the height of the Irish treaty negotiations in 1921, one of David Trimble's great political heroes, Sir James Craig, later to become the first prime minister of devolved Northern Ireland, emerged from David Lloyd George's office in Downing Street and observed with bemusement that there must be 'a verse in the Bible which says Czechoslovakia and Ulster are born to trouble as the sparks fly upwards'.

Europe in 1921 was still in the midst of the terrible post-war influenza epidemic, and Craig headed straight off from Downing Street to see his doctor, 'to be inoculated – I suppose against a Sinn Fein germ', as the cabinet assistant secretary Thomas Jones wryly noted.

Many things have changed on both sides of the border that Craig, Lloyd George and Michael Collins fashioned in those dramatic negotiations in London long ago. But eighty-two years later it is Trimble's turn to reflect that Ulster seems to be as much born to trouble now as it was then, while its Protestant leaders are as vulnerable as ever to a nasty attack of the Sinners.

Last week's assembly elections – in which Ian Paisley's Democratic Unionists elbowed past Trimble's Ulster Unionists for the first time in an assembly or parliamentary election – are a landmark setback for Tony Blair and his Irish counterpart, Bertie Ahern. They have underscored a lesson that, in one form or another, has been true since at least the time of Parnell – that every attempt to incorporate Irish nationalist aspirations within British political institutions will ultimately founder in some way on the rock of Ulster unionism.

From Gladstone to Blair, British prime ministers have thought that they could finesse the incorrigibles in Protestant Northern Ireland; they have tried every type of arrangement, from home rule, through partition, to repeated modern efforts at power sharing. But in the end, they have failed. This is not to pretend that unionism carries unique responsibility for the moments of crisis in which, in one form or another, it has refused to be pushed into arrangements it dislikes. Nor is it to deny that at various times there has been some progress and improvement. But that progress can be a deceptive light to steer by. It repeatedly suggests to nationalist and unionist alike that there is a linear progression in Irish history that is leading inexorably towards a 32-county united Ireland. Perhaps, one day, that will occur. Yet the history of the past 120 years consistently suggests the reverse.

The congenital optimists take a less drastic view of last week's results. They look at the votes cast and they point out, quite accurately, that most people in Northern Ireland voted for parties which support the power-sharing agreement of 1998. They look at the seats won, and they observe that perhaps seventy-one of the 108 newly elected assembly members support the agreement. They remember the 1998 referendum in which 71 per cent of Northern Ireland voters endorsed the agreement. And they cite a recent *Belfast Telegraph* opinion poll in which only 13 per cent of Ulster voters want to see the agreement abandoned and in which no fewer than 73 per cent of DUP voters said they wanted their party to cooperate in forming an executive government under the agreement's existing terms.

As it happens, Paisley dismissed that possibility out of hand in characteristic terms yesterday. But it is another self-deception to pretend, as some now do, that Paisley is the only remaining stumbling block to an era of 'new realist' cooperation between the DUP and the other big winner last week, Gerry Adams's Sinn Fein. Leave to one side the fact that a strategy based on waiting for the 77-year-old big man to retire would hand Paisley a personal veto on Northern Ireland's future that he would not be unwilling to exploit. The larger reality is that it is not in Paisley's hands to deliver such a historic compromise as this, even in the improbable event that he was suddenly minded, against all precedent, to do so.

Last week's results cannot and should not be talked out of existence just because we don't like them. They were indisputably Protestant Northern Ireland's vote for the agreement to be renegotiated. Sixty one per cent of Protestants want this to happen, according to the recent opinion poll. The DUP, which campaigned on this selfsame platform, hoisted its share of the poll from 17 per cent to 26 per cent last week. And a significant minority of the UUP electorate voted for Trimble opponents who take the same view.

Trimble did remarkably well in the circumstances, even increasing the UUP's share of first-preference votes compared with 1998. That he prevented his party's vote from haemorrhaging in the way that Brian Faulkner's did in the 1970s is a tribute to many things, including the greater resilience of the Belfast than the Sunningdale institutions. But it is also a tribute both to Trimble's own roots in hardline unionist movements, and in particular to his much-criticized brinkmanship tactics in the four years that he was chief minister of the power-sharing executive. Without them, it is hard to believe he would not have been swept away last week.

But the initiative is with Paisley now, whether for the aim of renegotiation or of outright rejectionism. It is with him, above all, because of the IRA's refusal to do and say the things on arms that Trimble and the British and Irish governments wanted. Behind that refusal, one presumes, is a view in the republican leadership that it is preferable, in the cause of securing a thirty-two-county united Ireland, to concentrate on eclipsing the SDLP and securing political hegemony in Catholic Northern Ireland in the long term than it is to make Trimble's leadership easier on the other side of the divide in the short term.

London and Dublin will clearly want to find a way of meeting Paisley's terms in some way if they can, in the hope that some sort of power sharing can emerge from the current suspension. Sinn Fein, though, can hardly be seen to agree. Adams has not brought his party to its present position in order to collude in what Paisley would be bound to present, at the very least, as the weakening of the agreement.

In his recent book on Irish home rule, the Queen's University Belfast historian Alvin Jackson argues that, just as with Gladstone in the 1880s, Blair's readiness for constitutional experimentation in 1998 owed its origin to the clash between Irish Catholic social and economic advance on the one hand and failed and discredited British-backed state institutions on the other. Gladstone failed because he faced an economically powerful and culturally self-confident unionism, Jackson argues, adding, 'It remains to be seen whether the war-weary, culturally disoriented and economically fragile unionist middle classes will accept the new home rule.'

Judging by last week's election results, the answer to that question, as the sparks still fly upwards, is once again no.

6 July 2004

SIMON HOGGART

Snake charmers

Alastair Campbell interviews Peter Mandelson, on television! What a feast of misinformation, mendacity, hyperbole, half-truths, evasions, spinning and whingeing self-justification we were promised!

And we got all that. But what was most striking about the interview, the second Alastair Campbell has done for Channel 5 (or Five as we are supposed to call it), was the way the pair circled round each other, waiting to strike. They can't help it. It's in their natures. They were like two cobras rising from baskets, twisting sinuously to the music. They knew they were of the same species, but even so, every now and again they could not help lunging at each other. For instance, Campbell said that Mandelson had acquired a 'huge' loan to buy a 'nice, swanky house in Notting Hill'.

Mandelson: 'It was nice, but it wasn't swanky – it was about half the size of your house in Hampstead,' and you could almost see the fang marks on Campbell's neck. Later, Mandy mused about the failings of the press. 'If you don't talk to them, if you don't return their calls, they think you're—'

'An arrogant, aloof git?' offered Campbell, purely in a spirit of helpfulness.

Mandelson's first statement on air was: 'I don't think I'm a particularly loathsome individual' – so clearly he was not afraid to plunge straight into controversy.

Campbell had prefaced the question with an avowal that Mandelson was – and is – one of his closest friends and 'a very capable minister'. 'So why,' he went on, 'does the Labour party loathe you?'

That was a facer. Mandy thought it was probably because he was 'a bit of a loner, a bit remote'. He didn't need to hang round the bars and tea rooms, because he had the leader's ear. 'I didn't need anyone else. I was not a retail politician,' he added. Well, of course not. No one had suggested that he could be bought!

The fact is that Mandelson and Campbell have always been courtiers, first of Neil Kinnock, then of Tony Blair. The monarch always thinks the courtiers are terrific, helpful guys. Those outside the charmed circle detest them; they themselves are deadly rivals for the affection and admiration of the king.

'If I am being honest, which I will be,' he went on, 'I don't think I've anything to lose by being honest at this stage in my political career ...' It was a fascinating insight. He talked about being honest as if it was something you might take up at a certain age, like angling or DIY, an optional extra tacked on to your life.

Alarmingly, he kept talking about himself in the third person. 'There has always been a fight within myself, and sometimes with others, about whether Peter is going to be Peter the Process Man, or whether Peter is going to be allowed to become Peter Mandelson, the politician and minister.' I wouldn't mind a ringside seat at that fight! What a grudge match – Mike Tyson versus Kylie Minogue.

Mr Mandelson resembles a toy I once had, the Visible Man. He had a perspex body so you could see the organs inside. Mandy has the Visible Brain; you can see the synapses working together. They have figured out that the future of the Labour party is Gordon Brown. The chancellor, who felt badly spurned and betrayed by Mandelson at the time of the 1994 leadership election, may soon be in power. 'Get in with Gordon!' screamed the synapses.

'He has the qualities and skills needed to be leader ... Gordon is a big person, he is a big politician,' Mandy told us, with an appearance of something close to sincerity. Nor could Mr Brown do any wrong. The news about the loan ('it wasn't secret, it was unpublicized,' he said, to snorts of laughter at the screening yesterday) had been leaked by his associates. 'That's not the same as Gordon,' he said, and at this point, Campbell burst out incredulously, 'You really believe that?' Why, yes, he really did believe it. He had even spoken to Gordon on the day, and had received some very good advice ('Don't resign').

But the real, deep well of bitterness began to gush over his second resignation, after the exposé of the Hinduja passport affair. He blamed Campbell for briefing the media against him. He accused him of 'a rush to judgement'. 'I think, as my friend of twenty-five years' standing, you might have given me the benefit of the doubt, and you chose not to.' He accused him of briefing the press wrongly on one day, then briefing wrongly, but in the opposite direction, the next day. He had created 'a sort of elephant trap ... into which I fell'.

Later Campbell told us that he thought Mandelson had not been bitter. If that is him being cuddly and forgiving, then I'd hate to meet him when he is bitter. In my view, though, for either to claim there was no ill-feeling between them was just a load of old cobras.

And what next week? Gordon Brown in conversation with Ed Balls? Richard interviews Judy?

20 August 2004

JENNI RUSSELL

Drilling down

We could start by feeling sorry for the schools minister, who is required to talk nonsense in the course of his job. This week David Miliband maintained that there were no credible questions to be asked about the annual rise in A-level passes. He claims that the rise in A grades is purely a matter for celebration; that the quality of the exam remains unchanged, and that anyone who questions this happy picture is simply trying to preserve middle-class educational advantage. On all three counts he is being disingenuous.

The rise in A grades means that applying to university is now a lottery. Parents of children with three As are furious when their children aren't offered an Oxbridge place, because they don't understand the statistics. It's not just that a higher proportion of people are getting A grades; far greater numbers are taking the exam in the first place. Twenty years ago, when 15 per cent of the population sat A-levels, a fixed proportion in every subject – 10 per cent – were awarded an A grade. So a top grade meant that a student was in the top 1.5 per cent of their age group. This year more than a third of the age group sat the exam, and more than a fifth got an A grade. So an A grade now puts a student in the top 8 per cent. No wonder the universities are having such an impossible time distinguishing between the clever students and the brilliant ones. Whereas three A grades were once a rarity, 22,000 students now get them.

Miliband contends that the huge rise in achievement is genuine, because standards have been maintained. He says there is not a scintilla of evidence that A-levels are any easier. In most subjects it is true that hard facts are impossible to find. How do you judge one English examination against another? Even if the questions look simpler, is the marking harder? But there is one subject which can be compared across the years, and that is mathematics. There, the evidence is incontrovertible; standards have been dropping for fifteen years.

In 2000, the Engineering Council delivered a devastating report on the maths skills of students entering maths, science and engineering courses. New students had been given an identical test every year for the preceding decade. As their A-level grades had improved, their mathematical understanding had declined. There was a stark example of just what that meant. The study compared the performance of students who in 1991 had narrowly failed their A-levels with students who had been given a C grade in 1998. The 1991 failures scored higher in the tests than the C-grade students did seven years later.

Miliband argues that this can be dismissed because the maths syllabus has changed. That is the point: the syllabus has been altered to make it easier, but the changes have left out skills mathematicians, scientists and engineers need.

The council was clear about the reasons behind this. It wasn't the fault of teachers; they were delivering many different courses to students with a wider range of ability than in the past. The problem lay with government decisions to make the syllabus less tough, and more accessible. At the same time, class sizes had been rising, while the supply of good teachers had fallen as the status of the profession had declined. The combination had been disastrous.

If that is the case with mathematics, the question is whether the same could be true of other subjects. Durham University thinks so. Its researchers have given an unchanging general ability test to first-year A-level students ever since 1988. The results show that students of the same ability are now achieving two A-level grades higher in every subject than they were fifteen years ago.

This grade inflation began with changes to the system twenty years ago. Until then, grades were awarded in the same fixed proportions, with 70 per cent passing and 10 per cent getting As. But in the mid-1980s, the government realized that this system, known as norm referencing, offered no scope for proving that standards were being raised. Instead it introduced criterion referencing, where examiners decided in advance that a paper of a particular standard would get a particular grade, regardless of how many other people achieved the same. The result has been that the proportion of passes and top grades has risen with every year, and 96 per cent of candidates now pass.

Examiners maintain that we can have absolute confidence in their marking, because they compare scripts from one year to the next, in order to ensure that a similar standard is being reached. That sounds reassuring. While norm referencing allowed us to judge students against their peer group, criterion referencing allows us to ensure standards are the same across time.

Except that it isn't so simple. In evidence to the Commons select committee inquiry into A-level standards eighteen months ago, the head of one of the exam boards, Kathleen Tattersall, admitted that A-levels are neither norm referenced nor criterion referenced. Instead they are 'soft criterion referenced'. What that means is that neither proportions nor standards are fixed in advance. It means that examiners can decide on a standard beforehand, but if too many people or too few then reach that standard, it can be adjusted. 'It is a system that has served us very well,' she said. It may have done. But it makes a nonsense of the idea that there are any absolute standards being maintained.

Soft criterion referencing means the government has created an A-level system that can deliver constantly improving grades with no firm reference to standards. It's what one would expect from a political mentality whose focus is less on education than on being able to demonstrate measurable improvements. A-levels are the culmination of a system which has drilled children through their school lives, at the expense of teaching them to think, learn and create. Miliband claims that when his detractors criticize him, they are implying that 'middle England' doesn't have the ability to succeed. But it is middle- and working-class England that suffers most from this concentration on regurgitation. It is working-class children who fall behind at every step of the rigid curriculum, and who are bitterly conscious of failure. The proportion of working-class students at university has remained almost unchanged since 1979.

The independent schools' watchdog has warned that even public schools, which once prided themselves on encouraging originality, are spoon-feeding their children to get them through A-levels with the highest marks. A Cambridge admissions tutor in English says that over the past three years he's found it pointless asking prospective students about the great novels; the exam demands mean they no longer read widely.

And in a sad illustration of just how narrow the marking has become, the eminent economist Lord Skidelsky failed a Russian economy paper when he took an A-level in Russian two years ago. The examination board said that his points were irrelevant, and that people who had too much knowledge of a subject often over-answered a question.

The argument to be had here is not an August diversion. It is a serious one. The current system is not producing what we need: a meritocracy of highly skilled, motivated people who have developed their talents. It delivers impressive statistics rather than students with impressive educations. When will ministers understand that there is a difference?

21 July 2004

MARTIN WAINWRIGHT

Behind the fridge

Europe's 200 million women yesterday acquired a new champion in the form of the United Kingdom Independence party MEP for Yorkshire and the Humber, Godfrey Bloom. 'I want to deal with women's issues,' he declared, 'because I just don't think they clean behind the fridge enough.'

Mr Bloom was speaking on his first day at the European parliament in Strasbourg as one of UKIP's eleven MEPs. 'I am going to promote men's rights,' he said, which was odd because he had just taken up a seat on the parliament's committee for women's rights.

For those women wondering why someone with Mr Bloom's views on their gender could deign to speak on their behalf, he said his mandate was clear: 'I am here to represent Yorkshire women, who always have dinner on the table when you get home.'

While the shades of Amy Johnson, the Brontë sisters and other famous Yorkshire women whirled beyond the grave, Mr Bloom unrepentantly went on local television – promptly syndicated – to make sure that his mission statement was understood. 'The more women's rights you have, it's actually a bar to their employment,' he said, citing his experience in the Territorial Army and a London investment firm for which he still works as a researcher. 'No self-respecting small businessman with a brain in the right place would ever employ a lady of child-bearing age.'

Mr Bloom, perpetually pin-striped and with an office answering machine that barks, 'Halt! Who goes there?', then briefly disappeared under a pile of furious responses from other MEPs, particularly from women. He was denounced as 'Neanderthal and absolutely terrifying' by Glenys Kinnock. Mary Honeyball, a Labour colleague on the women's rights committee, suggested an investigation of his business practices by a discrimination tribunal. But Mr Bloom, aged fifty-four, who took the last of Yorkshire's six seats in June, soon bobbed back up again with more on the same theme. 'It isn't politically correct, is it?' he said. 'But it's a fact of life. I know, because I am a businessman.'

Yorkshire was absorbing his view of its women last night, but there were knowing nods in Wressle, a small town near Selby where Mr Bloom has his party headquarters. UKIP's regional organizer, Tony Slater, was laid up recovering from a hip operation (and enjoying watching his friend on TV), but his wife said, 'It goes over your head round here; we've all heard it many times before.'

Mr Bloom, who fought two Westminster elections in East Yorkshire before reaching Europe, has made a name for one of the county's characteristics – blunt talk – while ignoring the other one – of 'seeing and hearing all, but saying nowt'. Friends of Mr Bloom, who is known to some as Godfrey's Bloomers, point out that for all his straight talking, his home life does not bear out any notion that women should primarily scrub and cook. His wife Katie is better known than he is – or at least she was until last night – as one of the country's leading horse physiotherapists and as a 'passionate' side-saddle rider. She was not available for comment, but she has come to his rescue before. When UKIP was charged with xenophobia, he countered robustly that his wife was half-Polish.

The party might soon find itself in need of more such excuses. After a month in the political sunshine that saw it dominate coverage of the European elections, UKIP has already had to suspend one of its MEPs, Ashley Mote, who is facing allegations of housing-benefit fraud.

Yesterday the party tried to laugh off its latest embarrassment. But the Tories – out for revenge – will be watching.

8 June 2004

MICHAEL WHITE

Alternate futures

The next prime minister of Britain went electioneering in Wales yesterday. Both of them. Gordon Brown arrived first, but Michael Howard stayed a little longer. After all, he is local.

The two politicians engaged in this largely unspoken duel to succeed Tony Blair did not meet, although their cars may have passed at high speed on the Severn bridge, going in opposite directions.

The chancellor's earlier unveiling of a Labour poster bashing the Tory record on jobs made the lunchtime news on Welsh television. Banging on about Europe at lunchtime in Bristol Mr Howard made Radio 4's *World at One* in London. There is a moral here for one of them.

Neither is a natural at retail politics, the art of canvassing strangers for votes. Mr Brown is too shy; Mr Howard is not shy enough. As he swept through Queen Street in Cardiff in bright sunshine, the Tory leader displayed his famous smile with the eagerness of an insurance salesman.

Mr Brown's technique is distinctive. To cover his shyness he laughs. Not any old laugh either, but a deep masculine laugh that goes on alarmingly like an unexpectedly active volcano. It makes him into a New Labour version of Oscar Wilde's Very Unselfish Giant, who will let all the children play in his garden provided they are properly supervised and have signed on for Sure Start.

When the chancellor arrived at Cardiff airport he sensibly realized that most voters present were concentrating on getting out of the country by polling day. He confined himself to a few: 'Nice to see you, how are you?' and 'What a lovely day.' He did talk to John Trew and his family because Mr Trew is a Labour candidate hoping to win a seat from the Tories in the Vale of Glamorgan.

'How's the baby?' asked Janice Trew.

'Doing very well, he's teething, he can't stand—' replied Mr Brown.

Whether he was about to say 'can't stand Tony' we will never know because Mrs Trew interrupted. 'That's a joy,' she said. The chancellor concurred.

The purpose of the visit, however, was to rubbish Llanelli-born Mr Howard's record as 'secretary of state for unemployment' in the early 1990s, as Mr Brown's host, Rhodri Morgan, put it. Wales had 120,000 jobless a decade ago when Mr Howard was employment secretary – three times today's rate. Mr Morgan is hugely popular and became Wales's first minister despite the efforts of Mr Blair, who preferred Alun Michael. But Mr Morgan is a bit scatty and has been in trouble for attending a golf conference in Newport on Sunday instead of going to the D-day commemorations. Yesterday he lavishly praised Mr Brown, who will overtake the Treasury tenure of the great Welsh radical David Lloyd George in exactly one week: 'You've done a brilliant job and I hope you carry on another seven years.' The chancellor took the compliment without flinching. But when Mr Morgan did his stuff again in Welsh for S4C television he left that bit out.

All councillors in Wales are up for elections in all twenty-two unitary authorities. There are also four MEP seats, down from five. Labour's Glenys Kinnock is certain to get one, plus a Tory candidate and a Plaid Cymru. Who gets the fourth depends on who you talk to: Labour or the Liberal Democrats, but not Ron Davies, the ex-cabinet minister, who is standing for Forward Wales, one of the many mini-parties. Labour may lose overall control of Cardiff city, a blow that would be softened by taking back Rhondda from Plaid Cymru and even neighbouring Caerphilly. Which is why the chancellor's car rushed him to the GE jet engine workshops at Nantgarw, slap on the border of the two councils. It is a sobering responsibility for the 800 skilled staff who take fifty-five days on average to check, clean and replace between 6,000 and 12,000 parts – all of them vital – on the huge jet engines that carry tourists from Cardiff and other airports.

Whereas Mr Howard campaigns in shirt-sleeves like an American politician, Mr Brown's crumpled blue suit – the only colour he wears – remained buttoned up in this well-ordered masculine world. He had two main lines of chat.

'How long have you worked here?'

'Thirty-two years,' replied tattooed Jim Best, who is thrilled to see him.

He then asked about commercial prospects.

'You've got to keep this place going,' said one man.

'Rhodri's the man with the money,' the chancellor swiftly countered.

In fact, his patter was earnest and policy-orientated as he parried most questions. He said little that Mr Blair would not have said in similar terms, except the bit about Wales having a different policy on student tuition fees.

Finally a burly man in a red shirt called Jim dropped the question. 'When are you going to be leader?' he asked.

'That's not today's story,' said the heir presumptive.

Later the group posed for a photo in front of a huge GE 90 engine, its carbon-fibre fan blades 3m (10ft) high, the muscle behind a Boeing 777. The modest chancellor did not take centre stage.

It was a symbolic moment. In conversation Mr Brown knew all about the Lloyd George record he is about to break, but made light of it. 'These things don't matter these days,' he said. But neither he nor anyone else appeared to know that nowadays British prime ministers fly in 777s.

Mr Howard wants the plane for himself. As the chancellor headed east along the M4 corridor for a visit to his Treasury colleague Dawn Primarolo's Bristol constituency, Mr Howard headed west to the (adopted) land of his fathers. His serious ambitions were plain by the way he tore through Queen Street shaking hands fervently with pensioners, couples and teenagers showing too much cleavage. 'Hello, how are you?' he asked everyone before urging them to at least think about voting Tory.

In the June heat, the blue Tory balloons, 'Let Down by Labour', which supporters were carrying for the TV crews, keep popping. It makes the Howard party sound like an Iraqi warlord, out shopping perhaps, on a day off. But Mr Howard means it. He wants to be prime minister. And, unlike his rival, has no need to hide his ambition.

16 August 2004

MADELEINE BUNTING

Moral Polyfilla

It's easy to laugh at the idea pioneered by Hazel Blears, the Home Office minister, to run Alpha-style courses for Labour party members to restore their idealism. Easy to scorn the idea of set texts, including key speeches by Tony Blair and Gordon Brown, being studied by the party faithful ahead of the weekend workshops. Blears claims it has worked wonders for the members who have already attended the first two and she wants the programme rolled out across the country.

Before the cynics pour withering contempt on the whole idea, Blears deserves some credit. First, she has recognized the gravity of a problem which is crippling the party – a crisis of purpose. Second, she's recognized that idealism is not an optional extra in political life, but an essential ingredient of progressive thinking – a truth on which no less a person than Tony Blair has built his entire political career.

Finally, she deserves some recognition for her bravery in treading into tricky territory; the debate on Blair's ten-year record between idealists and pragmatists on the left has become vicious. While the former fling their stock accusation at the latter of having sold out, the latter accuse the former of self-indulgence. In this furious argument on the Blair record – which one can already see in the A-level history papers of the 2020s – a million fewer children living in poverty is stacked against the escalating crisis in Iraq. A handsomely increased aid budget is up against the sham of half-truths which sold us a war on false pretences. What kind of qualification in moral accountancy could arbitrate this debate? Most, foxed and furious, shrug their shoulders, baffled by the paradoxes and inconsistencies.

I have little patience with those pragmatists who demand we 'get real'. We are entitled to judge New Labour and Blair on moral and idealistic grounds – because it is precisely on those grounds that they have consistently sold themselves to the British electorate.

Take three junctures in Blair's leadership when that has been evident. First, in his 1995 party conference speech, he declared that 'socialism ... is a moral purpose to life, a set of values, a belief in society, in cooperation ... it is how I try to live my life ... I am worth no more than any other man ... This is my socialism.' And he concluded: 'Let us rouse ourselves to a new moral purpose for our nation ... the coming election is not a struggle for political power; it is a battle for the soul of a nation.'

In 1999, in a speech in Chicago in the midst of the Kosovo war, he extended this interpretation of socialism to the global community and set five tests for intervention in another country (the war in Iraq didn't meet any of them). In 2001, in the immediate aftermath of 9/11, he famously declared that 'the starving, the wretched, the dispossessed, the ignorant, those living in want and squalor from the deserts of north Africa to the slums of Gaza, to the mountain ranges of Afghanistan: they too are our cause. This is a moment to seize ... the pieces are in flux, soon they will settle again. Before they do, let us reorder the world around us.'

Today, there's no evidence left in Blair of that early 1995 humility. The man who can lounge at the side of Silvio Berlusconi's swimming pool seems to be tone-deaf to the moral implications of his private life; it is a choice of holiday which infuriates precisely because it seems such a wanton squandering of a resource in which Blair is in short supply – his moral credibility. (An issue not helped by his wife signing on for fat fees for a public-speaking tour in the US – the size of the fees a consequence of her relationship to Blair rather than of her professional status.)

There is a painful irony that the most overtly idealistic politics for a generation should have led us into the most acute of moral quagmires in Iraq, one which will dog British politics for at least the next decade. Blair cast himself as the cheerleader of the biggest act of unprovoked US aggression for decades –

and every day the promised benefits of this illegal action become more illusory as daily life there becomes more dangerous, and necessities such as water, electricity, healthcare and education become increasingly precarious.

The 'reordering of the world' which Blair announced in 2001 is now all too real in the nightmare of new levels of tension and fury throughout the Middle East as events in Najaf unfold. The war in Iraq and the means by which he got his country into it – without the UN, without international consensus and with the manipulation of intelligence – has morally bankrupted Blair. Maybe the morality of all political parties gets tattered after a certain period in office, but the order of Blair's moral betrayal has gone well beyond that. No British political leader has pitched so high – and fallen so far short.

With the benefit of hindsight, the compelling attractions of Blair's morality, compared to the amorality of the Tories, blinded us. We asked the wrong questions of the young leader in waiting; the issue was not whether he was sincere. He was. What we underestimated was his remarkable capacity to convince himself of the moral rectitude of his own actions. We also gravely underestimated how much he wanted – and still does – to be a visionary leader. We didn't grasp the fatal element of narcissism which propels such moral ambition and we failed to predict how, in office, that could translate into arrogant hubris.

I feel a fool now. Looking back at those early speeches, I remember how arresting they seemed at the time. But now, after nearly a decade, I see that he was using morality to reconcile the irreconcilable – socialism and Thatcherite neo-liberalism. He recast socialism as a morality of community and mutual responsibility, which could be wrapped around the accommodation with neo-liberalism; it enabled him to fudge tough questions about inequality. Later, he used morality on the international stage to dress up a government bogged down in managerialism and public-sector reform.

The metaphor which comes to mind is morality as a kind of all-purpose Polyfilla which Blair has used to great effect to build the coalitions, and mask the internal contradictions of policies on both the domestic and international front. For a while, it looked good, but no longer. A morally bankrupted Blair can't resort to the language of crusades. The cracks are reappearing; without a common sense of moral purpose, New Labour will fracture into its constituent, warring factions. Blears's proposal may be timely and necessary – it's just that it is hopeless.

4 August 2004

MAEV KENNEDY

Unchanging Britain

There is still a Britain where every train runs on time from pristine stations, happy neighbours stand gossiping in spotless streets, the youths hanging around the market square are sharing a celebration cake instead of torching the bunting, and – a sight to cheer any UKIP politician – a woman is down on her knees scrubbing her doorstep. True, the barmaid at the Barley Mow looks to have had a tankard of cider too many and is about to topple backwards through the door of the public bar, and a burglar is sprinting across the racetrack, though a nice community copper is in hot pursuit.

Unfortunately the happy citizens are only four inches tall. Some of them have been hanging around their street corners every summer for seventy-five years.

Today, three tiny cheers will ring out around the world, from the twenty other members of the International Association of Miniature Parks, from Canada to Australia, as a rich man's toy in Buckinghamshire officially becomes the oldest model village in the world. Bekonscot, in the Buckinghamshire market town of Beaconsfield, admitted the first members of the paying public on 4 August 1929, and is still thriving.

All the profits went to charities from the start – the owner, London accountant Roland Callingham, certainly did not need the money – and to date it has raised more than £4m. Visitor numbers have fallen, but in the age of video games and white-knuckle theme parks, ticket sales are still brisk. Last year the village attracted 200,000 people, and more than 20,000 came last month. In the steamy heat this week it has been packed.

Tim Dunn, who has written the official guidebook to the village – he is only twenty-three, visited first as a toddler, and has been intermittently running the train system since he was thirteen – says the charm is the illusion of an unchanged world: 'Like most of us, Bekonscot has never really grown up ... It has remained virtually unchanged. Model steam trains chug around the railway and the Bekonscot fire brigade has never gone on strike. Bekonscot is truly a little piece of history that is for ever England.'

The authorities spotted this aspect of the village and in the Second World War Bekonscot was used for propaganda photographs, showing the gardener as air raid warden and tin-hatted fire crews standing by the castle. In the lean aftermath of the war there was something comforting about the safe little streets: most of Europe's model villages date from this time. The formula was copied all over the country, down to the awful puns – the baker is Ivan Huven, the greengrocer Chris P. Lettis. Bekonscot itself has gone back in time. The railway station is now an elaborate glass-roofed Edwardian vision, but was originally art deco, and other buildings originally in contemporary style have been remodelled to look more quaintly old-fashioned.

The real love of the village's creator was model railways. When Callingham's train set outgrew the house he moved it to the garden, and then the adjoining paddock. He and his head gardener, Tom Berry – who was to work on the village for another half a century – built the houses as landscaping around the train. The track was laid out beside the swimming pool, but when Callingham realized the guests at his bathing parties were more interested in the trains and houses, it became the village lake, complete with pleasure boats, beach and pier.

The children's author Enid Blyton was a near neighbour, and wrote a teeth-rottingly sweet booklet, *The Enchanted Village*: 'Mary cries out in joy, "It might be Fairyland! It's just as small anyway!"' Green Hedges, where she wrote most of her books, survives as a model in Bekonscot, built to mark the centenary of her birth in 1997, complete with the author sitting on a garden bench.

28 June 2004

HARRY GRIFFIN

Summit meeting

I have known the Arnside–Silverdale area since before the First World War, but had never been to – nor even heard of – the Pepper Pot. There is a photograph somewhere of me, aged about one and a half, in a pram, being pushed along Arnside promenade by my mother, wearing a huge, flowered hat – nearly as outrageous as those you see at Royal Ascot today.

Arnside looks much the same as it does today – without the traffic. But, the other day, kind friends decided to take the aged geriatric to see the Pepper Pot, a squat obelisk, commemorating the golden jubilee of Queen Victoria's accession, on top of Castlebarrow, a little hill overlooking Silverdale.

The interest in the walk was not in the obelisk but in the walk through Eaves Wood, a National Trust property crowded with oak, sycamore, beech, Scots pine, yew and almost any tree you could name, and carpeted with wild flowers in profusion. The view from the summit was disappointing to the west, the Lakeland hills being hidden by the foliage on the trees – although better, I'm told, in winter – but superb in other directions. Ingleborough, Josie's favourite mountain, boldly filled the sky to the east, while just below squatted the pleasant sprawling village of Silverdale, with the old church prominent.

But the outstanding feature of the view was the sight of the sparkling sands and channels of Morecambe Bay, the water dancing in the sunshine and the sands glowing and welcoming. The whole coast from Barrow to Blackpool was visible but, sadly, we also looked down on the spot where thirty Chinese cocklers lost their lives not so long ago. Beauty and tragedy together at a glance.

Harry Griffin died on 9 July 2004 at the age of ninety-three.

STATES

3 January 2004

JAMES ASTILL

Sixteen seconds

A little more than a week ago, the two rows of mud and clay brick houses facing each other across a narrow sandy track were home to about fifty families. Edalat Alley was a typical middle-income street in the Iranian tourist town of Bam, housing civil servants, shopkeepers and teachers. Many were related to each other, having moved in together fifteen years ago when the houses were built. Though a bit better off than most Iranians, the alley's residents shared many of their troubles. About a quarter of the men were unemployed, forcing many young couples to crowd into relatives' houses. Opium addiction, the scourge of the Baluchi people of eastern Iran, was rife.

But in sixteen seconds on 26 December 2003, that small world was obliterated by an earthquake. Fewer than ten of the alley's several hundred residents are still alive, and most of those have been dispersed to hospitals across Iran. As for the rows of neat houses, they are two mounds of dust, bricks and broken furniture. They end together in a bigger heap of bricks, concrete and twisted metal sheets: the remains of an orphanage where fifty-four girls perished.

Hamideh Khordoosta, aged twenty-two, was not in the house she shared with her husband – who is also her cousin – and a dozen other close relatives when the earthquake struck. She was staying with friends on the city's outskirts, having left her husband to his opium pipe in disgust.

Sitting amid the wreckage of the family's house, in a dusty brown headscarf and baggy jersey, Hamideh ticked off the relatives she had lost in the rubble: her grandmother; her sister; a dozen aunts and uncles, and most of their children. Her husband survived, though he is now paralysed with a broken back.

'Our sisters are dead, our children are dead, our parents are dead, our grief is endless,' Hamideh says, wiping away tears with a corner of her scarf. 'This is what it means to be lonely, having no one to share your sorrow.'

Early efforts to quantify the devastation of Bam have produced horrifying results. The registers record that 28,000 of the town's 80,000 people are dead and buried. The total death toll, including victims in nearby villages, could climb to 50,000, according to the government's estimate, the highest in any earthquake for twenty-five years. But global statistics do not describe the most bitter fact of the calamity: the near-complete eradication of countless communities of families.

'The sheer concentration of death is mind-blowing, it's unprecedented,' says Rob Macgillivray, emergency co-ordinator for Save the Children, and a veteran of numerous earthquake disasters. 'Communities have been virtually wiped out, whole extended families have been completely annihilated.'

Several factors meant that the quake, which measured a relatively modest 6.8 on the Richter scale, caused maximum carnage. One was its timing, at 5.10 a.m, on a Friday, the Muslim day of rest, when most of the townspeople were still in bed. Another, the most important, was the nature of Bam's construction – it is built mostly of mud bricks that crumbled to suffocating heaps of grey powder, leaving no pockets in which trapped survivors could breathe. The third factor was a consequence of the calamity. Most of the city's decision-makers, including every senior officer except the governor, and four out of seven senior Red Crescent officials, were killed, making the emergency rescue and relief operation slow to begin.

As the sole male survivor of a family of more than 200 people, Hamideh's husband is now rich, having inherited several houses and orchards across eastern Iran. Still she refuses to return to him: 'I will not cheat him or myself, because I do not love him,' she says. 'You cannot stay in love with an addict.' This leaves no one to share her grief or the agony of her week-old memories. 'I was pulling people from the rubble, but they were dead or dying all around me, people were dying everywhere,' she says, then sobs uncontrollably as she remembers pulling her neighbour's three-year-old daughter from the debris. The child's back was flayed, and when Hamideh poured antiseptic onto the wound, the girl went into a convulsion and died. 'For the first two days, there was nobody helping us,' Hamideh adds. 'The government said it was helping people but these were empty words. We had no one and I'm not a doctor. How could I know what to do with the child?'

Virtually all of Bam's survivors blame Iran's unpopular government for reacting slowly to a disaster it should have foreseen. Dissident politicians and journalists have fanned the flames, accusing the government of having no contingency plan. But, according to UN officials in Bam, and the evidence of its emergency response, the government did have a plan, which the Iranian Red Crescent carried out well in the circumstances.

Despite the slow start, within twenty-four hours of the quake, several thousand Red Crescent volunteers from across Iran were dispensing blankets and food in Bam. More than 90,000 tents were distributed within four days. University language departments emptied across the country, as students rushed to Bam to interpret for the thirty-four foreign rescue teams arriving to comb the rubble.

'The Red Crescent has been outstanding, absolutely first class,' says Ted Pearn, chief of the UN team co-ordinating foreign rescue and aid groups in Iran. 'I'd rate them one of the best organizations I've come across in my career. They took the bull by the horns, they welcomed international assistance. Overall, the whole operation has worked extremely well.' According to Mr Pearn, the international response was also sufficient.

Most of the rescue teams arrived hopelessly late, with only a handful – including four from Britain – arriving within forty-eight hours of the quake, when survivors are most likely to be found. But in the event, it mattered little. The teams rescued only one survivor from Bam's dusty rubble. Dozens of miraculous rescues have been reported, but only one of them has been officially confirmed. Foreign aid followed, with earthquake-prone Turkey the most generous donor.

'There's a tremendous amount of aid already in the country or on its way,' Mr Pearn adds. 'The biggest need now is information, on how many people are dead, on how many are in need.' The assessment is proving tricky, because most of Bam's survivors have left the city, back to the villages their families left a generation ago.

On Jamalidin Street, at the end of Edalat Alley, Mohammed Musafa, aged thirty-seven, was preparing to leave for his parents' village of Darestan, 20 miles away. The possessions he had scavenged from the wreckage of his home were loaded into a pick-up truck. His brother, his sister, their children, his wife and more than 100 of his relatives were dead. 'I have nothing to stay for,' says Mohammed, a secondary school teacher about to become a peasant farmer. 'I will return when the city is rebuilt.'

Across the road, tunnelling through the rubble of his family home in search of a carpet, Ali Rezah Mehri, aged twenty-five, has no plans to leave or to remain. Ali's parents, brother, sisters, brother-in-law and four nieces and nephews all died. He survived because he was up early on 26 December, driving his new Peugeot taxi. He used it to take his family's corpses to the cemetery. Someone stole the car while he was there.

2 January 2004

ANDREW MELDRUM

Unrecognized exodus

More than two million Zimbabweans have flooded into South Africa in the past nine years to escape the repression and torture of Robert Mugabe's vilified regime, but only eleven have been granted political asylum, the *Guardian* has discovered. And in the first nine months of last year the South African authorities arrested and deported 41,000 Zimbabweans back across the border. The total was more than all those repatriated between 1994 and 2002.

The startling figures reflect the growing humanitarian crisis facing Zimbabwean immigrants, and South Africa's dilemma over how to deal with them. Many Zimbabweans claim South Africa's reluctance to give them legal status has been compounded by the brutal treatment often meted out to those who try to make a legitimate claim. One man described how staff at a refugee centre demand bribes from queuing Zimbabweans, and routinely whip and hit those seeking asylum.

When the *Guardian* put these allegations to the director general of South Africa's Home Affairs department, Barry Gilder, he promised an investigation. 'There is no policy that I am aware of to discourage Zimbabweans from getting asylum here,' he said.

The influx of millions of Zimbabweans has overwhelmed South Africa, which has a population of 45 million, and created a substantial underclass of illegal immigrants who live a precarious existence – with no legal status they are not entitled to help from the South African government or from overseas. The South African government claims that only 1,471 people have formally applied for political asylum since 1994; it also conceded that only eleven had been granted refugee status.

However, Zimbabwean immigrants insist the reason why the numbers are so low is because immigration officials make it extremely difficult to apply. One immigrant, Tafadzwa Chimombe (not his real name, to protect his family in Zimbabwe), said, 'I've been to the refugee office six times but still not succeeded in getting the form needed to apply for asylum. They say they will deal with Zimbabweans once a week, on Tuesdays, but when we go there the guards hit people and use whips on us and order us away. It makes us ashamed to be Zimbabweans here in South Africa.' The South African government was actively preventing Zimbabweans from getting political asylum, Mr Chimombe said, because the South African president, Thabo Mbeki, supported the Mugabe regime. 'But we gave South Africans refuge in Zimbabwe during apartheid – why won't they help us now?'

Mr Chimombe has scars from the electric shock torture and beatings he received in Zimbabwe. A former captain in the Zimbabwe army, he was accused of sympathizing with the opposition, the Movement for Democratic Change, and subjected to days of torture at army barracks in Harare. 'My lips, tongue and testicles were swollen from the electric shocks, I couldn't even walk,' the 32-year-old said. Once he had recovered from the torture, he fled to South Africa. 'I am just trying to get papers so I am legal here. I cannot go back to Zimbabwe.' Although he has professional qualifications, he cannot get work without a permit; he was offered the application form if he paid a bribe of 500 rand (£50). And, while Zimbabweans were being forced to wait years for asylum approval, refugees from other African countries were getting their applications considered within six weeks, he said.

Several other Zimbabwean refugees described how they were tortured in Zimbabwe and then faced difficulties in South Africa. The treatment of Zimbabweans at the South African government's centre for political refugees, in the Braamfontein area of Johannesburg, was recently highlighted in a television documentary broadcast on South Africa's independent e-tv. A security guard was shown shouting, 'Get away, you Zimbabweans, we don't want you here.' The guard then flailed at the refugees with a rawhide *sjambok*, a short whip that symbolized the brutal ways of apartheid.

'They beat us and whip us,' said Pascal Moyo (his name has also been changed). 'It is terrible to be a refugee here in South Africa but it is even worse to go back. We must scramble and live by our wits.' To survive, Moyo collects glass and plastic bottles from refuse bins and sells them to recycling centres. (For women, prostitution can turn out to be the only way to survive.)

The international organizations do not assist people classified as 'economic refugees' so neither the United Nations High Commissioner for Refugees nor the International Committee of the Red Cross can help the Zimbabweans. Every week, hundreds are arrested and held at Lindela camp, before being deported by train. Rather than go back to further torture and persecution, many risk their lives by jumping from the carriages. Others just turn around and go back to South Africa, braving the crocodile-infested Limpopo river or finding ways to cross the barbed wire fence separating the countries.

'It's the infamous revolving door,' said Mr Gilder. 'No sooner do we deport them than they come back in.' He admitted that South Africa's entire Home

Affairs department was struggling with inadequate budgets, lengthy queues and corruption, and added, 'We have a legal responsibility, both by our own laws and international conventions, to offer asylum if there is a well-founded fear of persecution in the home country.'

According to Elinor Sisulu, the South African representative of the Crisis in Zimbabwe Coalition, the burgeoning numbers of Zimbabweans from across the border demonstrates that their country's problems are having a negative impact on the entire southern African region.

'It's a problem of huge magnitude. Zimbabweans come here and go underground. These people are not being treated like refugees, they are being treated like criminals. They call them economic refugees. At this point, I think everyone should be treated like a political refugee.'

29 December 2003

RANDEEP RAMESH

Kashmir's hopes

Mohammed Khan yearns to visit his uncle, who left the hamlet of Udoosa in Indian Kashmir for Pakistan more than a decade ago. The trip should be easy: a half-hour descent through paddy fields and lemon and orange groves followed by a half-mile walk along the road above the Jhelum river would get him to a bridge which begins in India and ends in Pakistan.

Mr Khan's problem is not geography, but history. The state of Kashmir is claimed by both India and Pakistan and they have fought three wars over it since it was split between them in 1947. He says: 'It is in the hands of these two big countries. The road has been closed ever since I can remember. The last kilometre on our side is mined and the Pakistanis used to shell the bridges and not let people cross.'

But a flurry of diplomatic initiatives between India and Pakistan, most notably a ceasefire last month on the de facto border known as the line of control, have raised hopes that the highway will be opened after more than half a century. The ceasefire was agreed in advance of a visit to Pakistan by India's prime minister, Atal Bihari Vajpayee, for a summit of south Asian countries from Sunday. The gathering is seen as a key opportunity for the rivals to consolidate a thaw in relations.

Udoosa is situated on a hillside pitted with semi-abandoned villages and blasted homes which have borne the brunt of decades of cross-border animosity. Opposite are the snow-capped peaks and dizzying gorges of the Jhelum Valley. There nestles the last Indian artillery position, just ahead of a 2-metre high barbed wire security fence being erected by the Indian army to prevent armed militants crossing into India. Beyond lies Pakistan.

'That village is with Pakistan,' said Mr Khan, pointing to a series of small houses dominated by a low-slung building topped with a green dome. 'All these years we could hear nothing but the shelling. Now we hear the *azaan* [the

Muslim call to prayer] from their mosque. I will be very happy if the road opens next.'

Built by the British at the end of the nineteenth century, the highway is the only all-weather road in the region and runs 78 miles from Srinagar, the capital of the Indian state of Jammu and Kashmir. Once the main route to Kashmir from central Asia and beyond, the road was blocked to hold back Indian forces at the start of the 1947 war between India and Pakistan. Now the traffic is thick with army trucks ferrying soldiers to their bases.

Twelve miles from the line of control and Udoosa, along a dirt track, is Uri, the last big town before Pakistan. It seems everybody in Uri has a story of being unable to attend a family wedding or a funeral across the border. Obtaining a Pakistani visa is difficult and making the lengthy journey via New Delhi is expensive.

'I have never met my three uncles in Pakistan, only seen them in pictures,' says Ajaz Ahmed, who runs a cake shop in the town. 'In 1947 my father was left behind in the rush of partition by his family. He only went to see his brothers in 1985 but they have never been able to come here and I have never been able to go there. I could not even visit when one uncle died.'

If Pakistan and India agree to open the road, many in Uri hope that not only will people from both sides be able to cross freely, but that trade will resume between Srinagar and Muzaffarabad, the capital of Pakistani Kashmir.

'Fruit is a big industry in Kashmir and if the road opens we could sell our apples and oranges in Pakistan,' says Mushtaq Ahmed Lone, a businessman. 'Before 1947, this used to be the main commercial hub of the region, and it could be again if the road opens.'

Such hopes rest on both countries continuing on the path to peace as well as taking the three months required to remove landmines and spread tarmac. The rapprochement between the two is remarkable, given that they came close to war little more than a year ago.

Kashmir stands to gain the most from any reconciliation. Its people have endured fourteen years of violent conflict between Indian security forces and armed Muslim separatists, who slip easily between Pakistani and Indian Kashmir. No Kashmiri family has escaped unscathed. Officially, since 1989 when the insurgency began, 30,000 people have been killed, but human rights groups say the figure is at least double that. In the last year the election of a new chief minister for Indian Jammu and Kashmir has seen the violence decrease but, nevertheless, police records show nearly 2,900 people have been killed.

For all the talk of progress, life at the other end of the highway in Srinagar is bleak. The city does not look like the capital of a state that is part of the world's largest democracy. Armed soldiers are everywhere: behind sandbags, at roadblocks and being carried on lorries. The rough methods employed during some of the army's operations have provoked anger, which in turn has fuelled the insurgency in Kashmir.

'The army and the paramilitary forces act with impunity. They cannot be prosecuted without sanction from the Indian government and this is only given in a very small number of high-profile cases,' says Pervez Imroz, a human rights lawyer in Srinagar.

At the recent funeral of a local chemist, Sartaj Ahmad, who was buried in the graveyard of martyrs in Srinagar, dozens of young men shouted slogans against Indian rule. The chemist was one of two men, unconnected to any separatist movement, later shot dead by Indian security forces in the poor district of Boatman colony on the northern outskirts of Srinagar after a gun battle between the army and an Islamist. Such incidents, described as 'regrettable' by the army, help create a culture of suspicion in Kashmir which leads many to harbour doubts that peace can ever be achieved through negotiations and confidence-building measures such as opening the road to Muzaffarabad.

'The question is about whether these things are sincerely meant and whether peace is achievable,' says Abdul Aziz Dar, who was a leading member of the militant group Hizbul Mojahedin, but who renounced violence after ten years in Indian jails. 'If not they will be seen as just part of a political game.'

9 January 2004

JONATHAN WATTS

Frozen frontier

The smugglers' signal comes shortly after midnight. From the darkness of the North Korean houses on the opposite bank of the icy Yalu river, a torchlight flashes twice. It stirs a Chinese woman, wrapped in thick winter clothing, to leave her ramshackle home and trudge across the snow towards the narrow stretch of water that serves as a border.

She is not alone. Here and there, shadowy figures can be seen on both sides of the misty river quietly carrying out an illegal – but thriving – trade in women, endangered species, food and consumer appliances that makes a mockery of North Korea's reputation as a tightly controlled and internationally isolated state.

Chinese border guards patrol the riverbanks, rifles slung over the shoulders of their thick green coats. But tonight at least they turn a blind eye to the flow of contraband goods and refugees that is keeping countless people from starvation and, according to some critics, Kim Jong-il's regime from collapse.

On the Chinese side, entire villages appear to be involved in the trade and nobody is particularly concerned about being caught. Chairs and sofas are left outside riverside homes so that lookouts can wait in comfort for the signal to make a delivery or pick-up. Local night markets openly sell the contraband goods procured across the border – ginseng, dog meat, bronzeware and timber. Traders also whisper that they can get bear gallstones – part of an endangered species. Selling these items is forbidden by law but they are highly prized in traditional medicine and fetch a good price. So do the Korean women whose sales are just as illegal and commonplace. Many locals know someone who has bought a wife smuggled from across the border. During the day, restaurants are filled with the chatter of illegal traders, who play mah jong until darkness falls and their real business begins.

'I can get you ginseng and dozens of bear gallstones from Korea if you can supply second-hand televisions,' boasts one Chinese smuggler, who says his network of employees and contacts across the border could handle 1,000 TVs a month. 'We wrap them up watertight and then float them over the river on inflatable dinghies. We have connections with border guards on both sides. They take a ten per cent cut and we get no trouble.'

At first sight, these illicit deals and cheap bribes seem a long way from the international negotiating tables in Beijing, where diplomats from China have been trying to bring the US, North Korea and other regional powers together to resolve the nuclear standoff on the peninsula. But speculation is growing among embassies, academics and locals that developments at the border could help to determine the outcome of the peace talks and the fate of the North Korean leader.

For many years, this north-east Asian boundary has been far more porous than many in the outside world believe. Since the start of the famines of the mid-1990s, tens, possibly hundreds, of thousands have fled across the Yalu in search of food. Those who stay behind depend on the huge amounts of food and clothing acquired legally and illegally in China.

Now that the temperature has dropped below zero, child beggars and day labourers cross back and forth over the frozen river. Such is the lack of controls that a local taxi driver says livestock are even led across the ice during daylight.

According to aid workers, the illegal trade and movement of people between the two nations have kept millions of North Koreans alive. Their evidence is circumstantial: those living close to the border are healthier than inlanders, who have no access to rice, fruit and meat smuggled out of China. The prices in Pyongyang's market are more expensive than markets near the border, closer to the main source of supplies.

For North Korea, which is under a virtual embargo, business with China is a lifeline. According to the latest government figures in Beijing, exports to North Korea rose 18.8 per cent to $43m (£23.5m) in the first eleven months of 2002. Imports tripled to about half that amount.

But no one knows how comprehensive those official figures are – let alone the extent of the smuggling business. When the *Guardian* requested details of the energy trade between the two countries, the Chinese government said the information was classified. The subject has always been politically sensitive and is becoming more so as China uses a combination of carrots and sticks to drive North Korea to the negotiating table.

In 2003 the Chinese government leaked reports that it had cut oil supplies to its neighbour for several days to pressure it into starting talks. Shortly after, Pyongyang agreed to a first round of negotiations in Beijing with the US. In September, after North Korea angrily denounced the outcome of expanded six-party talks, China quietly redeployed 150,000 troops to the border. Although the government called this a routine move, locals say the troops have now replaced local police in patrolling the riverbanks, a move equivalent to replacing the rotten washer on the leaky border so that the tap of illegal trade can be shut off at any time.

'Before, the smugglers and the local police were so close that they could always get round any attempted clampdown,' said a local resident. 'But the soldiers come from a different area. They don't mix with us. If they get an order to halt the illegal trade, it won't be so easy to bribe them. They'll shoot to kill.'

If China were to choke off the border trade, the impact would be devastating. According to a local church pastor, the degree of North Korea's dependence was apparent during the SARS crisis. 'The Korean government ordered the border to be sealed to prevent a spread of the infection. But they soon had to abandon that plan because so many people were either suffering or breaking the rules.'

The presence of the army also sends other disturbing signals to Pyongyang. Last year a policy paper is said to have circulated in Beijing, proposing Chinese military intervention to bring about regime change in North Korea. While this would fly in the face of decades of diplomatic and military passivity, its backers claim it would be a last resort to prevent a destabilizing war that could bring US troops closer to the Chinese border.

There are already signs of growing lawlessness near the border. Chinese residents say they have lost all sympathy for the North Koreans, who are now accused of robberies and murders. Some cross the border to raid warehouses and homes. Others – illegal immigrants who have been forced to live in the mountains for several years – have become bandits.

In one border village, all the locals could talk about was a raid on the trading depot two nights earlier and the murder of a policeman. In both cases, Koreans were being blamed. 'No one wants to help them any more,' said one waitress. 'They come to your house asking for food, but they're actually casing the joint. If they see something valuable, they return at night to steal it – and kill people who get in their way. I used to pity them. Now I hate them.'

1 March 2004

GARY YOUNGE

After Aristide

For the past few days the Haitian capital, Port-au-Prince, has been growing accustomed to a gruesome ritual. As night falls, the streets empty in fear of the wrath of the *chimères* – armed pro-Aristide gangs – on looting and shooting sprees. As day breaks, people emerge to see where the bodies have been left. Corpses can lie here for days until someone clears them up.

'It costs three hundred Haitian dollars [£21],' said a resident, Jocelyn, as she spread disinfectant outside Christ the King secretarial college on Saturday morning, where a body had lain for two days. 'I don't know who it is because they took all his money and papers.'

But yesterday the sun rose to a new reality. The president, Jean-Bertrand Aristide, was gone and, as word filtered out, the morning was punctuated by gunfire in the capital while others danced on the street in the rebel stronghold of Cap-Haitien. The first rebels to arrive in the capital went on a wild ride around town in cars and pick-up trucks, shot it out with an unseen gunman and hugged the people they came to liberate. 'Gonaives, Gonaives!' and 'Guy Philippe, Guy Philippe!' some residents chanted, using the names of the first town to fall in the revolt that dislodged Mr Aristide and the former police chief who led the revolt. Many rebels carried rifles or shotguns. Several of their vehicles carried small signs in the windscreens reading 'Liberation Front, Haitian Armed Forces'. 'We came here to work with the police,' their leader, Faustin Miradieau, said. 'We will recognize the authority of the new president.' They hugged and laughed with groups of officers from the Haitian national police, Mr Aristide's poorly trained 4,000-member force, whose members fled before the rebel advances in the north.

Mr Aristide leaves behind a country riven by civil war, paralysed by social chaos and crushed by poverty. The man once hailed as the 'Haitian Mandela' is now branded a dictator. The priest has become the pariah. This is the second time he has been forced to leave the country at gunpoint, but no one expects him to be returning any time soon. But those seeking a straightforward trajectory from good to evil will not find one in Mr Aristide. The very messianic qualities that greeted his ascent – in 1990, on being first elected, he found the people sweeping the roads before him with palm fronds – contributed to his downfall. The leaders of the death squads Mr Aristide disbanded now control much of the country and prepare to march on the capital. The country that assisted his return ten years ago, the United States, encouraged him to leave.

In a country where the media is either unreliable or unavailable, fear travels faster than fact. Early yesterday morning the *chimères* stopped journalists to ask if the rumours about Mr Aristide's departure were true. Within an hour they were shooting at the press, blaming them for besmirching their president's name.

Two days of relative calm preceded a storm of looting, murder and mayhem. Police guarding Haiti's main prison near the National Palace ran away, some discarding their uniforms to avoid detection. The jail emptied. An estimated 2,000 inmates, including murderers, melted into the crowds. Looters hit a police station in Petionville, an upmarket suburb of the capital, carting away police hats, T-shirts, helmets and other bits of police uniforms. On a main thoroughfare, a barricade of burning tyres sent up a wall of thick black smoke.

Haiti has had more than thirty coups and nineteen years of American occupation in a 200-year history blighted by dictatorship at home and international isolation. Mr Aristide, for most of his political life, espoused social justice and practised the politics of authoritarianism. As a radical priest in the 1980s, he called capitalism a 'mortal sin' and encouraged his flock in the shantytown of La Saline to do the holy work of fighting repressive regimes. But he also praised the smell of burning tyres – a reference to 'necklacing' where supporters hung flaming tyres on opponents' necks. In 1988 the Salesians expelled him from their order, accusing him of inciting violence and exalting class struggle. But what worried the Catholic Church endeared him to the Haitian people. In 1990 he won a democratic election with a landslide. Before he could be inaugurated he had first to see off a coup attempt. Before his first year was out he had been overthrown and exiled to the US.

Many of those who now oppose him say that those characteristics that made him a popular priest also made him an awful politician; he neither compromised nor made strategic alliances, but laid down the law and expected it to be followed.

'He hasn't changed,' said Jean-Claude Bajeux, the director of the Ecumenical Centre for Human Rights, and Mr Aristide's former minister of culture. 'We made the mistake of thinking he was a political leader. But he does not know or understand what a political party is for.'

Mr Aristide's three-year exile in Washington DC altered his politics and he sought to accommodate US interests. 'If you have a populist without a real agenda, you're feeding a demagogue,' said Lawrence Pezzullo, a former US special envoy to Haiti. As unrest grew, Mr Aristide relied increasingly on armed gangs.

The name of his party, Lavalas, is Creole for torrential floods. In the 2000 legislative elections the party swept everything before it, committing widespread fraud that led to a freeze on millions of dollars in aid. Despite winning the presidential elections in the autumn of 2000 with 92 per cent of the vote, Mr Aristide had by then lost much of his democratic legitimacy. This led swiftly to instability and then insurrection. Last month the rebels seized several towns, many of which the government took back with the help of armed gangs. When, last week, the rebels took the second largest town of Cap-Haitien and refused to negotiate, it was clear Mr Aristide had lost his authority.

The question now is what will replace him. The political opposition is a broad-based coalition of students, human rights activists and business people. The armed opposition is run by former death squad leaders. Having achieved their primary aim of getting rid of Mr Aristide there is little upon which they will agree.

8 June 2004

EWEN MACASKILL

Death at dawn

For hundreds of thousands of refugees like Souad Omar Mousa the rain that fell yesterday in the Darfur region of Sudan is something to dread. 'If I was in my village, I would welcome it,' she said. 'But here we are exposed.'

Home for Mrs Mousa is now the Kalma camp, near Nyala, one of hundreds scattered throughout Darfur. Refugees live under straw matting or in the open. In what the United Nations describes as the world's worst humanitarian disaster, the arrival of the rains means that life for the refugees will become even more grim and the death toll will almost certainly rise.

About 30,000 are estimated to have been killed in the last year, victims of a government-armed militia that has terrorized and destroyed villages throughout Darfur, where 1.2 million have been displaced, with a further 100,000 taking refuge in neighbouring Chad. A UN official who has travelled extensively throughout the region said yesterday, 'If you go a thousand kilometres from here to Chad you will not see a single village intact.'

During a three-hour flight over Darfur, hundreds of blackened and scorched villages were starkly visible against the red desert. Mrs Mousa walked for three days to reach Kalma after the Janjaweed militia attacked her village, Shatee, west of the Mara mountains, two months ago: 'They came at dawn, at four a.m. They came on horses, donkeys, camels and Land Cruisers. They burnt the houses and killed the men and many of the male children. I don't know if my husband is alive or dead.' She fled with her four sons and three daughters, but one of her children, Omar Abdul Rahin, seven, died on the way.

The refugees claim the government is engaged in ethnic cleansing, using the Arab Janjaweed to force out black Africans. The Sudanese government denies the charge, blaming rebel forces rather than the militia, and has allowed few journalists into Darfur to see what is happening.

Kalma is one of the better camps because of the presence of Medecins sans Frontières, the international medical relief charity. But the death toll is still very high, way above what aid agencies regard as crisis point. There are about ten deaths a day, most of them children. Tom Quinn, the MSF medical team leader in the camp, said he went to five graveyards ringing the camp last week and counted 131 mounds of earth, gauging the size of the body by the length of the mound. 'Of the one hundred and thirty-one, only thirteen were adults,' he said. There was a desperate need for aid, especially plastic sheeting to provide some protection from the rain. He complained of obstruction by the government, saying that 30 tonnes of medicine has been lying at Port Sudan since early May. The rain, he added, was another concern – 'This whole area will be flooded' – and even if the camp survived there would be pollution, malnutrition and disease.

A British delegation led by the international development secretary, Hilary Benn, yesterday had a confrontation with the governor of South Darfur, General Hamid Mussa, who insisted that the instability in the region should be blamed mainly on rebel forces. Mr Benn questioned him about allegations that the government had provided the militia with weapons. One of General Mussa's ministers replied that weapons were readily available throughout Sudan because of wars in neighbouring countries.

The camps throughout Darfur range from places like Kalma, which at least has medical facilities, to Meshtel in the north of the country in which refugees are living in the open and are forcibly removed at frequent intervals by the government. In addition Meshtel is beside a river, which will almost certainly flood when the rains arrive.

The refugees arriving at all the camps tell of fresh attacks. Aisha Yunis Suleiman, aged thirty-five, reached the Kalma camp five days ago from Mugdi. She said her village had suffered an aerial bombardment in which her husband had been killed and that the militia had gone into the village immediately afterwards. Asked who had been responsible she said, 'The government.' She would only return to the village 'when it is secure'.

Mrs Mousa too will not go back until she is sure there is peace. She was prepared to risk the devastation and possible death from the rains because, she said, 'There is a bigger risk of dying in the village.'

29 July 2004

DAVID FICKLING

Down in the Outback

The fresh lick of paint on the toilet blocks can't cover up what's wrong with Ninga Mia. In this Aboriginal shantytown in the shadow of one of the world's biggest gold mines, living conditions are probably as grim as they get in Australia. A third of houses lack bathrooms and toilets, and even those that have these basic facilities are overcrowded and often insanitary.

'This is the richest square mile in Australia and our people are living here in substandard conditions,' says Maria Meredith, the manager of Ninga Mia's Aboriginal corporation. Behind her the Kalgoorlie Super Pit looms over the town in a towering escarpment, while machinery from the mine's lime kilns clanks constantly in the background. The pit is big enough to swallow up the City of London, and the 26 tonnes of gold mined from it every year are worth £182m on world markets. 'Our people, they're the ones that showed them the gold in the first place, but what sort of contribution goes back into the community?' Ms Meredith asks.

The facts of Aboriginal health in Australia are a pressing and constant concern. Whereas Australia as a whole ranks between Sweden and Iceland as ninth in the world for life expectancy, indigenous Australians come between the Cambodians and Sudanese at 178th. Those born Aboriginal can expect to die twenty years younger than their non-indigenous compatriots. Aboriginal infant mortality runs at nearly four times the rate of the general population, putting it on a par with Russia and Sri Lanka, despite a nationwide record that is better than Britain's. If you are indigenous, you are seven times more likely to catch meningitis, ten times more likely to catch tuberculosis, forty times more likely to catch syphilis and sixty-seven times more likely to catch gonorrhoea. If you are an Aboriginal child, you are twice as likely to be born with a low birth-weight and five times more likely to have a mother younger than seventeen. If you also live in a remote outback community, the odds are evens that you will have scabies and two to one that you will have other running sores. Remote Aboriginal communities record the highest rates of roundworm infection in the world, and one 1997 study found hookworms in 93 per cent of children in one community.

In the offices of Bega, Kalgoorlie's Aboriginal-controlled health centre, the chief executive, Greg Stubbs, shakes his head at the clinic's registration figures. Health services normally see a pick-up in attendance as patients hit their late fifties and start encountering more problems, but Bega has a dramatic drop-off. Just one-twelfth of their 7,000 clients are over fifty-five. 'They're not turning up because they're dying,' he said. 'It's only just over sixty years ago that Aboriginal people round here have come into this civilization, and our people just haven't been able to cope with the huge changes. They don't go hunting for bush tucker any more, they go to the shops and buy Western food. They don't get the exercise they should.'

Six hours' drive east of Perth in the heart of Western Australia's prosperous goldfields, Kalgoorlie is where the two sides of Australia's health divide come face to face. Money flowing from the mines and from heritage tourism makes its white population richer than the national average, but Aborigines live in a different world. Ninga Mia, a community on the town's outskirts, where 150 people live in often squalid conditions, does not even appear on the maps handed out by the tourist office. Services at the settlement have slowly improved over the years. When it was set up in 1983, its dwellings were corrugated-iron sheds without power or water, and until twelve months ago 49-year-old Beth Nelson was still living in a fibreboard shelter with no toilet or bathroom.

Les Calyun and his wife Marianne, both thirty, are moving out of their dilapidated house, having spent six months living there with their three children. 'It's pretty poor,' he said. 'We haven't got a front door. I got some board and put it up. There's a toilet but it's not working though, gets blocked all the time. The window went out so I had to stick that bit of plastic over it there.'

Poor housing exacerbates other problems. Dusty and unhygienic surroundings mean that deaths from respiratory problems are four times more common among indigenous Australians; deaths from heart disease and strokes are three times more common. Diabetes, fuelled by the change in diet and lifestyle, causes death ten times more frequently, and in some communities affects more than half of all people.

Neil Thomson, professor of public health at Edith Cowan University in Perth, said poverty, racism and dispossession were at the heart of the problem. 'It's almost a classic example of the impact of social factors on health. If you were dispossessed and marginalized in this way, how would you cope?'

The same factors intensify the problems of violence endemic in most Aboriginal communities. Aborigines are forty-five times more likely to become victims of domestic violence and 40 per cent more likely to commit suicide. Add in the effects of car accidents and fights, and violent deaths are three times more common. Even the most well-appointed buildings in Ninga Mia are overcrowded. A house the size of a large bedsit typically provides a home for seven or more people, often accompanied by a regular stream of distant relatives from more remote communities.

The sheer scale of the problem often seems to confound public health experts. Treating Aboriginal poor health can be like picking up the pieces of a shattered society: less about handing out the right pills than it is about healing the chaos that has resulted from colonialism and dispossession.

Health workers admit that some of the biggest challenges simply involve educating people about health. Aware of the resentment caused by generations of white paternalism, they see practical as well as ethical problems in trying to tell people how to live their lives. At the same time, they know that the lifestyles of Aborigines in rural Australia are often making them ill, and that people don't realize their health is poor because they have never known it to be good. Working on a painting in the back of a stripped-out old van in Ninga Mia, 61-year-old Dinni Smith fights off a hacking cough to insist that he has never been sick.

The tragedy of Aboriginal ill-health is that its causes are well understood and could be prevented without the need for dramatic technological breakthroughs. 'Talking about the health system is a misnomer in this case,' said Neil Thomson. 'The problem is the failure of the health system to take responsibility and advocate broader change, as well as just delivering services.'

Many white people in Kalgoorlie resent Bega's attractive new clinic as a sign of government largesse to Aborigines, but in truth health spending per head on indigenous Australians is only 20 per cent higher than overall, coming to just over A$3,065 (£1,200) for each person. Given the extraordinary difficulties surrounding Aboriginal healthcare, even conservative estimates calculate that the A$1.245bn annual budget needs to be boosted a further 20 per cent. A 2001 report by the government's official spending equity body went further and said it should be doubled.

Kalgoorlie may seem a long way from the Canberra bureaucracy where such decisions are made, but it is far from a forgotten backwater. Australia's health minister, Tony Abbott, flew into town on Tuesday for a pre-election meet and greet with local movers and shakers, and the treasurer, Peter Costello, also popped in last week. Neither found time to visit Ninga Mia.

10 August 2004

SIMON TISDALL

Charge sheet

The US charge sheet against Iran is lengthening almost by the day, presaging destabilizing confrontations this autumn and maybe a pre-election October surprise.

The Bush administration is piling on the pressure over Iran's alleged nuclear weapons programme. It maintains Tehran's decision to resume building uranium centrifuges wrecked a long-running EU-led dialogue and is proof of bad faith. The US will ask a meeting of the International Atomic Energy Agency on 13 September to declare Iran in breach of the nuclear non-proliferation treaty, a prelude to seeking punitive UN sanctions.

Iran's insistence that it seeks nuclear power, not weapons, is scoffed at in Washington. John Bolton, the hawkish US under-secretary of state for arms control, says there is no doubt what Tehran is up to. He has hinted at using military force should the UN fail to act: 'The US and its allies must be willing to deploy more robust techniques' to halt nuclear proliferation, including 'the disruption of procurement networks, sanctions and other means'. No option was ruled out, he said last year. Last month in Tokyo, Mr Bolton upped the ante again, accusing Iran of collaborating with North Korea on ballistic missiles.

Israel, Washington's ally, has also been stoking the fire. It is suggested there that if the West fails to act against Iran in timely fashion, Israel could strike pre-emptively as it did against Iraq's nuclear facilities in 1981, although whether it has the capability to launch effective strikes is uncertain.

The US has been pushing other countries to impose de facto punishment on Iran. Japan has been asked to cancel its $2bn investment in the Azadegan oilfield and Washington has urged Russia to halt the construction of a civilian reactor.

Condoleezza Rice, the US national security adviser, said at the weekend there was a new international willingness to confront Tehran, but declined to rule out unilateral action if others did not go along. That will fuel speculation in Tehran and elsewhere that the Bush administration may resort to force, with or without Israel, ahead of November's election. Options include 'surgical strikes' or covert action by special forces.

Such a move would be a high-risk gamble for George Bush. After the WMD fiasco, there would inevitably be questions about the accuracy of US intelligence. In the past Iran has vowed to retaliate. Although it is unclear how it might do so, the mood in Tehran has hardened since the conservatives won fiddled elections last winter.

'I think we've finally got the world community to a place, the IAEA to a place, that it is worried and suspicious,' Ms Rice said in one of a string of interviews with CNN, Fox News and NBC television. She vowed to aim some 'very tough resolutions' at Iran this autumn. 'Iran will either be isolated or it will submit,' she said.

Officials in London say she exaggerated the degree of unanimity on what to do next. Britain, France and Germany are the EU troika, which has pursued a policy of 'critical engagement' with Iran, despite US misgivings. Jack Straw, the foreign secretary, has invested considerably in resolving the issue, travelling to Tehran on several occasions. A diplomatic collapse would be a blow.

'There has been no such decision at all,' a Foreign Office spokesman said yesterday of US efforts to take the dispute to the Security Council. 'The dialogue [with Iran] is ongoing and the government still believes that negotiation is the way forward at this stage.' But Britain is in danger of being dragged down a path of confrontation that it does not want to travel.

Nuclear weapons are not Washington's only worry. The US charges include Iran's perceived meddling in Iraq, where the blame for the surge in Shia unrest is laid partly at Tehran's door. It also takes exception to Iran's ambiguous attitude to al-Qaida and Tehran's backing for anti-Israeli groups such as Hizbullah. The recent Kean report on 9/11 detailed unofficial links between some of the al-Qaida hijackers and Iran. Investigations into other terrorist attacks since 9/11, including this year's Madrid bombings and failed plots in Paris and London, point to an Iran connection, though the extent of any government involvement is obscure.

While the Bush administration is set on a tougher line there is no consensus even in Washington on what to do. A report by the independent Council on Foreign Relations says that, since Iran is not likely to implode any time soon, the US should start talking. 'Iran is experiencing a gradual process of internal change,' the report says. 'The urgency of US concerns about Iran and the region mandate that the US deal with the current regime [through] a compartmentalized process of dialogue, confidence building and incremental engagement.'

That suggestion was mocked by a *Wall Street Journal* editorial as 'appeasement'. Hawks say the nuclear issue is too urgent to brook further delay. And therein lies the rub. Bringing Iran in from the cold is a time-consuming business. But the Bush administration, as usual, is in a hurry.

DEBITS

16 June 2004

LARRY ELLIOTT

Brown's quiet satisfaction

It was with quiet satisfaction rather than a fanfare of trumpets that Gordon Brown edged past David Lloyd George this week to become the longest serving chancellor since the nineteenth century. Following Labour's drubbing at the polls, a round of celebratory interviews was deemed too politically provocative, with Mr Brown fearing that it would look like the start of a leadership bid.

The quiet satisfaction, on the other hand, stemmed from the fact that the Treasury stewardship of Lloyd George, rather than that of any of his Labour forebears, is the one particularly admired by Brown. Lloyd George is the current incumbent's role model for the way he unashamedly used the post for radical ends, ushering in the embryonic welfare state with a series of social reforms while keeping a tight rein on the nation's finances (at least until the First World War intervened).

In some senses, the desire to hark back to the last great Liberal chancellor rather than Snowden, Dalton, Cripps, Callaghan or Healey is understandable enough since Labour second lords of the Treasury have spent most of their time managing crises. But the similarities go deeper than that.

Introducing his self-styled People's Budget in 1909, Lloyd George said: 'Out of the money raised by taxing superfluities, funds will be established to secure honourable sustenance for the deserving old, and to assist our great benefit societies in making adequate provisions for sickness and infirmity, and against the poverty which comes to the widows and orphans of those who fall in the battle of industry.'

All very Brownian: the Scottish Presbyterian in him would like the bit about taxing superfluities, the reference to the deserving old chimes with the chancellor's own distinction between the diligent and the workshy, while he too has been using the Treasury to fight against poverty. And just as the economy of Lloyd George's day had to cope with the United States and Germany starting to outpace Britain in the race for economic hegemony, so today there are those who fall in the battle of globalization.

The comparisons do not end there, either. Lloyd George was the pre-eminent figure in Asquith's star-studded cabinet, and after more than seven years at the Treasury, containing eight budgets, his ambition and talent took him, via brief sojourns at the ministries of munitions and war, to the top of the greasy pole. During world wars, chancellors are inconsequential figures responsible only for writing the cheques, so for Lloyd George a change of job (he kept the occupancy of 11 Downing Street) was a promotion. For Mr Brown, every other job than prime minister is demotion, as both he and Tony Blair are acutely aware.

The chances of Mr Brown fronting a putsch against Mr Blair, as did Lloyd George against a weakened Asquith in 1916, are slim; the chancellor knows

Labour's history is littered with assassins who have received contumely rather than praise. The Lloyd George example is hardly encouraging, in any case, since his toppling of Asquith split the Liberal party and hastened its replacement by Labour as the party of the left. But just as there have been parallels, so too there have been differences between the two longest serving chancellors of the past 100 years.

Mr Brown normally rattles through his speeches in just less than sixty minutes, while the People's Budget clocked in at a jaw-dropping four and a half hours. According to Roy Jenkins in his book on chancellors, it was 'singularly ill-delivered', although it is amazing anybody was still awake to pass judgement.

The sums involved in what was the most contentious budget of the twentieth century were also staggeringly modest by today's standards. Lloyd George needed to raise £164m in revenue – the sort of petty cash Mr Brown would trouser from the taxpayer in a couple of hours – in order to build more Dreadnought battleships for the arms race with Germany and to pay for old age pensions. His means of doing so caused an uproar. Not for Lloyd George the safe option of stealth taxes, of nibbling away at the taxpayer in the manner of a modern chancellor. This was an in-your-face package from a chancellor bent on making a virtue of redistribution: there were higher taxes on unearned income but new child allowances for those with incomes of under £500 a year; there was the introduction of a super tax on those earning £5,000 or more – the equivalent of getting on for £500,000 in today's money – and there were the taxes on land that especially angered the landed gentry, whose opposition to the budget in the House of Lords prompted a full-scale constitutional crisis.

And if, in these days of spiralling oil prices, Mr Brown is cursing the chancellor who first thought of taxing motorists, he has Lloyd George to thank for his predicament. The People's Budget introduced a sliding scale car tax, with a swingeing impost (equivalent to £2,000 today) on the idle Edwardian rich swanning around in their limousines, and excise duty of threepence (just over 1p) on petrol.

In retrospect, it was all downhill for Lloyd George after the People's Budget, with none of his seven others matching it for radicalism. But that one budget has gone down as a seminal moment in modern political history – ushering in the era of the welfare state and big government.

Mr Brown's approach has been different. There has been no great confrontation, no whizz-bang moment since the bombshell of Bank of England independence four days into his chancellorship; rather a measured approach, which Mr Brown has dubbed 'prudence for a purpose', but really boils down to using the fruits of steady economic growth to tackle poverty.

Lloyd George's 1909 budget was called 'a monument of reckless and improvident finance'; Mr Brown has done his utmost to neuter his critics by allowing the rich to get richer, and cloaking his redistribution in language designed to appeal both to the voters and to the arbiters in the financial markets.

In that respect, the most significant of Mr Brown's eight budgets was that of 2002, which announced increases in spending on the NHS to be paid for by higher national insurance contributions. The thinking behind the move was that after running the economy prudently for almost five years the time was right politically for higher direct taxes to pay for improvements in public services.

Even then, it was national insurance that took the hit. Income tax, described by another former chancellor as 'an engine of gigantic power for great national purposes', has remained the great untouchable. But those were Gladstone's words and he delivered a record twelve budgets. By his standards, Mr Brown is still a beginner.

15 June 2004

FELICITY LAWRENCE

Superpowers

Four giant supermarket chains now exert unprecedented control over what we eat and where we buy it. But, plied with their half-price Euro 2004 beers, we seem to be comatose over what this creeping takeover is going to mean for our communities and our lives.

Tesco, Asda, Sainsbury's and the newly merged Safeway/Morrisons group command over three-quarters of British grocery sales. This extraordinary concentration in power in one of Britain's most important corporate sectors is not yet complete, however. Tesco has become dominant, almost unstoppable, with the latest figures giving it a share of over 27 per cent (a 25 per cent share of any market is normally considered enough to trigger a monopolies inquiry). Sainsbury's is struggling. Most in the industry assume that further consolidation is inevitable.

'The slide rule is being run over two to three companies even now,' Professor John Bridgeman, former director general of the Office of Fair Trading, said at a Lancaster University seminar last week. The warning from Bill Grimsey, chief executive of the Big Food Group, which owns Iceland shops, was even more stark. We are at a point, he argues, where what we do now about supermarkets will set the terms of our social legacy for the future. We can either act to curb monopolization or allow choice to be dramatically reduced. If we fail to act, Grimsey says, the affluent could find themselves with a choice of 'Tesco, Tesco or Tesco', while the disadvantaged are denied affordable access to good fresh food.

If these sound like the words of a rival on the run, the fates of Bicester, Brackley and Buckingham are worth considering. Tesco is the only superstore operator in each of these three neighbouring towns. The recent acquisition of the One Stop chain of convenience stores by Tesco – incredibly, unopposed by the competition authorities – has given it four stores and a dominant position in Bicester town centre as well, plus stores in the centre of Brackley and Buckingham. Residents have to travel significant distances by car to reach alternative superstores.

This helps explain an apparent paradox in new research by Lancaster's School of Management, presented at last week's seminar. Although in theory we have more choice, most of us in fact feel more constrained than ever as we struggle to fit buying our food around our busy household routines. Today's big supermarkets typically offer 40,000 to 50,000 different products. In a brutal battle for position, they are also cutting prices. So why aren't we happier with them? The reality is that most people's choice boils down to driving to the nearest supermarket. We have no way of comparing prices in different stores over the range of what we buy or really knowing which company is cheapest for us. Since most things are unmarked except on the shelf, we usually can't remember what they cost. Nor do we have time to master the layout of anywhere unfamiliar. Any idea of being able to choose between shops is abandoned the minute we have parked the car. So in reality, unprecedented choice comes down to agonizing between twenty different boxes of over-processed cereal or six different thicknesses of loo paper.

More troubling is the picture the Lancaster research paints of the impact of supermarket power on vulnerable households. These include families on low incomes, but also single-parent households and the elderly across all income groups. Those who depend on buses or lifts struggle to reach the superstores as competitive pressure closes down local shops. They feel excluded from many bargains which depend on being able to buy goods in bulk. They resent the fact that those who are richer or more mobile get the better deals. For the elderly, the sheer physical distances involved in walking through huge hyperstores is too daunting. Those who feel excluded in these ways are not a fixed group: we move in and out of exclusion as our personal circumstances change. Cheaper food, which seems an indisputable good, is not so great if the poor end up paying more because of it.

There is now a coalition of interests which want to see curbs on supermarket power, from the National Federation of Women's Institutes to farmers, independent shops, environmental groups and trade unionists. Their concern goes beyond social exclusion. Concentration has allowed the big four to abuse their buying power and squeeze suppliers and competitors. Price cuts are not funded by cuts in profits – Tesco turnover increased by 60 per cent in the five years to February 2003, and group operating profit by 75 per cent. Its margins increased over the period. Those who bear the brunt of the cuts are at the bottom of the chain. British farmers have been driven out of business or pushed to the margins of survival as supermarkets source whatever is cheapest and fly it in from around the globe. But this is not what most shoppers would choose – when asked, they say they prefer British farm food.

The supermarket system of centralized distribution that has turned our motorways into warehouses has also spawned a new industry: packing. As suppliers and farmers have been squeezed, the pain has often been passed down the line, to migrant workers paid less than the minimum wage and treated like slaves. No one knows how many are working in the food sector in this country today. A conservative estimate puts the number at over 100,000. Most migrants move in and out of the food, agriculture and construction sectors. One well-placed source, with no anti-migration axe to grind, puts the total across the sectors at nearer 2 million. Given that many of them work double shifts, seven days a week, small wonder our productivity figures look good. And this is one reason why the government has been so limp about supermarket power. Increased productivity and deflation in food prices helps hold down inflation, and while corporate profits soar, the incentive to interfere is not great.

The competition authorities – now technically independent of government – have done little better. They no longer apply a broad public interest test, but (driven by European competition law) judge what is competitive on the narrowest of definitions: price. When the competition commission conducted an inquiry into supermarkets in 2000, it decided that large one-stop grocery stores formed a separate market from convenience shops and should therefore not be seen as being in competition with them. It was, as Professor Bridgeman acknowledges, a 'huge flaw' and failed to anticipate the way the big four would take over smaller chains.

The 2000 inquiry did at least call for a statutory code of practice to stop abuse of suppliers. In 2004, we are still waiting for the Office of Fair Trading to review the watered-down voluntary code eventually introduced. It has by common consent done nothing to help.

If we are to prevent irreversible damage to our towns and communities we need a change of direction now. The definition of the market should be changed so that Tesco, Asda, Sainsbury's and Safeway/Morrisons can no longer buy up small chains. A statutory code of practice that stops supermarkets bullying suppliers and abusing their power is needed urgently. Government should also recognize that the public interest in competition matters goes far beyond prices. It must include consideration of environmental and social good. With supermarket executives from the big four – and Tesco in particular – able to whisper directly into the ears of Downing Street (two of its directors came straight from Whitehall), shoppers might want to send their own message, by voting with their feet and buying elsewhere.

10 November 2003

NILS PRATLEY

The boy done good

Albrecht the Hun was James Murdoch's early contribution to the art of cartooning in the pages of *Harvard Lampoon*, the Ivy League university's student-produced satirical magazine. Albrecht is a gentle soul who prefers poetry to mass slaughter. He doesn't do what is expected of him.

James Murdoch also knows what it is like to be labelled. In his thirty years, he has been branded the Rebel, the Shy One, the College Drop-out, the Artistic One, the Music Industry Flop, the Internet Wunderkind and the Daddy's Boy. A few of those labels were the result of his – highly successful – attempt not to look like a son of Murdoch while at Harvard. In the Albrecht years, James Murdoch variously sported a beard, dyed blond hair and a stud above his eyebrow; two tattoos have presumably been harder to remove during his evolution into suited executive. Cod psychologists used to recount the story – attributed to his mother Anna – of how the young James once asked, 'Is Daddy deaf?' such was his inability to engage his father. But his college friends say there was more to James than a severe case of younger-son syndrome.

'He was always working and was incredibly prolific, whether it was painting, drawing or building things,' says Mark Roybal, a member of Murdoch's arty and musical crowd at Harvard. 'He used to build these automated puppets and then shoot them on film. James was definitely disciplined about his academic studies and he got good grades. He's an incredibly intelligent guy – he got a lot out of college but he outgrew it.'

Indeed, he famously left a year before completing his four-year course in visual entertainment studies. But these were formative years for James Murdoch. When he married Kathryn Hufschmid, a former PR executive and model, three years ago his best man was his old college room-mate, Jesse Angelo. (Students of News Corp, incidentally, should note the name: as well as being the best mate of the boss's son, Angelo has enjoyed a rapid rise within two Murdoch publications, first the *Daily Telegraph* in Sydney and now the *New York Post*, where he edits the Metro edition.) James is also a trustee of *Lampoon*, helping out with ideas and still visiting regularly, according to the magazine's president, Colin Jost: 'He's a funny guy, very gregarious and pleasant to be with.'

But gregarious only up to a point. Bruce Churchill, who was chief operating officer at Star under James, says that the public attention he will now receive in London will be new. 'He will deal with it fine, but for him it will be a new thing,' he says. 'He and Kathryn are not public people. They do not swan around at parties.'

Restaurants and intimate gatherings seem to be more James's style. 'When he's in New York, we'll go out for dinner,' says Roybal. 'He's a dear friend to me and my wife because he cares about what we are doing and he remembers little details. He's got a broad kind of intelligence and it's taken him from building puppets to running BSkyB.'

BSkyB shareholders can, then, at least be confident they are getting an amiable, rounded individual. But can he run a company?

It is harder to add garnish to his early years in business. Rawkus Entertainment, the hip-hop label James founded with two friends after Harvard, was far from an overnight success. One former employee paints a picture of a typically chaotic start-up.

'When I arrived I was told to make my own arrangements for a desk and chair,' says Jeff Gottesfeld, a promotions specialist who came with one of Rawkus's first signings, the delightfully named Whorgasm, who promptly flopped. 'I think Whorgasm just signed because they wanted a shot of Murdoch money,' he adds.

Two years after the launch, James accepted his father's offer to buy the business. Some reports say Rawkus was making a small profit, some that it was loss-making. What is not disputed is that it was one of the smallest deals in the history of News Corp – annual turnover was barely above a couple of million dollars. In fairness, though, the postscript should record that Rawkus is now a highly fashionable, if still not mainstream, New York hip-hop label.

James's return to the family fold came in 1996, and the internet was the thing. The following year he was made president of digital media with the task of launching websites for important parts of the empire, such as Fox Sports and Fox News in the US, and investing in internet ventures. He travelled to conferences and was said to have received one-on-one tuition from new media gurus.

What James did not do – unlike elder brother Lachlan – was blot his copybook. Lachlan and Kerry Packer's son were the driving forces behind One.Tel, an Australian telecoms company that crashed amid huge debts, lawsuits and embarrassment. James had no involvement with One.Tel and the closest he came to a major mistake was his enthusiasm for News Corp to buy PointCast, a software developer, for about $400m. Rupert Murdoch, having invited the vendor to his California ranch, was astonished to find he would deal; PointCast, its software unravelling, was sold the following year for a mere $7m and James learned a lesson.

By the time he gave the Alternative McTaggart lecture at the Edinburgh television festival in 2000, he had lost his innocence about new media and sounded as sceptical as his father. 'If I have to read another article about "surviving in the digital era" or "the new realities of the new economy" or some other angst-ridden twaddle I'll have to fucking shoot myself,' he said.

At the age of twenty-seven, with no direct experience in television or Asia, James was made chairman and chief executive of Star in 2000. At the time, it looked a poisoned chalice to some: Star had lost an estimated $500m in the previous five-and-a-half years. But it was also an opportunity. Star's signal reaches from China to Australia; China was enjoying phenomenal economic growth; and Star was well invested and employed some of News Corp's top executives, such as Churchill and chief programmer Steve Askew. Star is now profitable and has made some undoubtedly clever strategic moves, especially in India where its Hindi version of *Who Wants to be a Millionaire?* was a sensation.

'There were positive trends already working in their favour, but James and Bruce did a good job in driving the operating business,' says Richard Greenfield, media analyst with Fulcrum Global Partners. 'I was impressed by James's array of knowledge about the business, especially about Asia where you are talking about a diverse group of operating environments.'

In a region where family names count for something, James travelled widely, talking to politicians, employees and partners. He also made an infamous speech in which he condemned Falun Gong, the growing spiritual movement in China, which has been persecuted by Beijing but seems harmless to most Western observers. James described Falun Gong as 'an apocalyptic cult'.

Hong Kong has its share of playboys, but James was not one of them. Ray Bashford, editor of the *South China Morning Post* at the time, says, 'The impression he gave was that he was just working his butt off to establish himself within the empire. There wasn't much frivolity or displays of wealth. He was very discreet. When I saw him in restaurants it was usually with a set of young fogeys, US business types.'

In Hong Kong, James also discovered an athletic streak, taking up mountain biking and karate. He and his wife had a child and he made virtually his first stab at raising his personal profile, posing in Hong Kong's street markets for an interview with the Asian edition of *Time* magazine. In retrospect, that *Time* interview is most interesting for his revelation about how he landed the Star job. Murdoch senior told his younger son to 'think about China' and a few days later asked if he liked Chinese food. 'And that was kind of it,' James confessed. 'It had been decided.'

The BSkyB selection process was hardly more demanding, many share-holders think, however much the harrumphing Lord St John of Fawsley protests. And that's the real point about James Murdoch, now master of Sky's Isleworth HQ. He's clearly smart and has learned from experience, but let's not pretend he rose purely on merit. It had been decided.

James Murdoch duly became chief executive of BSkyB with only minor protests from some shareholders. In August 2004, however, his first major presentation to the City on strategy was greeted disdainfully. BSkyB's share price fell by a fifth in a day, removing £2bn of the company's stockmarket value, as Mr Murdoch outlined plans to spend more on marketing as growth in subscriber numbers slowed.

7 April 2004

MATTHEW FORT

Salt

It happened to olive oil. It happened to bread. And now it is happening to salt. The stuff is diversifying, climbing up-market and going chic, sleek and expensive. Once there was just kitchen salt and table salt. It came in round containers and on the label was a picture of a small boy running after a chicken trying to sprinkle salt on its tail. That salt was white as snow and ran fine and free as sand. Not any more.

Salt comes in flakes, in flowers, in crystals. It comes grey, pink, white and blue. It comes from rocks, from deserts, from lakes, from tidal flats, from mines, from barely accessible mountain fastnesses. It comes from Essex, Wales, the Guérande, the Camargue, Portugal, Spain, Australia and now the Himalayas.

The latest designer salt to hit the market is L'Himalayen, complete with a Journey Notebook. 'The product of unpolluted ancient seas dried up over 200 million years ago,' claims the packaging. 'Naturally rich through water filtering by mineral-rich magma over millions of years.'

L'Himalayen may not have quite the exclusivity of Oshima Island Blue Label salt, about which Jeffrey Steingarten wrote in his memoir *It Must've Been Something I Ate*. This can be bought only by members of the Salt Road Club, with a longer waiting list than the MCC; but L'Himalayen still has something of the rare, the exclusive and the utterly daft about it.

But then salt has always attracted keen attention. Wars were fought for it and fortunes built on it. It has been used as a currency (have you ever wondered about the origin of the word 'salary'?), a taxable commodity, religious symbol and a preservative, a glaze for pottery. No wonder Jesus Christ turned to salt for an analogy when he said, 'Ye are the salt of the earth: but if the salt have lost his savour, wherewith shall it be salted?'

The Romans built the Via Salaria from Rome to the Adriatic coast to bring salt to the city. Benvenuto Cellini created one of the greatest of all Renaissance artefacts, a gold *saliera*, or salt cellar. (Sadly it was stolen from the Kunsthistorische Museum in Vienna in 2002 and has not been seen since.) According to Mark Kurlansky in his book *Salt*, the shortage of salt contributed to the collapse of the south at the end of the American civil war. Mahatma Gandhi conceived of the salt march as a means of challenging British imperialist control, with Indians asserting their right to gather salt. The Chinese created a museum devoted to it – the Zigong Salt History Museum.

Nearer to our own time, salt has become, if not the Great Satan that is fat, at least a minor devil, contributing to high blood pressure, heart disease, fluid retention, kidney stones and sundry other modern afflictions. We are supposed to consume no more than 4g of it a day, yet we regularly gobble up far more. But what is it? Salt in its essential form is a compound of sodium and chlorine – and all of it (pay attention, class) is sea salt, whether collected from evaporating sea water or mined as rock salt, which is simply the dried-up remains of prehistoric seas.

It may contain other trace elements as well – magnesium, calcium, iodine and sulphur among them.

It also turns up in some rather unexpected places, and by that I don't mean industrial pizzas, burgers and other fast foods. Gastro-physicist chef Heston Blumenthal recalls, 'We wanted to make a celery-based sauce, but when we tried reducing pure celery juice to the concentration we were looking for, it became so salty we couldn't use it.'

While the diversity of its distribution makes it a marketing man's dream, does one salt really taste very different from another? Steingarten maintains that it does, and in 2000 set up an experiment at the bi-annual meeting of scientists and super-foodies at Erice in Sicily to prove his point. This he did, at least to his own satisfaction: he was the only one in a group that included Blumenthal and American food science writer, Harold McGee, who correctly identified the salts in question. The experiment was repeated back in Britain at the research centre in Leatherhead with inconclusive results. Or rather, the most exclusive salts did not live up to their billing.

Blumenthal remains a sceptic: 'I'm not entirely convinced. There doesn't seem to be that much difference in flavour between one salt and another, unless you start adding other ingredients such as seaweed. But there may be a different degree of saltiness.' Some salts, he says, taste saltier than others. He does use different salts for different purposes in his kitchen.

He turns to free-running, fine-grain salt for seasoning purées, veloutés and soups, and, where texture and saltiness are called for, sprinkles Fleur du Sel de Guérande on meats, fish and foie gras just before serving, because different salts dissolve at different rates in contact with different environments. He also recommends incorporating a little salt in chocolate and crumble toppings as it helps bring out sweetness.

Tom Aikens, multiple-award winning chef at the recent London Restaurant Awards, uses four salts in his restaurant. Maldon salt goes on the tables. Fleur du Sel de Camargue is sprinkled on bread before it is baked, 'for the texture and because it doesn't burn like some other salts. I don't know why.' He seasons dishes before and after cooking with fine-grain salt, and puts coarse crystal salt into dishes requiring long cooking, such as braises; he also puts it into stocks and uses it for curing. 'Old-fashioned kitchen salt is absolute filth,' he says. 'It has a nasty, bitter aftertaste.'

'What they used to call table salt is a thing of the past,' agrees Zeenat Anjari, the buyer for Flaneur, the upmarket delicatessen in Clerkenwell in central London. 'There is definitely a surge of interest in salts with subtle and unique flavour profiles. This isn't simply a matter of fashion. People who are really interested in food are looking to the quality of the raw materials they use.'

Sarah Loxton, product developer for Marks & Spencer agrees: 'Salt has been on our radar for some time. It is the latest gourmet item. The more people understand about food, the more they look for the best, just as they have with olive oil or balsamic vinegar. They want to know where it comes from and how it's produced.'

'It's a little ironic, I suppose, just when we're being told to lay off the salt that there is this upsurge in interest in it. The good thing is that the purer the salt the more intense the flavour and the less you need. Our top salt comes from Wales. It is hand-harvested and filtered and cleaned in water.' She warns that the next store cupboard staple being lined up for the gourmet treatment is pepper.

It is tempting to satirize the growing salt phenomenon by suggesting that it won't be long before there are extra virgin salts, designer salts and single-estate salts. There will be specialist salt boutiques to sell them and restaurants offering diners a choice of salts at their tables. Too late. At Thomas Keller's fabled French Laundry in California the foie gras fanatic is offered a choice of five salts with which to season the dish.

It's enough to turn the satirist into Lot's wife.

WINNERS

23 October 2003

DUNCAN MACKAY

Track and fraud

When, one beautifully warm and sunny day last June, Dr Don Catlin turned up for work at his laboratory at the University of California in Los Angeles, there was an unexpected package waiting for him. Ripping it open, he was surprised to find that it contained a syringe containing a barely visible residue of a strange-looking substance.

Handling it carefully, he wondered what it might be. Then he remembered that, a few days earlier, an official at the United States Anti-Doping Agency (USADA), an independent organization charged with overseeing the implementation of the country's drugs-in-sport policy, had received an anonymous call from someone claiming to be a 'high-profile' athletics coach. They had said that they had information on a new strain of designer anabolic steroid which was so powerful that athletes only had to inject themselves with a couple of drops under their tongue and it could help make them run faster, throw further, jump higher. What Catlin had been mailed was the smoking gun.

He and seven other scientists at the lab set about finding out everything they could about the substance. Time and time again, they ran it through a high-resolution mass spectrometer, the dope-busters' main weapon in the war against drugs in sport. The machine bombards molecules with a beam of electrons to fragment them. This process produces a graphic picture, or 'spectrum', which provides a molecular fingerprint of the substance. By testing and re-testing the sample, the scientists managed to break the drug's code.

'We start to piece together from the spectrum what the molecule could look like,' says Catlin. 'We draw pictures of it. Finally it all comes together and we say, "OK, this steroid [molecule] that I just drew on the paper fits what we think is in the syringe." Then, to prove that, you make the steroid. We synthesized it here. We started from scratch and we made the molecule, which turned out to be THG [tetrahydrogestrinone].'

Now that Catlin understood the chemical make-up of the drug, he set about devising a test for it. He was already excited that he could be on to something huge when he received a call from the headquarters of USADA in Indianapolis. The organization's chief executive, Terry Madden, wanted to know whether he should authorize the freezing of urine samples collected from athletes during the US championships held in Stanford a few days earlier. He figured that if Catlin was on to a drug that a cabal of chemists, coaches and athletes thought they did not know about, then the odds were that competitors there had been using it.

One of the most successful people at these championships had been Remi Korchemny, a septuagenarian, half-Ukrainian émigré who once coached the 1972 Olympic 100m and 200m champion Valery Borzov and who now ran the

KMA Track Club with Victor Conte, the founder of the Bay Area Laboratory Co-operative (BALCO), a nutrition company based in San Francisco. Like a contented granddad, Korchemny had watched proudly from the stands as his star pupil, Kelli White, had raced to victory in the 100m and 200m to qualify for the US team for the world championships to be held in Paris in August.

Competition is so tough among female sprinters in the US that Korchemny knew that coming out on top in their trials meant she would start as favourite for the world event. In Britain's Dwain Chambers, a 26-year-old Londoner he had been coaching full-time since May, he already had the Paris favourite for the men's 100m, the blue-riband event of every championships.

Korchemny had made a good living since coming to settle in America in the 1980s and had established a reputation for helping players in a range of sports with their fitness training. But track and field remained his passion and more than thirty years after watching Borzov power to victory at the Olympics in Munich in the red vest of the Soviet Union, Korchemny was excited that he stood on the verge of establishing himself as the greatest coach in the world.

White and Chambers were members of the KMA Track Club, an organization set up by Korchemny and Conte to help market BALCO's most popular product, a zinc and magnesium supplement, which, since 1999, had grossed the company about $100m (£60m) worldwide. Conte rubbed his hands in anticipation of what success for White and Chambers might mean to him and his company in terms of increased visibility and profits.

Conte would not be the only financial winner. Athletics long ago threw off its amateur shackles and is now a multimillion-dollar industry where the top performers earn Premiership-style salaries and those associated with them share in the wealth. Few had done better financially than Maurice Greene, the 2000 Olympic 100m champion, and his team of advisers. Another coach, John Smith, had turned him into the world's fastest man, rescuing him from a life working in a burger bar. Smith exploited Greene's marketability by setting up Handling Speed Intelligently with a loud and brash lawyer, Emmanuel Hudson. It was an organization designed to market athletes that Smith coached and the pair made thousands of dollars out of Greene, who at his peak was able to command an appearance fee of $100,000 every time he stood on the start line of a big race in Europe.

Korchemny's star was in the ascendancy just as that of his main rival Smith was in freefall. The former world record holder for the 440 yards turned soap opera actor had enjoyed almost unbroken success stretching back to 1988, when he had coached Quincy Watts to the Olympic 400m gold medal. Greene had been his biggest success story, though. As well as the 2000 Olympic 100m gold medal, the sprinter had won three consecutive world titles and set a world record for the 100m. But Greene had appeared to lose his magic spell and Smith had no one to replace him.

Smith's decline had been accelerated by a series of scandals involving him and some of his best-known athletes. The most damaging involved Ato Boldon, who in 2001 had tested positive for a banned stimulant but escaped with a warning. Then Smith was accused of assaulting Anjanette Kirkland, the world 100m hurdles champion, whom he had coached but had subsequently ceased to work with, in a bar room brawl, although no charges were ever brought.

Those close to Greene continued to talk him up as the world championships approached, but a man who once appeared invincible seemed incapable of recapturing his best form and restoring Smith's reputation as the best coach in the world. Thus it was an extremely confident Chambers who left London at the end of July for a training camp with Korchemny in Saarbrücken, Germany, where he planned to fine-tune his preparations for Paris.

Even when a team of officials from the world governing body, the International Association of Athletics Federations, showed up on 1 August to carry out a random drugs test on the training group, Chambers did not believe he had anything to fear. But thousands of miles away, back in Los Angeles, Catlin had been working diligently and had finally established a scientifically validated test that meant he could identify THG in urine samples.

As Catlin began testing the samples that Madden had had the foresight to freeze, he realized the scale of his achievement. Up to twenty of the most famous names in athletics showed traces of THG. The biggest doping scandal in sport was about to hit the front pages – as Chambers discovered yesterday when his became the first really high-profile case thrown up by the new test Catlin has produced.

In more than forty years of trying to stamp out the use of performance-enhancing drugs, scientists had come to accept that for the most part they were going to be one step behind those who wanted to cheat. This is not, however, the first time that Catlin had enjoyed a significant victory in the battle. In 2002, he had surprised a group of competitors at the Winter Olympics in Salt Lake City when he had developed a test for darbepoietin, a synthetic hormone that had just come on to the market to help cancer patients with anaemia, but which had been abused by unscrupulous athletes seeking to gain an edge by using it to increase their oxygen-carrying capacity. Three cross-country skiers – Larisa Lazutina and Olga Danilova of Russia, and Johann Muehlegg of Spain – were caught as a result of Catlin's test and all lost medals.

But, depressingly for those who believe in the purity of sport, the truth is that those who know what they are doing can usually get away with it. It is a point illustrated by Charlie Francis, who was the coach of Ben Johnson when the Canadian tested positive for steroids and was stripped of the Olympic 100m gold medal he had won at Seoul in 1988. Once Johnson had been unmasked as a cheat, Francis admitted his compliance in helping him to beat the system and wrote a book, *Speed Trap*, which is considered to be the most insightful piece of work on the subject of doping in sport.

Francis has continued to follow doping trends and remains arguably the most knowledgeable authority in the world on the subject. In an article for *Testosterone* magazine shortly after the Sydney Olympics in 2000, he wrote a feature in which he revealed what one successful group of American sprinters had allegedly been taking during the run-up to the games. His list included the steroids Anavar and Halotestin, along with ATP, embryonic calf cells, insulin and erythropoietin, a blood-boosting drug used in the treatment of kidney patients. 'Please note that this programme was for the year 2000 and has no doubt been changed since,' said Francis in his article.

The Olympics return to Athens in 2004 – their spiritual home and the place where they are supposed to be reborn. But increasingly it appears that the only race that will count is the chemical race. If the scientists and administrators lose, what hope is there for the sport? Will sponsors want to back it? Will TV want to show it? Will spectators and armchair enthusiasts take it seriously? Will anyone care about drugged-up designer athletes? The most worrying thing for those who want an end to this chemical race is that Catlin will not always be so fortunate as to have the evidence packaged up and slipped in the post to him.

24 November 2003

MATTHEW ENGEL

Rugby's roots

The morning after is the time reality sets in, and reality comes no colder than it did yesterday at St Catherine Meadow, home of Spartans Rugby Football Club. Here we were on day two of the Great English Rugby Boom. And nine aspirant Jonny Wilkinsons, plus one chunky ten-year-old prop forward, all from local primary schools, turned up for the normal Sunday morning session of mini-rugby, the form of the game supposed to unearth the lads who will win the World Cup again in 2015.

Unfortunately, the adults failed to make it. The gate was locked and the club was deserted. The kids had a makeshift knockabout in the bleak car park, practising their scrummaging like young stags in the rutting season, while the parents wondered whether English rugby was now too hungover to attend to normal business.

Then word came through: mini-rugby cancelled; breakdown in communication; apologies. 'Rugby's going to have to get its act together,' seethed one mum. And if rugby can't get its act together here, it can't happen anywhere. For this is Gloucester, the heartland of the English game.

All over the country, people who don't know the difference between a wing three-quarter and a ha'penny stamp spent Saturday night dancing on tables, 'doing the Jonny' with their arms, yammering on about 1966 and pledging undying allegiance to a game that mixes nitpicking complexity, simple artistry and even simpler violence. But among true rugby folk, reaction to England's victory over Australia was at once drunker – and more sober.

This is a city where there are more than a dozen high-class clubs, their strength still based largely on the city's selective rugby-playing grammar schools. Here the sporting landscape is dominated by the Premiership rugby team, the Cherry-and-Whites, and the soccer team – Gloucester City FC of the Dr Martens League Western Division – is so overwhelmed that they only make page twenty-seven of the Saturday Pink 'Un. And the crowd who watched the game in the most rugby-crazed pub in the country's most rugby-crazed town on the most rugby-crazed day in English history cannot possibly have been out boozing on Saturday night. The limits of human endurance are such that they must have been comatose.

Opposite Kingsholm, the Gloucester rugby ground, an all-ticket crowd started drinking pints round about 8 a.m. in the White Hart, the pub run by the former England forward Mike Teague. Much the same was going on down the road in the Queen's Head and the Kingsholm Inn, and in the other 14,997 English pubs reputedly open for the occasion, although elsewhere the drinking may not have been on the same heroic scale.

For these were no fairweather fans. When the whistle blew for infringements, many of them actually understood why. In this pub all five screens are tuned to rugby even when Old Fartonians are playing Lymeswold on Sky Sports 49. And the customers, many of them with forearms like oak trunks and the capacity of oil tankers, represented the spirit of old rugby, that game of sang-froid and singsongs. And they were paying homage to this new game of Woodward and Wilkinson, in which England practise beforehand and go on to win.

At the height of the drama, the White Hart reacted the same as everywhere else. They explained Australia's last-minute penalty in the usual technical terms: 'The referee's a twat.' In extra time strong men nuzzled closer to each other for reassurance. Some tried to turn away, but there were too many screens; there was nowhere else to look. And when victory came, a 'Yes!' rang out that could have been heard all the way to Sydney. Their emotions were drained, even if their bladders were not.

Someone said to Teague that it had worked out well for him: 'Think of all the extra beer you sold in extra time.'

He reacted with contempt. 'Think of the prize!' he said righteously. 'The greatest prize of all!'

In any case, he was still selling just as much beer in mid-afternoon. But by now a certain thoughtfulness had crept in. 'In a way I feel resentful about all the people jumping on the bandwagon,' said Steve Barrett, a Gloucester season-ticket holder who sounded mighty perceptive for someone who had drunk six pints of Guinness washed down with four of Strongbow. 'But how else will you get people into rugby except by winning something like this? For me, I don't want the day to end. I'm supposed to go into town to go shopping but I know if I go out it's just another wet Saturday, and it's over. The world always stops for football. I want it to stop for rugby, too. I think today it's at least sort of stuttered.'

Barrett wanted to go over to Kingsholm to savour the moment there, but Gloucester were away and the ground was closed. The nearest game was down the road at Spartans, in a bleak clearing between Tesco and the railway line, where 100 diehards were watching the local derby against their most feared neighbours, Gordon League. Here, rugby did not feel like a boomtime sport. 'Fifteen years ago I was captain of the Spartans' Fifth XV,' said one spectator, Carey Phillips. 'Now they're struggling to put out two teams.'

Spartans lost, 16–15. So it was a night of mixed emotions in the club Portakabin: it did not go on especially late. The chairman, Mike Bubb, came down yesterday morning to clear up and, incidentally, let in the mini-rugby kids so they could at least have a run on the field.

'Everyone's glad to see England win, but grassroots rugby depends on volunteers,' said Bubb. 'You've got to have people willing to give up their weekends. I'm here eighteen to twenty hours a week sweeping the leaves up, clearing the drains and changing the lightbulbs. You need clubs like this to get the next Jonny Wilkinson. And no one's giving us the money to do it. That's the reality of rugby.'

23 February 2004

DONALD McRAE

The real McCoy

The face might have looked a terrible mess, as if someone had used a baseball bat to fracture its cheekbone in three different places, but Tony McCoy was far more worried about his head. Pacing restlessly around his warm house in Oxfordshire last Wednesday afternoon, when he should have been out riding on a cold and bone-hard track at Leicester, McCoy was oblivious to the latest physical damage he had done to himself after falling heavily at Plumpton two days earlier. The real pain was locked inside his obsessive mind.

'It's doing my head in,' he sighed and stared despairingly at the massive television screen. Incessant footage of that afternoon's racing from exotic Leicester and Musselburgh was being beamed mercilessly into his kitchen. His hand cupped his shattered left cheek as if he were trying to comfort himself. 'I've got to get away.'

McCoy had just decided he would fly to Dubai with Mick Fitzgerald that night. Fitzgerald was recovering from the broken arm he had suffered while racing at Kempton earlier this month. Sending McCoy's assistant, the former jockey Gee Armytage, on a mad scramble for a last-minute flight appeared to be an act of impulse, but the reason for his sudden departure was more deeply rooted.

Martin Pipe, the trainer for whom McCoy rides most, had picked up two more winners at Leicester. McCoy, had he not been injured, would have ridden both and increased his tally of 159 winners this season. Richard Johnson, his closest rival in the race to become champion jockey this April, was only seven wins behind him on Wednesday.

Each day McCoy was away from racing gave Johnson more opportunity to narrow that already meagre gap. The frustration, on only his second day without a horse, was slowly killing McCoy. He smiled grimly at the suggestion that his five-day trip to Dubai might be seen as a welcome rest from the track. He was not going to Dubai to drink or lounge next to the pool, or eat an expensive meal in a fancy restaurant. That, he said darkly, was the only good thing about his horrendous fall last Monday. Even if he wanted to succumb to a tempting sliver of boiled chicken, his shattered cheek made it too sore for him to chew properly. And so, rather than a winter vacation, McCoy was literally fleeing from the trauma of being made to step back from his obsession with winning. 'I've got to get away,' he repeated.

We made a start by retreating from the kitchen and the giant plasma screen to find a quieter room. With his escape almost assured, McCoy finally relaxed. He sank back into a chair and we began, of course, with the face.

McCoy has always cut a haunted figure, his taut features and sunken eyes a result of the starvation he endures every day. Yet the new blue and purple dents and cuts that marked the left side of his face had become a source of comic wonder to those closest to him. McCoy's humour was just as black.

'They call me Elephant Man now. A fair few people have suggested I use this as a good excuse to get some cosmetic surgery to improve my looks. They're probably right but I don't care what my face looks like. You don't race with your face, do you? If it was down to me I would be out there this minute, riding hard as ever.' McCoy considered the doctors and friends protecting him from himself. The word 'bastards' lingered on his dry lips. He swallowed it instead and shrugged. 'I know they're doing the right thing for me in the long run. But they can't stop me for ever. I'll be back racing next week.'

The risk, for McCoy, is enormous. Should he fall again on the same cheek the damage could be irreparable. Yet compared to defending his status as champion, as the greatest jump jockey of all time, the danger seems irrelevant to him. With his latest injury following the two months of racing he lost after breaking his arm at Worcester last June, McCoy has endured a raw old season – peppered by two controversial bans for excessive use of the whip. His appetite for winning, however, is still voracious. It explains why he is chasing his ninth successive champion's title, having secured his 2,000th career win last month.

'It's all that matters to me. The desire to win is driven by my fear of losing. That – losing – is just the worst thing in the world.' Injury, according to McCoy, ranks as 'the second worst thing in the world'. Yet barely forty-eight hours after falling at Plumpton, McCoy was ready to relive the bleak moment. 'I fell while riding Tanterari in an earlier race. It was real head-over-heels stuff. I wasn't marked up but it didn't help. A heavy fall always takes its toll. I then went out on Polar Red. He's a good horse but he just took off a bit early and landed on top of the fence. I shot forward and I was left hanging on his head. If the horse goes down as well they usually protect you a little. That didn't happen this time. I took all the impact. It's the most dangerous kind of fall. And I've broken enough bones to know when I've broken something new. I thought, "Shit, I'm going to be out for a long while." But as I walked back to the weighing room it didn't seem so bad. They still rushed me to hospital, where they said I'd need an operation on my face. As soon as they start talking about operating that increases your time away from the track. But on Tuesday, even though the cheekbone had broken in three places, the surgeon decided to leave it alone. You can imagine how happy I was when he said that.'

McCoy's determinedly casual response can be traced back to the number of broken bones he has endured. 'I've broken my leg and my arm. I've shattered my collarbone. I've broken my shoulder. I've fractured vertebrae and my ankle. I should count up all the bones I've broken one day. But I would need to set aside a little time. I guess the hardest was when I broke my leg in Ireland in 1993. I was only eighteen. This mad horse, Kly Green, charged a rail. My left leg snapped. You could hear the sound, they tell me, a hundred yards away. I knew straight away the leg was gone. Bones were splintering through the jodhpurs. I just lay on that cold ground, moaning. Jim Bolger, the trainer, came over. He looked at me and said, "You're fucking soft." He was deadly serious and it probably did me a lot of good in the long run. It made me think about pain and not wanting to give in to it. Jim was a hard boy all right but he was a good trainer and someone a lot of young people could learn from. If you set your mind to it, you can stand anything.'

McCoy weighs a little over 10 stone for every race he enters. The will it takes to boil down to such an unnatural mark for a strong man who is broad-chested and, at 5ft 10in, far taller than most jockeys, is as eerie as it is perversely riveting.

'What have I eaten today?' McCoy said as he repeated the inevitable question. 'I actually haven't eaten much. I've had two pieces of toast.' It was just after 4 p.m. when McCoy totted up his intake for the day. He looked awfully pale, but he still smiled. 'The mouth's far too sore to eat. It's the one consolation to all this bother.'

Asked how much harm he might be doing to his body, the jockey nodded more seriously. 'I know it's physically not good for me. Taking so many bangs to the head is not good for me either. But racing always excites me and never frightens me. It's my life. So I don't begrudge the sacrifices or feel sorry for myself. But it is hard in the mornings when I have to lie in a scalding bath and then run in a sweat-suit or go to the sauna just to shift six or eight pounds. It's cruel. I'm turning thirty this year and so I can't do ten stone no more. My body is much more muscly and I'm far stronger. Getting down to ten stone three or four is very hard now. But that's what you have to weigh if you want the best rides.'

McCoy has long had the very best rides. Yet Martin Pipe has had, by his exacting standards, a patchy season. 'If a yard has a great year,' McCoy said, 'they pay the penalty the next because they're not well handicapped. But maybe our horses have not been the usual calibre recently. That's why I can't mess about too long with this injury. I have to hold on to the champion jockey position this year. But Richard is breathing down my neck. He works really hard and so it's going to be very tight this time. Beyond that, I would still love to eventually ride three hundred winners in a season. I don't know if it's possible. I used to ride a bit for Venetia Williams and Jonjo O'Neill but they've got their own jockeys now and so my potential winners have been cut. I managed two hundred and eighty-nine winners when I broke Sir Gordon Richards's record. That was the high point of my career because it had stood for fifty-five years. Now I've done two thousand career wins I'm already looking for the next two thousand. I feel I can go on at this rate for another nine or ten years. Easy. As long as I keep winning I can take all this other stuff – the weight and the broken bones and all that crap. I've just got to keep winning.'

McCoy was flying again, even if he had yet to leave for the airport. 'C'mon AP, you better get packing,' Fitzgerald chided soon after he arrived, having slipped the plaster cast from his broken arm as an exultant sign that he could be back in time for Cheltenham himself.

'Relax,' the previously twitchy McCoy said. 'I've got to get my photo taken.'

'Jesus,' Fitzgerald laughed. 'I was thinking no one would recognize us in Dubai and you're getting pictures of you as the Elephant Man splashed all over the papers.'

With things of beauty suddenly on his mind, and almost in a holiday mood, McCoy thought of his beloved Arsenal and asked, 'Did you see that first Reyes goal against Chelsea the other Sunday? Wasn't that just beautiful?' He turned his smashed-in face away from the racing on television and looked into the camera.

The two famous and battered jump jockeys arrived home last night. While they were away Johnson won five more races to cut McCoy's lead to two. This morning McCoy will meet Dr Robert Hencher, one of London's leading maxillofacial surgeons, to reassess the displacement in his fractured face. If, as McCoy fervently expects, a satisfied Hencher turns him over to Michael Turner, the Jockey Club's resident doctor, then he could ride again tomorrow or Wednesday. Sedgefield on a Tuesday afternoon in February or Doncaster on a cold Wednesday will have never looked more beautiful to Tony McCoy.

28 June 2004

MARTIN AMIS

Possession's all

I must have been the only fan on earth who thought (for a full hour) that the England team had flopped out even earlier than it did: to Croatia. They like their football just fine down here, or they do when Uruguay is playing – or were playing, and winning their two Olympic Golds and two World Cups (the national team is now pitifully weak).

These days they are far, far more savagely engaged by how Penarol did against Nacional than by anything achieved by their distant ancestors: the Spanish, the Italians, the Portuguese. When you catch any mention of 'Eurocopa' down here, you know you are dealing with an intellectual.

Still, the tournament is ebulliently and chaotically covered by Fox Sports (pronounced 'folks spwarts'), which chose, last Monday, to show France v Switzerland in precedence to the simultaneous fixture, England v Croatia. I kept the TV on, ready and warm, and could hear from several rooms away the demented commentator's minute-long 'Goooaaal!' and his crazed ditties about Zinedine Zidane and Thierry Henry.

I tiptoed in twice, early on in each half. During visit one, they briefly showed Croatia's first goal; during visit two, they briefly showed Croatia's second. And I thought: that's that. After the final whistle they stuck with the French celebrations and the same looped Adidas ad for about half an hour, while I submitted to the caustic hormones (familiar enough) of the failed jingo.

I was saying to myself: this is the punishment for the game against France. But I was also belatedly saying that the demeanour of the Croats, after their second strike, had not been the demeanour of a team that was now leading 2–0, or even

2–1. They would have been a wriggling heap of nudists; they would not have been hurrying back to the centre circle with the self-effacement of men who still had honest work to do.

Then Fox Sports flashed up the group placings: England with six points and a goal difference of 8–4. Then they flashed up the scoreline: Scholes (Scholes!), Rooney, Rooney, Lampard. Ten minutes later I sat back, with a bottle of Don Pascual, and feasted on the win. This, I submit, is the only bearable way of watching an England match, confident in the knowledge that, however hard they try, they can't possibly mess it up.

It was a genuinely charged performance, too, and the dynamo was the terrifying Wayne Rooney. When he smashed in his first goal, from that distance, from that angle, it was the way he shaped that stayed with you – like a gorilla, with fully demonstrative menace. Zidane twists, Henry glides; Rooney thunders. He is neither vicious nor undisciplined, but his is a game of applied violence. The sportsman he most resembles is not another footballer: it is the pre-decadent Mike Tyson. Behind Rooney, the midfield was for once as potent as it looks on paper. When the match was over it was possible to believe that the debacle against France had been survived, forgiven. Zidane in injury-time: that was just a nightmare. It never really happened.

But it did happen, and England v Portugal was, with variations, its grisly recurrence. When Owen scored in the third minute, the euphoria was soon qualified by the following intuition: with time added on, England were now going to spend an entire football match in frazzled defence, dropping back ever deeper, the beleaguerment solidified by ever-more paranoid substitutions. As Rooney limped off, after twenty-odd minutes, you felt you were complicit in an act of unilateral disarmament. But by now it was taking some doing not to notice a qualitative difference between the teams: the abysmal gulf in technique.

The days when an England player's first touch could often be mistaken for an attempted clearance or a wild shot on goal – those days are over. The deficit is not in individual skill, it is in collective skill; it is in the apparently cultural indifference to possession. In 2004, football is no longer a dribbling game, still less a long-ball game (and how many balls did we float to our two haring midgets up front?); it is a possession game. The 'clearance', as practised by England, is simply an anachronism. When an international defender heads it away, he heads it to a team-mate. When we 'clear' it, we just clear it, for two or three seconds.

After the match Eriksson talked of 'possession' as if he thought of it as foreign frippery – as if he had succumbed to the masochistic machismo that says: You didn't score that time, did you? Have another crack.

During the second half it was a full-time job not noticing what the chasing game does to a side's morale. Pass it to a team-mate? We couldn't even throw it to a team-mate. A Martian, looking on, would have wondered at the mysterious discrepancy: whenever the ball went into touch, it seemed that it could only be reintroduced to a player in a red shirt. Portugal's equalizer was both completely inevitable and richly deserved. And then the crouched supporter was left to believe that England, this booting, blocking, sliding, nutting, hacking behemoth, this hysterical combine-harvester, was about to transform itself into an instrument of attack.

That it did so was a great tribute to the real but fading virtues of passion and will. It granted us the ritual of losing the shootout. Beckham 'bravely' (i.e. vaingloriously) went first, and inspired his team by ballooning the kick without falling on his arse – which is what he did in Istanbul last October. (This time he blamed the penalty miss on the penalty spot, as, with infinite inanity, did Eriksson: 'I complained personally to the UEFA official responsible about the penalty spot.')

How, by the way, did it ever get about that Beckham was good at penalties? He utterly lacks the steel for it. Maybe Scholes has it – but Scholes was off, physically spent. And if such a thoroughbred is out of gas at this point in the summer then so is everybody else in the Premiership. As a first step, on even-numbered years every player in the England squad should be rested for ten games a season, by FA law.

As a second step, we must settle down to learning how to keep possession: how to retain the football. It is the best defence, it is the complete defence, as Brazil showed us in the quarter-finals of the last World Cup. The penalty shootout is a tawdry lottery, but any kind of win, for England, would have been a tawdry lottery, and would have meant the prolongation of illusion. Consider the statistics. For the main body of the match, Portugal have claim to twice as much possession, twice as many corners and half as many fouls. At this level, we're no good, and we have to start again.

5 July 2004

RICHARD WILLIAMS

Russian steel

No one could miss the salient features of the game that made Maria Sharapova the new Wimbledon ladies' champion on Saturday. The imposing serve, the unrelenting desire to hit the chalk with every drive and the urgent speed with which she covers the width of the baseline were there for all to see. Only in close-up, however, does the really telling detail reveal itself. Look at her fingers and you will see that, however radiant her smile, the nails of this seventeen-year-old Russian girl are bitten to the quick.

As she took the title from Serena Williams on Saturday afternoon, a lot of people woke up to the fact that Sharapova is the real thing. But her fingernails had already been telling the story. She may have a contract with a model agency but this is no would-be catwalk queen who fills the hours during rain delays by getting out her pots and brushes and giving herself a manicure. For all her considerable beauty, this is a young woman with the priorities that made champions of Maria Bueno, Billie Jean King and Steffi Graf.

Somewhere out there, someone – possibly Clive James, who once expressed a desire to be bathed in the sweat of Gabriela Sabatini – is already writing a poem about Sharapova. It might start with a description of the moment when she tosses the ball up to serve and, as it reaches it apogee, a line through her left arm and right leg forms a perfect perpendicular. Or with the intensity of her preparation for each point, in the way she walks back towards the stop-net, frowning as she pauses to refocus her thoughts before turning to face her opponent, eyes narrowed.

Beauty is to be found there, for sure, and in many dimensions, to be envied by those who had it in one form but not in others. What really marks out Maria Sharapova, however, is the sheer strength of her will, as the champion of 2002 and 2003 discovered when, having taken a pasting in the first set, she seemed to have fought back into a position from which her hat-trick might be completed.

Sharapova saw off the challenge, as she had seen off those of Ai Sugiyama and Lindsay Davenport in the preceding rounds. And of all the things the number thirteen seed said last week in response to a crescendo of media interest as she laid waste to the hopes of more experienced players, nothing resonated more profoundly than her answer to a question about spending time on the practice courts. 'I'm not interested in getting better,' she said. 'I just want to win matches.'

What an attitude to take on to the court. What a wonderful example of getting priorities straight. What a rebuke to those obsessed by the minutiae of the game. And she followed it up on Saturday when she was asked how she had beaten the defending champion.

'To tell you the truth,' she said, 'I don't know what happened in the match. I don't know how I won. I didn't think who I was playing. I was just concentrating on what I was going to do, just on myself. I knew that the power was within me and that, if I put my mind to something, I would do it. That's what I thought about the whole match.' She had not studied Williams's early matches, she said. 'I didn't watch her play throughout these two weeks. I did not have a big tactic going into this match. I was just there to play my game and figure out a way to win and figure out what I needed to do just to get used to her game a little bit. Did that pretty fast.'

Which is not to suggest that the technicalities of the game lie beyond her scope of interest. No one who has spent the bulk of childhood at Nick Bollettieri's tennis academy could be less than well grounded in the mechanical aspects of the game. In Sharapova's case it extends to a constructive awareness of her own deficiencies.

'I think my opponents have always considered my forehand to be my weakness,' she said. 'That's what I found out. But thanks to those opponents, my forehand's getting a lot better.'

It was good enough on Saturday to cause serious embarrassment to Williams, who glimpsed a first break point at 30-40 in the second game of the second set but then found herself sprawling in the dust beyond the baseline. Chasing a deep crosscourt forehand at the end of a long rally in which she had been pulled from side to side and lured fore and aft by the guile and power of Sharapova's driving from both wings, finally one attempt to apply the brakes and shift her weight had proved too much.

In a way this was the final Wimbledon might have enjoyed in 2002 and 2003, had it not been for injuries and the fact that the Williams sisters find the business of playing against each other in a big match so emotionally demanding as to ruin the competitive spectacle.

Serena responded quickly to a suggestion that the experience of playing Sharapova on Saturday resembled that of competing against her own sister. 'Yes, it was, actually,' she said. 'Like Venus, she has a good reach and a good serve. And today she had a really good serve.'

But Sharapova had a great deal more than that to offer. For a teenager who giggles a lot and likes to go shopping, she demonstrated a will to win that was nothing less than astonishing. As the match went on it became like an invisible second skin. Afterwards she was asked whether she had ever needed to work on the mental side of her game.

'It's always been there,' she replied. 'I've always wanted to compete and I've always wanted to win.'

And no coach had ever suggested that she needed to work on it?

'Never,' she said, and smiled again.

19 August 2004

STEPHEN MOSS

A new hero

Today, the Oval Test match begins. Normally, apart from a few Thermos-toting obsessives from Dorking intent on getting to the Harleyford Road early for the 10.30 a.m. start, that would mean little. In the week that the Olympic flame was ignited and the Premiership kicked off, it should mean nothing: a sideshow in the global sporting funfair. But, happily, this year is different. England are winning, are playing exuberant cricket and have found a new superstar: Andrew 'Freddie' Flintoff, the man who has achieved what appeared to be impossible and made cricket sexy again.

Since Ian Botham retired more than a decade ago, England have been looking for a new hero. The phrase 'the next Ian Botham' has been hung around a succession of players' necks and gripped so tightly that they were strangled. David Capel, Derek Pringle, Ronnie Irani. Remember them? Thought not. But Flintoff, after a stuttering start, is living up to the hype. Now twenty-seven, he has matured into a destructive batsman who can play long innings, a fiery fast bowler who can disconcert the opposition (witness the way he bounced out the great Brian Lara on Sunday), and a brilliant slip catcher. He is three players in one, the talisman of an increasingly confident team, the hope for the Ashes clash that will dominate next summer.

More than that, Flintoff is a player who transcends his sport, one of those rare talents who can attract new converts. Cricket can sometimes seem a trifle slow: Groucho Marx was once taken to Lord's to see a match and, after an hour's play, turned to his host and asked when it was going to start. A Test match can last thirty hours – twice as long as Wagner's *Ring* cycle. But Flintoff overcomes the prejudice against a long, slow, meandering game that, even after five days (or ten days in the case of one famous Test in South Africa in 1939), can still end in a draw. He is the sport's great hope for a golden future.

Flintoff has been called a *'Boy's Own* hero', and never was the phrase more appropriate. First, there is the utter simplicity of his approach. When he bats, his principal desire is to hit the ball as hard and as far as possible. He has already struck almost fifty sixes in Test matches and there is no doubt that he will end up as the six-hitting record-holder. Babe Freddie! When he arrives at the crease, his adoring fans start baying for him to smash the ball over the ropes. He has even said that sometimes this puts too much pressure on him, forcing him into wanton aggression too early in his innings. But mostly, he does it anyway: it's the way he plays.

There was a very Freddie moment at the Birmingham Test match earlier this month when he launched a six into the upper tier of a stand (while making an extraordinary, match-winning 167). Who should be under the ball but his father, Colin? Dad promptly spilled the catch, for which Flintoff junior gave him a fearful ribbing in his end-of-play interview with Channel 4. Which is the other key point about Flintoff: he is funny, unaffected, unchanged by stardom. He is still the big, brawny boy from Preston who likes a pint and a laugh, and most of all loves the game of cricket.

Flintoff is a cricketing Alf Tupper. For those readers who didn't read *Victor* comic circa 1967, Tupper ('the Tough of the Track') was a loveable but tenacious Brit who worked as a welder, lived on fish and chips, and invariably won gold for his country, beating all manner of dodgy Russians, egotistical Americans and Vorsprung durch Technik Germans. It was not enough to win: the winner had to be simple, straightforward, approachable and level-headed, an ordinary bloke like you or me. Win the 1500m? Anyone could do it – just eat an extra portion of cod.

Now, of course, it's not cod you have to eat to win gold, but a cocktail of designer drugs dreamed up in California. And Roy of the Rovers is earning £100,000 a week, shagging his way around the fleshpots of Melchester and playing in a team dominated by footballing mercenaries with unpronounceable names.

Cricket hasn't quite succumbed to the twenty-first century, thank God. The top players do dye their hair, drive sports cars and wear designer sunglasses while they bowl, but they do not indulge in the worst excesses of the modern sportsman. Their saving grace is that they spend so long on the field that they don't have the time to prop up bars or get into fights at nightclubs.

Cricket is still played by recognizable human beings. Flintoff is an ordinary genius. *Wisden*, which this year named him as one of its five cricketers of the year, called him 'a farmhand delighting in the coconut shy'. He brings the characteristics of the village green – a violent swing of the bat, uncomplicated fast bowling, laughter and a sense of well-being – to the Test arena. In an age of paranoia and doubt, Flintoff is liberating, a cold beer on a hot day. If a Test match is, indeed, a sporting *Ring* cycle, Flintoff is our Siegfried: innocent, fearless, the superhuman shaper of events.

Flintoff has only come of age as a cricketer in the past eighteen months. He made his debut for England in 1998, but struggled with both bat and ball. He was young, callow, unfit and intimidated by the big names in the England team. His most memorable early moment was when a TV camera panned across the dressing room and spotted a page-three photo in his corner. He was a boy in a man's world.

As a youngster, because he was big and immensely powerful, he always played in teams a couple of years above his age group. He still was – and he knew it. After one decent performance against Zimbabwe, he gave himself a public pat on the back. 'All right for a fat lad,' he said. The humour, self-deprecation and sense of perspective have always been there, in the bad times as well as the good. You only have to see Flintoff interviewed – hands in pockets, smiling, unfazed by the fact that he has just slayed another dragon – to sense that he is rooted. He is unlikely ever to use the third person, as sportsmen who get above themselves are sometimes wont to do.

In those first years as an England player, Flintoff's 'normality' was part of the problem: he was too keen on lager and pizzas, not working hard enough at his game. 'Fat Freddie' was becoming a joke. His manager, 'Chubby' Chandler, and former Lancashire team-mate Neil Fairbrother read the riot act: he was wasting his talent, was in danger of throwing his career away. He got the message, cut down on the lagers, lost a couple of stone, even took up Pilates to strengthen his bad back.

This year he has been transformed. His career statistics are still not exceptional: almost 2,000 runs, averaging 32.3 per innings; 85 wickets at a cost of 37.15 runs per wicket. As averages go, they are very average. But this year, he has been phenomenal: a batting average of 55.5 and 30 wickets at 25. Even those figures do not tell the whole story: it is the way he makes his runs, the fire with which he bowls, his playful swagger when he fields. He makes everything seem possible. His team-mates now keep saying they feel they can win from any position, no matter how bleak. They have self-belief. Flintoff is their alchemist.

On Monday, it was Flintoff who was at the wicket when England took an unassailable 3–0 lead in the Test series. He had batted sensibly for a couple of hours; then, with victory in sight, he wound himself up and sent the ball into the stratosphere for two huge sixes (where was his father?). To show that he was not just a biffer, he finished the match with a delicate late cut and Old Trafford went wild. A ground on the final day of a Test is often a funereal place: but on this occasion 14,000 had come to celebrate England's new messiah and his team progressing to the promised land. The other Old Trafford is only half a mile away, but for once it was cricket that was getting the attention.

His nickname – now universally used except by his mother and his wife-to-be Rachael, who for the moment are sticking with Andrew – was coined by John Stanworth, the coach of the Lancashire second XI. When the strapping fifteen-year-old turned up one day, Stanworth shouted, 'It's Fred Flintstone.' It seemed perfect for a larger-than-life figure who would, before the fitness regime, have loved nothing better than to tuck into a dinosaur-burger with extra cheese.

The most endearing facet of Flintoff's character is that he is so obviously a team man. His hundred for England in a hopelessly lost cause against South

Africa at Lord's last year meant little to him; he could barely bring himself to acknowledge the applause when he was eventually dismissed.

Five years ago, the obituarists were sharpening their pens. English cricket appeared to be in its death throes as a national game. 'The script for English cricket now seems to be more like the Book of Job than anything else,' wrote *Wisden* editor Matthew Engel in the 2000 edition of the famous almanack. 'The English crisis is now the greatest crisis in world cricket.' The England team were the worst in the world. Football – both the sport and the soap opera – dominated the media, filled the sports pages to bursting point, was in danger of creating what Engel called a sporting 'monoculture'. County attendances were pathetic (Derbyshire had just over a thousand members, of which sixteen were dogs). There was less and less cricket being played in schools, especially state schools. You rarely saw cricket being played in the streets, as you once had.

Cricket was deemed slow, irrelevant, meandering; a nineteenth-century game that offered little to the slick new twenty-first. Neville Cardus's 'background music to an English summer' seemed to have no place in the age of rap. It was the game of country vicars and posh blokes with pipes and tweed suits: E. W. Swanton, CMJ, Blowers, a hangover from the world of squires and blacksmiths. It was history. And then along came Freddie.

It would be foolish to ascribe the rebirth of English cricket to one man. Coach Duncan Fletcher must take much credit; ditto former captain Nasser Hussain, whose Taliban-like sense of discipline made England competitive again. Michael Vaughan, the current captain, with his choirboy face and endearing tendency to drop easy catches, is allowing his team to play joyous, uninhibited cricket. Ray Illingworth and the hard-bitten Yorkshire old-timers must wonder what's going on out there.

But it is Flintoff who is the symbol of the game's extraordinary renaissance. When he struck the winning runs to wrap up the series win against the West Indies, it was impossible not to share the collective pleasure. Middle-aged men threw their Thermos flasks in the air; young women, abjuring the joys of small-bore shooting on TV, jigged; the many children at Old Trafford dreamed, 'That could be me.' Alf Tupper had triumphed. It is always said of the great cricketing entertainers that they empty bars. How, these days, the breweries must fear Freddie Flintoff.

2 August 2004

DONALD McRAE

Ambitious tilt

'A-T-H-E-N-S,' Michael Phelps says quietly as he spells out the name of the ancient city he has carried inside himself for so long. The 6ft 4in American swimmer with the size 14 feet and the even bigger hope of becoming the sensation of the 2004 Olympic Games pauses dramatically. He can remember all the moments when he has stared at those same six letters.

'Back in the winter, at 5.30 a.m., when I didn't want to get up and train on some cold and dark morning I'd still make myself snap on the light and look inside my swimming cap. "Athens" is stitched on the inside. I'd get up then. I'd grab my bag and head for the pool. I've been doing that 365 days – year after year. I can't remember the last day I didn't train. Thanksgiving, Christmas Day, New Year's Day. I haven't missed one of 'em for years. And every single day I got that word, Athens, running right round my head.'

A week on Saturday, on the first day of Olympic competition, Phelps will take to the pool in Athens and begin his outrageously ambitious tilt at sporting history. Marketing men, merchandisers, sponsors and television executives around the world are all lurking and smacking their greedy chops at the prospect of an amiable and strangely unspoiled nineteen-year-old matching their voracity as he tries to swim down the record seven gold medals Mark Spitz won at the 1972 games in Munich. Speedo has guaranteed Phelps a cool and instant $1m if he fulfils the seven-gold fantasy.

Last month, having dominated the US trials, Phelps confirmed that he will swim the butterfly over 100m and 200m, the 200m and 400m individual medleys and the 200m freestyle in Athens. He also hopes to feature in three American relays, which means that Phelps could swim twenty races in eight days. There is, after all, another Olympic record to chase. In the 1980 Moscow games, the Russian gymnast Aleksandr Dityatin won three gold medals, four silvers and a bronze. Eight medals of different colours may be more plausible than seven straight golds but even this target is the product of hype rather than a reflection of Phelps's own calm expectations.

'The whole seven-gold deal was between Speedo and my agent. They agreed it. If I bring back only one gold people are going to say it's a disappointment. But not too many of them own an Olympic gold medal so if I get one I'm going to be happy. That's the important one – the first gold. I'm just focusing on that for now. After that, the best thing is to keep my options open. I don't want to put a limit on anything. The more you dream the more you achieve. So on the inside I'm real pumped about Athens and what might happen – but I try not to think about it too much. I leave that to everyone else.'

While the statistical possibilities are intriguing, Phelps himself emerges as the real story. He comes from a broken home in Baltimore, a gritty redbrick and blue-collar city more usually associated with a downbeat cop series like *Homicide* than the sunlit pools of California which the moustached and bronzed Spitz represented. His father, Fred, a policeman, and his mother, Debbie, a schoolteacher, separated when he was only seven.

Echoes of a traumatic past are heard in his sister Whitney's memories that, on her way to being picked for the US swim team at the age of fourteen in 1994, she used the pool as a refuge from trouble at home: 'I didn't have to listen to people yelling. It was my escape. I took a lot of anger and beat it out – just me and the bottom of the pool.'

Phelps, meanwhile, says, 'I feel most at home in the water. I disappear. That's where I belong.'

Phelps and his father apparently argued bitterly just before last year's world championship in Barcelona. Fred Phelps, supposedly, missed his son's high school graduation party after he had been told that two complimentary tickets to Spain were going to his estranged wife and eldest daughter, Hilary. The spat, since resolved according to Phelps, did not diminish his astonishing performance in Barcelona – where he won four gold medals and smashed five world records in a week, proving that, for all the promotional bluster, Phelps has an almost eerie ability to block out distractions. His coach, Bob Bowman, has spoken of the need sometimes to 'physically shake' the swimmer to drag him out of a trance-like reverie just before a big race.

'I was in a zone in Barcelona,' Phelps agrees when he recalls breaking two world records in the space of forty-five minutes. 'That night was very big. I went into it with the clear aim of becoming the first man to set two world records in two different events on the same night. When it happened it was extremely exciting. It showed that it's possible to shoot for something and accomplish it – but I was so tired at the end I could hardly climb out of the pool. Athens is going to be even more physically and mentally draining.'

A psychological battle has been brewing between Phelps and Ian Thorpe – the world's best swimmer for so long. In Barcelona they raced each other only in Phelps's favoured 200m medley. He cruised away from Thorpe in an imposing swim. More tellingly, Phelps won one more gold than the trio picked up by the Australian.

Four years ago, at the Sydney Olympics, the Thorpedo was unstoppable. He won three golds while the fifteen-year-old Phelps finished fifth in the 200m butterfly final. 'It was a different time. Thorpe was incredible while I was just proud to have made the US team. But I ended up disappointed because I wanted a medal. It was a learning experience – my first international meet and my first time out of America. When I got back to school in Baltimore no one asked me about the Olympics. Everybody just asked whether I'd seen any kangaroos hopping around or koala bears up in the trees. I told them Australia was the same as America – except the people were nicer.'

The Australians have since become more vitriolic. 'Look,' said Don Talbot, the Australian swimming coach in Barcelona last year, 'I don't wish to denigrate Michael Phelps – he's a great talent – but those who talk about him in terms of being as great as Ian must be out of their minds.'

Thorpe himself dismisses Phelps's pursuit of a mythic seven gold medals in Athens by insisting, 'It's unattainable for me and it's unattainable for anyone.'

Phelps counters: 'He's saying it's impossible for him. That's all. I'm trying something for me. In Barcelona I was honoured to have the chance to race against him. He's mainly a freestyle swimmer while my strength's in the butterfly and medley. But he took me on in one of my events. I won that time but in Athens I'm going to do something I've always wanted to do – swim freestyle against Thorpe.'

When Phelps races the imperious Thorpe towards the end of his eight-day marathon in Athens he will almost certainly be exhausted. He might have picked up three of a likely four gold-medal haul by then but he will struggle in Thorpe's best event – especially as another Australian, Grant Hackett, and the Dutch world champion Pieter van Hoogenband will also push him hard:

'The way I look at it, this is an opportunity for me to swim in probably the fastest 200 free in history. I'm going to be, at the very least, competitive. It's going to be some race.'

The Thorpe–Phelps stand-off will almost certainly be billed as the swim of the games – and perhaps even the clash of the whole Olympics. Thorpe, whom Phelps replaced as the world's swimmer of the year in 2003, will be desperate to assert his authority over the aspiring king of the Olympic pool.

Phelps, for now, is happy to highlight the difference between their current lives. While Thorpe is used to personal invites from Tom Cruise and Giorgio Armani to movie premieres or fashion shows, Phelps lives a more anonymous life. Asked whether he would choose to strut down the red carpet with Nicole Kidman on his arm or simply put another woofer in his beloved old Cadillac, Phelps is amusingly evasive. 'I dunno. Tough one. Seriously. I'm used to just hanging out at my mom's and fooling around with my car. I can walk around downtown Baltimore very easily. It sometimes seems as if no one knows who the hell I am. I hardly ever get stopped in public. In a way it's good because I can live my life the way I want. But in another way it's kinda disappointing because there's a total lack of recognition for swimming. I think it's a real pity because we have so many talented American swimmers and they never get the same publicity Thorpe is given in Australia – where swimming is taken more seriously than in any other country.'

Athens will probably change everything – and the signs are already there with the American money men putting him and Cindy Crawford together on stage last month as he announced his Olympic schedule – but for now Phelps remains stimulating and engaging company. It's hard not to like a guy who can eat eight fried eggs, eight slices of toast and a whole melon for breakfast and then, with barely a burp, consider the cultural clash embedded in his contrasting passion for gangsta rap and swimming. How many other swimmers in the relentlessly white pool can talk cogently about the machine-gun rapper Twista or name-check Notorious B.I.G.'s 'Ready to Die' as the bleak inspiration which motivates them during his daily 10-mile thrash through the water? 'I just like the sound of hip hop,' Phelps says. 'I love Jay-Z and 50 Cent and I'm a huge Biggie [Smalls] fan. I listen to rap on the way to practice and whatever I've been playing just loops through my head as I swim.'

During the last month 'Overnight Celebrity' by Twista has filled Phelps's head more than any other track. It seems a curiously appropriate ditty by a warp-speed rapper, the fastest mouth in the business for the fastest kid in the water. While Phelps has been a swim-star for years, a series of glittering performances in Athens will turn him into a mass-market celebrity.

'Away from the Olympics I've got a pretty quiet life,' he confesses. 'It's kinda boring. I haven't got a girlfriend and I can't do the kind of things all my friends are doing as college students. I swim, listen to hip hop and work on my car. But, in my opinion, that's still a pretty good life. I don't know whether I'd want to trade it for anything.'

His ambition as a great swimmer, however, will transform his life later this month. He might not win the impossible seven but Phelps, the flying Twista of the pool with a giant 6ft 7in armspan, will cut an irresistible figure in Athens. And, afterwards, Cindy Crawford will probably want to see him again. But she'd better be ready to hang out in Baltimore where Michael Phelps, hopefully, will still eat eight fried eggs for breakfast and listen to Biggie Smalls in his old Cadillac while, in true bling bling style, he counts the gold medals hanging round his neck.

Phelps won eight medals, six of them gold. Thorpe won four, two of them gold. Phelps will have another opportunity to win Speedo's one million dollars in Beijing in 2008.

LOSSES

He can't say sorry

How wrong does a man have to be before he will apologise of his own volition? My boyfriend has mucked up more travel plans, broken more household objects, misrecorded more TV programmes, burned more food and created more difficulties for more people through his thoughtlessness and inefficiency than me and my female friends have altogether in our entire lives. "Oh, sorry – that was my fault." Can he be trained (not just to say it, but to *feel* it) or should I just break up with him now? *Name and address withheld*

Sounds like a pretty good ploy to me to avoid ever being lumbered with travel plans and cooking. However if you want him to say sorry, then just ask him to. If he refuses, ask him why he refuses. If he won't tell you, say, "Sorry, Goodbye." It amazes me that you are so relaxed about his clumsiness, and yet so wound up about an apology – but there, who can ever fathom the female mind?

From Ann Widdecombe's G2 Advice Column

7 July 2004

JESS CARTNER-MORLEY

Haute couture

When Yves Saint Laurent retired, his business partner, Pierre Bergé, predicted that haute couture, the most expensive and exclusive tier of fashion, where dresses are handmade and cost upwards of £10,000, would die without him. His words, dismissed at the time as sour grapes, now seem prophetic.

Just eighteen months after Saint Laurent's last show, the Paris couture season, which began yesterday, has dwindled from a grand week to a scant two-and-a-half days. Versace, Givenchy and Ungaro are all notable for their absence this season; Balmain, Nina Ricci, Paco Rabanne and Louis Feraud had already bowed out. The Japanese designer Hanae Mori, seventy-eight, has announced that her show tomorrow night will be her last and that her couture line will then close; it is rumoured that Valentino, who is seventy-two and has no obvious successor, may bow out in the near future. And like a rat deserting a sinking ship, Yohji Yamamoto, who in recent years has piggybacked the haute couture season, taking advantage of the presence of the international media in Paris to display his ready-to-wear line, has switched the date of his show from this week to October, and the better-attended ready-to-wear shows. The couture businesses of lauded designers including Christian Lacroix and Jean-Paul Gaultier – the man hailed as the successor to Saint Laurent, and who now holds his prestigious closing slot – are known to be under increasing financial pressure.

Old-fashioned is perhaps the politest way to describe haute couture. Many prefer archaic. Announcing his decision to quit, the designer Emanuel Ungaro, a great couturier who trained under Cristóbal Balenciaga, declared that haute couture 'no longer answers, as before, to the tastes of contemporary women'. Price tags are at least ten times that of Bond Street designer labels; each piece requires a number of fittings and takes several months to make. No change to traditional dressmaking methods is countenanced – zips, for example, are banned. There are, at a generous estimate, only 300 women in the world who buy couture clothes, and few of those are young.

However, it would be premature to declare couture dead as long as John Galliano, who yesterday presented his haute couture collection for Christian Dior, is on the scene. Over a thousand people yesterday packed a marquee in the Bois de Boulogne to watch an electrifying bootleg of styles: pneumatic corsets, inspired by Zsa Zsa Gabor and the pin-up girls of the 1950s, ermines, velvets and plush silks, reminiscent of traditional royal portraits, and intricately handpainted and embroidered with designs stimulated by classic Sèvres porcelain and Fabergé eggs. It is hard to envisage Oprah Winfrey, or any of the other high-achieving modern women in front row, wearing a Wedgwood blue ballgown, which combined the ultra feminine bustiness of *Dangerous Liaisons* with stately, billowing Henry VIII cloaks.

But no matter – Sidney Toledano, CEO of Christian Dior, recently told *Le Figaro* that the purpose of the Dior couture shows, which cost the company €2m (£1.3m) each season, are 'to stamp our mark on the media'; the shows are attended by 180 photographers and images are beamed around the world. He compares couture week, a small event with a global profile, to the Cannes film festival.

Undoubtedly, haute couture currently enjoys vast publicity. The current cover of *American Vogue* shows Nicole Kidman wearing Christian Lacroix haute couture, and it has become a staple of the red carpet, favoured for its uniqueness by actresses who are petrified of being cheated of publicity because they are wearing the same dress as a colleague or a rival. Chanel haute couture has become a popular choice at the Oscars, and was worn at Cannes by Diane Kruger at the premiere of *Troy*, in which she played Helen, the most beautiful woman in the world.

Donald Potard, president of Jean-Paul Gaultier, has tentatively suggested a way to modernize and so rescue haute couture. He has floated the idea of a halfway house between couture and ready-to-wear – outfits would be displayed in stores (which haute couture is not) but then be made to order, albeit with one fitting rather than three or four.

A similar 'hybrid' idea is being considered at the house of Emanuel Ungaro. This is not a solution that will please the purists but it may be the only way to keep couture alive.

29 March 2004

JOHN VIDAL

Apples

Donkey Orchard on the edge of Kingsbury Episcopi in Somerset has been in Rodney Male's family for almost two hundred years and the two-hectare field of ancient cider apple trees, with evocative names such as Old Morgan Sweets, Kingston Black and Newton Wonders, would in many countries be classed as a national treasure. The orchard's crooked, hollow-trunked trees have great bushes of mistletoe in their high branches and many house jackdaws, woodpeckers and rooks. Lambs and ponies graze under the trees, which, in a few weeks' time, will be a blaze of soft pink and white blossoms.

But the exquisite old English orchard, celebrated since Celtic times and promoted by modern governments and tourist boards, is under a threat that some rank as the ecological equivalent of the dissolution of the monasteries. This autumn hundreds of orchard owners around Britain will reluctantly call in contractors to grub up and burn their trees. Donkey Orchard will fall, so will its only slightly less venerable neighbours, Boar's Field and Orchard Anne.

Mr Male and the other growers fully appreciate the environmental, cultural and landscape value of their trees but say they have no option because of the government's proposed farm payment scheme. If felled before 1 January, orchards will be classed as 'farmland' and be worth an automatic yearly £340 a hectare, in perpetuity; but any left standing will be worth no more than the land value and, crucially, will not be considered for farm payments.

'I can't afford not to rip them out,' said Mr Male, whose great-grandfather planted Donkey Orchard in the early 1800s. 'Just one apple tree in a field may class it as an orchard, and that will mean no payment, ever. People like me will clear out all the old, less productive orchards. Plenty are thinking of it. We're obviously not going to risk keeping them.'

The scheme, claimed by the Department for Environment, Food and Rural Affairs (DEFRA) to reward environmental good practice rather than production, will be paid according to acreage in England. But although people growing sugar beet, potato and asparagus – crops with no great environmental benefit – will be rewarded, uniquely in Europe Britain has chosen to exclude orchards. Apple, plum and cherry growers, who have never received state subsidies, say they are less worried about the acreage payments than the loss in capital value of their farms and smallholdings.

'We will see the biggest bonfires since foot and mouth disease, only they'll smell better,' said John Thatcher, who runs Thatchers' cider works in Shepton Mallet and buys in thousands of tonnes of apples a year.

Julian Temperley, owner of 150 acres (60 hectares) of traditional cider apple orchards and Britain's largest cider distillery, in Kingsbury Episcopi, said, 'What's the government got against old orchards? This is going to be an environmental, landscape and wildlife disaster.'

Simon Russell, spokesman for the National Association of Cider Makers and Matthew Clark's, Britain's second largest commercial cider makers, said, 'There is a real risk that people with older orchards will now grub them up.'

The potential loss of the old orchards will add to the vertiginous decline of fruit growing in Britain over the past fifty years. From an estimated 80,000 hectares given over to orchards in 1945, there are now just 20,000 left and perhaps 1,000 to 2,000 hectares of traditionally managed ones grazed by animals for six months of the year.

In the past five years, according to DEFRA, more than 10 per cent of all British orchards have been lost. From 1,500 registered apple and pear growers in 1987, there are now just 500. Counties such as Essex, Cornwall and Kent – the latter once known as the 'garden of England' for its orchards – have lost up to 90 per cent of their fruit trees. At least 60 per cent of all orchards were lost in the past thirty years largely because supermarkets preferred to buy just one or two varieties in bulk from France, the US and New Zealand.

'The price of apples has hardly risen in ten years. There are now just five commercial apple farms left in the whole south-west,' said William Hebditch, of New Cross Farm in South Petherton, Somerset.

The loss of one old orchard can mean the extinction of an apple variety, said Sue Clifford, of Common Ground. 'You don't just lose trees. You lose the recipes, the songs, the work, the festivals, the landscape, and all the wisdom gathered over generations of how you grow them.'

The apple is Britain's national fruit. The Celts worshipped it, Glastonbury was called Avalon, 'the Isle of Apples', every cottage had a tree or two, and for

12 May 2004 Chancellor Gordon Brown at the Foreign Office before giving a speech about competitiveness in the enlarged EU. (Dan Chung)

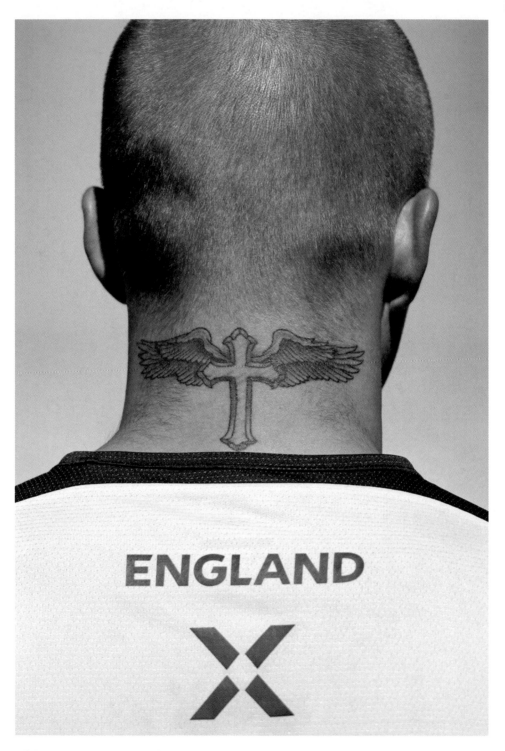

12 June 2004 David Beckham displays his latest tattoo – a cross on the back of his neck – as he trains in Coimbra ahead of the game tomorrow. (Dan Chung)

29 May 2004 Melvyn Bragg at the Guardian Hay Festival, 2004, Hay on Wye. (David Levene)

5 April 2004 Ken Livingstone, mayor of London. (Sean Smith)

generations farmworkers were paid in cider. Britain's national apple register lists more than 6,000 varieties of English apples, some, it is thought, local to just a single parish or even a farm, and all developed to grow well in particular soil conditions. But according to a Friends of the Earth survey, only 38 per cent of the apples sold last year in Tesco and Asda, the country's biggest chains, were British, while convenience stores scored lower, with 27 per cent.

'Buyers want lorry-loads of the same product, the same size, same price, week in, week out, which, with our traditional English varieties, is very difficult to do,' said John Breach, chairman of the British Independent Fruit Growers Association.

Mr Temperley thinks it is not too late to alter the payment scheme and avoid felling. 'Safeguarding the orchards would cost perhaps a million pounds, about 0.01 per cent of the total agriculture package. I can point to fifty acres near Kingsbury alone which will be felled this autumn – the most traditional orchards left in Britain. They harbour wildlife, give employment and are far more interesting in every way than grassland. The county will be a poorer place without them.'

Yesterday the government said it was taking the issue up with the European Commission. 'We are aware of the concerns and are in discussion with the Commission and with fruit growers,' said a spokesman for DEFRA.

27 December 2003

PAUL WEBSTER

Cézanne's hills

Under a sky full of sleet above a dull, brown stretch of the Seine, an effort of imagination is needed to link the hillside above this village west of Paris with some of the most colourful works of the impressionist painter Paul Cézanne.

From next year, it could be even more difficult to make the connection after a move by the local council to remove rows of chestnut trees and build seventy-eight houses on a skyline that the Aix-en-Provence painter immortalized in his *Le Coteau de Medan* – the steeply rising riverbank above the village, which attracts thousands of art lovers.

While it is an exaggeration to claim, as some locals do, that the low, curving hill on the road to Claude Monet's Giverny is the Île-de-France's answer to Aix's Mont Sainte-Victoire, views of the village are as recognizable today from the opposite bank of the Seine as they were when Cézanne visited his childhood friend Émile Zola 120 years ago.

Zola, like his fellow novelist Victor Hugo, was an obsessive photographer and left behind his own shots of Medan from the spot on the right bank where Cézanne placed his easel during regular visits. Zola's house, with its statue of the creator of the Rougon-Macquart dynasty, is the most visited site in a village of 1,480 people which has preserved the tranquil atmosphere treasured by the impressionists, most of whose works were painted along the Seine as far away as

Rouen and Le Havre, although an increasing amount of tourist river traffic stops offshore from Medan to admire Cézanne's perspectives. Inevitably, the plan to build upmarket housing has caused a national row unlikely to end whatever the conclusions of a public inquiry, which finished on Christmas Eve. Those against include Pierre Bergé, the co-founder of Yves Saint Laurent's fashion empire, who heads an association dedicated to Zola's works. He has promised to use his fortune to oust the right-wing mayor, Serge Goblet, if permission is given to change the skyline, and has strong support in the village led by Jean-Pierre Aubin de Malicorne, who heads an association called the Real Friends of Medan.

'This site is as precious to us as Sainte-Victoire is to the people of Aix,' he said, recalling that the picturesque reputation had attracted many writers and artists, including the Nobel prize-winner Maurice Maeterlinck, who settled there. 'It is a wonderful viewpoint to admire the Seine and the colourful barge traffic heading to and from Paris. The river cruise traffic is growing rapidly and will one day be as important as that on the Rhine. Those houses are going to take away the charm from an internationally known landscape.'

Defenders of the Cézanne legacy include a Canadian airline pilot, Silvere Le Blond, Zola's great-great-grandson, but if the municipal elections of two years ago are anything to go by, nearly two-thirds of the village backs the mayor and wants the new houses to generate more revenue through taxes and to boost local traders.

Mayor Goblet said he would make no comment until the public inquiry made its report to the environment ministry, which will decide whether the Coteau de Medan merits permanent protection. But in the past, he has said that, despite claims of 'cultural sabotage', it was impractical to list every site painted by the impressionists because their mark can be found in any number of communes situated among the forests and hills bordering the Seine.

27 November 2003

RICHARD WRAY

Swordmakers

Despite the success of the *Lord of the Rings* films and the swashbuckling epic *Pirates of the Caribbean*, British householders no longer want to know the location of their nearest swordmaker. They are more likely to want to find a local lifestyle guru or laser eye surgery, according to the compilers of the latest Yellow Pages classified directory.

Although perhaps not as highbrow an indication of cultural change as the introduction of new words into the Oxford English Dictionary, the creation of new categories in the country's largest telephone directory does highlight the increasingly hectic lifestyles people now lead.

Included in the new Yellow Pages, which will start appearing on people's doorsteps towards the end of the year, will be babysitters, lifestyle management and concierge services, supermarket home delivery services and home stagers –

the latter category helps homeowners ready their property for sale, rather like having a personal version of Carol Smillie. If the local lifestyle guru is unable to alleviate the stresses and strains of modern living, help is at hand in the new category of convents and monasteries. Categories deemed too antiquated for the new directories, which list 1.9 million businesses, include links with the past such as manufacturers of anchors and bellows, tin smiths and swordmakers.

Also on the way out are several hangovers from the fashions of the 1970s and 1980s. Belt and suspender manufacturers obviously no longer warrant the attention they received during the eighties, when red-braced yuppies ruled London's Square Mile, while caravan manufacturers also failed to make the cut. Some rather specialist categories such as feather and down suppliers and butterfly farms and breeders are also being axed, to be replaced by laser eye surgery and mobile beauty therapists.

Used car dealers are only now being given their own category. They will sit side by side with another new category – car recycling centres.

17 October 2003

FRANCIS SPUFFORD

Concorde

Long before the dawn of real aviation, Leonardo da Vinci started to speculate about uses for the flying machines that were taking shape in his imagination. With them, he thought, people might 'seek snow on the mountain tops and bring it to the city to spread on the sweltering streets in summer'. Out of the brazen August sky over Florence, cool flakes from the Alps might flutter down; passers-by sweating in Renaissance Rome might lift their faces to be refreshed. It was an idea that became grimly ironic from almost the moment that flight became practical at the beginning of the twentieth century. As soon as they were invented, planes were pressed into service to kill city dwellers, rather than to refresh them. Out of the sky over Guernica, over Dresden, over Hanoi, high explosives rained.

But from time to time, in particular projects, flying has eluded the irony in Leonardo's dream, and served the civil delight of which he first thought. Concorde is one of those projects. It is a marvel, a genuine exercise in the technological sublime. British Airways staff call it 'The Rocket', and building it was indeed the European equivalent of the Apollo programme, a gasp-inducing, consciously grand undertaking that changed the sense, in those who contemplated it, of what human beings were capable of.

When Britain and France agreed to build Concorde in 1962, no one knew how to design a supersonic passenger plane. Of course there were proven military jets that flew at Mach 2, but those were one-seat aerial hotrods in which a fit young man could hurl himself around the sky for a couple of hours, followed by days, if not weeks, of maintenance work on the aircraft. A smooth ride, a commercial level of fuel economy, an aircraft reliable day after day: these were all mysteries to be solved from scratch.

An effort of applied futurism produced a plane that handled like no other, soared to the stratosphere like no other and was sculpted like no other, so that for the three decades Concorde has flown, it has continued to look more modern than anything else on an airport runway. As it retires, it still looks as if a crack has opened in the fabric of the universe and a message from tomorrow has been poked through. Only it is clear now that the tomorrow in question was yesterday's tomorrow.

The technological leap involved in building Concorde helps to explain how the cost of the project kept multiplying over the years of the plane's development – aided by some poor management and by some foolish late changes in the specification, until the price tag too was sublime and worthy of a gasp. By some reckonings, Concorde ended up being designed not once, nor even twice, but two-and-a-half times, because of a decision to make the production model 20 feet longer than the prototype, and the constant jostling of redesigned components against neighbouring components, which then also had to be redesigned.

At a witness seminar on Concorde held at the Institute for Contemporary British History in 2000, one of the civil servants participating remembered the example of Concorde's ever-expanding wheels: 'They discovered that the weight had gone up to the point where the wheel had to be larger to meet the runway requirements, but the wheel was a tight fit in the wing. So a bulge had to be produced in the wing. The result of that was that the air resistance was greater than it had been, more fuel was required, and to carry that fuel a heavier structure was required. Because a heavier structure was required, an even bigger wheel was needed.'

And at every revision, the designers were aiming at an extraordinarily narrow window of technical viability. As eventually completed, Concorde has a payload capacity of only 7 per cent of its take-off mass, a ratio more reminiscent of a satellite launcher than a normal airliner. It can cross the Atlantic, but only just. London–New York and Paris–New York are possible; Frankfurt–New York is not. Yet perversely, Concorde works at all because, in one limited sense, its British and French designers were modest. They were required to leap into new structural and technological territory, but beyond that, they successfully confined themselves to solving only the next problem, filling in only the immediately adjacent bits of the unknown.

Take Concorde's chosen cruising speed of Mach 2.2, for instance: it was just about at the safe limit of what a conventional aluminium structure could stand in the way of atmospheric heating, so long as there were a few pieces of more resilient steel and titanium covering the sensitive nose and wing edges. If they had tried to build a plane that flew at Mach 3, they would have been looking at a skin temperature at cruise altitude of 250°C, enough to melt aluminium, and the whole plane would have had to be executed in unproven, exotic materials.

Here was where the Americans went wrong with their abortive government-funded Supersonic Transport: Boeing spent the 1960s trying to construct a super-duper, all-new Mach 3 SST, and ended up with nothing at all. The

Russians, meanwhile, made the contrasting mistake with their Tupolev-144, aka Concordski, and attempted a quick and dirty solution that didn't refine military technology enough. The Tupolev's engines were twice as heavy and burned fuel twice as fast as Concorde's. It only had the range to get halfway across the Atlantic.

The real flaw in Concorde was not technological. It was social. The whole project was based on an error in social prediction. Those who commissioned it assumed that air travel in the future would remain, as it mostly was in 1962, a service for the rich, and the gilded upper-crust celebrity rich at that, the jet set as they were when the phrase was first coined. Concorde was built to move Princess Margaret, Noel Coward, Grace Kelly and Ian Fleming around the world. Since this pattern of use was assumed to be a given, the natural next move was to accelerate the aeroplanes.

But at the same time as Britain and France were betting on supersonic speed as the next step in aviation, one of the bosses of Boeing, unconvinced that the SST programme was really the way forward, pushed through the development of a subsonic plane that could carry 400 passengers at a time. The Boeing 747 – just as bold a leap into the unknown as Concorde, just as extreme in its departure from the norm – was the right plane for the future that actually arrived. It allowed airlines to serve the mass market for air travel that burgeoned in the 1970s. Boeing sold the hundreds of planes that the Concorde consortium had hoped to. With its cramped tube of a cabin and its tiny payload of passengers, Concorde could not be adapted to suit the more varied needs of a world in which it had become normal for millions of people to fly. It was a Batmobile when the market demanded a bus.

Most observers expected Concorde to expire in the early 1980s. It survived only because new management at BA found a way to exploit the flipside of the plane's failure. Lord King, the Thatcher favourite brought in to prepare the airline for privatization, would never in a million years have endorsed the building of a big-ticket dream-machine like Concorde, but he could see that an accident of history had deposited an asset on his tarmac that none of the competitors had. The total lack of demand for the plane could be repositioned as a badge of exclusivity.

The experience of sitting on one of Concorde's Connolly-leather seats for two-and-a-half hours could be sold as one of the super-luxury items – like a Rolex, like a Ferrari, like couture clothing – whose price is completely divorced from its utility, and instead testifies to how desirable the thing is. The economics were still tight, but with the £900m development cost to the taxpayer written off, Concorde's current account could be made to balance, and the plane soared on for twenty more years, gorgeously excessive, gloriously, redundantly superlative.

I'm glad it did. Passers-by in the hot streets of London and Manhattan would stop when they heard the rumble, and tilt their heads to see the unmistakable silhouette go by. It scattered intimations of grace, which could fall into a frantic urban day as coolingly as any flurry of cold white stars. It dropped (as it were) snow, not bombs.

2 October 2003

TIM RADFORD

Lions

Collectively, the householders of the world could be about to put the cat out. African lion numbers have fallen by 90 per cent in the past twenty years, according to a recent report. There are only about 23,000 alive today. That's the number of seats at Barnsley football club stadium.

The tiger is also an endangered species. At the highest estimate, there are fewer than 8,000 left. To put that number in perspective, about that many people work on Ministry of Defence sites in Wales. There are probably only 15,000 or so cheetahs in the whole of Africa. The Iberian lynx is down to about 600.

And it's not just the cats that we're putting out. The Cross River gorilla subspecies, for example, which lives on the border between Nigeria and Cameroon, is down to about 200 at the most. That is fewer than the number of British men who each year develop breast cancer. There are fewer than fifty Chinese alligators surviving in China. Most books give an estimate for sperm whales of 1 to 2 million, but a paper published last year gave an estimate of 360,000. The most recent estimate for southern hemisphere minke whales is about half the total estimate of 760,000 derived from surveys in the late 1980s.

Lions, cheetahs and lynxes share certain characteristics with many other threatened creatures: they are large, they are carnivores, they are fussy about where they live, they need a large range, they have small litters and a long gestation period, and they are hunted. This makes them natural candidates for extinction in a world in which human numbers have soared from 2.5 billion to more than 6 billion in fifty years. The planet's population grows by more than 80 million every year. There are roughly 240,000 extra mouths to feed every day.

Each of these humans has a personal ecological footprint: that is, each appropriates an average of 2.1 hectares (5.2 acres) to provide water, food, energy, housing, transport, commerce and somewhere to tip the waste. (Americans on average take up almost 10 hectares each.) Even though the rate of growth in human numbers is beginning to decline, the wild things are being pushed towards oblivion at an ever faster rate. That is because the numbers of individual households – empty nesters, yuppies, singletons and one-parent families – is exploding, even in those countries with low population growth. That means yet more pressure on the wild to provide timber, gravel and lime, plant fibres, food and water.

Survivors in an increasingly human world need a different set of characteristics. They must be small herbivores that produce large numbers of offspring very swiftly, adapt happily to concrete, tarmac and fossil-fuel pollution and are prepared to live anywhere. So the typical wild animals of the twenty-first century, as one American biologist predicted more than thirty years ago, 'will be the house sparrow, the grey squirrel, the Virginia opossum and the

Norway rat'. The lion, denied the lion's share, could slope off into the eternal night.

The big animals are merely the most visible of endangered species. One-eighth of all bird species are at serious risk of extinction. At least 13 per cent of the world's flowering plants could be about to perish. One-fourth of all mammals are to some extent endangered and around thirty species are down to their last thousand members. There are nineteen critically endangered primates, and sixteen species of albatross could be about to fly away for ever. These are sober estimates from the International Union for the Conservation of Nature about animals that are already well studied. But biologists simply do not know how many species there are on the planet. The big ones are easy to spot; the smaller ones are literally beyond counting. About 1.8 million little birds, beasts and beetles have been named, but there could be 7 million or even 70 million.

Five years ago, John Lawton, a population biologist and now the chief of Britain's Natural Environment Research Council, tried to take the measure of biodiversity in the Cameroon. He and colleagues marked out a few plots of forest and started trying to count the species in eight taxonomic groups. They spent 10,000 hours on the research and then abandoned it: the job would have kept 1,200 taxonomists busy for years.

'We surveyed birds, butterflies, ants and then all the way down to itsy-bitsy nematode worms,' he says. 'The percentage of species we found that were actually known and described by taxonomists was inversely related to their body size. In other words, we didn't discover any new birds. We found a new subspecies of butterfly. And 90 per cent of all the nematode worms had never been seen by a scientist before. It was just a huge effort: the number of scientist days it took to identify the things was again inversely related to their body size; the smaller the critters were the longer and longer and longer it took to sort them out.'

The Earth's most heart-rending problem comes with a catch-all title – biodiversity. These six clumsy syllables sum up the totality of life on Earth, from subterranean fungi to wind-borne spores, from cloud-forest beetles to Arctic bears, from ocean algae to tubeworms in the abyss. Many of these creatures quietly underwrite human economic growth: they oxygenate the atmosphere, cleanse drinking water, fix nitrogen, recycle waste and pollinate crops. A team at the University of Maryland once calculated that nature delivered goods and services worth $33 trillion to the global economy every year. The gross national product of the whole world at the time was only about $18 trillion.

One school of thought argues that if the big, beautiful beasts – the charismatic megavertebrates – are going, then thousands of small, nondescript creatures could go with them, with unpredictable consequences. There are almost apocalyptic predictions about rates of extinction. Edward O. Wilson, one of America's most distinguished biologists, once calculated that 27,000 species of creature went extinct every year in the tropical forests alone. A few years later, a team of biologists at Stanford University suggested that populations of plants and animals were being wiped out at the rate of 1,800 an hour. These may be wild overestimates, but even the most conservative biologists tell a bleak story: this, they say, is the sixth great extinction of life in the history of the planet. The first five extinctions, recorded in the ancient rocks, were all natural: from volcanic catastrophe, climate change, asteroid impact, or even deadly radiation from an exploding star. But this one, they all agree, is the unwitting work of humankind.

Robert May – Lord May of Oxford, president of the Royal Society, a former government chief scientific adviser and once a research partner of Edward O. Wilson – reckons that at the very least, the rate of extinction is now 1,000 times faster than the 'background' rate of extinction over hundreds of millions of years, recorded in fossils from Cretaceous, Jurassic and Triassic rocks. Should people care? Most conservation action by bodies such as the WWF concentrates entirely on the charismatic big vertebrates, such as the panda and tiger, rhino and lion. Could we live without them?

'Maybe we can, but if people aren't going to care about them disappearing, who is going to give a stuff about the insects and fungi until the consequences emerge?' May says. 'A stronger argument is that we are not sure how much we can simplify the world and still have it deliver all the services we depend on.' Lions won't be extinguished, he says. 'They will be kept in reserves and zoos. But the question is, whether you are keeping a lion or whether you are keeping a Latin binomial, *Felis leo*, and that is a question that is awkward to ask.'

The lion, according to Georgina Mace, director of science at the Zoological Society of London, was the one animal conservationists had not been worried about. Until recently, it had been widespread in Africa, though it had all but disappeared from Asia. There are two ways of alarming conservationists, she says. 'One is that you are incredibly rare and you just sit on a remote island, being a species that is found nowhere else and there are just fifty of you, but you could have been rare for ever and ever: that is the nature of the life you have. The other way of being of conservation concern is to decline very quickly, and we have been much better at spotting the former rather than the latter. But the latter is probably the one that is going to affect most species. If you are just sitting there being very rare, people are usually protecting you.'

The lion, as she sees it, is not an isolated case. The population of bluefin tuna had crashed by 95 per cent before anybody noticed. The passenger pigeon once existed in tens of millions, but was wiped out. The American buffalo almost disappeared. There would once have been lions by the million.

'Carnivore numbers fluctuate. If you are looking in one place, you'd see them come and go. Actually, what they are doing is moving large scale across the landscape, occupying areas where there is abundant prey and then moving somewhere else; they are quite hard to monitor. You think, oh, they are rare here – and then you suddenly realize that actually, they are rare everywhere.'

The bitterest irony is that animal populations are dwindling and extinctions accelerating despite a thirty-year campaign to establish parks and wildlife reserves in all the great wilderness areas of the world: the rainforests, savannahs, estuaries, deserts, mountains, grasslands, wetlands and so on. These wildernesses cover 46 per cent of the land surface, but hold just 2.4 per cent of the population. More than 10 per cent of these places are now protected by national and international edict. Yet ultimately they cannot protect the wild things. Poachers look to make a killing in both senses of the word. Big animals stray and become a menace to small farmers, who drive them off or kill them. And the tourists turn up, bringing even more of mankind and its expensive ways into the wilderness. A study of the Wolong Reserve in China – opened decades ago to protect the giant panda – revealed that the panda was still in decline and that more humans had moved in, cutting back the bamboo forest for roads, homes and tourist services. The lions in Africa – and all the creatures in Africa's national parks – are still being hunted, hounded or harassed by humans.

There are some who argue that some species will only be saved in zoos (indeed, London Zoo played a big part in saving the almost-extinct Arabian oryx and restoring it to its native wild). But Mark Collins of the UN world conservation monitoring centre in Cambridge says he cannot accept the idea that the lion might survive only in safari parks, or that zoos could be the last resort as the saviours of species. The big wilderness reserves exist, and they could be made to work.

'I feel we have sufficient knowledge of how to manage these key habitats. It is just a matter of political will,' he says. 'I do not accept that the doors are closed. We have parks, and even outside parks, we have the technology and the knowledge to manage most of these habitats like forests and so on, properly. It's just that we are not actually doing it.'

Life's richest places are also those where humans are poorest. Africans are already struggling against hunger, poverty, Aids, malaria, cattle diseases and – in many cases – civil war. Nobody knows how this one is going to end. 'It is all very well for you and me, but if I was some poor, oppressed farmer in Africa I am not so sure I would look kindly on the elephants that trample my crops,' says May. Nor have Europeans and Americans held up much of an example. When Western governments began pressing African and Asian nations about the fate of the elephant, developing nations retaliated by suggesting that the Atlantic cod, too, should be protected. The point is well made. Developed nations with sophisticated fishing technology have knowingly put cod and tuna at risk, and had begun to wipe out the barn door skate and great white shark as their nets swept through the seas. 'There is a real irony,' says Mace.

The lions of Africa – and the wild creatures further down the food chain – can only be saved by money and political will from both national and international communities. The developing nations do have an incentive to protect their biodiversity. It represents potential wealth, one way or the other. Some extinctions of already rare creatures are inevitable. But spend on the lions, says Lawton, and you could save a lot more besides. Committed spending saved the black and white rhino – targets of poachers as well as victims of human pressure – but the sums of money invested were critical.

'If you create big, effective reserves for these charismatic guys at the top of the food chain, huge numbers of other creatures we don't even know exist could just slip through to the end of the century on the coat-tails of the lions,' Lawton says. 'So it is a matter of putting enough resources in. In a world which is prepared to spend an extra fifty-five billion pounds on a war in Iraq, we are talking about peanuts.'

6 September 2003

JONATHAN WATTS

Old Beijing

Mao moved them in and now money is moving them out. The residents of Beijing's maze-like *hutong* neighbourhoods were the heroes of the Chinese revolution, but they are now being evicted so that the property developers who hold sway in today's China can build high-rise residential blocks for a new generation of nouveaux riches.

For more than a hundred years, the smoky-grey, walled courtyard of 39 Dongsi 12th Lane has provided a refuge from the waves of imperial oppression, communist revolution and capitalist rapaciousness that have swept through China. Located in a *hutong* alley in the heart of Beijing's old city, the tiled-roof compound is just a two-minute walk from the choked-up streets and noisy construction sites that pollute the capital with dust and noise.

But you only have to duck through its narrow gateway to escape into a small oasis of pomegranate trees, gourd vines and neat rows of potted plants, where elderly men play Chinese chess, housewives hang their washing and schoolchildren bury their noses in homework.

For eight centuries such quadrangle buildings, arranged in the tree-lined maze of *hutongs*, were the distinctive feature of life in Beijing – once the world's most sophisticated city. But they are now being destroyed in their thousands as the Chinese capital undergoes one of the most dramatic transformations in the history of urban planning.

In a headlong rush to cash in on China's spectacular economic growth and to modernize Beijing before the 2008 Olympics, the old single-storey neighbourhoods are being flattened by developers keen to secure the high-value land on which they are situated. In their place come sleek high-rise buildings and apartment blocks, almost indistinguishable from those found in cities around the world. The destruction of an ancient heritage and a traditional way of life is belatedly raising alarm bells inside the Chinese government, but even with growing official support, conservationists are fighting a losing battle against the bulldozers and public indifference.

Number 39 Dongsi 12th Lane is at the forefront of efforts to maintain the *hutongs*. This summer, the quadrangle – once home to a Qing dynasty emperor's kung fu instructor and now home to twenty-six families – was the first to be listed by the Beijing municipal government in its most ambitious conservation campaign yet. Numerous stories have appeared in the Chinese media about the property, which is marked with a blue plaque declaring it to be 'protected courtyard'.

Yet many fear it is too little, too late. According to the *Beijing Weekender*, a third of the 62sq km old city has already been demolished. Beijing says it will protect 200 homes, but more than 10,000 others are being knocked down every year, reducing the number of *hutongs* from their 1980s peak of 3,600 to fewer than 2,000 today.

'If they don't stop, Beijing as an historical city will cease to exist,' warned the writer Hua Xinmin, a leading campaigner for the protection of the *hutongs*. But there is little that opponents of development can do. Under Mao Zedong, the courtyards – like all land – were taken into state ownership. Their wealthy owners were replaced by the families of Communist party cadres as a reward for their loyalty. Now, however, they are at the mercy of a state that is obsessed with economic growth. With no ownership rights, residents, many of them retired, have little legal redress when their homes are listed for demolition by property speculators, to whom the *hutong* buildings are valueless. 'They only want the prime real estate they occupy,' said Liu Xiaoshi, a senior architect and former member of Beijing's urban planning bureau. 'But the new properties are no substitute for the culture and spirit of the ones they replace.'

Despite such concerns, the priority of the municipal authorities is modernization not conservation. Beijing plans to spend $22bn (£14bn) on beautifying the city in time for the 2008 Olympics. The construction boom has attracted architects from across the globe to work on such lavish projects as the $300m bubble-shaped opera house, designed by Frenchman Paul Andreu, which is being built opposite the Forbidden City; and what will be the city's tallest building, a $600m headquarters for the state broadcaster designed by two Dutch architects, Ole Scheeren and Rem Koolhaas. Elsewhere the transformation is more prosaic: narrow *hutong* streets knocked down for wide boulevards of office blocks and shopping malls filled with Starbucks, McDonald's and KFC outlets.

As more new buildings go up, a growing number of courtyard residents are being moved into high-rise apartment blocks in the suburbs. Many go willingly, glad to swap a cramped life of foul communal toilets and smoky coal stoves for spacious flats with private bathrooms and central heating. Others attempt opposition, but their petitions and court orders are ignored by the powerful developers.

Residents appear fatalistic. 'There's not much we can do if they want to redevelop our home,' said Li Ruiling, whose home for thirty-eight years on Dongsi 12th Lane backs on to a construction site for a new subway station. 'And preservation is no solution because we'd have to move out while they fix the place up and then it would be too expensive to move back in.'

Though the central government is belatedly recognizing that their homes and their way of life are cultural treasures, it is no longer able to rein in the runaway development it has unleashed. Many observers fear that Number 39 Dongsi 12th Lane may end up among the last of the *hutongs*.

'The central government says it has stopped the destruction of the courtyards, but the reality is that on the ground they are still knocking them down,' said Edward Lanfranco, the author of a book on Beijing. 'Small pockets of courtyard areas may survive, but the future for old Beijing is likely to be a Disneyland area for tourists. Meanwhile an eight-hundred-year-old way of life will have disappeared.'

30 August 2004

SIMON HATTENSTONE

The last stop

Tony Boyce applied for the job on the Wednesday. On the Sunday, he was told that he'd got it and that they would fly him over from Barbados to London to work on the next available bus: 'They were ready for me, but I wasn't ready for them.' He was still at school, still living with his grandmother, and wasn't sure if she would cope by herself. That was forty years ago, when the sixties were just beginning to swing. 'I was so excited,' he says, 'especially when I saw the red buses from the air. People always talked about the red buses in London.' On Friday, Tony will be made redundant, along with all his fellow conductors on the 73 route. On the same day, conductors on numbers 9 and 390 will also lose their jobs. By the end of next year, there will be no working Routemasters and no conductors left in London. The old jump-on, jump-off bus will be a thing of the past, a tourist attraction at best.

Tony is leading me through Tottenham bus garage, home to the 73, and up the stairs to the canteen. He is tall and thin and elegant. 'I was brought up by my grandmother, and leaving her was quite a shock for me. She understood and told me to go, and said when I got here I could look after her back home. I sent money because my grandmother had looked after me, so it was my duty to look after her.'

It was a time of mass migration from the Caribbean to England. West Indians such as Tony were invited here to do blue-collar jobs on the buses and railways and in the National Health Service. 'They wanted us here for economic reasons because the people in England wouldn't do the jobs. That's why we were here.' His mother was already in England, working in Birmingham, when he arrived. She was thirty-eight years old, and had just had a baby with a new partner.

It was only when he got here that he realized things were done differently in England. 'What surprised me most was on the first morning I said good morning to everybody, and everybody looked at me as if to say, "What are you doing?" That's our culture back home, to say good morning. Then I realized it wasn't the thing to do.' He smiles and laughs. 'That was a big shock. But then again, England is a big country, and back home in Barbados you knew everybody.'

Does he think people ignored him because he was black? 'No, it was more cultural. But yes, of course I experienced some hostility. It has improved, but you still get the odd one. There's this guy, every time he gets on the bus he starts trouble with black people. Every time I get him I know he's going to upset some person. He's an older fella, and I'm surprised nobody has hit him. He told me last week I was a nigger and I was a coon.' Did he tell the man to get off the bus? 'No, I think it's a mental problem. So you can't do that to a mental person, can you? And for that one person, you've got millions who are not racist, so that's the way I look at it.'

Tony has witnessed much change since he started on the buses. There was the social and sexual liberation of the 1960s ('It was the time of the mini-skirt. That was something!'), the industrial strife and three-day week of the 1970s, the austerity of the 1980s, Cool Britannia of the 1990s, and the irony of the 2000s – that while 6 million people are now using London buses every day (up from 4.2 million four years ago), there is no place for conductors like him. According to Transport for London they are an anachronism.

Tony has had a wonderful life on the buses. 'I love it, and the people love me, too.' There is always a tiny minority of troublemakers, but if anybody ever tries it on with him on the bus, his regulars will come to his rescue. In the end, he says, it comes down to respect and love. 'To me there's no difference between a baby in your arms and an old lady who's got a stick: to me they all need respect, and that is what I will give. If one person upsets you, don't take it out on the next person who comes along. You have to treat everybody as individuals, and if you can't, you have problems. On my bus, most people, if they are sad when they get on, they will get off happy. I smile with them.'

He nurses his mug of tea in his big hands. I ask him how he cheers people up. He struggles to explain. 'I can't do it right now, it's impromptu. I can just make people laugh when they are sad. I remember one man, who was so sad, and when he got off the bus he was the happiest man. All his muscles in his face lit up with joy, and when he got off he said, "I've never met a person like you." That's the main thing people will miss me for – making them smile. People have cried when I've told them we're leaving.' He pauses, sups his tea. 'Yessssssss!' he says contemplatively.

Has he any plans for the future? Well, he says, he's sixty years old, so he thinks he deserves a break. 'I don't think I will look for much work now because I've done forty years in the country. I'm going to have six months to a year's rest and after that I'm going to think what I will do.' He will get a decent redundancy payoff, although he doesn't know what it works out at. He says he has never been much bothered about money. How much does he earn a year? 'To be honest, I don't know.' He gets the giggles. 'Like I say, it's OK if my hours are all right.'

Tony is a Methodist and has a diploma in religion; he may use his time to do a degree. Could he become a minister? 'I don't think I will become a minister, but I'll always get to help people.' In a way, I say, conducting is a form of ministering. 'Yes, I think so,' he says. 'Everybody needs help at some time.' He tells me of the policeman who got on his bus one Christmas somewhat the worse for wear. 'He was drunk, drunk, drunk, and he said, "Look after me, I'm drunk," and I said, "That's good, man," because it was Christmas and he was happy. And I looked after him not because he's a policeman but because he's a human being. He got off at Catford.'

Transport for London and the ten private companies that run London's buses say there is no longer any need for conductors – buses will be run by the driver, and customers will buy tickets from the machine at the bus stop before boarding. Tony disagrees. 'What happens with vulnerable people now? On the new bendy buses, the driver can't get up and help people in difficulty. I think it comes down to two things – politics and profit. After the bus company became privatized, those two things ruled, like in every industry.'

Before Tony goes off to work, he introduces me to Flo Twumasi, who is sitting in the canteen eating her lunch. He says she will be happy to talk to me. But she isn't. 'Why should I talk to you?' she says. 'How will it help save my job?' I say I have come to the garage to look for conductors to speak to because Transport for London said it was unable to help me – they had asked the companies who run the buses and they had replied that their employees were tired of talking to the press and wanted to get on with their work. She laughs when I tell her that, and says, 'What work?' Now she seems happy to talk.

Flo is forty-seven, and came to Britain from Ghana in 1980 to join her husband who was working here. She has been a conductor for eight years: 'We have our good days and our bad days, but I'd say the majority are good.' A good day, she says, is one without hassle, one in which she will see her regulars and they will talk. 'I love the sociable part, chatting to people. Most of my regulars are friends.' Does she see them out of work? 'Nooooo. As soon as I come off the bus, that's it.'

What's the worst side of the job? 'Working late at night, and standing on the platform – that is scary. Very scary.' Luckily, she says, she has never been mugged. When she gets home at night, she is exhausted, and her feet are sore. Does her husband massage her feet? 'Noooo,' she giggles. 'Nooo. I just have a bath and wait for the next day to come round.' Does she think that collecting money is the main part of the job? 'Oh, you collect the money and check the passes, but then there's safety, keeping the gangway clear, and all the questions people ask ... Of course, I don't like the fact that conductors are going because I'll be out of a job, but what can I do? The thing is, who am I? My opinion does not count.'

Flo hasn't got a clue what she will be doing in a few weeks' time. Is she scared? Yes, she says, she has to support her son who is at university studying systems engineering, but hopefully he will be earning soon, and thankfully her husband is working, and she still holds out the tiniest hope that they will find another job for her on the buses. Doing what? 'I don't know. Nothing really. I just keep my hopes high,' she says, and laughs, a little despairingly.

On the next table in the canteen, Adjei Kwaku, also Ghanaian, asks if he can talk to me. He is forty-four, and came to Britain when he was twenty-seven. He has done a series of odd jobs, is married with four children, and has been a conductor for three years. He talks quietly, intensely. 'The conducting job is very stressful. Very stressful,' he says. 'Passengers don't respect conductors or drivers. Most people think you don't need any qualifications to be a driver or conductor. Let's take you, for instance. If you are in an office and somebody comes into the office and spits at you, would you be happy? Because that's what happens on the buses, they spit on conductors and drivers. I was spat on just because I told a man the bus was full. I did not allow him to come on the bus and he spat on me. It's my job. And I was upset when I got back to the garage and didn't feel I could work, and I was told, "If you don't finish the day's work, we'll only pay you for the work you've done." I didn't finish the job, I was too upset.'

Isn't it amazing how London has changed, I say, how it has become a multi-racial melting pot. He nods, and says yes, it is good, but there are still problems: 'One Jamaican lady told me I was a fucking African, and I said to her, "Where do you come from?" and she said, "Jamaica is not Africa." Sometimes the passengers are very horrible – you have to control your temper. Having been a bus conductor I can do any kind of public work, because I've got the experience of how to deal with the public.'

Is there anything he likes about the job? 'Yes, I like it because I see a lot of people and some of them are very kind, they talk to you nicely. But sometimes we go to work with a miserable face and somebody will come on the bus and tell you to smile, you know what I mean. That person doesn't know what's going on in your life, though.'

When he and his colleagues were told about the redundancies, he says, Arriva told them they would train them for other jobs, such as revenue inspectors or drivers. But he doesn't know anyone who has a new job to go to. He has just been sent a form asking if he is looking for alternative employment, but he doesn't hold out much hope. What kind of payoff will he get? 'The package is not good. For the three years I have worked I will get three thousand pounds. I'm looking for other work, security, whatever. Actually, I have decided to join the community police.'

Adjei is glad that they are getting rid of the Routemasters: 'I think it is a good thing because people fall off the bus and they can die. Almost every month you hear of someone falling off the bus and hurting themselves.' But if there is no Routemaster, and no dangerous platform, and no passengers hopping on and off, and if machines are dispensing tickets, doesn't that mean the companies are right when they say conductors are outdated? 'Most of the ticket machines don't work. So if people come on the bus and the ticket machine is not working, the driver won't let them on. Three days ago I had a man on my bus and he wanted to buy a one-day pass and there were no machines working, so what does he do then?'

Back in Ghana, Adjei passed A-levels in English, maths and science. Has he considered going back to college? 'I would like to go to college, but how can I at my age and with my children?'

Bob is sitting at the same table drinking tea with us. Bob isn't his real name, but he still works for the company as a driver and doesn't want us to use his real name in case he is victimized. He has worked as a driver of one-man buses, a driver of the 73 Routemaster and a conductor. 'Driving without a conductor is very difficult. When you're doing the one-man bus, you do so many jobs. When you are on the 73 you feel more relaxed, more concentrated on the driving. As a one-man bus, apart from the problems on the road, your controllers put so much pressure on you. Most of them don't even talk to you nicely. You are not supposed to run early, and then when you run late, they ask why you were late. Now when we get to a bus stop and someone delays you, you have to make time for the person, and it might take five minutes, and at the end of the day you will come in five minutes late and the controller will ask you where you lost your time.'

When a machine is out of order, he is expected to take the customers to the next stop, where they can get off the bus to buy a ticket and get back on again. He laughs at the thought of twenty customers in search of a working machine.

He takes out a book of dockets he has been given. 'This is called the customer service card,' he says. It is to be used when customers can't get a ticket at the next machine or because they don't have change. 'You fill it in and give it to the person. So if the fare due is a pound, you write down a pound and tear it off and give it to the person to go and pay with.' Where do they pay? He holds his hands out, and says he hasn't got a clue. The customer service card is transparently flawed. There is no space to write the customer's address, and even if there were, how would the driver have the time to wait? Without conductors, how will the bus companies keep a record of customers who owe money? 'We have no idea. I think they are going to give every person the benefit of the doubt.'

Bob talks about his trade union, the Transport and General, dismissively: 'We have to forget about the union because they are not helping us in any way. Drivers want conductors to stay. I think if Ken Livingstone or Transport for London [had] allowed conductors on bendy buses, it would have been brilliant. It would have made the job safer and more comfortable for the driver.'

Bob, also Ghanaian, says he enjoys working as a conductor, but prefers driving because the money is so much better. 'As a driver, the basic is about eighteen thousand, and the conductor gets about twelve thousand basic.' Today he is doing overtime from 12.30 p.m. to 3 p.m., then his real shift starts at 5 p.m. 'You have to kill yourself to earn the money,' he says.

I arrive at Archway bus garage, hoping to find conductors who work on the 390 Routemaster, which is also to be scrapped on 3 September. Unfortunately, the conductors were moved to King's Cross a year ago, Eleni Da Silva tells me. Eleni is sitting with her feet up in the canteen waiting to go to her afternoon shift. She is Brazilian, a driver, and wearing black leather fingerless gloves. Nowadays she is a one-woman driver, and says it is so much harder to focus on the roads than in the old days. 'You keep having to check on the tickets, and often people come inside and you can't work out what type of tickets they have.' Not only was it more fun having a conductor, she says, she also felt less exposed. 'If something happened to me, he could be my witness, I wouldn't need customers.'

Does she have a favourite bus? 'Yes, I liked the number 10 Routemaster more than any other route.' Why? 'I like the bus. It was very nice to drive. I want to go on it again before it goes away, actually. It was just good to be there. Good experience. The Routemaster is more solid, heavy, everything about the bus really, everything about the journey I liked, too.'

Eleni then poses on the bus for the photographer.

'You'll have to unbutton your shirt. I had to,' conductor Jim Stokes teases.

'Ooooh, yeah!' Eleni says enthusiastically.

'And don't forget to flash a bit of leg; this is the *Guardian*.'

A Transport for London spokesman says that, frankly, he is tired of all the sentimental rubbish that has been talked about the scrapping of the Routemasters. 'We're being portrayed as if we've got some evil masterplan, but there are four good reasons why the Routemasters are going. First, age: the newest buses are thirty-six years old and they were designed for a seventeen-year working life. Second, they are ten to fifteen per cent more expensive to run than new buses: it's true that they use less fuel, but they also carry fewer passengers. Third, people are twice as likely to be injured on Routemasters as on other buses.

Fourth, accessibility: we have a commitment under the government's Disability Discrimination Act to a one hundred per cent accessible fleet and we reckon ten per cent of our customers have some kind of disability.' He says it is important to remember that even now, Routemasters only account for 300 buses in a fleet of 7,500.

As for conductors, he says, again, it's easy to be dewy-eyed, but the fact is that their main job of collecting fares had disappeared. And while many passengers think conductors provide security on the buses, he says the reality can be very different. 'When conductors get involved in people's arguments, they often get assaulted. Transport for London is actually boosting security by increasing both the number of CCTV cameras and the number of police officers on buses.'

Jim Stokes is fifty, and a conductor on the 390. He has worked on the buses for fourteen years. If he had managed one more year, he and his wife would have got a free pass for life.

He says society has changed since he started, and it is reflected by what he sees on the buses. 'When we started on the 139s, they were a lovely bunch of people, commuters – they would park their cars out in West Hampstead because there were no parking restrictions. They were polite, they always had their fares ready and you could communicate with them. But unfortunately on the 390s, like the 10s which we also used to run, the attitudes have changed.' How? 'They are more arrogant. We pass the King's Cross area where we get a lot of drug addicts, and they try to give us hell. We have to adapt to their attitudes, which is a change, because it makes us rude and voluble when we don't want to be. They're down-and-outs.' Do you have to be tough to be a bus conductor? 'These days you do,' he says.

The trouble, he says, is that so many people don't want to talk. Why? 'It's mainly because they're foreign. They either don't speak the language properly or if you go up and talk to them because you fancy them or you just want to be sociable, they pretend ... they're just not interested.' Is he chatty by nature? 'I can be, but at the moment I keep myself to myself; that way I don't get no complaints.' Has he been getting complaints? 'Everybody gets complaints: that we're ringing the bell too early, or the driver's driving too erratically and they're throwing everybody over.'

Jim talks in a nasal tone, like Ken Livingstone, and has a similar anorak quality. Like most conductors, however, he doesn't have much time for the mayor of London, who said that he was going to put a conductor on every London bus before deciding to scrap them wholesale. He accepts that there is a problem with the safety and accessibility of the Routemaster, but doesn't believe that is the real reason they are being decommissioned: 'Well, we've been told that no firm likes to pay two wages with the one bus; that, I think, is the moral of the story. But according to the EU, we're having far too many platform accidents.' Jim has had three accidents on his bus – 'not fatal, but very serious. One was completely drunk, another girl fell off ... they get off in the wrong direction to which the bus is going and they hit the ground hard. It's OK if you get off in the same direction that the bus is travelling, and if you can run fast enough you can slow yourself down without any injury. But get off the wrong way and you go straight to the floor.' The new buses do have undoubted advantages, he says. 'They can dip the fronts to make the platform lower for the old-age pensioners, and they can carry wheelchairs and pushchairs, which is good.'

So they will, in fact, be better than the old Routemasters? 'No, they'll never be better than Routemasters. Because the Routemaster's a narrow bus, so it can get through tighter traffic, it can load up twice as fast, it can travel a lot quicker because it doesn't take as much loading-up time, and it's good for public morale.' What does he mean? 'They are a centrepiece for us and the community. The public love them, they are a tourist attraction for London: the big red bus and the black taxis.'

I ask him what he has liked most about his job. 'Every trip you go down the road is completely different. Even though it's the same road, it's different people, so you're getting a second chance, so to speak. Well, I believe so, anyway. And we carry some of the world's prettiest women, and that is one good plus on our job. We do, you know.'

Englishman Jim earns £17,000 a year and says his wage has depreciated over his working life. 'When I started I was earning more money in real terms. It wasn't until Margaret Thatcher started playing around and then we lost Christmas bonuses, attendance bonuses, London weighting ...' He says he will get a decent payoff, £18,000 after fourteen years. 'But when I've spent the cheque, it will be murder.' Is there nothing on the horizon? 'Nothing at the moment. It's all low-paid, five-pound-an-hour jobs – cleaning, security, shop work.'

As we talk, the bus starts to move out of the garage. 'Where are we going, Len?' Jim says to his fellow conductor, Lennie Ishmael.

'He's just checking the steering, I think, Jim.'

Lennie is fifty-six years old, from Guyana, and is wearing more gold than P. Diddy. He tells me he is a driver and conductor, but at the moment is restricted to conducting duties: 'Unfortunately I was held up for drink-driving in my car and I was suspended for five years, so at the moment I'm on suspension, but I'm still conducting.' He is going to court to try to get his licence back before he is made redundant. 'If I get back my licence before the third I will get back my job, and if I get a licence afterwards, I will have to take the redundancy money. The minimum you can serve when you get suspended for drink-driving is two years, and in October it will be three years since I was suspended.' (Lennie calls later to say that he didn't get his job back.)

He agrees with Jim that people aren't as polite as they used to be: 'As time goes along, people maybe value money more and they don't want to pay, even if you ask them. They tell you point blank they don't have to and they're not paying. And they forget their pass at home, and things like that, and it's very hard to get them to pay. Now people won't pay even if you stand over them and demand that they do.'

After the bus arrives back at the garage, Jim leads me out and shows me how to get a bus to Aldwych and points to a Routemaster. 'See that bus?' he says. 'ALD 971B. It's the fastest bus in London; there isn't one that could touch it. All the other buses are regulated to do twenty-eight to thirty miles an hour, but that one isn't. We love it. You never finish late on that bus.'

Down at Aldwych, a row of number 9 Routemasters form a neat line. Luz Mery is sitting on her bus talking to somebody. Would I mind waiting while she finishes her chat? she asks. She is Colombian and has worked on the buses for three years. Yes, sure, she says, there are tricky customers ('My God, I have difficult passengers!'), but the good ones more than make up for it. 'I meet many people who speak Spanish, or sometimes people bring me things. One day a passenger gave me cake ... I had never seen her before. It was so nice. See the lady I was talking to? This is my friend now. We meet here on this route, on the number 9, and now she's a good friend.' What will she do when she is made redundant? 'I don't know. I have a problem now. I need to work and I need to move – so how can I look for work?'

One bus down the line is Englishman Mark Mundy, who is about to set off for Hammersmith. It has just started sheeting down with rain. 'I only took up conducting temporarily because I was out of a job, and I said I'd only do it for three months, but I've ended up doing it for four and a half years.' Why does he think he is being made redundant? 'Well,' he says, swinging off the metal pole at the platform, 'Livingstone had to go with the safety regulations or whatever. But obviously they're saying: why should they pay two lots of wages when they can get away with one lot? Just one of those things, innit?'

Yes, he says, he has enjoyed the jobs, but it's not all roses. 'We only get four weeks' holiday after two years ... and you don't get full sick pay unless you do five years' work.' He apologizes, and says he hasn't really got time to talk, then moves down the bus to work. Within twenty seconds he has doled out a couple of tickets, given a young man directions and helped an elderly lady with a steady hand.

PEOPLE

MICHAEL WHITE

Ronald Reagan

The pundits who yesterday claimed a place for Ronald Reagan in the pantheon of great US presidents spoke truer than many of them seemed to realize when they said he had restored America's self-confidence and made the country what it is today. As he boasted at the time: 'It's morning in America.' He won two landslide elections off the back of that boast, despite the vast federal deficit and being terror-bombed out of Lebanon, despite the self-deluding gaffes and much skulduggery, including support for what we now call Islamist terrorism. So Reagan's greatness is a bold claim, but a fair one.

The former Hollywood actor turned fortieth president did indeed become the symbol of America's final victory over the Soviet Union in the Cold War. Side by side with Margaret Thatcher, he also led the right-wing reaction to the settlement bequeathed to the boys who stormed the D-day beaches by FDR's New Deal and the 1945 Attlee Labour government. From being the solution, the state became the problem. Much of the confusion inherent in current US policy – from Kyoto to Baghdad – stems from that flawed insight. As such, Reagan has a lot to answer for at the bar of history, as much at home as abroad. You do not find poverty anywhere else in the First World quite like you can find in America in the big city slums or the black districts of mid-size towns. You can find it in the former USSR, of course, but that too is a charge for which Reaganomics must bear some blame.

Yet yesterday's emotional response to the 93-year-old president's passing was not all fake sentimentality or cynicism. Ronald Reagan was a happy warrior whose easy-going 'Aw, shucks' style could make people smile who never voted for him. 'Wake me up in an emergency,' he used to say, 'even if I'm in a cabinet meeting.' He watched a lot of old movies and went to bed early. But it was always a mistake to underestimate him. When I arrived in Washington during his 1984 re-election campaign, the Democratic challenger, Walter Mondale, thought he could make an issue of Reagan's age, seventy-three at the time. Then Reagan used one of their TV debates to promise not to make an issue of young Mondale's (fifty-six). The whole country laughed and Ron was back for four more years.

In 1988 there was half-serious talk of changing the constitution to allow him four more. You had to be there to understand his hold on the American people. But right-wing US Republicans do not export well. Among the uptight elites of Europe Reagan was always 'that cowboy'. Even Mrs Thatcher – who owed him for his support in the Falklands – had her doubts, voiced only occasionally in public, over the deficit or the 1983 invasion of Grenada.

Reagan knew that the appeal of individualism, both noble and selfish, would defeat the Soviet fox. Armed with 'evil empire' rhetoric – which he believed – and a chequebook, he outspent it. Missile defence tests were fiddled, then as now, but worked. All this was combined within a bundle of contradictions. Though a believer in Armageddon, Reagan himself was not particularly religious, but his influential wife, Nancy, had an astrologer. He was a divorcee, and personally tolerant. And his own family was a dysfunctional prototype of the Osbournes.

The first Reagan press conferences I attended required a correction box so cringe-making in next day's *Washington Post* ('the president misspoke on the following points ...') that I assumed the old boy would have to resign. But it didn't matter. On the big occasion, the *Challenger* disaster or D-day 1984, he could touch people's hearts. His letter revealing his Alzheimer's condition ('I am one of millions of Americans ...') is a model of grace. Foreigners often fail to grasp that an American president is head of state as well as head of government. 'He's much better at being the Queen than he is at being Mrs Thatcher,' I used to explain, condescendingly, on my visits to Britain. She was so busy, so formidable; he was, well, laid-back. He made it seem so easy. I was wrong about that, too. The old actor was just acting.

Ronald Reagan died on 6 June 2004 at the age of ninety-three.

27 April 2004

VERONICA HORWELL

Estée Lauder

Estée Lauder, who has died aged ninety-seven, was a generation younger than those other cosmetic empresses Elizabeth Arden and Helena Rubenstein; and had less old-world imperial ideas as to how beauty could upgrade female status. She proposed that a woman might, through managing her appearance, join the beautiful people, agelessly photographable in couture clothes, about to host the perfect house party on the Riviera or Palm Beach for, say, the Princesses Diana and Grace, and a Vanderbilt or two.

Lauder's advice suggested, without any contempt, that men were suckers ('You can get anything you want from men with perfume'), and that women should control their looks to control their lives ('Before you were married, you played at being glamorous and exciting, you were the greatest little actress in the world; now what are you? Nothing – go do something about it, honey'). Hers was a work ethic for the complexion. 'Not by hoping or dreaming, but by working for it' was Lauder's slogan, and later her company's mission statement.

She was born Josephine Esther Mentzer, in Corona, Queens, New York, the daughter of Hungarian immigrants. Her father, Abraham, managed a hardware store, and, as a child, she gift-wrapped hammers at Christmas time. Her mother, Rose, retained her Hapsburg empire faith in spa treatments and unguents; while Uncle John Schotz, a skin doctor who arrived from Vienna at the outbreak of the First World War, brought over 'a little bottle of oil and told me never to use anything else'.

In those days, perfumes were closer to hooch distilling in the bathtub than laboratory chemistry, and cosmetics were mostly pharmacists' concoctions. So Schotz stirred his potions on the kitchen cooker, and flogged them locally. His young niece promoted one of them as Super-Rich, All Purpose Cream (which sounds like the brisk, unexotic labels of her Clinique brand more than half a century later), but her proper career began after she married an Austrian-born businessman, Joseph Lauter, in 1930.

She knew what she wanted, which was to be calmly rich in servant-run houses in Manhattan and Eaton Square; she did not then know how to achieve it. She even tried acting and thought Joseph enough of a liability to divorce him in 1939, taking their son Leonard with her. Four years later, she rectified the mistake, remarrying Joseph, who had, by then, changed his name to Lauder, and having a second son, Ronald. The couple, as equal partners, founded the firm of Estée Lauder in 1946 – Estée was the Frenchified version of Jo's middle name.

But they were not then on a fast track. When the adult Leonard joined them in the 1950s, they were still operating out of a room above the Stork Club in New York; Leonard recalled how his mother would put telephone callers on hold, then change her voice to pretend to be whatever department they demanded. If out-of-town buyers actually arrived, she would lead them out on to the terrace for a lunch served by waiters from the club.

Estée's original insight was to understand how the best shops filtered reality, responding artificially to the seasons and selling not so much goods as a temporary fantasy existence. Thus the Lauders wanted to retail the output of their two small factories, not through pharmacies, but in department stores. At Saks Fifth Avenue, the first store to stock her products, in 1949, Estée made up customers, forty a day if that was what it took to shift product. 'Touch your customer, and you're halfway there,' she said.

She once 'accidentally' spilled Youth Dew, her pungent body scent, on the carpet in the Galerie Lafayette in Paris as an olfactory business card; she kept on at Harrods for years to be allowed into their perfume department. Youth Dew was credited with transforming the company's fortunes; following its introduction in 1953, annual sales rose from $20,000 to $800,000 by 1958.

By the time Estée's name became familiar in the mid-1960s, after Leonard took out a loan to finance the firm going international, she was into her fifties, and knew how women used skincare and cosmetics as a psychological, as well as practical, defence against the marks of age. 'Time is not on your side – but I am' was another Lauder slogan. She offered make-overs and advice even to hackettes conducting interviews – 'White is a godsend, honey, it's black in a dim-lit room that makes you look old and tired' – and concentrated on fragrances and compacts (her own were of gold and platinum).

The money rolled in and, with it, the desired style of living. Lauder came to exemplify the American concept of graciousness she had dreamed about: starched collars on Paris dresses, tiaras at the New York Met, philanthropic foundations dispensing charity, tête-à-têtes with the Duchess of Windsor. A Lauder cream, the duchess remarked gratefully, put a girdle round your face. Estée loathed rival cosmetic baron Charles Revson, of Revlon; she thought he was vulgar. He didn't have class, he wasn't aspirant and he cut a meaner deal than she did. President Richard Nixon offered her the post of US ambassador to Luxembourg and, in 1978, the French awarded her the Légion d'honneur.

Joseph, who said his wife's epitaph should be 'Here lies Estée Lauder / Who made it / And spent it', died in 1983, but their sons and the creative team kept updating the company image. The firm added a male range, Aramis, in 1964, and, four years later, responded cleverly to the baby-boomers, who wanted beauty to be more scientific, by launching Clinique in outlets offering a quasi-medical consultation with white-coated saleswomen.

Clinique packaging remains a twentieth-century classic: pharmacy bottles and full-metal-jacketed lipsticks, like silver bullets for the handbag. Prescriptives (1979) and Origins (1990) matched market changes towards playful colouring and earthy ingredients; in the mid-1990s, the firm shrewdly acquired two cult companies, developing cosmetic lines for high-fashion professionals.

The corporate face morphed with the times too – presciently when the then little known Elizabeth Hurley was chosen as model for a re-launch in 1995. Even half-dressed to shock, she looked like a lady by Estée's definition, and the grande dame herself stood by Hurley during a scandal, loyalty repaid when an image of Hurley romping with a dog sold gallons of an old-style Lauder scent. The company went public the same year, and Leonard succeeded his mother as chairman.

Estée Lauder made her last spot-lit public entrance at the firm's fiftieth anniversary party at the New York Museum of Modern Art in 1996. By then, she had a personal fortune in the region of $400m, and was listed in *Forbes* magazine among the 400 richest Americans. She was frail, but visibly proud of the family achievement – 9,900 employees in more than 100 countries, turnover of $3bn a year – and equally of grandson William (head of Clinique) and granddaughters Aerin (head of development) and Jane (Clinique). 'My body is inside her,' Estée said of each of the girls.

But in the photographs of that party, Estée herself glows brighter than her descendants. She always was a dab hand with rouge, since, without it, 'We blondes fade at night.'

Estée Lauder died on 24 April 2004 at the age of ninety-seven.

15 April 2004

RORY CARROLL

Thabo Mbeki

For the democratically elected leader of a country it was a strange motto but Thabo Mbeki seemed to relish it: 'No one likes me; I don't care.' It started as a terrace chant of defiance by fans of Millwall, the London football club loathed by rivals, and at some point South Africa's president made it his own.

He never articulated it so bluntly, of course, but the evident disdain for what others thought of him shone through. Whether addressing the ANC party faithful or captains of industry, there would be no jokes or effort to connect, no projection of personality. It has done him little electoral harm. This week Mbeki is poised to win a second five-year term when he leads the ANC to a crushing victory at the polls, maintaining and perhaps strengthening its political dominance since apartheid fell in 1994. As leader of the region's economic and diplomatic powerhouse, he is the most important man in Africa.

Curious, then, that Mbeki, aged sixty-two, is so unloved. In recent weeks he has reinvented his public persona by playing with children and dancing, an astonishing departure that has won rave reviews, but for a decade, as Nelson Mandela's deputy and then as president, he abhorred the common touch. Give him an opportunity to empathize with the poor and sick, and he would retreat into technocratic jargon. Give him a baby, and he would plop it into the nearest lap.

'We've got a government of the people, for the people, by the people, led by a president who doesn't like people,' satirist Pieter-Dirk Uys quipped on a theatre stage last week. The audience boomed with applause. Black South Africans as well as their white counterparts are not 'wildly enthusiastic' about the president, according to Bob Mattes of the Cape Town-based polling group Afrobarometer, which is why his approval ratings of 55 per cent trail his party's.

Mandela's well-documented coolness to his successor was visible again last week in their awkward sharing of a podium in Johannesburg. His ex-wife, Winnie Madikizela-Mandela, detests Mbeki. She keeps a photo of the time he knocked her hat off at a rally – she tried to kiss him; he shoved her away – tacked to her office wall like a trophy. Even his parents, ANC stalwarts, did not love Mbeki in a conventional way and encouraged him to regard the movement as his real family.

Why is Mbeki unloved? And does it matter? 'There was no way Mbeki was ever going to be adored the way Mandela was. So he advanced his career in a different way, by getting people to respect him, even if they did not like him,' says Mark Gevisser, a Johannesburg-based author whose biography of the president is to be published this year.

A Western diplomat agrees, claiming that Mbeki decided in the early 1990s there was no point competing for the adulation inspired by Mandela and so opted to play the technocrat and intellectual, the master of detail who would turn ANC promises of a better life for all into reality while sponsoring a pan-African renaissance.

To those who knew him in exile, as a student at the University of Sussex, a spokesman in the ANC's London office and a leader-in-waiting at the ANC's headquarters in Lusaka, Zambia, the change was startling. The young charmer who loved Monty Python, whose camaraderie and intellect persuaded Western governments to impose sanctions and white Afrikaner leaders to accept the unsustainability of apartheid, vanished. He kept the pipe, and the penchant for Scotch, but became aloof upon entering government.

'I was hugely impressed by his intelligence, his sense of humour. I don't know what happened after 1994. I don't think any of us know him,' said Uys, speaking after his one-man show.

Does the president's personality matter? Electorally it is largely a non-issue, says Mattes, the pollster, because South Africans vote for parties, not candidates. But its impact on government policy is profound and complex, say analysts. On one level Mbeki is refreshing. Here is a politician with no time for image consultants or soundbites. The rest of the ANC dances and sings at rallies but he is usually happier in his chair. Wooden, certainly, but if a continent needs a leader with more competence than charisma it is Africa.

Good governance is not about popularity, so arguably there was no better man to deal with the horrible surprise in 1994 that the newly elected ANC government had inherited no bulging coffers to fund the houses, piped water and electricity it had promised the poor. The minority white regime had bequeathed a distorted siege economy close to collapse, which required long, painful fixing. 'Mbeki is an exceptionally intelligent man, one of the sharpest and brightest analysts I have ever met,' says Allister Sparks, a leading commentator. 'Since he was deputy president he was the one driving the transformation of the economy.'

In effect, that meant dumping the ANC's wholesale nationalization in favour of pro-market policies. Ten years later poverty and unemployment are worse but there is a new black middle class and an economy that is stable and poised, according to the government, to deliver jobs and hope.

Mbeki knew the ANC's coalition partners in the trade unions and Communist party would not forgive him, but he went ahead anyway, according to one observer, adding that his one-time rival for the leadership, Cyril Ramaphosa, would have cared too much about popularity to pull it off. 'He often acts as a prophet in the wilderness,' Gevisser says. 'His career is full of conflict. Even though he was the crown prince he always had to fight for his own position.'

Born into modest means in rural Eastern Cape, from boyhood Mbeki was groomed for leadership and apprenticed to a series of father-figure grandees, including Oliver Tambo. The problem, according to one observer, was that he grew up treating relationships in terms of power and ascendancy, and divided people into those to be buttered up and those to be intimidated. Now he is president there are fewer to butter up.

Some white South Africans worry over time their country could slide into a Zimbabwe-style one-party state, but Mbeki's businessman brother, Moeletsi, says democracy is secure: 'Governments in South Africa don't have so much power.' Even so, it was unfortunate that the president narrowed policy debate, according to Judith February of the Institute for Democracy in South Africa. 'The Mbeki style is "I know what's best for the country".'

One issue, HIV/Aids, has wrecked confidence in his judgement. An estimated 5.3 million South Africans have the virus, and some 600 people die daily. Mandela ignored the pandemic in office but hopes were high that his successor would respond. Instead, Mbeki, unafraid to be unpopular, fell for dissident scientists and crypto-scientists who denied HIV caused Aids, and warned that anti-retroviral drugs could shorten rather than extend lives.

Civil society groups and medical organizations were blocked from setting up treatment projects. Hundreds of thousands were dying on his watch, to the horror of a world which had feted the ANC, yet still Mbeki stayed firm. Under pressure, he 'withdrew from the debate' and this month the state finally started a national treatment programme – just in time to neutralize HIV/Aids as an election issue. Some critics suspect the president wanted to spare the exchequer by letting the virus decimate the poor and unemployed. Others think he was sincere in challenging mainstream science and that he remains convinced he will be vindicated. Either way, the saga left the impression that if people did not like the president, he felt the same about them.

Now comes the twist. In the past few weeks of campaigning, the candidate Mbeki appears reborn. Instead of orating at rallies he has been canvassing door to door, visiting townships, sitting on floors, listening. It has been a shrewd re-branding exercise but appears to have awoken something. Long after the sun has sunk and television crews have left, Mbeki has continued, eager to engage with ordinary folk. To his surprise and delight some have cheered and jostled to touch him.

South Africans have glimpsed another leader, one who cares what they think, and for that they seem to like him. The shame is he could have endeared himself long ago if only he had cared enough – or had confidence enough – to try.

30 March 2004

JOHN EZARD

Peter Ustinov

So joyous and immense were the hopes that once rested on the actor, raconteur and humanitarian Sir Peter Ustinov, who has died in Switzerland aged eighty-two, that the final balance-sheet of his life was bound to seem an anticlimax, both to himself and to those who saw the skyrocket of his early talent.

To his contemporary Richard Attenborough, and to many others, 'There was no doubt that he was the genius of our generation. We regarded his potential to be as great as Chekhov or Shaw.' But, Attenborough added, when Ustinov was nearly seventy, 'He hasn't yet written what he is capable of – largely due to his diversity of talent.' He never did, and he knew it. He had to be content with the immense joy that he did give, apparently effortlessly, and with being the most consistently funny raconteur of his time, recognized as a peer by virtually all other humorists, such as Frank Muir, who called him 'one of the best-loved people in the world'. From his late teens until old age, with a steadily wider audience, he enriched the gaiety of nations and added to the public stock of harmless pleasure. His global public will be, as Dr Johnson said of David Garrick, 'disappointed by that stroke of death' which eclipses his gaiety.

His mother was convinced he would be a great creative genius. By the standards he set himself, those of the old European high culture of his mixed ancestry, he fell depressingly short. His genius turned out to be mainly for life-enhancement. His London stage debut at the age of eighteen is still a legend sixty-four years later. He had West End audiences and the leading theatre critics of the day convulsed with laughter at a brief revue sketch. One of his later party pieces was to imitate every orchestral instrument in Beethoven's *Eroica* symphony.

His early impact as a comic performer was comparable to that of Peter Cook, John Cleese and Rowan Atkinson, but Ustinov also proved to be a playwright of substance, a film director, a novelist, a heavyweight newspaper columnist and an Academy Award-winning actor. His conviviality and breadth of interests gave him access to most of the world's VIPs. His close friends ranged from Mikhail Gorbachev to Yehudi Menuhin. He published more than twenty books and harvested countless awards and honorary degrees. His career was like a firework display, which never seemed to end. The highest-rising rockets and the great, all-illuminating Roman candles ran out eventually, but the squibs and firecrackers were still entertaining; and the occasional extravagant set-pieces remained gorgeous.

He was haunted by his father's remark about his literary debut – 'It is not even drama; it is vaudeville' – and in the end, he may have fallen below his mother's expectations. But – along with a few others, including Spike Milligan, Tony Hancock and perhaps the early Mel Brooks – he came as close to genius as any humorist in his time. Late in life he kept calling himself a failure, while sounding remarkably comfortable about it.

'There was only one saving grace,' he wrote in his autobiography *Dear Me* (1977), which sold a million copies, 'and that was that I was irrevocably betrothed to laughter, the sound of which has always seemed to me the most civilized music in the universe.'

His parental heritage was hard to live up to. His father was Jona 'Klop' Ustinov, an opportunistic journalist, half-Russian, half-German, 'the best raconteur I have ever met', according to Dame Rebecca West. Until recently, Klop, whose nickname meant 'Bedbug', was remembered chiefly for running a German news agency in London after the Second World War. But in 1999, a study drawing on unreleased MI5 files disclosed that, as an agent for British intelligence before the war, he warned the government seven months in advance of Hitler's intention to invade Czechoslovakia. In 1938–9 Klop was press officer at the German embassy in London. The ambassador, Joachim von Ribbentrop, was a confidant of Hitler. Ustinov passed on material not only proving Nazi intent, but showing that Hitler's private remarks about the British prime minister, Neville Chamberlain, were littered with schoolboy obscenities. Chamberlain's combined anxiety and rage over this 'contributed materially' towards his introduction of military call-up early in 1939, according to the study. Klop had made a small difference to history, something that his son never managed.

Peter's mother was the painter and ballet designer Nadia Benois, of Russian, French and Italian blood. Her uncle was the theatrical art director, painter and librettist Alexander Benois, co-founder of the magazine *Mir Iskusstva* (*The World Of Art*), out of which sprang Diaghilev's Ballets Russes. Another ancestor through this bloodline was the Italian-born early nineteenth-century Russian composer Catterino Cavos.

Ustinov was born in Swiss Cottage, London, an almost perfectly spherical 12lb baby and only child, descended, as he later said, 'from generations of rotund men – it was the 214th prize in the lottery of life'. He was, according to his family, reading at eight months and displaying his father's gift for mimicry by impersonating Lloyd George at the age of two. His first drawback was his shape, which led to nicknames at school. He 'learned how to survive by emphasizing the clumsy and comic aspects of my character', a ploy that became lifelong. His second was his poor maths and science, which prompted him to leave Westminster School without taking exams. But he had already earned his first writing income by selling the *London Evening Standard* a teasing news story about Ribbentrop's son, a fellow pupil. He was already starting to write plays.

His mother got him into the London Theatre Studio, an acting school run by her friend, the eminent director Michel St Denis. The actor Dirk Bogarde, who shared a dressing room with him, remembered 'a rough-haired, scatty boy, blindingly ambitious, streets ahead of any thing I'd ever come across ... he scared the shit out of me'. St Denis diagnosed 'a dangerous facility which would need counteracting with discipline', a complaint drama critics were to make all Ustinov's life.

In 1939, his flair burst out almost overnight in two sketches in a revue at the Players' Theatre in London. One sketch, spoken mainly in invented Swahili, satirized a talk he had heard at school by a cleric on 'Christian soldiers in the heart of darkest Africa'. The second was a monologue by Madame Liselotte Beethoven-Fink, an imaginary, Austro-German lieder singer, 'grimly mustering the remains of a charm that never existed', as James Agate, the most influential theatre critic of his time, wrote. Agate called it 'an immense piece of acting, too macabre and too true to be merely funny'.

This was enough to launch him in the theatre. A friend sent Agate a draft of Ustinov's first play, *House Of Regrets* (1940), a tragicomedy about Russian émigrés not unlike his own family. The critic announced in the *Sunday Times*, 'A new dramatist has arrived.' By 1942, just after his twenty-first birthday, the new dramatist had two plays running in the West End, *House Of Secrets* and his comedy, *Blow Your Trumpet*, although the latter flopped.

Simultaneously, thanks to the Second World War, Private Ustinov was serving rather insubordinately in the Royal Sussex Regiment. After six awkward months, a transfer to the Army Kinematograph Service enabled him to work as an apprentice scriptwriter on Carol Reed's films *The Way Ahead* (1944) and *The True Glory* (1945), and to direct his first film, *School For Secrets* (1946), about the invention of radar. In 1944 his play *The Banbury Nose*, the story of an English upper-class family written backwards in time, led Agate to hail him as 'the greatest master of stagecraft now writing in this country ... He has as much wit as [Noel] Coward'. In 1946 he played the detective, twice his own age, opposite John Gielgud in a legendary stage version of Dostoevsky's *Crime and Punishment*. Then he directed and starred, as a cowardly Italian conscript, in *Private Angelo* (1949), a film that won him recognition as a film character actor of flourish, wit and an unusual understated pathos.

In 1950–1 he gave four film performances of this kind: in the French Resistance biopic *Odette* with Anna Neagle; in the comedy *Hotel Sahara*; in *We're No Angels* as an escaped convict alongside Humphrey Bogart; and as Nero in the Hollywood epic *Quo Vadis*, which earned his first Oscar nomination. But the film laid bare an inhibition possibly implanted in his schooldays or by his quarrelling parents; he could not portray passionate feelings without looking foolish.

In retrospect, though, 1952 was his true *annus mirabilis*. It saw the first night of his most successful play, *The Love of Four Colonels*, a Cold War satirical burlesque in which Russia, America, Britain and France partition the land in which the Sleeping Beauty lies. Welcomed as a small, if slightly verbose, masterpiece, it ran for years all over the world and became a staple of amateur dramatic societies. Almost simultaneously, he was diverse and prolific enough to collaborate on BBC radio with Frank Muir, Denis Norden and the actor Peter Jones on the improvised series *In All Directions*, which is regarded as a forerunner of *The Goon Show*.

In 1956, he had another durable stage hit with *Romanoff and Juliet*, another Cold War satire, later filmed. In 1960 came his best film acting as Batiatus, the self-disparaging slave dealer in Stanley Kubrick's film *Spartacus*. Fellow actors still analyse the almost throwaway technique of understatement with which he upstaged Laurence Olivier during that player's prime and held his own with Charles Laughton, a grand master of underplayed idiosyncracy. It won him an Oscar for best supporting actor – as did *Topkapi* only four years later.

But his heyday was slipping away. Although he appeared in twenty-one more films during the next thirty years, he had no more triumphs; nearly all the films were abysmal. On the stage, the tolerant, discursive, boulevard theatre in which he had flourished was disappearing. The turning point was the most ambitious project of his life, his effort in 1961 to do justice as film director and producer to Herman Melville's naval allegory of good and evil, *Billy Budd*. It shot Terence Stamp to stardom but was a near-disaster, partly because to guarantee backing, Ustinov had to miscast himself as the idealistic but impotent authority figure, Captain Vere. He was hamstrung by his awkwardness about passion. The performance was a melodramatic embarrassment, as he acknowledged.

But there was a deeper problem. Ustinov was keen to discuss – as he tried to do in his novels and prose – good, evil and other themes from the old European culture from which he came. In attempting *Billy Budd*, he felt he had 'at last succeeded in fighting my way through to my own heart'. Yet it began to seem clear that audiences wanted him to be just a funny, foreign fat man. The exotic, clever Europeans he played so well were novel and exciting to the public when such people arrived in Britain and the US as refugees in the war years; by the 1960s they had been absorbed into their host cultures. As a pundit he was handicapped by verbosity. But his talents also straddled too many nationalities for a mass public.

In 1998 he had a critical success in Moscow directing an opera at the Bolshoi. It went unreported in Britain, but in Russia was headlined 'Englishman Saves the Bolshoi'. He said, 'I've never been accused of being English before. It seems rather painful, especially coming from my original country.'

Gradually he relaxed – and slightly coarsened – into the role his new admirers seemed to want: a globetrotting, tax-exiled celebrity who told uproarious tales in funny foreign voices, and star of the Hercule Poirot film series, which allowed him painfully little range or scope. He became, as he once said, 'a dancing bear', and worked hard at it. Into his late seventies, he travelled arduously for television programmes and gave a spate of good interviews to publicize them. Succeeding the late Orson Welles as a foreign member of the Académie Française, he delivered a tribute to the film director that was full of barely disguised autobiography. He said, 'The observer might think that the young man of twenty-five, who had succeeded in leaving the rest of the race so far behind in the first hundred metres, was indeed capable of every victory he could ever wish for. Yet ...' He also said of Welles, 'He could have hung up the chains of the dancing bear and given himself over to contemplation and quiet – something he enjoyed but for which he rarely had the peace of mind.' His own life would have been sadder if the wellspring of laughter inside him had not run so deep.

But in addition to being a celebrity, he shuttled about on behalf of UNICEF, the world children's agency, and was president of the little-known World Federalist Movement. Last year, he was honoured with a graduate college named after him at Durham University, where he was chancellor.

He was married three times: in 1940 to the actress Isolde Denham, with whom he had a daughter, the actress Tamara Ustinov; in 1954 to the actress Suzanne Cloutier, with whom he had a son and two daughters; and in 1972 to the freelance political journalist, Hélène du Lau d'Allemans.

Petrus Ustinov died on 28 March 2004 at the age of eighty-two.

30 March 2004

CORRECTION

Edward Heath

Sir Edward Heath is a sprightly eighty-seven, rather than spritely (headline, page 3, yesterday). Spritely: elf-like, dainty. Sprightly: full of vitality, lively (Collins).

31 October 2003

STEPHEN BATES

Gene Robinson

If you didn't know one thing about Vicky Gene Robinson, the US Episcopalian cleric who this weekend will be consecrated diocesan bishop of New Hampshire, you could mistake him for any one of a thousand vicars or a hundred bishops. Indeed he is just like them. Certainly it is hard to see him, as he was described by his old hometown newspaper the *Lexington Herald-Leader* in Kentucky last weekend, as the most controversial Anglican leader since Henry VIII.

Canon Robinson, aged fifty-six, is diminutive, benign and sandy-haired, beaming genially out at the world through rimless spectacles. He has enough charm to woo the most recalcitrant member of the congregation into joining the flower rota. Even his most committed critics concede that. And he has the steely determination to defy some in his diocese, many in the US Church and a chorus of congregants and primates around the world to become the Anglican communion's first openly gay bishop.

Kendall Harmon, canon theologian of South Carolina and one of Robinson's doughtiest, most reasonable, critics, says, 'I think he's avuncular and quite charming. We converse civilly by email. But he's wrong. I think he's wrong to be in a sexual relationship outside marriage and I'd say that if he was a heterosexual as well.'

Robinson is not the first gay bishop, of course, or gay priest. There are plenty of those around the world, even in churches within an Anglican communion in which some leaders – such as Peter Akinola, the Archbishop of Nigeria – believe that homosexuals are worse than beasts and say they could not sit in the same room with them. So much for the Church's policy of listening to gay people. Homosexuals are clearly even worse than women, whose ordination did not ultimately split Anglicanism, the difference being that many evangelical and conservative opponents of Robinson know women. Some are even married to them.

The opponents just have a seemingly insuperable problem with men who lie with men – even men in monogamous relationships who want to be Christians – and are prepared to split the Church if Canon Robinson becomes Bishop Robinson on Sunday afternoon. Despite the huffing and puffing from this month's Lambeth conference at which thirty-seven Church leaders warned that his consecration (but not, apparently, his continuation as a lesser priest) would tear the fabric of the communion, not one has been in touch to ask him to step down. Not the head of the US Church, Presiding Bishop Frank Griswold – who voted for his election in August – nor Rowan Williams, the Archbishop of Canterbury, who leads the worldwide communion. Perhaps they know it won't make any difference.

Mindful of the police security that surrounds him after death threats from Christians, Robinson told the *Guardian*: 'The only thing that would keep this from going forward is if I cannot be there for some reason. I have taken the appeals that have reached me very seriously. There have been thousands of emails and letters – two or three times as many in favour as against, including from non-Christians and Jews – and I read every one until the language and the rhetoric became more escalating and obscene. I had a really beautiful postcard from England, showing the high altar of Durham Cathedral, and on the back they'd written: "You fornicating, lecherous pig." This has strengthened my faith. God seems so very close right now that prayer almost seems redundant. I feel absolutely surrounded by his love and his presence is almost palpable to me. I am calm and at peace and I am prepared to move forward.'

Robinson may feel particularly touched by God because when he was born in 1947 to tobacco sharecroppers in Kentucky he was paralysed and not expected to live. Thinking it would not matter, his father gave him the names he and his wife had planned for a daughter – hence the Vicky. Instead, the paralysis went and he lived. His mother Imogene said this week that she believed God had spared his life and guided him ever since: 'To me he's always been a wonderful boy. We've been proud of him all his life.'

This rhetoric about God's personal intervention is not the sort of stuff you would get from the bland men who sit on the Church of England's bench of bishops. Nor is it the language of those who regard Robinson as defying God's law by living in sin with his partner of thirteen years, Mark Andrew, an official in the local health service. The tactics of some opponents have been quite disreputable, including a transparent attempt to discredit him on the verge of his election at the Episcopal general convention in Minneapolis. He was accused of 'inappropriately touching' a man at a public meeting – an assault that transpired to be a hand placed on the complainant's shoulder. Then there was the pornographic website that could be accessed from a teenage helpline that Robinson had helped to set up a decade ago – the 'smoking gun' in the words of one over-excited hack – that turned out to be an inadvertent link added many years after his connection with the service ceased.

But it still goes on. The evangelical *Church of England Newspaper* until recently regularly smeared Robinson by saying he had abandoned his wife for his partner. The facts are rather different. He was married for more than a decade, although his wife Isabella knew he was gay. The couple had two daughters and the young clergyman had therapy to try to 'cure' his orientation. It didn't work and in 1986 they separated, divorcing the following year. Afterwards they attended a church service at which they asked each other's forgiveness, promised to raise their daughters together and handed back their wedding rings. Robinson did not meet his partner until three years later. It may be significant that both his former wife and his daughter Ella gave him their full support in his election as bishop – the other daughter, Jamee, was giving birth at the time.

Robinson, ordained thirty years ago, has been a priest in New Hampshire for nearly all his ministry. There are only 15,000 Episcopalians in the state, and they elected him as their next bishop in the summer from a field of 150 candidates. Had the election taken place a few weeks previously his appointment would not have had to have been confirmed by the general convention but would have passed through a church committee on the nod, so perhaps avoiding the worldwide controversy. Nevertheless, when the storm broke, the fact that Robinson had been democratically elected by his own parishioners placed him in an immeasurably stronger position than Jeffrey John, forced in July by the Archbishop of Canterbury to step down from the suffragan bishopric of Reading because he was gay, although celibate. The archbishop appointed Dr John, knowing him to be gay, and then backed down when evangelicals complained.

Yet Robinson has become a hate figure for some conservatives. The redoubtable Baptist minister Fred Phelps will travel from Topeka, Kansas, to stand outside the consecration with his 'God Hates Fags' banners. Mr Phelps describes Robinson as a 'disgusting, detestable, loathsome, filthy, abomination – the Great Whoremonger'. To another section of the community, however, Robinson's appointment is a sign of hope. His appearance by videolink at the Lesbian and Gay Christian Movement's conference in Manchester last weekend was greeted with a standing ovation.

'To raise the issue of homosexuality above the Nicene Creed and belief in the

Trinity seems to me to border on idolatry,' he said. 'If this is all about the authority of scripture why haven't people threatened to leave over the Church not obeying Christ's commandment to reach out to the poor? A third of the parables and a sixth of Christ's words in the Gospels are about wealth possession, but we don't hear too much about that.'

11 October 2003

DAN DE LUCE

Shirin Ebadi

She is small in stature but a force of nature in and out of the courtroom. Shirin Ebadi is a one-woman human-rights machine, inspiring students through her law faculty lectures, forcing judges to acknowledge contradictions in Iran's legal code and lobbying parliament to protect the rights of children born out of marriage. She has already embarrassed the conservative clerics ruling Iran but yesterday's announcement from the Norwegian Nobel committee will make life more awkward for the defenders of the country's rigid laws. For Ms Ebadi and her colleagues the Peace prize is like a shot in the arm for their efforts. 'I think this prize gives me and Iranian people more courage to work for human rights and peace,' she told the BBC in Paris.

What must have the hardliners worried is the following Ms Ebadi has among the vast youth population, who see her as a courageous heroine standing up to a theocratic system. 'I'm so happy,' said Reza, a graduate student in Tehran. 'I am proud to be an Iranian today.'

With young women becoming educated in unprecedented numbers, Ms Ebadi senses society is changing in ways that the conservative establishment does not understand. 'Sixty-three per cent of entering university students are women. They see that the laws are not suitable for the conditions that are emerging,' Ms Ebadi, who has two grown-up daughters, told the *Guardian* recently. 'Because so many women are protesting against their conditions, things will have to improve.'

Along with several other lawyers, Ms Ebadi has launched a non-governmental organization, the Centre for the Defenders of Human Rights, which will benefit from the Nobel prize of $1.3m (about £780,000). 'She is one of the most active lawyers in Iran, working to promote human rights for women, children and all citizens,' said her colleague, Mohammad Fayfzadeh. 'She has performed brilliantly.'

There was a time when the 56-year-old Ms Ebadi was fighting a lonely battle. After the 1979 revolution that toppled the regime of the shah, Ms Ebadi was told she would have to step down as Iran's first female judge: 'The head of the court told me I could not work as a judge because I am a woman. He said it was forbidden by sharia law.' Now prominent lawyers and MPs agree that women should serve as judges. 'Many women are now working as legal advisers to judges. It's only a matter of time before we have female judges. We have been fed so many things in the name of Islam and sharia law.'

She uses sharia law, which forms the basis of Iran's laws, to argue that there is no legal foundation for discriminatory rules that give women an inferior status. She cites the writings of senior clerics and other areas of the law that have been freshly interpreted to adapt to modern circumstances.

In one case Ms Ebadi has fought against 'blood money' provisions that put the value of a woman's life at half that of a man's in financial compensation. 'I accept these cases to show what the consequences of inadequate, inappropriate laws can be,' she said. Through her lobbying in parliament and the courts, Ms Ebadi has also succeeded in her campaign to grant legal rights to children born outside of marriage though they are still denied the right to any inheritance: 'I am still fighting to get that changed.'

In a country where many dissidents have been discredited or forced underground, Ms Ebadi stands out for her single-minded commitment to human rights without ties to partisan politics or polemics. She has spent time in solitary confinement and received a suspended sentence of fifteen months for videotaping an interview with a former paramilitary. In the interview, the paramilitary described an assassination attempt against a member of the cabinet and other methods of repression. Ms Ebadi, who works late hours in her office alone, acknowledges the threat she is facing: 'Defending human rights in Iran has unavoidable dangers.' The most chilling event for her was when a document leaked out from the intelligence ministry that included names of intellectuals who had been murdered in mysterious circumstances. It was a list of political enemies apparently singled out for liquidation. 'I'm like any other human being,' she said. 'I experienced fear. It comes to you like hunger, you don't have a choice. But I have learned how to overcome this feeling and not let it interfere with my work.'

She wears the head scarf or *hejab* as required by Iran's dress code and though she has no affection for it, she sees it as a low priority among a long list of women's grievances: 'There are much more important issues that need to be addressed.' Ms Ebadi credits the Islamic revolution's strict dress code and segregation of the sexes at university with opening the door to emancipation. Once the universities became a place where a father could send his daughter without worrying about 'moral corruption', society began to change, she said. 'There is a saying that modernity is born on the street. And when a woman steps out on the street, she cannot be a traditional woman any more.'

4 October 2003

HYWEL WILLIAMS

The Pope

Ever since that surprise October election twenty-five years ago, Karol Wojtyla has been Christianity's main event. The papacy has been his best and longest gig – a chance for this former actor and occasional playwright to play his best role (and real self), that of the gleeful contrarian. Doctrinally, he's rejected modern liberalism as so much cocky materialism. Administratively, he's cold-shouldered Vatican 11 – collegiality and all that – as the boring preoccupation of second-rate academics. Now the show is nearing its close. Earlier this week Josef Ratzinger, the cardinal in charge of enforcing Roman Catholic doctrine, said the faithful should start to pray for Wojtyla. But this is a papacy that has long since sent its friends to their knees. Its style has been relentlessly hostile towards modernity, castigating all questioning as faithlessness. A Wojtyla encounter with the risen Christ might well elicit the inquiry: 'John Paul, John Paul, why do you persecute me?'

Although the rock-star-like appetite for the world tour remains unsated, the eighty-three-year-old body is giving out. And the Pope's nomination, with immediate effect, of an extra thirty-one members of the college of cardinals is a sign that John Paul is preparing for his final act. These are overwhelmingly the Pope's men, raised and advanced in the career structures established over the past quarter of a century. And it is that college that will elect his successor. Long after his death, the Catholic Church will remain a John Paul affair.

'Be not afraid!' – the keynote phrase in his address to humanity on the eve of the millennium – is also the key to the man. He is a political activist who knows that the world can be changed as long as you are well organized and mentally sorted. Not for him the cultivated pessimism of some Catholic intellectuals. He has a powerful record of opposition to totalitarianism in both its fascist and its communist form. And from that struggle he has learned the central lesson of his life: evil only seems to triumph, but faith-driven politics can win through. It's a life example that rebukes the sceptical timidity of 'professional' politicians.

Looking at a Catholic world transformed by his own optimism of the will, he is undismayed. While dark forgetfulness claimed those other 1980s Cold War warriors, Reagan and Thatcher, John Paul persisted. Josef Ratzinger, in most respects his alter ego, foresees a fortress and minority Church, a slimmed-down body entirely on-message. But Wojtyla's instinct is that the twenty-first century will be the great Christian century – a real springtime for Catholic humanity, despite all the present evidence of a decline in communicants and vocations. For vision and consolation he turns away from Western Europe – populated for him by bourgeois and parochial wimps. Africa and Latin America are where the action lies: continents of peasant vitality and all signed up for the voyage on that ark of salvation.

And the peasant Church is attractive to Wojtyla because it accepts so unquestioningly the Pope's exclusive custodianship of the keys of heaven. He has gone through the ecumenical motions with Protestant churches – but no more. When he meets Rowan Williams today, he will, in his view, be shaking hands with an amiably muddle-headed university professor who has been deluded into thinking that he is a priest.

Throughout his priesthood the Pope has been absolutely faithful to the idea that Christianity offers the world a sign of contradiction. His inspirational side comes from his apocalyptic sense that the world stands under judgement. Wojtyla glories in the fact that the Church is the light that stands out against the surrounding darkness, and that the faithful are really called to a life in which they are bound to be misunderstood and persecuted by secular ideologies. He is shaped by anti-fascism and sees clearly how national socialism was an alternative theology, a system of nature worship that uprooted the cross and replaced it with the forest. And the best of him is in those impassioned encyclicals that have called down papal judgement on the developed world's capitalism. He was an anti-globalist long before the idea was taken up by secular liberals.

As a social thinker he has followed and developed the Catholic Church's teaching – established since the late nineteenth century – that capitalism has to be regulated by both Church and State. The rights of individualism, in this perspective, run easily and heedlessly into gratification of the self. Against such Anglo-American capitalism, John Paul has always expounded passionately the Church's philosophy of the communal, of workers' rights as organized in trade unions and in political parties. It's an aspect of Catholic truth that shows how the Church is the body of the risen Christ and also the body of believers. Like classic socialism, it has the dynamism of a mass movement – which is why liberalism, with its rather cultic attachment to individual rights, is very alien to it.

When it comes to the need to defend the rights of nations as well as individuals against the rule of might, Wojtyla has been a Catholic hero. From the defence of Polish independence right through to the condemnation of American aggression in the Middle East, the papal words are always a powerful reminder that the very notion of international order is rooted in Catholicism. This papacy has upheld and advanced the Catholic intellectual tradition of examining scrupulously what makes a war just or unjust.

But the contradiction's greatest sign is within Wojtyla himself. He is the intellectual theoretician and defender of peasant Catholicism: the former professor with a penchant for the prophecies of Fatima. And he has behaved in ways calculated to justify the most arrant Protestant demonization of Catholics as hypocrites. He has ensured that the laity lives in a terrible system of double standards about birth control, while the paedophilia scandals, particularly in the US, are a direct result of his own arrogant system of centralized Church government. Local bishops, denied autonomy, kicked the problem upstairs, where it was allowed to fester. The catastrophe illustrates Wojtyla's attachment to sixteenth-century counter-reformation Catholicism, top-down rule from the centre. The result is that his Church is as sclerotic as the Kremlin that he helped to dispatch – and for the same, bureaucratized reasons.

And in his beloved Third World, it was Wojtyla's own decision to go on the heresy hunt against liberation theology – that most potent gospel-intoxicated witness to the truth that the Church's first mission is to the poor. Liberation theologians galvanized Latin American Catholicism – and were then personally crushed by the Pope. What followed, especially in Brazil, has been a Catholic tragedy. The poor have left the Church and flocked to the mass evangelical sects with their pie-in-the-sky consolations.

World-transformers are not easily disentangled. Their strengths tend to be part of their weaknesses. In much the same way, Christianity's own history shows that its superstition can't be easily separated from its truths. But the sadness of this papacy is that it is so haunted by one man's war. For although his papacy was so triumphalist-baroque in style, this Pope has been incorrigibly a man of the underground resistance. He decided to fight totalitarianism in the secular world by cultivating a corresponding totalitarianism on Peter's throne. Ecce Papa – a man of iron.

31 July 2004

RICHARD EYRE

Our patron saint

A friend of mine had a framed photograph of Marlon Brando hanging on the wall in her hallway for many years: Stanley Kowalski in *A Streetcar Named Desire*, body curved sinuously, arms folded across sweat-stained grey T-shirt, hands pushed defensively under biceps, eyes direct and challenging. A few weeks ago, on the day that Brando died, the picture fell from the wall, breaking the glass.

It wouldn't be much of an exaggeration to say that for my generation of would-be actors Brando was a saint – and I don't mean a secular one. We revered him, genuflected before his image, scavenged for anecdotes of his life, attempted to imitate him, attempted to be him. I even possessed a sacred relic – a few frames filched from a 16mm copy of *On the Waterfront*, which I kept in my wallet for many years.

Even though he gave very few performances in which he didn't seem to be taking his revenge on the studios or the director or the audience, I still regard Brando as the best film actor ever. He was mercurial, feline, melancholy, witty and, like all great actors, androgynous. He had an almost mystical authority, the beauty and sexual promise of a Caravaggio youth, dangerous to men and women, gay and straight. For us, in the early 1960s, he showed what Keats had meant: beauty was truth, truth beauty; that was all we knew and needed to know. That I am now disappointed by his waywardness, selfishness, laziness, greed, misogyny, meanness of spirit and disdain for his genius does nothing to diminish the fire of my passion.

Each age defies knowledge of evolution, imagining its revolutionary ways of seeing will endure. When Brunelleschi and Masaccio invented perspective in the early fifteenth century they were as certain that an artistic limit had been reached as the passengers on the first railway trains were that their bodies would disintegrate if they went faster than 30mph. But each generation comes to regard yesterday's novelty of vision as today's archaism. Acting is no less immune to such creationist theology.

Brando was my discovery of perspective. He showed me that people reveal their characters as much in the details of their gestures and posture as by what they say or – as importantly – don't say. It seems odd that actors, engaged in a craft dedicated to imitating nature, should need to discover naturalism. Couldn't actors before Brando see that people didn't behave and move and talk like, well, actors? Which is why I felt so exasperated by the many tributes that referred to Brando as 'the Great Mumbler' or a 'devotee of The Method'. The first accusation made him seem like a fool, the second a follower of a dubious religion.

To deal with his mumbling first: watch him in *Reflections in a Golden Eye*; or as Mark Antony in *Julius Caesar*; or as Fletcher Christian in *Mutiny on the Bounty*. In the latter he was haughty patrician with a perfect English accent that he'd culled from a young upper-class English actor called Tim Seely, whom he befriended for the duration of the film and cruelly dropped as soon as his purpose was achieved. 'I played many roles in which I didn't mumble a single syllable,' he said in his autobiography, 'but in others I did it because it is the way people speak in ordinary life.' And, defying the image of the self-indulgent narcissist, he said he was well aware of how restricting it was: 'It served the American theatre and movies well ... but you cannot mumble in Shakespeare. You cannot improvise.'

If Brando was not a mumbler, neither was he a Method actor. Temperamentally he could never have been part of a group, still less a collective that resembled a cult. The Method emerged from a New York company of playwrights, directors and actors called The Group. In their programme for training actors lay the genesis of the Actors Studio, founded by one of The Group's directors, Lee Strasberg who, as Arthur Miller once told me, was 'so bad that they had to find something for him to do'.

With Stanislavsky as his model, Strasberg encouraged his actors to systematize their work: the catechism of 'impro', 'emotional memory', 'private moments' and 'relaxation exercises' became their credo. What could only have meaning as empirical practice became a method – or worse still, The Method. Brando's teacher was not Strasberg but Stella Adler, an actress from The Group who had studied in the US with two Russian ex-pupils of Stanislavsky. 'In ordinary life,' said Brando, 'people seldom know exactly what they're going to say when they open their mouths ... They pause for an instant to find the right word, search their minds to compose a sentence, then express it. Until Stella Adler came along few actors understood this.'

There are as many 'methods' of working as there are actors. Some lose themselves in research, as if to elevate the business of acting into a pseudo-science. Others improvise and paraphrase. Others still literally become the character, on set and off. In the days when it mattered to him, Brando researched parts; he inhabited them. He ushered in an approach that is now widely followed by most professional actors, who are following Stanislavsky's pragmatic methods even if they never invoke his name.

Brando got bored by acting. He found the childlike part of it – the impersonation and dressing up – increasingly silly, not a proper activity for a grown man, too feminine by half. Brando, for all his womanizing, seems to have disliked women as much as he disliked the feminine in himself. Whatever the causes, he was cursed by hating the thing that had made him famous. When I made a series about twentieth-century theatre for the BBC, *Changing Stages*, I wanted him to talk about acting. The producer rang him in Los Angeles and he talked to her amicably for about forty-five minutes, said he would happily talk on most subjects for my programme but couldn't imagine anything more boring than talking about his life as an actor. But I did speak to Kim Hunter, the Stella of the Broadway production of *Streetcar*, about him. 'He was an absolutely marvellous actor to work with,' she said. 'His sense of truth about what he was doing just brought the best out of you. And he would tell you if you were missing a word out of a speech. He cared about commas.'

Marlon Brando died on 1 July 2004 at the age of eighty.

5 *August 2004*

OLIVER BURKEMAN

Misstep

In Wembley Park, where the suburbs of north-west London finally surrender to the trunk roads and exhaust fumes, the day that Vipula Prasanna died was an otherwise unremarkable one – a quiet Sunday in May that started foggy and never got much brighter. As almost everyone involved in the case would remark at some point over the following weeks, a few seconds' difference and it would have stayed unremarkable. Prasanna, a forty-year-old Sri Lankan, wouldn't have reached the tube station exit barrier at precisely the same time as Michael John-Charles and John-Charles's five-year-old son. And the fine boundary that separates a general atmosphere of aggression from outright violence on the London Underground might never have been breached at all.

Instead, this is what happened: a few minutes before 11 a.m., Prasanna, who was planning to visit a cashpoint before attending a Buddhist temple, reached the barrier a few footsteps ahead of John-Charles, a former dancer on his way to see his mother, who was visiting from the Dominican Republic. Then Prasanna stopped, realizing that the gates immediately ahead of him were for passengers entering the station. He turned to his left, scanning for the exit gates, found them, and changed direction. John-Charles and his son had been heading directly for the correct gates; in the few seconds it took Prasanna to cross several feet of yellowed floor tiles, they had caught up with him, and the three converged at the barrier.

In the next moment, a fifteen-year-old girl on a school trip heard someone shout something about a shoe. A Nigerian woman, on her way to church, remembered John-Charles telling Prasanna that if he didn't apologize, he would get hurt. James McShane, a station attendant, turned towards the noise and saw a confrontation at the ticket barrier. John-Charles's face was inches from Prasanna's, one witness recalled, and John-Charles was screaming, 'Do you think you can step on my son and get away with it, you fucking cunt?' McShane remembered that Prasanna 'might have sworn back', but mainly his impression was that the Sri Lankan was 'trying to defuse the situation'.

By now, the three had made it through the barrier, and CCTV footage shows Prasanna extending his arm as if imploring John-Charles to see reason. On the narrow, cracked pavement outside the station, no longer in view of the cameras,

Prasanna turned to the five-year-old, witnesses said, 'leant forward and touched the young boy ... in a gentle and reassuring manner'.

'Don't you fucking touch my child,' John-Charles shouted, and clenched his right hand into a fist.

Two hundred and thirty-eight people were violently killed in London in the year to June, some for reasons just as trifling as stepping on somebody's foot – like the fifteen-year-old knifed to death in Fulham in June, apparently for his mobile phone. But something about Vipula Prasanna's death on 2 May seemed to shake even seasoned police detectives and lawyers. It wasn't just the sense that anyone could have been the victim, but a troubling flicker of a thought that it wasn't all that hard to imagine being the perpetrator, either. 'It's just sad, really sad,' says one veteran official connected with the case, before adding bluntly that there have been times on the tube when he has felt like punching people, too.

Not that the official would want you to believe that he might have done what John-Charles did in the moments after he delivered an upper-cut to Prasanna's jaw. The blow, though not fatal in itself, pushed one of Prasanna's teeth through his lip, and sent him reeling backwards. He hit his head on the pavement, where he lay motionless. More than one witness said they saw 'the life go out of [Prasanna's] eyes'. But John-Charles apparently ignored him, striding off with his son down the road, past the Food King and the funeral directors' towards a nearby council estate. Prasanna was carried by air ambulance to the Royal London Hospital, in Whitechapel, and attached to a life-support machine. Three days later it was switched off.

A day after that, according to John-Charles's legal team, the 38-year-old was driving past Wembley Park station when he saw the police boards requesting help in finding a suspected murderer. He recognized himself in the CCTV photos, called a solicitor and made arrangements to surrender the following morning. Police say he told them little, though it did emerge that the foot-stepping incident might have happened earlier in their journeys, at a different station.

Last Friday, John-Charles was jailed for manslaughter at the Old Bailey, and the curious details that emerged about him then seemed somehow to intensify the poignant randomness of the two trajectories that crossed at Wembley Park. John-Charles had worked as a professional dancer, appearing, his defence counsel said, with 'several major singers' on *Top of the Pops*. He had apparently trained for the ballet, and was described – in a detail the newspapers jumped on – as the 'first black student to enrol in the Royal College of Ballet'. (This was also, however, one of the many details of the case that seemed to collapse at the slightest prodding: there is no Royal College of Ballet, and John-Charles was not a student at the Royal Ballet School or the Royal Academy of Dance. His lawyers declined to clarify the matter.) After dancing – and before giving up on the arts altogether, and moving into computers – he had tried singing, even recording his own album. A single called 'No Chorus', by a Michael John-Charles, was released in January 1998, in the same month as Catatonia's hit 'Mulder and Scully'.

News of Prasanna's death made a forceful impact in Sri Lanka – not so much because of its randomness, but because of the way it seemed to strike at the foundations of some long-held Sri Lankan ideas about the British character. 'The British are known as gentlemen,' says Prasad Gunewardene, who covered the story for Colombo's *Sunday Observer*. 'Maybe it was unintentional, but it has brought down the standards of the Britishers among the people of Sri Lanka. They don't expect British people to assault a person who is already pardoning himself.'

Prasanna's family heard the news on his wife's birthday. At their modest home in Colombo, Sudanthika Prasanna answered a phone call she expected to be from her husband – but the voice at the other end was that of Irene Fernando, his former London landlady and a fellow Sri Lankan immigrant. 'I was sitting there, and the police inspector was over there,' Fernando recalls, speaking this week, after John-Charles's sentencing, and gesturing around the small front room of her semi-detached house ten minutes' drive from the spot where Prasanna was attacked. 'They don't speak English, and the police didn't speak our language. So it was down to me to tell them he was on life support.' Soon after, at the Royal London, Fernando held a mobile phone to Prasanna's ear so that his four children, aged between four-and-a-half and twenty, could talk to their unresponding father. 'Oh my God, they were screaming,' Fernando remembers. '"Don't turn off the machine! Don't turn off the machine!" But the doctors decided they had to, and who am I to argue?'

By the time he died, Prasanna had been living in the UK for four years, working mainly in a souvenir shop on the Edgware Road and a discount store in Brixton, sending a portion of his wages back to Colombo each month. 'And perfume and make-up,' Fernando says. 'His daughter [twenty-year-old Sashika] would say, "Send me this, send me this." I told him, "You can buy them in Sri Lanka – what do you want to send them from here for?" But he'd say they liked British things.'

Prasanna had arrived as an asylum-seeker, but his application had been refused twice by the Home Office. His friends say that he had no interest in staying illegally any longer, and planned to return home in July.

'And now the problem is for the children,' says Anura Medagadara, sitting in an office at Willesden Community Hospital, the broken-down NHS establishment where he works as an orderly. Medagadara, a small, jowly man in his thirties, barely knew Prasanna, but is active at the Buddhist temple he sometimes attended, in the London suburb of Kingsbury. After the attack, Medagadara raised about £5,000 for Prasanna's family through the London tabloid *Newslanka*. Much of it was spent bringing Sudanthika and her youngest son, Divyanjali, to London in June, to co-ordinate the return of Prasanna's body to Colombo: 'In our culture system, they always need the body.' Sri Lankan Airlines gave them discounts, but now little of the money is left.

According to Gunewardene, at the *Sunday Observer*, Prasanna's funeral in Colombo on 26 June drew almost 1,000 mourners, and took nearly three hours to process 4 kilometres from the family home to the cemetery. In the family's only interview, Sashika told Gunewardene she thought that her father had been phoning to wish her well in an imminent exam. 'He had hope in me and wanted me to study well,' she said. 'Who will assault a man who tenders an apology for an error that he had made? Do British people behave in such a dastardly manner?' For her part, Sudanthika seemed as angry as she was upset. 'We want Prime Minister Tony Blair to ensure justice,' Gunewardene quoted her as saying. 'Englishmen are known to be people with manners.'

In the end, the fate of John-Charles was decided by a turn of events as random as the encounter that killed Prasanna. The night before he gave his plea, the judge who had been scheduled to hear it, Michael Hyam – who might well have ended up deciding his sentence – suffered a heart attack and died. The next morning, every judge in the Old Bailey crowded into Court Number Four to pay their respects. Shortly afterwards, in an adjoining courtroom, John-Charles's defence lawyer announced that he would be pleading guilty to manslaughter. Last Friday, he received a sentence of three years, half of which was suspended; given the time he has already served in custody, he should be free by September next year.

The sentence reflects the clear lack of homicidal intent on John-Charles's part, but Prasanna's friends in Britain are understandably furious. 'I never heard of anything like this in my country,' says Medagadara, who expresses his anger with bursts of nervous laughter. 'In Sri Lanka, the killer would get real punishment. A lifetime sentence. He's getting three years, he comes back. Yeah, it's manslaughter, but if he didn't attack, Prasanna would never have fallen down. Prasanna would never have gone to the hospital, and never died.' He sighs. 'But it doesn't matter now.'

On the grey day of Prasanna's death, Wembley Park station was closed until after 6 p.m., but things have long since moved on. The ticket barrier where the confrontation occurred is closed as part of extensive renovation works; passengers are currently diverted through a side passage. Most of the surrounding area, in fact, feels like a construction site – from the cranes along the side of the railway tracks to the giant swooping arc of the new Wembley Stadium nearby. On the street outside the station, the spot where Vipula Prasanna's head hit the pavement is unmarked.

28 July 2004

DUNCAN CAMPBELL

Open to all

The funeral, like the man, was 'open to all'. Two hours before the ceremony to say farewell to Paul Mackintosh Foot was due to take place at Golders Green crematorium in north London yesterday afternoon, they had started gathering in their hundreds.

There were the banners of the Socialist Workers party and the unions, of the anti-war and the anti-racism movements, all the causes in which the journalist, revolutionary and campaigner Paul Foot had been so pivotal and with which he was so proud to be associated before his untimely death at the age of sixty-six last week. There were the victims of miscarriages of justice, like Vincent Hickey, Jim Robinson and Colin Wallace, for whose freedom he had battled, and the countless trade unionists and campaigners whose picket lines he had addressed or whose mistreatment he had exposed.

Everyone on the short march up the hill to Hoop Lane seemed to have a personal memory. One remembered writing an anti-Vietnam war pamphlet with him in 1964 and another, a journalist with a lovely west country home, recalled 'Footie' telling him not to worry, that after the revolution it would be 'kept as a regional headquarters'.

There was his uncle Michael Foot and a handful of MPs – Tony Benn, Jeremy Corbyn, George Galloway, Bob Marshall-Andrews – with whom he had found common cause. There was a triumvirate of former *Mirror* editors, and a former ambassador to the US, Peter Jay, and comedians and actors and film directors. And there, walking past the Nostalgia Steel Band as it played, were teachers and printers and dockers and journalists, hundreds of those who, for the last three decades, would have expected a march on such a handsome summer's day to have been addressed with passion, wit and intensity by their favourite orator.

But this time he was present in a wicker coffin draped with a red flag and a Plymouth Argyle scarf, a tribute to the football team and one-time lost cause, which he followed with the same eternal optimism and enthusiasm as he fought all his other causes. More than 2,000 walked with the coffin and many more were already at the crematorium to greet him.

'For God's sake, cheer up!' his old friend, Jim Nichol, told the mourners who filled the hall as hundreds of others listened to the service outside. 'In the integrity department, he set the benchmark.'

Richard Ingrams, his old schoolfriend from Shrewsbury days and his first editor at *Private Eye*, had memories that stretched back more than fifty years, memories of 'cricket matches, plays and concerts and happy hours spent browsing in second-hand bookshops ... He devoted hours to helping the powerless victims of the system ... I trusted his judgement implicitly.' Describing his old friend as a 'devout atheist', Ingrams said Paul Foot had been much upset to discover, after he suffered a near-fatal aneurysm five years ago, that some of his religious friends had been praying for him – and even more indignant to hear that some of them thought that their prayers had been answered when he survived to go on campaigning and writing. 'But there is nothing to stop us now from praying that our beloved Footie may now rest in peace,' he said.

Lindsey German, of the Socialist Workers party and the Stop the War Coalition, of which Foot had been a founder and enthusiastic member, spoke of his ability to bring both history and literature to life. She hoped his legacy would be to inspire others 'to fight to change the system and to make it a better world'.

His three sons, John, Tom and Matt, did what they knew their father would have wanted them to do: they made the mourners laugh despite their grief, with tales of the man who loved C.L.R. James and Gazza, Shelley and Ian Botham, and who was capable of 'a fine off-drive and an excellent forehand', as well as rallying the troops on a cold, damp miners' picket line or enthusing the marchers at an Anti-Nazi League gathering.

'He would have hated anything pompous,' said John. Tom said there was 'no one I knew I would rather spend my time with'. There was the playing of a recording of one of Paul's and his young daughter Kate's favourite songs, one as old as many of the mourners, 'I'm a Gnu', sung by its composers, Michael Flanders and Donald Swann.

There was a final, passionate rendition of 'The Internationale', with many a clenched fist raised and with no need for most of those present to read the words printed out on the programme of the call to the starvelings to arise from their slumbers.

Before that, his three sons had read from his beloved Shelley's poem 'The Mask of Anarchy':

Rise like Lions after slumber
In unvanquishable number –
Shake your chains to earth like dew
Which in sleep have fallen on you –
Ye are many – they are few.

Yesterday they were many, not just those who had flown from across the world or travelled down from Scotland and the north to say their sad goodbyes, but those who had written to his family with their private memories of someone who had touched their hearts. They were the many – the very many – who loved and were inspired by Paul Foot.

Paul Foot died on 18 July 2004 at the age of sixty-six.

4 August 2004

SIMON HATTENSTONE

Peter Pan

I almost faint when Peter Duncan opens the door. It's an apparition. A quarter of a century on from his *Blue Peter* debut, he is unchanged. His hair is still brown, his eyes mystic blue and he's even wearing a pair of shorts. If anything, age makes him more boyish. The cheeky-chappie presenter became, in the mid-1980s, the macho cheeky chappie, who did crazy things for the television camera on *Duncan Dares*; then the risqué cheeky chappie who did crazy things for the movie cameras; and then the mature cheekie chappie who did crazy things for his family, like take them round the world and film the experience. Now, at fifty, Duncan has reinvented himself again – he is the role-model cheeky chappie who is Britain's new Chief Scout.

He bounds enthusiastically from one room to the other, making iced lime drinks while talking ethics in modern society, DIY and his own football genius. In another life, he would be a Labrador.

Bloody hell, I say, you've not changed. 'Uh, no. Yes. No. Yes, I haven't aged yet. It might all come in a rush. I can slip from playing young juves to old men just like that.' It's a classic Duncan sentence – diffident but ultimately decisive. Duncan seems like the archetypal public school boy – likeable, benignly assertive and Panglossian. But he's not. In fact, he went to secondary modern, and left at fifteen to join the panto with his parents who were actor-managers. Now Duncan has four children of his own.

He talks about what attracted him to the greasepaint – the sense of community, being part of a team while still expressing yourself as an individual. In a way, he says, the same is true of everything he has done in life. 'The dichotomy in my life has always been the idea of being useful and doing useful things at the same time as being slightly self-infatuated with your own creative expression.' He often uses words like dichotomy.

Bet your wife, who was a social worker and is now a midwife, has no truck with that bollocksy, artsy-fartsy me-me-me world, I say. He grins. 'I'd like to see that in print,' he says, before agreeing.

Perhaps *Blue Peter* was the perfect halfway house for him – it meant he was doing something socially useful but he could also indulge his ego. 'Yes, I think it's true, and one has to recognize it is a dilemma because as you get older, you get more interested in – dare I say it, I'm sounding like an actor now – being more purely creative.'

The great thing about *Blue Peter*, he says, is that it's always been about ideas, and often the ideas originate from the kids, and it is truly interactive. He wasn't too sure about becoming a presenter at first – after all, he was a serious actor – but he says they were fantastic years. 'There was the adventure side, and the thrill of travel, and the live TV. I loved it.'

He is thinking about his role on the show, and says it's not so different from what he will be doing with the Scouts. He's a true pro – when he thinks we're talking too much about *Blue Peter* he easily, casually, turns me back to the Scouts. Yes, he says, as a *Blue Peter* presenter he was a figurehead and as chief scout he will be a figurehead.

Were you surprised when the Guides approached you? 'You mean the Scouts?' he says gently. Oh yes, I say apologetically, telling him I never quite managed to get to grips with the movement. 'Yes, but … that's where it all went wrong! See, the Scouts for the last twenty years has been co-educational, it's been boys and girls, and, no matter how often you say it, people still forget that.'

Martin, who is sitting on the corner of the sofa stroking one of Duncan's cats, is a field development officer employed by the Scouts Association. He is here to help out with facts and figures. Yes, Martin says, people don't realize quite how much the movement has changed over the years – these days you don't have to pledge your allegiance to Queen and Jesus, and the set-up is more informal, inclusive and internationalist. Duncan is scouring the Scouts manual as Martin talks. 'Yes, there are 28 million scouts worldwide now.'

The problem, Martin says, is not so much with global scouting; it is with British scouting. In modern Britain, where so many families are brought up by single parents or where mum and dad work full-time, parents simply don't have time to help out, and without parents doing their bit you cannot have a booming movement. Duncan believes that parental lack of interest is due more to social change. 'In the last twenty years, it's been the rise of the individual as opposed to the group. Everyone wants to be an individual. So you need to get people to realize there is value – adults I'm talking about – that you can learn something from working in a group.'

He can't stand the way modern Britain is so cynical and illiberal. 'The only thing that binds kids together who are thought to have problems with anti-social behaviour is that they are all told, "You can't do this and you can't do that." The Metropolitan police now want to put a curfew on anyone under sixteen being in the West End after 9 p.m. What extraordinary thinking. Where is that thinking coming from? Quite extraordinary.'

He is lost for words, and stumbles around until he hits on the right one. 'I mean, love. There is something about love that is missing from their life.' He finds it sinister how people blame the 1960s, which was all about love, peace and understanding, for the collapse of moral authority.

Duncan assumed that when Labour came to power, their apparent desire to dictate life to the masses was a bluff to appease Middle England, but now he thinks it's for real. And, he says, spending money on negatives such as anti-social behaviour orders is a waste. Mid-sentence, he has another brain wave. 'It would be better to form an elite SAS squad of scouts, call it something else, just people who are trained and go into the community.'

Ultimately, it's all about embracing life rather than condemning it, he says. A couple of years ago he decided to go off round the world with his family and record their experience with a camera. 'Having done all that travelling with my kids, I can see what it engenders in them. Once you've met your mate from Iraq, the last thing you want to do is ...' He trails off. 'When we go to war or when we see what society is doing to their contemporaries they get very angry because they've seen stuff.' He looks at Martin. 'It's funny, I'm worried that I'm becoming boring because in a short time I've become passionate about it. Must change my tune, must slip in a few more gags.'

Martin giggles at the idea of Duncan becoming a Scout bore. 'That's a good idea,' he nods good-naturedly. 'We can have a new section in the mag called Scout Boring.' But seriously, he says, that's why they have appointed Duncan to the honorary position of Chief Scout – to show the world that the Scouts is a forward-looking, fun organization. And, of course, there is the bonus of Duncan being a newsworthy name. Indeed, the *Daily Mail* has made much of his previous career as a porn star in the film *The Lifetaker*. Actually, Duncan confides, it wasn't really a porn film – he barely took his top off and even then he was in shadow.

As well as his other qualities, what does make Duncan well qualified to be chief scout is his alpha-maleness. However bonkers the challenge, he has always been up to it. He shows me a trophy commemorating the time he drove across the Irish Sea in a Volkswagen for *Duncan Dares*. Is there anything he is scared of, or useless at? 'Well, my wife would say my DIY skills are crap, but she's wrong!' As for fear, he doesn't do it. 'There's a scouts' trek up Everest in 2007, and they don't know it yet but they might have this old bloke tagging along ...'

Duncan's wife, Annie, arrives back home. He goes out to have his photograph taken. What does she think of him as new chief scout? 'Well, it will be very interesting to see how an organization like the Scouts deals with him. The kids will love it, but some of the more staid people ... he might raise eyebrows from time to time, but that may not be a bad thing.'

Duncan is in the garden climbing trees for the photographer. I ask him if he thinks of himself as a man or a boy. 'Ermmm ... transition. I may become a man this year ... Maybe when I get inaugurated in September, maybe that will be my inauguration into manhood.'

'Oh God, he's not in the tree, is he?' Annie shouts from the kitchen. 'Just be careful, will you, Pete? Don't do anything silly.'

MEDIA

ROY GREENSLADE

Black pays the price

It was impossible to wipe the smiles off the faces of Conrad Black's legion of critics yesterday. When a bullying, bombastic, verbose and vain man falls from power, it's not surprising that champagne corks should pop.

For those who have followed Black's recent fortunes, the outcome was inevitable. From the moment an American investor identified the odd matter of 'fees' paid into a private Black concern, the wheels began to come off. Black huffed and puffed, threatening here, promising there, lampooning his detractors, but he couldn't hide from the authorities any longer.

It is a great irony that he has championed the very economic system which has brought him low. Black has repeatedly called on the world to share his adoration for capitalism's free market. Yet it is the ruthless application of the free market by his rival, Rupert Murdoch, which lies at the heart of his problems. They began the day Murdoch launched his price war in 1993, reducing the cover price of *The Times*. 'I love Rupert,' Black once told me, 'but the guy is trying to drive the rest of us out of business.' Within days of that conversation, Black was offering his readers cut-rate subscriptions, thereby reducing his circulation revenue by millions each year.

In a vain bid to keep the *Daily Telegraph* above a million sales, he also gave away too many copies and suffered further problems when advertising revenue fell during the recession. Gradually, profits from the cash cow that was the *Telegraph* group have dwindled to almost nothing, a fact hidden by Black's opaque accounting systems.

Observing Black's predicament has been like watching a replay of Robert Maxwell's final months when his empire crumbled. There are fascinating similarities: both exhibited megalomaniac tendencies; both set up complicated arrangements in which their public companies were surrounded by satellites of private companies with impenetrable accounts; both punched way above their real financial weight. Of course, nobody is suggesting that Black has been guilty of stealing from his company's pension funds. But no wonder the revelations about unauthorized payments have prompted jokes about Baron Black of Crossharbour needing to change his title to Double-Crossharbour.

Black over-reached himself, living out the image of a global media tycoon without the substance to sustain it. He was, it must be conceded, damned good at building his image by employing a potent mixture of bluster and dissembling overlaid with irascibility.

Black seems to prefer insulting people to praising them. When I used to meet him regularly outside the Brompton Oratory after his Sunday devotions, it took little prompting to goad him into a diatribe against his latest enemy. Some of his free character readings of rival owners were both rude and very funny. He was in similar form at a media lunch a couple of months ago. Asked to say a few words, he began his over-long and repetitive defence of President Bush by launching a silly attack on certain journalists for failing to understand that his company was in good health. Bernard Shrimsley, the former editor of three national papers, asked if he planned to sell the *Daily Telegraph* to Richard Desmond. There was a long silence until Black, in a booming baritone crescendo, said, 'Never ... never ... never ... never ... never ... never.' We laughed but, as the shrewd Shrimsley remarked afterwards: 'It won't be long, then.'

In one sense, Black won't be selling to anyone – he probably won't be in a position to decide what happens to his papers. Desmond, the pornographer who owns the *Express* and who fought a battle with Black over the income from their jointly owned printing centre, would certainly not be Black's first choice.

But it would be churlish to suggest that Black's proprietorship of the *Telegraph* has been all bad. He breathed life into a dying monster when he bought it in 1985, playing the role of white knight to its owner, Lord Hartwell, then acting as cuckoo to evict the Hartwell family from their Fleet Street nest. However, the *Telegraph's* best years under Black occurred when he was in Canada. Once he came to London and settled himself into the press baron position of political meddler, his stewardship was more haphazard. His harrying of Max Hastings, his first editor, is a matter of public record.

While some of his maverick entries into editorial affairs were amusing – such as his preference for women in short skirts – his pro-Israeli and anti-European Union sentiments have been controversial. His paper has also undermined Tory party leaders ever since his heroine, Margaret Thatcher, was deposed.

Black respected Thatcher because they shared monetarist economic views. Now it seems that the great, free market ideologue is to lose his business because he forgot the first rule of his beloved capitalism: only the fittest survive.

1 July 2004

DAVID McKIE

Hard facts into high art

If you thought that road rage was a modern phenomenon, think again. Some time in 1826 – that, at least, was when the *Dorset County Chronicle* picked the story up from an Edinburgh paper – two horsemen, the heads of rival county families, came face to face in a narrow lane. Each asked the other to move aside, but neither would budge. After a while, one produced a newspaper and proceeded to read it from cover to cover, a process that took three to four hours. As he finished, the other courteously asked if he might now borrow it. How the confrontation ended is not revealed. Perhaps they simply died there.

More than fifty years later, the novelist Thomas Hardy copied this tale into a notebook which he had labelled 'Facts From Newspapers, Histories, Biographies and Other Chronicles (mainly local)'. Much of his material came from his local paper in Dorset, the *Chronicle* – and not just from recent editions. He'd persuaded the editor, a trusting fellow, to lend him the files from the late 1820s, taking them home, where he and his wife laboriously and not always quite accurately copied them down.

He seems to have felt guilty about this process, as if fearful that his reputation might be damaged if it were known that incidents, episodes and characters in his books had drawn on these simple sources – so much so that he marked the notebook 'to be destroyed uncopied'. Even then he erased and excised some entries (though it's possible to deduce what is missing from the newspapers he was using). But despite his instructions, this notebook was not destroyed, and it has now appeared in an edition called *Thomas Hardy's 'Facts' Notebook*, perceptively introduced and meticulously edited and annotated by Dr William Greenslade of the University of the West of England, Bristol.

Some episodes in the novels are clearly based on these newspaper stories: the selling of Henchard's wife in *The Mayor of Casterbridge*, for instance; Henchard's bankruptcy hearing; and his wrestle with Donald Farfrae, clinging closely to the account that Hardy had read in the *Chronicle* files for 1829. Some of these connections were known already; others were not. But there's more to this book than a mere guide to sources. It's a portrait of a great writer at work, selecting, shaping and picking up fresh ideas – mostly from newspapers but also from books (Horace Walpole's letters, Captain Gronow's then celebrated reminiscences).

Some of what he records seems so trivial you wonder why he bothered. Elsewhere he picks up the sort of anecdote that so many people enjoy reading out of newspapers. The road rage story is one; another is an account of a man with such an aversion to cats that he carried strychnine with him to kill them. But the aspects of a story that Hardy fastens on are not always those that would catch the eye of the general reader. Indeed, there is one account of an aristocratic abduction in which one of the most intriguing ingredients – the fact that the abducted woman later married the magistrate who sent her abductor for trial – is recorded in Greenslade's footnote but is not in the notebook.

Abductions are one of Hardy's passions, along with jiltings, elopements, suicides, accidents – especially if a coach is involved – confidence tricks, highwaymen, horse thieves, men of good birth and background reduced through drink or debt or whatever to squalid poverty, and people who, sharing a room or even a bed in an inn with a stranger, wake up to find they've been robbed – or never wake up at all.

But he's not just looking for stories. Ploughing through the files from the 1820s, he is trying to get a sense of how the everyday world of Wessex has changed over the past half-century; a process symbolized, Greenslade points out, in the relationship between the rough-hewn, old-fashioned Henchard and the modernizing newcomer Farfrae. Newspapers, it is sometimes said, are the first draft of history, and here, in a sense, they're the first draft of Thomas Hardy.

How proud the pressmen of the 1820s would have been had they known that their reports had helped to shape and flesh out the work of one of England's greatest novelists. There's another aspect of newspapers in Hardy's notebook, though, rather less flattering to those in the trade. According to a reference in the *Chronicle* in 1826, the editor of the *Leicester Journal* in 1750 was so short of news that he started to serialize the Bible, getting to chapter ten of Exodus before anything occurred that was worth writing about.

15 May 2004

IAN MAYES

Images and rights

A picture carried across five columns on the front page of the *Guardian* on 10 May had this descriptive caption: 'A naked Iraqi prisoner cowers in front of barking dogs held by US soldiers in Abu Ghraib jail.'

A number of readers questioned the way the picture had been presented and a few said the *Guardian* should not have used it at all. The paper has carried more than fifteen different pictures of prisoners in Abu Ghraib since it published the first on its front page on 30 April – a hooded figure with wires attached, standing on a box. What was different about this one? Unlike almost all of those used earlier, in which the heads of the prisoners had been hooded by their guards, the face of this man was quite clearly visible. He would probably have been recognizable to those who knew him. He would certainly recognize himself.

One reader wrote: 'Please could you explain to me how the photo of a naked Iraqi prisoner on your front page does not infringe his human rights?' A reader of the *Guardian* online, writing from Germany, said: 'Please, please replace the image of the naked Iraqi on your front page and world news page with something less upsetting. It is shameful enough that he has been abused in such a way, but for you to broadcast his humiliation to all your online readers worldwide is certainly adding insult to injury.'

Although readers did not always say so, it seemed to be the fact that the man's face was shown that increased the degree of distress communicated by the picture. 'I realize that you have printed such pictures before on this terrible subject and I know that it is important for us to receive this information,' one wrote. 'Nevertheless, I object to [this picture] because I feel it is now bordering on voyeurism – it feels like incitement, somehow, or as if we all have a part of this man's shame and humiliation. I do not wish to be in any way associated with this sort of inhumanity, and by blazoning it on the front page of the paper it makes us all implicated.'

There is, I suggest, some confusion here between the crime and evidence of the crime. Publication of the photograph does not infringe the man's human rights; but it does graphically convey an infringement of his rights. Taken with other photographs, and we now know there are at least 1,800, many showing greater abuses, the picture has an imperative that demands prominent publication – and demands it, apparently, regardless of all consequences (for instance the further excitement of anti-American feeling in the Arab world). The story has been rightly persistent.

All right, one reader said, but 'why didn't you use a black box to cover the naked prisoner's eyes – as convention demands of civilized societies – in order to give him a certain degree of respect, masking his identity, while still getting the story across?'

A glance across the other British newspapers reveals the confusion – or let us call it differences of opinion – on this. Some pixellated (electronically masked) the prisoner's face. Others did not.

You might ask yourself the question: 'If this had been done to me would I want the world to know about it – would I want the world to know it had been done specifically to me?' To put it another way: 'Would I, given all the efforts of the perpetrators of these abuses to ensure the anonymity of their victims, want to be consigned to anonymity by a newspaper which had had the opportunity to get me out of it?'

In fact, as the *Guardian* reported on Thursday this week, prisoners who, despite the hoods placed over their heads, have been able to recognize themselves in these photographs, are now beginning to come forward to identify themselves and to testify to their maltreatment. The editor of the *Guardian* strongly defends the decision to carry the picture as it was received by the paper and not to mask the face. He feels the paper made a mistake at the beginning of the Iraq war when, after a request from the Ministry of Defence, it pixelated the face of an Iraqi soldier who had surrendered to US marines. He said that to have continued to do that, or to do it systematically, would change the face of war reporting.

We do not know what the particular prisoner in the picture had done or was alleged to have done. Would it, should it, make any difference? Who is diminished by the revelation of such an abuse: the prisoner, his guards, or, as the reader I quoted earlier seemed to sense, all of us? Was it more or less uncomfortable because we were asked to look the prisoner in the face?

3 February 2004

MARTIN KETTLE

Threat from within

Having read the Hutton report and most of what has been written about it, I have reached the following, strictly non-judicial, conclusions: first, that the episode illuminates a wider crisis in British journalism than the turmoil at the BBC; second, that too many journalists are in denial about this wider crisis; third, that journalists need to be at the forefront of trying to rectify it; and fourth, that this will almost certainly not happen.

The reporting of Lord Hutton's conclusions and of the reactions to them has been meticulous. The same cannot be said of large tracts of the commentary and editorializing – nor of much of the equally knee-jerk newspaper correspondence. Much of this comment has been sullied by scorn, prejudice and petulance. The more you read it, the more you get the sense that the modern journalist is prone to behaving like a child throwing its rattle out of the pram because it has not got what it wanted.

Since in some quarters it has become almost obligatory to dismiss Hutton out of hand, it is necessary to reassert that the law lord did an excellent job in conducting his inquiry so briskly and transparently, and to stress that his report is overwhelmingly consistent with the evidence he received. This is especially true of what became the crux of the inquiry: the alleged sexing up of the Iraq dossier; Andrew Gilligan's reporting; and the dispute over the naming of David Kelly.

From the start, though, too many newspapers invested too heavily in a particular preferred outcome on these key points. They wanted the government found guilty on the dossier and on the naming, and they wanted Gilligan's reporting vindicated. When Hutton drew opposite conclusions, they damned his findings as perverse and his report as a whitewash. But the report's weakness was its narrowness, and to some extent its unworldliness, not the accuracy of its verdicts.

There was rattle throwing from the right of the pram – 'a great disservice to the British nation' (Sir Max Hastings in the *Daily Mail*) – and from the left – 'Lord Whitewash' (Paul 'We are paid to be cynical' Routledge in the *Daily Mirror*). But the worst example, appropriately enough, came from the man who has a good claim to be the author of the entire problem between Downing Street and the BBC, the former *Today* producer Rod Liddle.

Liddle is the man who hired Gilligan. He is also the man of whom a former colleague said (as told to *Today*'s historian): 'Rod didn't want conventional stories. He wanted sexy exclusives ... I remember Rod once at a programme meeting saying, "Andrew gets great stories and some of them are even true" ... He was bored by standard BBC reporting.'

Liddle's article in the current *Spectator* exemplifies this approach, and incarnates a great deal of what is wrong with modern journalism. Liddle's article is sneering (Lord Hutton's Ulster brogue is mocked, and he is described as anachronistic and hopelessly naive), and unapologetic (the best Liddle can manage is that Gilligan's famous 6.07 a.m. report went 'a shade too far'). Above all, Liddle's piece is arrogant, embodied in his remarkable final sentence: 'I think, as a country, we've had enough of law lords.'

Think about the implications of that. To Liddle's fellow practitioners of punk journalism, it can be excused as sparky, or justified on the grounds that it is what a lot of other people are saying. To criticize it is to be condemned as boring or, like Hutton, hopelessly naive. To me, though, it smacks of something bordering on journalistic fascism, in which all elected politicians are contemptible, all judges are disreputable and only journalists are capable of telling the truth, even though what passes for truth is sometimes little more than prejudice unsupported by facts.

Liddle is an extreme case, if an influential one (he was ubiquitous in the studios last week, acting out his juvenile Howard Marks fantasy). But he is the iceberg tip of a culture of contempt towards politicians (and thus of democracy) and judges (and thus of the law) that is too prevalent in British journalism (think Jeremy Paxman, for instance, both as interviewer and author). Too much of the initial response to Hutton has wallowed in that fashionable but ultimately destructive cynicism.

Fortunately, however, not all of it. Amid the excessive condemnation of Hutton and the equally exaggerated (and frequently self-interested) dancing on the BBC's imagined grave, there were other voices, which deserve to be heard more widely. So, hats off to the *Economist* editorial that skewered Gilligan for a report that was 'typical of much of modern British journalism, twisting or falsifying the supposed news to fit a journalist's opinion about where the truth really lies. Some in the British media have described such journalism as "brave". Sloppy or biased would be better words.' Bravos, too, for Saturday's signed article by the *Financial Times* editor Andrew Gowers, which described this 'dreadful misadventure' as a wake-up call for British journalism, and said it 'should prompt us to resist the easy, superficial certainties of *parti pris* opinion and rediscover the virtues of accuracy, context and verification'. A round of relieved applause also for the BBC's acting director general Mark Byford for his direct response to David Frost's question this week that 'mostly right isn't good enough for the BBC'.

There is certainly a threat to modern journalism, but it does not come from Hutton, or even from Tony Blair. The over-reaction to Hutton has had the unintended consequence of ensuring that Blair cannot be seen to intervene further against the BBC. Providing Byford continues as he has begun, the BBC's independence is safer now than it would have been had Hutton spread the blame around more evenly.

The threat to modern journalism is real, but it comes not just from without but also from within. It comes not just from the manipulations, favouritism and half-truths of the discredited, and partially abandoned, Labour spin culture, but also from the media's disrespect for facts, the avoidable failure to be fair, the want of explanation and the persistent desire for melodrama that are spin's flip side.

A month ago, the Phillis report on government communications set out some ways that the post-Campbell political world could clean up its act. These need to be followed through. But do we in the media have an equivalent awareness of the equally urgent need to raise our own game? I do not believe we have even begun to realize the damage that some modern journalism is doing to the fabric of public and private life. As Rod Liddle might say (but wouldn't), I think, as a country, we have had enough of such things.

31 July 2004

MARK LAWSON

Political football

In the most public discussion of linguistics apart from Bill Clinton's use of the term 'sexual relations' and Andrew Gilligan's ad-lib of 'knowingly', the future of the England football coach may depend on the interpretation of three words: 'This is nonsense.'

Leaks from sources both friendly and hostile to Sven-Goran Eriksson suggest that this was his response when the Football Association told him of newspaper rumours that he had bedded an FA secretary. It seems that his employers may have taken this as a denial of having had sex with Faria Alam, while what the coach meant was that the intrusive questioning was nonsensical.

This would be consistent with Eriksson's claim in an official statement that he 'at no time either categorically denied or confirmed' the relationship. And it would not be the first time that such a misunderstanding had occurred. A political spin doctor once told me that, when young and naive, he had asked his candidate about rumours of bisexuality. He took the response – 'I can't believe you're asking me that' – as a denial, but, when the tabloids found the other man, it turned out that the words had been a defence of reticence.

It's tempting to call Eriksson's use of language Clintonian, and the former US president is the public figure he most resembles in libido and lingo. But, whereas Bill's 'sexual relations' depended on a most generous interpretation of what counts as sex, Sven's 'This is nonsense' is a genuine double entendre. To bear his meaning perfectly, it would ideally have been 'This is a nonsense' – but this was a man speaking in his second language.

And, if the comment did express outrage at the line of questioning, there was nothing disingenuous about it. Sven and his assistant, Tord Grip, genuinely fail to see sense in the obsession of the British press with his sex life. Culturally, the gap between Scandinavian liberalism and the British newspapers' furious puritanism towards celebrities is as big a mismatch as England v Liechtenstein.

The argument of Sven's press enemies is that he has brought the FA into disrepute and abused a position of trust. But, as has been confirmed by the recent scandals involving David Beckham and Wayne Rooney, football is a sport that encourages sexual athleticism.

Although moralists might wish it otherwise, Sven's erotic adventures have probably improved rather than reduced his reputation with the testosterone-heavy young men he manages. And, unless his affair at the FA involved rape, coercion or harassment (which the woman's tabloid exclusive yesterday seems to make clear it did not), then there clearly is a case for privacy. Even the usual justification for sexual scrutiny of celebrities – that they have used their private life to build their image – clearly doesn't apply in this case as Sven has always made clear that his sex life was a penalty area for interviewers.

However, when Sven and Tord express bewilderment that the coach might be thrown out over matters unrelated to the game, they are missing the point; the newspapers calling for Sven's head are engaged in a displacement assassination. Driven almost crazy by Tony Blair's stubborn continuation in office – through Iraq, Hutton and Butler, heart scares and by-elections – these titles have taken consolation in trying to pick off another public figure. The attack on Sven is politics by proxy.

Toppling this alternative boss will give a brief pleasure to frustrated newspapers, but the likely consequences would leave the media unable to claim even a draw: the coach would get millions in compensation and soon reappear in charge of a club, while England might have to begin a World Cup campaign with an unproven boss.

What has happened this week is that a standard created by the media to topple politicians is now being applied to a football manager. But, even in politics, the presumed connection between fidelity and efficiency was long ago disproved. In America, the divorced John Kerry runs against an incumbent who is desperately trying to wrap himself in the mantle of a twice-married president, Ronald Reagan.

In football, as in politics, the record suggests that what is nicer for a wife has not been better for the country. The two most apparently uxorious recent England managers – Kevin Keegan and Graham Taylor – have been weakest on the field, while the more romantically chequered Bobby Robson, Terry Venables and now Sven have come much closer to winning cups.

For the FA, being battered into appointing someone who regards their wedding day as a more important date than 1966 would be bad husbandry of its money. If Eriksson is forced out, it should be because of his poor use of substitutes, not as a poor substitute for Tony Blair.

22 July 2004

BRIAN WHITAKER

Control Room

Just before the war in Iraq, when journalists were rushing off to become embedded with the military, Jehane Noujaim, an Arab-American film director, decided to embed herself among journalists. She arrived with a couple of mini-DV cameras in Qatar, the tiny Gulf state that gave birth to al-Jazeera – the Arab world's favourite TV news channel, denounced by the Bush administration as a purveyor of lies, lies and more lies. The result is *Control Room*, an 84-minute documentary, billed as a fly-on-the-wall look at the workings of al-Jazeera.

The film was much praised when it opened in the US. The *New York Times* wrote: 'You are likely to emerge ... with your certainties scrambled and your assumptions shaken.' This may be especially true for *New York Times* readers in view of all the scare stories about Iraq that the paper published before the war but has since retracted. It may also be a shock for folks in Tennessee to discover that al-Jazeera, on the inside, is much like any other TV station: banks of flickering screens, hot lights, knobs, buttons, trailing cables, and people trying – with varying degrees of success – to do a professional job.

People on this side of the Atlantic who don't get their news from Fox and CNN, or care what Donald Rumsfeld thinks of al-Jazeera, may find *Control Room* less of an eye-opener – though that doesn't make it less worth watching. It is far more than a documentary about a TV channel. It's about two opposing perceptions of the Iraq war – Arab and American – and on that theme it's as good a film as anyone is ever likely to make. It explores the issues with depth and subtlety, and the central characters have rounded, complex personalities; they are not cardboard protagonists.

On al-Jazeera's side is Hassan Ibrahim, an overweight reporter of Sudanese origin who once worked for the BBC. Genial and sophisticated, he opposes the war but readily mocks Arab fantasies. 'The problem in the Middle East is that everything is [seen as] an Israeli conspiracy,' he says. 'Everything! If a water pipe breaks in the centre of Damascus it will be blamed on the Israelis instead of blaming it on incompetence.'

The US military is represented by Lt Josh Rushing, a press officer at Centcom which – conveniently for the film – based its wartime HQ in Qatar, some 20 miles from al-Jazeera's studio. Rushing is a rare species: a decent and patently sincere PR man who has promised himself that he will get through the war honestly, without spinning. Encountering Ibrahim for the first time, he sets out the American case, saying that Iraq has weapons of mass destruction and 'the will to use them against us'. Ibrahim asks: 'When did Saddam threaten the US with weapons of mass destruction?' It's a cunningly straightforward question to which the hapless press officer has no answer beyond repeating what he has already said – that Saddam has 'the will'.

At first, Rushing seems out of his depth, unprepared for the political complexities of the situation he has been thrust into. He just doesn't get it. Or, looked at another way, he thinks the problem is that the Arabs don't get it. 'This guy Saddam,' he says, 'is probably the biggest threat to Arab Muslims that exists on the planet today. He's probably killed more Muslims than anyone on the planet today. No question about it, so al-Jazeera should be reporting him as that.'

Harvard-educated Noujaim worked for MTV's news and documentaries division before leaving to make *Startup.com*, the real life boom-and-bust tale of a website. She arrived in Qatar 'kind of looking for the eye of the storm', but without a clear idea of what she wanted to do. 'It's the people there who inspired the story,' she says. Even then *Control Room* almost didn't happen. 'I sat in the guard's office [outside al-Jazeera] for a week trying to get a pass to visit the general manager.' Once inside, everyone seemed far too busy preparing for war to talk to her. It was only when Ibrahim found her sitting forlornly in the cafeteria and volunteered to look after her that the project took off.

Over several weeks she amassed 200 hours of film. Deftly edited highlights from this, together with news footage from Iraq and clips of Bush and Rumsfeld, gradually built into a narrative that follows the war from its start to the fall of Baghdad. With the war as its framework, the film unleashes a debate about objectivity, which, as one of al-Jazeera's staff observes, is 'almost a mirage': intentionally or not, all journalists bring some personal baggage to their work. Deep down, American journalists will always be Americans and Arab journalists always Arabs.

They also have to consider what viewers expect of them: the demographics, as TV people call it. 'When I watch al-Jazeera, I can tell what they're showing and not showing. Same when I watch Fox on the other end of the spectrum,' says Rushing in the film. 'It benefits al-Jazeera to play their nationalism because that's their audience, just like Fox plays to American patriotism for the exact same reason.'

The big question, though, is how far journalists should go in pandering to their audience. 'I am representing my station but I am also representing my people,' says a correspondent from Abu Dhabi TV, one of al-Jazeera's rivals. 'The way I deal with spokesmen has to reflect what my people are feeling.' Samir Khader, a senior producer at al-Jazeera, on the other hand, is all for breaking taboos: 'To shake up these rigid [Arab] societies ... to tell them, "Wake up! Wake up!" That is the message of al-Jazeera.' He asks his researcher to find an American who can analyse US policy on his news programme, but the American unexpectedly rants about the war being a plot to grab Iraqi oil and Khader cuts the interview short. 'That wasn't analysis, that was hallucination,' he grumbles.

If al-Jazeera is not the ruthless propaganda machine that Washington imagines, neither is Centcom. Its efforts to control the news agenda look ham-fisted even when opportunities for a publicity coup drop on to its plate. As the troops enter Baghdad, Centcom talks instead about Jessica Lynch, the US soldier 'rescued' from an Iraqi hospital bed. On another occasion, a spokesman introduces the now-famous 'deck of cards' showing the most-wanted Iraqi leaders but refuses to let anyone photograph the cards or take a closer look. Furious reporters then get on their satphones and explain to unconvinced news desks that they have got only half a story.

Watching the news clips of Bush and Rumsfeld, it's easy to imagine that a clash of civilizations is under way, but at ground level the film offers reasons for hope. Despite the politics, senior producer Khader wants to send his kids to school in the US, while Ibrahim invites Rushing home for dinner. Rushing, in turn, agonizes over the realization that he is less distressed by the sight of dead Iraqis on TV than dead Americans. Though the film doesn't mention it, Rushing never got a military permit for dinner with Ibrahim's family, presumably in case they kidnapped or poisoned him.

Since *Control Room* came out, Rushing – one of the best adverts the marines ever had – has been gagged by the military and al-Jazeera isn't exactly over the moon about the film either. Spokesman Jihad Ballout described the film rather tersely as 'the director's creative interpretation' – which of course it is. 'I was trying to find the most emotional moments because that's what drives the story,' Noujaim says. 'The goal is to come as close as possible to an emotional truth.' The irrepressible Ibrahim, meanwhile, has toured the US giving interviews and turned into a minor celebrity. He has also had that long-promised dinner with Rushing. Not at his home in Qatar, but in LA.

ARTS

15 May 2004

SIMON CALLOW

A god without a cloud

Alan Strachan is right to point out that when John Gielgud's obituaries were written, and his place in the theatrical pantheon assessed, Michael Redgrave was inexplicably omitted from the list of Britain's greatest twentieth-century actors. The fine and judicious biography he has written does an important service in restoring a major figure to its rightful place in the theatrical landscape. It must, however, be said that both the career and the man emerge if anything somewhat more enigmatic than they were before.

Inevitably, Redgrave, whose last major creation was Jaraby in *The Old Boys* (directed by Strachan) at the Mermaid in 1971, is remembered by fewer theatre-goers than the other great actors who all had Indian summers well into their seventies. His distinguished body of film work – including superb performances in *The Browning Version*, *Dead of Night* and *The Stars Look Down* – is perhaps better known, and fortunately now includes the television film of the Chichester festival production of *Uncle Vanya*, which preserves his nonpareil performance in the title role, generally regarded as the crowning glory of his work in the theatre.

If nothing had survived but this one performance, both electrifying and heart-breaking, he would on the strength of it have joined the ranks of the Immortals. The character's life is inhabited with profound complexity but also a kind of transcendent poetry: absolutely real but on an epic scale, the reality of life itself, not merely of one life. His co-star, the director of the production, is Laurence Olivier, whose Dr Astrov is itself a brilliantly achieved, deeply felt performance. But Redgrave's achievement is of a different order. He does what only the very greatest acting does – he opens up the secret places of the human heart, allowing us to glimpse truths about ourselves that we can barely acknowledge, in Vanya's case the overwhelming sense of waste, the impossibility of love, the death of hope. Redgrave knew about such things. As if at destiny's behest, his early life shaped him to experience loss, disappointment, rejection.

He was unique among the great actors of the twentieth century in that he was actually born into the theatre. Both parents were actors, as were many of his forebears. His father, Roy, was a feckless charmer of a barnstormer who made his way to Australia, where he triumphed in outback melodramas, occasionally featuring live sheep; his mother Daisy and the infant Michael joined Roy, somewhat against Roy's will, and stayed with him for a little while, during which time the boy made his stage debut, running on at the end of a sentimental monologue to cry, 'Daddy!' In fact, he couldn't bring himself to utter the word and instead burst into tears, a nice metaphor both for his relationship with his father (from whom they parted shortly after and whom he

© Andrzej Krause, 2004

© Andrzej Krause, 2004

© Martin Rowson, 2004

© Steve Bell, 2004

© Steve Bell, 2004

© Martin Rowson, 2004

never saw again) and for the unusual degree of emotion he was to bring to his own work as an actor.

His childhood, back in England, was as unsettled as the life of a single parent who was a jobbing actress on tour could hardly fail to make it, and he was constantly given over to the care of aunts (and 'aunts'), frequently depending on the kindness of landladies. Then, quite without warning, his mother married a very respectable and comfortably-off businessman and their lives changed hugely for the better – in the material sense, at least. Redgrave was plunged into the inevitable Oedipal alienation, in addition to resenting what he felt to be the bourgeois nature of their new life. He was sent to a minor public school where he was blessed with an inspired English teacher who staged plays to a high level of excellence. He also experienced the usual intense crushes on various fellow pupils; before long he had been to bed with men and with women.

Both sexes were understandably smitten by this immensely handsome, elegant, witty and infinitely vulnerable young man. At Cambridge, in the late 1920s, he had long-term love affairs with several men, moved in Bloomsbury circles and was in touch with many of the Apostles; this was the epoch of Burgess (who designed a play for him) and Blunt (with whom he co-edited a magazine). He was confirmed in his left-wing political attitudes, though never formally a Marxist. He was not an especially diligent scholar, but absorbed a very wide culture, particularly during a visit to Heidelberg, which was rare for an actor at the time. He became a schoolmaster, plunging immediately into directing and acting in school productions, playing Hamlet, Lear and Samson Agonistes. By the age of twenty-six he felt strong enough to enter the fray professionally, playing a vast range of roles in the course of a year at William Armstrong's Liverpool Rep, where he met and married Rachel Kempson. Within a year he had been snapped up by the Old Vic and was playing Orlando opposite Edith Evans's Rosalind, one of the great romantic partnerships of the decade; a year after that he was cast in the leading role in *The Lady Vanishes* for Alfred Hitchcock, his film debut. Four years into the business he was an established star in both media.

Despite his splendid physical and vocal equipment – the nearest thing to an *acteur noble* this country has produced – he did not quite fit into a pre-existing mould. 'What sort of actor do you want to be, Michael?' Edith Evans had asked him. 'Do you want to be like John, or Larry, or Peggy Ashcroft, or me? What sort of standards are you aiming at?' He was in fact that unheard-of phenomenon, an English leading actor who was not an extrovert, always seeking to create from within. Like Charles Laughton, with whom he had surprisingly much in common, he was always in touch with his inner drama, and his best work possesses a sense of fathomless pools of complex life within. Unlike Laughton, his relationship to his own body and his face was not anguished; it is in fact very often the gap between the nobility of his appearance and the turbulence inside which gives his acting its extraordinary tension.

He was desperately needy in his sexual and emotional demands. 'I am shallow, selfish (horribly), jealous to a torturing degree, greedy, proud and self-centred,' he wrote to John Lehmann. 'I have grasped at people's love and done vain and stupid things to get it; I am at times hideously immoral.' An example is the passionate affair he had with Edith Evans during and even after the run of

As You Like It, starting when Rachel was seven months pregnant with her first child Vanessa, and continuing thereafter for nearly a year, an affair of which Rachel remained ignorant till the publication of Bryan Forbes's biography of her some forty years later.

Later, the affairs were with men, including at least four long-term relationships, all of which Rachel was told about to the accompaniment of copious tears, and all of which she learned to live with: indeed, she even learned to live with the lovers themselves. He was so infatuated with Noel Coward during their brief affair that it was with him and not Rachel that he spent his last night before beginning his wartime naval service. She was curiously tolerant, almost unnervingly so. In addition to the marriage and the official lovers were unending one-night or indeed one-afternoon stands, for which purpose he had rented an office off St Martin's Lane, plus pick-ups in parks and stations; later, territory not covered in Strachan's book, he was to go into darker and darker realms sexually, usually fuelled by large quantities of alcohol. These encounters were always accompanied by terrible remorse and vows of renunciation, always broken, sometimes on the very day of the diary entry that records them. This is something that goes well beyond simple bisexuality or mere promiscuity. It is an irresistible compulsion, driven by unshakeable guilt and the constant need for endorsement. It was inextricably bound up with his art: 'I like attempting parts of men, as it were, in invisible chains.'

The miracle is that for so much of his career, until he was stopped in his tracks by Parkinson's disease shortly after his sixtieth birthday, he remained so productive and so constantly illuminating in his work; he maintained an elegance and splendour through some of his most demanding roles and despite the unremitting intensity of his private experience. His classical roles – and in one glorious season at Stratford he played King Lear, Shylock and Antony – were absolute re-inventions of the characters, but the re-invention was completely unselfconscious: he worked from profound inner promptings, his transformations organic and radical.

As a director, too, he worked with exceptional taste and intelligence; and finally as a writer he produced two of the finest books in the language about acting, and a haunting novel, *The Mountebank's Tale*, about an actor and his doppelgänger, whose epigraph (by Rilke) seems to tell us something very personal about the enigmatic Redgrave himself: 'I can only come to terms with inner cataclysms; a little exterior perishing or surviving is either too hard or too easy for me. In the life of the gods … I understand nothing better than the moment they withdraw themselves; what would be a god without the protecting cloud, can you imagine a god worse for wear?'

30 April 2004

LUCY MANGAN

Goodbye, dear friends

Our parents had 6 May 1954, the day Roger Bannister ran the first four-minute mile and provided amateurism with its last hurrah. We will have 6 May 2004, another end to another glorious era. That's the day when the last ever episode of *Friends* will air in the US, the day we will bid a fond farewell to a sitcom that spoke for a generation. My generation.

I spent my twenties growing up with the shiny sextet, and their departure from my life is, in its own way, a small bereavement. As the show gears up for its own last hurrah, the stubborn streak of sentiment in me that has resisted erosion by the ten years of rapier wit from the six master ironists demands a moment's pause to reflect on what has gone before.

When *Friends* launched in April 1995, I was in my penultimate year of university and, like all those who were still then being labelled, in cruelly reductive but none the less tragically accurate fashion, Thatcher's children, woefully ignorant of the wider world. We paid scant attention to the then fresh-faced leader of the opposition (Tony, was it?) who was intent on removing from his party's constitution something called Clause 4, whatever that might be.

Within weeks, *Friends* established itself as 'appointment TV', although I'm not sure the phrase had even been coined at the time. Friday pub visits were postponed until 9.30 p.m. Early parties would pause at 9 p.m. for the half hour to enable us to catch up with Joey, Phoebe, Monica, Ross, Chandler and Rachel, characters who would soon become so famous that they would make Hawkeye, Radar, Murphy Brown and the gang at Cheers look like footnotes in television history.

When the series first began, the six friends were a little older than me and my friends. They had already made the transition from university to the working world, although the uninitiated might have had difficulty discerning any interruptions to the coffee-drinking and gossiping to earn a crust. It was a bright, colourful, charmed life – and we wanted it.

The odd thing was, we got it. We fell into step with the six and stayed with them for the next decade. It was the only programme around that really showed us ourselves. Ourselves with better wardrobes, better apartments and much, much better upper arms, of course, but being such a hip, young, media-savvy generation, we discounted these superficial differences for the televisual conventions they were and appreciated the show for what it was – a mirror up to nature. A cracked and distorted mirror, perhaps, but then we're dealing with cracked and distorted times. How we loved seeing ourselves reflected sixfold! Not just because in these benighted times you don't exist until you've been identified by a phalanx of marketing mavens and immortalized on TV, but because, goddammit, we're only human and we all need narratives for our lives.

Here was a group of people who lived like my friends and I did – largely the products of fractured families, unshackled and uncomforted by religion, unconstrained by dependents, uninterested in politics and incapable of embracing an ideology, even if it came with a lifetime's supply of free lattes. But for all that, not bad people. Not, at least, the selfish, amoral, Reaganite/Thatcherite soulless products of an atomized culture, as the newspapers had been painting us. We were just trying to have a laugh, hold down a job and, yes, 'be there' for our friends.

The Simpsons and *Roseanne* had already redefined acceptable notions of what a close and loving family could look like now that *The Waltons* was a meaningless anachronism, but *Friends* took it a stage further and made the case for all of us who had peopled with select companions the void left by parents. Writer Ethan Watters later identified this very modern phenomenon as the creation of 'urban tribes'; friends who were taking the place of family for a generation that was no longer expected to settle down straight after graduation and that could no longer look to parents, church or politicians for guidance and support while they finished the increasingly lengthy business of growing up.

But the greatest part of the show's appeal was its implicit acknowledgement that Monica, Ross, Chandler, Phoebe, Joey and Rachel were as adrift as we were, navigating the sewage-strewn seas of modern dating without a compass, failing to centre their moral gyroscopes and generally flailing desperately towards the dry lands of social competence. In short, it was confirmation that everyone was making everything up as they went along. We hadn't been left off the circulation list for some Big Book of Modern Rules. There were none. Oh, sweet relief to see these six twenty-somethings looking at the glittering fragments of possibility and reacting not with intoxicated glee but with desperate twistings of the lens to try to bring them into some sort of comprehensible pattern. And failing.

As a – naturally – complex and fascinating, multi-faceted viewer, you could see yourself reflected in each of the characters, according to your ever-fluctuating needs. Rachel (at least before Jennifer Aniston and her increasingly implausible musculature drove an unignorable wedge between audience and character) was your quotidian self: nice girl, rubbish job, unthreatening levels of wit and intellect. Joey was the more primal version; he might prioritize sex and pizza more consistently than you, but you couldn't pretend you didn't understand where the man was coming from. Monica was the successful, organized, capable side of you – albeit one constantly under threat of being suffused with neuroses. Ross the paleontologist, with his lesbian wife, hapless air and string of failed dates, clearly represented our shared sense of being constantly buffeted and victimized by the forces of modernity beyond our control. Eccentric Phoebe represented the possibility of escape – of being oblivious to the stresses and strains that habitually do for the fully sentient. And Chandler. Ah, Chandler. I don't know how he played in Peoria, but I would hazard a guess that he was the character with whom the British audience most readily identified. His decision to deal with the world solely through the medium of sarcasm, and to conduct all his relationships via wisecracks lest his carefully sealed emotional core be breached, I suspect resonated more deeply with viewers in this sceptic isle than it did with less fundamentally misanthropic audiences. We know what we like, and honest, open communication ain't it. We understand that mordant irony is an inviolable constituent of the modern human condition, and we worshipped his facility with the form.

Like all good friends, Ross, Rachel et al have kept pace with us over the years. Initially, they were single and happily so, to the weeping gratitude of all those of us who gibbered in fear at the possibility that the saddening, maddening Bridget Jones and Ally McBeal were unavoidable destinations ahead. Short, then longer-term relationships started to turn up for them and us. We survived them, and could fancy we did so with the same poise and panache as our fictional counterparts, even if we weren't always able to recover in twenty-seven minutes (not including the ad break). I can't be the only one who roused herself from a tear-sodden pillow with the words: 'If Phoebe coped with David going to Minsk, I can cope with this.' If I am, then I will, of course, be slashing my wrists in shame as soon as I get home.

Unfortunately, nothing this good lasts for ever, and eventually the group had to start reflecting the sad truth that people change. The buggers grow up, couple up and sell up to start new lives as adults elsewhere. I suppose at the back of my mind I always knew that a decade of *Friends*-ship was the very most one could hope for, and I can't complain about managing to maintain my own similarly self-indulgent lifestyle for just as long. The essentially temporary and fleeting nature of it has, after all, always been part of the charm. Nevertheless, I watch with increasing awe and horror the avalanche of wedding invitations pouring on to my mat – or, at least, the place where my mat would be if I lived that kind of domestically ordered life.

I have felt for Joey as he, likewise, has watched his best friend marry his other best friend and stood by as the others pair off. As I have watched my friends embark on squeezing out squalling infants while I simply struggle to get myself safely into work, so Joey has had to watch Rachel and Ross produce their own enemy of promise, the promise that they would always be available for biscotti and ballgames for as long as he and we all needed. It's more than a little disconcerting to discover that at some point during the past decade my personal development arrested to such a degree that I now identify more with a man who once happily troughed through a trifle/shepherd's pie combo without noticing anything amiss than with my original correlate, the well-meaning control freak Monica. But there it is.

The time has come for us all to shake hands and acknowledge that the good times, as we once knew them, are over. But it's hard. To lose one friend may be a misfortune, but to lose six is wholesale abandonment. And the fact that I'm as powerless to stop it happening within my real-life tribe only aggravates the wound. Although I know we all have to move on, and fully intend to once I have spliced my DNA with that of a genuine adult, with every engagement or pregnancy that is announced within my group, I feel the fissures widen, my delight become ever more heavily laced with fear and visions of a lonely, black-hearted future abound ever more plentifully. But, just as I'm learning to forgive Rachel and the rest for their imminent desertion, I'm hoping that I'll learn to forgive my friends, too. We've all been through too much together over the years to let bitterness poison us now. So I raise a latte to you all. Goodbye then – and thanks for all the laughs.

3 October 2003

MARTIN KETTLE

Bach at his best

In general, says András Schiff, he does not re-record the piano repertoire at all. 'This work, though, is very close to my heart. Closer than anything really. This is the exception.' This work, exceptional in every sense, is Bach's *Goldberg Variations*, arguably the greatest of all keyboard works. Schiff has just re-recorded the variations for ECM. Twenty years ago, the Hungarian-born pianist made a much-acclaimed studio version for Decca. Now, as he nears his fiftieth birthday, comes this second version, recorded in Basle, a live performance like all Schiff's current recordings.

Schiff, it turns out, is not just good at playing the *Goldberg Variations*. He talks a pretty mean performance of them, too. He has provided what he calls a written 'guided tour' to the variations to accompany the new disc. And when we meet in the north German city of Bremen, where he has just given the latest of what he calculates as 'several hundred' lifetime performances, he gets straight down to explaining the work yet again.

The *Goldberg Variations* form the final part of what Bach, in his characteristically practical way, called the *Clavier-Ubung*, or keyboard exercise. But Schiff insists that we should not let such a utilitarian title mislead us. 'Bach is a very modest man,' he says. 'He does not boast. He has no ego whatsoever. So this is a very modest title.' The exercises are a collection of every genre and form of composition for the keyboard, but they culminate in the variations. They are 'the best of him', Schiff says, the 'pinnacle of his whole output for keyboard', the '*ne plus ultra*'.

When Schiff performs these variations, he explains, there can be nothing else on the programme. The *Goldbergs* must stand alone, played with all repeats, a performance that takes about seventy minutes. 'It would be an absolute sacrilege to play anything else. And I never play an encore. And I would prefer it ideally if there was no applause at the end, just a wonderful silence. Unfortunately there is almost always someone who wants to show how well he knows the piece by applauding at the instant the final note has been played.'

Nowadays, the *Goldbergs* are a universally revered piece. It wasn't always this way. 'These variations were a well-kept secret for most of the nineteenth century,' Schiff says. 'Beethoven knew them, of course. There would be no *Diabelli Variations* without the *Goldberg Variations* – they're obviously the model. But mostly they were studied, not played in public.' Not until Wanda Landowska resurrected the work for the harpsichord at the start of the twentieth century did the *Goldbergs* take their current position as a pinnacle of the literature.

Getting into Bach's mind as he wrote them is a challenge that Schiff eagerly accepts. 'I think he didn't really think very highly of the variation form. He was a man of his time in that respect, too. He viewed the variation form as an entertainment form, very extroverted and very brilliant. But Bach was a man of great integrity. He despised cheap success. He wrote very few variation-form pieces.' The *Goldberg Variations* begin and end with a so-called aria, which is one of the most sublime statements of calm in all European music. Its return at the end, after thirty variations, is one of the profoundest moments in all Bach. But Schiff has a good tip for the listener beguiled by the simple dignity of the aria's tune. Listen instead, he cautions, to the bass. It is the true guide to the work as a whole. 'The way to think of it is by thinking of Bach as an architect rather than as a painter. Beware of the tunes. Concentrate instead on the ground bass, which is the solid foundation of everything else. Where I live now in Florence, we have this most beautiful cathedral with its dome and cupola by Brunelleschi. But it would not be there without the foundations to hold it up. Similarly in music there is a tendency to follow the top line. I think always in music we should start with the bass.'

The structure of the *Goldbergs* can seem austere and academic. The key to the variations is the number three, says Schiff. After the aria, the thirty variations are arranged in ten groups of three. In each group, Schiff argues, one variation represents 'the physical', one 'the emotional' and one 'the intellectual'. 'The first is very virtuoso, a toccata-like piece. The physical side represents for me the joy of playing. It has to have this element. Then there is the emotional side. It can be a dance piece perhaps, or a singing piece, like the thirteenth variation, which is a particularly beautiful ornamented song in the major key, or its sister piece in the minor, the twenty-fifth variation that Landowska called the 'black pearl'. And then every third variation represents the intellect, and these are all in the form of canons, each at an increasing interval, starting with the canon in unison and working up to the canon in ninths.

'We have to get rid of the idea that he was writing these variations as a monument to himself,' Schiff continues. 'He was not at all concerned with posterity, and it is important not to treat every bar too reverentially.' That is especially true, Schiff suggests, of the thirtieth and last variation, the so-called 'Quodlibet'. 'We are expecting a variation that is true to the structure of the piece, which would be a canon in tenths. Instead, Bach produces 'a most human climax', a movement whose title means literally 'what pleases'. The ground bass is still there, of course, but the character of the movement is formed by two folk tunes that would have been easily recognizable to Bach's contemporaries.

'One of these songs is about cabbages and turnips. The other is about how long it is since he has been away. I feel it's all very sociable and merry, like a family get-together. I can imagine Bach and his family all sat round the table with a glass of beer. I have heard performances which are deadly serious here. But that completely misses the point. There is the most profound humour here, the kind of humour that we later find in Haydn and Beethoven. A great artist does not have to write only about man's sufferings, you know.'

The great Bach pianists are constantly drawn back to the *Goldberg Variations*. Glenn Gould famously also recorded them twice, at the beginning and end of his life, producing wildly different readings on each occasion. The late Rosalyn Tureck recorded them over an even longer span, first in the 1950s, the last time in 1999.

Now Schiff is joining this distinguished club. He is frank about what he sees as the shortcomings of his great predecessors. Gould, he says, is 'an artist you should admire but not copy'. Nobody can approach him in articulation, Schiff says, 'but at the expense of the singing way of playing the piano. Gould himself sings, but his piano never sings. But maybe that's the way he wanted it. There was nothing he couldn't do.' Tureck, on the other hand 'had this high-priestess aspect, which is totally legitimate but not something I follow or share'. Bach, says Schiff, can be presented 'in a very forbidding way, but I don't think this is my way'.

We shake hands as I leave. Schiff is going off to practise. 'Back to the *Goldbergs*, yes,' he says. 'I will play for half an hour and go through the things I didn't like in last night's concert. It's like climbing. I'm a few hundred feet higher up the mountain than I was before. I can see things I did not see then. But I'm still nowhere near the top.'

2 October 2003

DAVID McKIE

Don't toy with me

Simon Callow's moving tribute in last Saturday's *Guardian* Review to Rupert Bear contained one distressing error. Reviewing a biography of Alfred Bestall, who for many years devised and illustrated Rupert's adventures, he wrote: 'It is a very different world from the knock-about poster-painted realm of Noddy and the other extrovert denizens of Toytown.'

Wrong location there, I'm afraid. Noddy, Big Ears and the rest of that gang lived in Toyland. Toytown was the creation of a now largely forgotten figure called Sydney George Hulme Beaman. Beaman had begun as an actor but, having time on his hands, he took to carving wooden puppets, who, as he gazed on them, started to take on characters of their own. (Curiously, Noddy began the same way, when Enid Blyton's publisher introduced her to a set of puppets created by a Dutch artist, and she started to weave fantasies round them.)

Like all good children's stories, Toytown was built around a small group of core characters, with others intervening from time to time. In the BBC *Children's Hour* series that made Beaman temporarily famous, the chief of these was Larry the Lamb, whom I used to find pretty tedious as a child. This was partly because the actor who played him was required, whenever an appropriate vowel occurred, to bleat; but even more because he was so insufferably deferential. 'Please, sir, Mr Mayor, sir,' he would constantly wheedle, and 'I'm only a little lamb ...'

I have seen it suggested that Larry was shrewder than he let on, and was busy, under cover of such devices, manipulating those he appeared to flatter. At the time, though, he often seemed more of a creep than a sheep. But any defect in Larry was redeemed by the crew around him. His good friend Dennis the Dachshund always spoke as if in simultaneous word-by-word translation from the original German. ('The furniture,' Dennis exclaimed, 'too large was into the house to go.') In the war years, Dennis achieved the difficult feat of becoming a figure at once definably German and totally sympathetic. There weren't many of them around in those days.

Then there were Mr Mayor, the town boss of Toytown, whose statue in a hat more appropriate for an admiral dominated the town square; Ernest the policeman ('the constable frowned very hard, and wrote for a long time in his book, trying to look as important as he could'); a dazzlingly accident-prone magician; a wild and woolly inventor; and best of all, Mr Growser, the epitome of every curmudgeonly soul who ever took up his pen to write a letter to the editor, signing himself 'Disgusted'.

Toytown, as the titles of some of the stories indicate (*The Disgraceful Business at Mrs Goose's*; *Dreadful Doings in Ark Street*; *Dirty Work at the Dog and Whistle*), was full of mischief. In *Mr Growser Moves House*, which I picked up in Woking this week for rather a lot of money, Mr Growser decides it is time to leave his home in Noah Street. 'Noah Street,' he tells the Mayor, 'is a disgrace. Are you aware, sir, that hardly a morning dawns without my finding either a stone has been thrown through my window, or a tapioca pudding thrust through my letterbox?' No episode was ever complete without Mr Growser undergoing some kind of public humiliation and uttering, on radio at least, the cry that became his trademark: 'It Ought Not To Be Allowed.'

Though the title page of *Mr Growser Moves House* says that it's by S.G. Hulme Beaman, the cover admits that the truth is a little different. This series was issued some thirty years after his death with the help of Betty Hulme Beaman – his widow, perhaps.

It had taken him some while to establish himself. His breakthrough was the acceptance of a cartoon strip called Philip and Phido by his neighbourhood newspaper, the *Golders Green Gazette*, in north London. He was over forty when his Toytown stories began to appear on the radio. And within three years he was dead, at forty-four, of pneumonia.

The Times gave him just one sentence at the end of its obituaries column. His local *Hendon Times* had nothing to say, not even in 'Golders Green Spangles', its weekly column by Spartan. The *Golders Green Gazette* was more generous, recalling the part it played in his success by the publication of Philip and Phido, and noting that his studio at home had a model city peopled by Toytown characters beautifully carved in wood.

But he died in 1932, long before his radio series achieved its greatest successes, long before satisfied customers bought up the books that Betty completed. For him there was none of the money that Noddy would make for Blyton; his will was worth £979 gross. No blue plaque has been placed on his house in Sneath Avenue, Golders Green – the sort of solid suburban street in which stones are never thrown through respectable citizens' windows nor tapioca puddings pushed through their letterboxes. And now this very newspaper has cruelly assigned the world that Hulme Beaman created to Blyton. In the words of perhaps his greatest creation: It Ought Not To Be Allowed.

12 September 2003

JOHN PATTERSON

Invasion of the movie snatchers

They keep springing up like old friends from the distant past: *Get Carter, Traffic, The Ladykillers* and, this weekend, *The Italian Job.* Except they're not our friends. They're like those pods in the basement in *Invasion of the Body Snatchers*: evil, soulless versions of people we think we know and love.

They are all (or in *The Ladykillers'* case, will be) American remakes of well-known British originals, of films or TV dramas that earned sterling reputations or heavy receipts or rave reviews in their country of origin. Thereafter, they're left to languish in culty obscurity, often for decades, until some 23-year-old in a Hollywood studio spots their retread potential and alerts Legal Affairs to snag the remake rights. The process that then ensues, involving the usual squadrons of hacks and shaky-handed script-surgeons, is analogous to removing the spine from a kipper, throwing the meat away, then building a whole new fish around the bones. A stupid and pointless procedure indeed, especially when one examines the mutant results for firmness of flesh, freshness, odour and edibility.

Certain questions inevitably arise. Firstly, what is so wrong with American movie-making that its practitioners feel compelled to plunder the cinematic heritages of other countries for new – or, pardon me, old – plots and stories? Is it because they have so thoroughly strip-mined their own cinematic and televisual culture that they must now start on ours? Certainly, if you've sunk to the level of remaking TV shows like *Scooby-Doo* and *McHale's Navy* you are millimetres from the bottom of the barrel, and it's time to seek fresh fields to defoliate.

But given the generally dismal quality of most new British films, what will there be for the Americans to remake in twenty years' time? *Maybe Baby? Greenfingers?* What deformities of deformities will they be shooting back at us by then? Trapped between the immovable, sclerotic Hollywood behemoths and the levelling anarchy of European co-production financing arrangements, which way can British cinema jump if it wants to remain viable instead of functioning as Hollywood's Airstrip One?

Peter Collinson's original *Italian Job*, released in 1969, managed to be so unreconstructedly English – or so unreconstructibly London – that it sank its own chances at the American box office. American viewers of my acquaintance need moment-by-moment explanations to comprehend it. And that doesn't make them stupid or insular; quite the contrary, it's a pretty stupid and insular movie in the first place. And *Job One* was simultaneously so fiercely Eurosceptic, albeit *avant la lettre*, that today it feels like a blueprint for twenty subsequent years of football hooliganism, pissing in foreign fountains and all those things that prompt the French to call us *les fuckoffs*.

The Italian Job is not American. It's not European. It's English, for good or ill, and Little English at that. If it voted, it would vote for Enoch Powell (you can't help noticing that it's the black driver's fault that the bullion-loaded bus ends up hanging over that cliff). If it sang, it would sing, in lusty tones, Bruce Forsyth's annoying 1968 export-drive anthem, 'I'm Backing Britain'. It was made as Britain, or non-hippy Britain, was convulsed by the orgy of nostalgia and national self-examination, with occasional stabs at revisionism like Angus Calder's *The People's War*, caused by the thirtieth anniversary of the Second World War – an orgy that also included Michael Caine's other duff movie of that year, *The Battle of Britain*.

For me, these are the things – the cultural environment, the social surroundings – that make Collinson's movie so fascinating to watch, and that partly redeem it. Certainly it's not the lame, dated jokes, the lazy writing, the slack narrative pacing, the boring matiness of the male ensemble or the overall emptiness of the film. I can't cut it any breaks today just because it knocked me out as a ten-year-old watching it on BBC2. But its many faults make it an ideal candidate for the remake treatment, the rule being, of course: only remake crap, because remaking *Citizen Kane* is just asking for trouble.

So we get the remake, thirty-three years later and, oooh, about 33 per cent better than the original. F. Gary Gray and his rewrite goons have shifted heaven and earth to maintain an appositely Italian connection – a twenty-minute opening heist set in Venice – before relocating their completely new story to Los Angeles, proud home of the 10-mile traffic-snarl. Caine's Charlie Croker becomes Mark Wahlberg's Charlie Croker II, while Noel Coward's coercive and inflexible Mr Bridger becomes Donald Sutherland's benign and fatherly John Bridger. The Mini Coopers they hold on to; everything else they flush down the pan.

Like I said, the kipper and the bones. Except this time it almost succeeds, possibly because slick, meretricious stories work better if they're gussied up by pros, instead of being dreamed up by erratic guys like Caine and Collinson over brandies.

Precisely the reverse was true of *Get Carter* 2001. Hollywood took a great British film and, with consummate alchemical skill, transformed solid gold into mushy dogshit. The only good thing it did for world cinema was to kill off Sylvester Stallone's career. Steven Soderbergh's remake of the Channel 4 series *Traffik* was an altogether more substantial and intelligent achievement (at least, on first viewing), perhaps because Soderbergh plays clever little games with his source material, much as he did with *The Limey*. That latter movie, which was not a remake but a compendium of types and scenarios from 1960s British gangster classics, Soderbergh described as '*Point Blank* and *Get Carter* remade in the style of Alain Resnais'. This conveniently neglects the fact that John Boorman and Mike Hodges were at least the equals of Resnais when they made these particular films, but denotes a level of respect for the originals not evident elsewhere. Indeed, it's difficult to think of a British film-maker of the same age whose grasp and understanding of British cinema history exceeds Soderbergh's. We ought to worry about that.

Soon enough we will be faced with Joel and Ethan Coen's remake of Alexander Mackendrick's Ealing classic *The Ladykillers*, which will make for quite the conflict of loyalties when I nervously take my place in the cinema. Although the Coens will undoubtedly make something highly original, I can't help but feel a certain lowering of the spirit as they enter this particular game, no matter how brilliant they are. What will an American version of an Ealing comedy look like? And will we dare to gaze upon it? Of course we will. We all trooped off to see *Sleepy Hollow* and *From Hell*, which were basically inflated remakes of Hammer Studios pictures. Can we be far from the American remake of *Carry On Up the Khyber* or *Confessions of a Driving Instructor*?

The alleged special relationship between British cinema and Hollywood is a lot like the alleged special relationship between Downing Street and the White House. It doesn't exist. At least not in any way that favours us, the junior partner. From Beverly Hills and Bel Air, we look like just another jumped-up little market in the north of Europe, bigger than Denmark, smaller than Germany. Yet the language that we and Ireland, alone in Europe, share with America induces us to believe that we have some mysterious umbilical connection with Hollywood, that we can make hay in their movie markets with our inward-looking, class-obsessed little films and our no-mark knock-offs of their better-funded genre pieces. This delusion has deformed British cinema for decades, and largely blinded us to our other identity as Europeans. We can seek to please both markets, but in the main we opt to genuflect in the direction of the Hollywood sign.

Unfortunately, Hollywood has changed enormously since the glory days of the 1960s, when British films (made often, as we tend to forget, with US money) were able to storm the US box office regularly. Back then, studios were reeling from incompetent, geriatric management, bitter takeover battles that dropped them into the hands of rapacious multinationals interested only in the bottom line, and creative near-impotence. They were glad of the chance to distribute and profit from the *Alfies*, *Darlings* and *Ipcress Files* we sent their way.

These days, in a culture of opening weekend receipts, production schedules offering ten or twelve effects-heavy blockbusters per year instead of thirty variously budgeted productions, and an overly youthful, intellectually dormant mass audience, we have to work to get their attention. Also absent is the old sense of continuous cultural exchange between Hollywood and other national cinemas. This process benefited and enriched both parties. New movements or schools of film-making in other countries tended to see Hollywood as a monolith against which one could productively bang one's head. Soon enough, Hollywood would absorb, or co-opt new aesthetic styles and approaches, usually discarding much of their political content.

Thus Italian neo-realism, favouring non-actors and location shooting, was absorbed by American film-makers like Jules Dassin to create films like *The Naked City*, in which location shooting and documentary styles became merely aesthetic innovations, like Technicolor. Later, the French would build their new wave on their pronounced love for American studio pictures, tempered with political dissent of varying degrees. Hollywood returned the favour with *nouvelle vague*-ish movies like *Bonnie and Clyde* and *Five Easy Pieces*. The Italian cinema of the 1960s, from Antonioni to Visconti to Sergio Leone, saw its stylistic innovations poured into films from *The Godfather* to *High Plains Drifter* to *Heaven's Gate*. With The Beatles raising the British profile in the 1960s, there was suddenly a willing American audience for the hugely influential Bond and

Beatles movies, and, no less importantly, the Hollywood studios set up well-financed offices in London and other European capitals to fund promising local productions.

In the 1970s, the Germans would revitalize their own cinema by confronting the coca-colonialist legacy of a movie market saturated for twenty years with US product, and making films that, especially in the case of Wenders and Fassbinder, displayed a profound ambivalence towards America and American cinema, often as their main theme. (Until *Paris, Texas*, Wenders's entire career was built around this cinematic attraction-repulsion.) Many directors from these movements would spend time in Hollywood. Other centres of production and innovation – Lodz, which gave us Polanski and Skolimowski; Budapest, which spawned Miklos Jansco; and the Soviet film industry – ensured that new and influential voices continued to emerge and enrich world cinema.

Well, you can kiss all that goodbye. The give-and-take, the cultural exchange, that's all over. What gets given is not worth having half the time, and what gets taken is no longer innovation or formal advances, just the plots of our old movies, good or bad. With the now thoroughly corporatized studios churning out heavily test-marketed, lookalike movies every weekend, American cinema for the most part is as insipid as fast food and as depressing as mass tourism. Homogenization has proceeded apace ever since *Jaws* and *Star Wars* and the monochrome platitudes of Ronald Reagan. Test-screening audiences are treated like corporate shareholders who must be appeased first, last and always, meaning movies are altered to suit the whims of housewives, students and truants. The rating system dictates that most movies must fit within the confines of the PG or PG-13 rating (lose a third of your take if you snag an R-rating).

All these things, along with the perennial problems of creative bankruptcy, executive timorousness, and plain old rotten film-making, have led us to the summer of 2003, which offered US audiences a dumbass action movie and a laugh-lite comedy each weekend, and precious little else to leaven a starchy diet. All energy is expended on that first weekend, after which the audience either finds out how bad the movie is and stays away in droves, or misses a great movie that can't be adapted to a throw-shit-at-the-wall-and-see-what-sticks approach to marketing.

Globalization and the primacy of American exports mean that, whether or not these movies succeed domestically, they are then force-fed to the world market, clogging two or more screens per Ukrainian, British or Greek multiplex, cancelling out space and appetite for domestic products. And the films that we make, if we wish them to succeed in the American market or to net a US TV sale, must adhere as closely to all these narrow parameters as possible, thus feeding the decay, internationalizing it, making it the standard. You send us your crap; we'll slavishly imitate it and sling our homemade or subtitled crap back at you. If we can't compete at the blockbuster level, as we seem to be attempting to do with, say, Anthony Minghella's *Cold Mountain*, we'll settle for a niche in the independent market, and bring home nickels instead of dollars.

The need to appease the American market is a Europe-wide problem, but in Britain, because of those delusions of equality with America, it seems more acute, less a new trend than the same one that has bedevilled British cinema since the days of the quota-quickie and the Eady Levy.

Myopic, movie-phobic financiers seem always to have been the bane of British directors and their aspirations, forever imposing imported American stars on resolutely British films and demanding mindless alterations. Audiences don't exactly beat the drums for more domestic movies. Our collective cinematic folk memory extends no further back than *Star Wars* or *Bonnie and Clyde*. And we leave our greatest directors, and particularly the ones who want to make specifically British movies, out in the cold, scratching for pennies, starved of funding, scorned and traduced for having ideas in their heads.

If Britain subsidized the kinds of movie that otherwise couldn't get made – as the German government did very cheaply in the 1970s as a matter of national prestige – then Terence Davies might have made fifteen films instead of five, John Boorman wouldn't be scraping together his budget from eighteen different sources and blowing it on as many lawyers, and Mike Hodges wouldn't have had to endure the insults attendant upon the miserable reception afforded his stunning *Croupier*, which had to be filmed largely in Germany. We may bitch and moan about American audiences and distributors, but it took American audiences to see the value in *Croupier*, and to shame its backers into releasing it properly in Britain. You'd think Hodges might have had less of a struggle making his superb new thriller *I'll Sleep When I'm Dead*, but not really. It's worth mentioning that the American success of *Croupier*, and the very existence of *I'll Sleep When I'm Dead*, the best British movies of their respective years, were both largely due to the untiring efforts of producer/marketing whizz Mike Kaplan, an American. There's a last trace of that give-and-take.

So it's their fault, but it's also ours. If British cinema is reduced to a library of old movies – from which the invaders wish to steal only the premise, the best jokes or just the title – then we are as much to blame as they are. We have permitted our movie industry to become a supplicant to a gargantuan and scarcely human corporate movie culture that sees us as carrion to be picked over. We could have an entirely different, rich and vivid movie culture in Britain – there are plenty of isolated examples of it cited here – but we prefer our craven relationship with the snoring giant over the water. It barely matters to me that they made a half-decent remake of *The Italian Job*. What worries me is that sooner or later they'll be buying *Performance*, *If…* or even *Croupier*. Kippers, one and all.

2 July 2004

JOHN MULLAN

Comma wars

The only surprise is that something like this did not come sooner. Write about grammar, of which punctuation is but one elaborate and beautiful part, and you open yourself to attack. You always take the risk that your medium will undo your message. Write a book whose subtitle is *The Zero Tolerance Approach to Punctuation* and you invite a little of that laudable intolerance upon yourself. When your book has sold more than 1.5 million copies, the invitation becomes irresistible.

As well as its massive sales – a complete surprise to author and publisher – Lynne Truss's *Eats, Shoots & Leaves* enjoyed a critically friendly reception in Britain. The reviewers themselves liked to be thought of as 'people who love punctuation and get upset about it' (the book's description of its intended audience). High-profile curmudgeons such as John Humphrys recommended it. But now a fellow 'stickler' (Truss's name for those who truly care about punctuation) has taken the author of this surprise bestseller to task for her own grammatical failures. In a long article in the *New Yorker*, Louis Menand condemns and attempts to anatomize Truss's 'strange grammar'. So inaccurate or incorrect is Truss's punctuation, he says, that 'it's hard to fend off the suspicion that the whole thing might be a hoax'. He continues in the same withering vein: 'Either Truss needed a copy editor or her copy editor needed a copy editor.'

Menand writes with the borrowed authority of a magazine that is renowned for its code of 'correctness', in matters both of fact and of style. As he explains (and those acquainted with American journalism might recognize this), 'The British are less rigid about punctuation and related matters ... than Americans are.' So British readers are hardly likely to object to Truss's 'British laxness'. According to Menand, 'About half the semicolons in the book are either unnecessary or ungrammatical, and the comma is deployed as the mood strikes.' Unless a semicolon is dividing items in a list, he explains, it should be used only between clauses that can stand as complete sentences. Truss not only flouts this rule, she shamelessly tells the reader that she is doing so.

You can hardly blame Menand for hugging himself when he finds the first mistake at the book's very beginning, in its dedication. Here, he delightedly discovers, 'a nonrestrictive clause [that] is not preceded by a comma. It is a wild ride downhill from there.' Does he have a point? He feels no need to tell the *New Yorker*'s notoriously literate readers what a non-restrictive (I like a hyphen there, myself) clause is, but, to judge his attack, you'll need to know. Truss's dedication mentions 'the striking Bolshevik printers of St Petersburg who, in 1905, demanded to be paid the same rate for punctuation marks as for letters'. To put it simply, Menand says that there should be a comma after 'Petersburg'. Without that comma, the dedication is to some striking printers who made the demand, as opposed to some other striking printers who didn't. Only with a comma is the dedication to all the striking printers (as Truss presumably intends).

It is true that the rule about a comma before a non-restrictive clause ('the house, which is Victorian, is dilapidated') and not before a restrictive clause ('the house that I own is dilapidated') is there in Fowler's *The King's English* but is not mentioned in Truss's book. Some of Menand's other points seem less like hits. He complains about a misplaced apostrophe in 'printers' marks', but couldn't the printers be plural? He complains of inconsistency. 'Sometimes, phrases such as "of course" are set off by commas; sometimes, they are not.' (Would you use those two commas, by the way?) But inconsistency might simply be appropriate variety. He complains that Truss uses parentheses to add independent clauses to the end of sentences (so do I, sometimes).

The *New Yorker* does not encourage letters of rejoinder, but Andrew Franklin, Truss's editor at her publishers, Profile Books, is happy to answer back. He is not to be outdone in witheringness by Louis Menand. The problem is mostly the critic's humourlessness. 'If you have no sense of humour,' Franklin thinks, the success of Truss's book will be a mystery to you. Misunderstanding the purpose of her book, which is not a style guide but an entertaining 'call to arms', Menand has pedantically reached for a non-existent rule book. 'I think he's a tosser. You're welcome to use that,' Franklin remarked when I quizzed him for his views on Truss's antagonist. 'I'd never want to spend an evening in his company.' Rules in English 'are more complicated and sophisticated' than he can dream of, he adds. Good writers can break the rules, provided they have learned them before they break them.

Why should it have so provoked one of the *New Yorker*'s leading writers? 'A twisted colon' is one of Franklin's explanations, but he also has a weightier cultural analysis. The attack is 'deeply xenophobic'. An American critic who is used to his readers having their eyes only on American culture has seen them reach for an idiosyncratic English book for a discussion of grammar. So far the book has sold 800,000 copies in the US, about as many as it has sold in Britain. For the arbiter of matters literary and linguistic in the *New Yorker* chair, it is, Franklin guesses, just too much.

Menand certainly has one explicit objection to the book's Englishness. He points out that it has not been altered for its American edition, and is 'virtually useless for American readers'. They order things differently over there. Quotation marks always go outside stops. And the title of Truss's book, according to American grammatical mores, should have a comma before the '&': Eats, Shoots, & Leaves. So are those American readers poor saps, duped into buying a guide to a language they do not write? Franklin retorts that the 'trivial differences' between British and American punctuation are mentioned by Truss, who anyway wrote a separate introduction for the US edition.

Certainly it is the case that it is Truss's breeziness, even her happy facetiousness, that has made her book a bestseller, not her description of how to use apostrophes. The book's success is all about it not being a style guide. After all, those style guides are all out there and none of their authors has ever been able to retire on the royalties from even the most helpful. It is the combination of concern with jokiness, irritating to some, that has attracted readers. Style guides list rules and conventions, but you can actually read Truss's book.

So her confessions that she breaks some rules are all to her purpose. Menand's own article turns into a meditation on the nature and the elusiveness of a writer's 'voice', and a voice is what – for good or ill – Truss manages to give you. Menand says that a writer's voice has nothing to do with his or her punctuation, but his own prose has a voice that is certainly, in part, a function of his punctuation. He combines colloquial idioms and contractions with a certain fastidiousness – some might think fussiness – in his use of commas. (Look back at that earlier example.)

Funnily enough, this is something Truss talks about in her book. Her chapter on commas begins by examining the famous 'clarification complex' of a past editor of the *New Yorker*, Harold Ross. Ross was always trying to get contributors to use more commas and admitted in a letter to H.L. Mencken that he had 'carried editing to a very high degree of fussiness here, probably to a point approaching the ultimate'. He itched to put in commas wherever he could. Perhaps Menand has inherited the itch, and perhaps it is a matter of taste and not correctness.

27 August 2004

EMMA BROCKES

Think pink

Think pink! Think pink! When you shop for summer clothes
Think pink! Think pink! If you want that *quelque chose*
Red is dead, blue is through
Green's obscene, brown's taboo!
(Kay Thompson in *Funny Face*, 1957)

Musicals are pretty silly. The people in them find they can do things, amazing things, like dance on the ceiling or build a barn using acrobatics in the place of more traditional construction methods or get plucked from a crowd to sing a song to which they know all the words or choreograph entire streets of people or rollerskate – things that, before they felt a show tune coming on, they simply couldn't do. The men in musicals wear more make-up than the women – Howard Keel leads the field in *Calamity Jane* – and the women have more drive than the men. Is there any scene more monstrous in film history than that of Barbra Streisand, as Yentl, sailing under the Statue of Liberty hollering, 'What's wrong with wanting more?' in a film not only starring, directed, produced and co-written by the woman, but one in which, despite the Broadway pedigree of her co-stars, she awarded all the songs to herself? Yes, all of them. That, my friends, is the magic of musicals.

The history of the genre is to some extent a history of America's relationship with itself: musicals aspire with an almost ideological fervour to the condition of being American. Stern lessons are taught about self-reliance, about how to 'shine', as orphan Annie puts it, 'like the top of the Chrysler building'. From the homely moral of *The Wizard of Oz* ('if you ever go looking for your heart's desire, you needn't look further than your own backyard'), to the vicious ambition of *42nd Street* to Aunt Eller's pioneering-spirit speech in *Oklahoma* – 'lots of things happen to a woman: sickness, or being poor or hungry or being left alone in your old age, and you can stand it. There's one way: you gotta be HEARTY!' – all peddle the show-must-go-on machismo of American conservatism. But they are subversive, too; they poke fun at their own nostalgic values and this conflict is their great source of power, one always missed by people who hate them. 'Let me tell you something, son,' says Walter Matthau in *Hello, Dolly!*, 'I've worked hard and I've become rich, friendless and mean. And in America, that's about as far as you can go.'

If musicals amused people in the 1930s, hypnotized them in the 1940s and 1950s, and more or less died out in the 1970s, they have, despite their recycled storylines and arch dialogue, never really wanted for fond audiences. Seventy years after *Top Hat* was made, who can fail to be charmed by Fred and Ginger gliding around in evening dress to Irving Berlin's 'Isn't This a Lovely Day (To Be Caught in the Rain?)'? Or fail to sigh for Ava Gardner as she gazes, with beady-eyed madness, across the Mississippi at the end of *Show Boat*, her happiness evaporating to the strains of 'Ol' Man River'? Martha Graham once said, 'It is not the job of the musical artist to be larger than life, but to be as large as life.' Musicals are in essence about luxury: of dress, of movement, of talent, of emotion. What is sadder than a sad song, or happier than dancing?

'Don't you ever let yourself go?' said Fred Astaire to Cyd Charisse in *Silk Stockings* (1957).

'Go where?' she said.

'I don't know. Just go, go, GO! Don't you ever feel so happy that you just want to dance all round the room?'

'Happiness,' replied Charisse, speaking for straight men everywhere, 'is the reward of industry and labour. Dancing is a waste of time.'

'I like wasting time,' said Fred.

After a long, slow decline, the film musical appears to be coming back. There are at least five in production at the moment, among them *Rent* and *The Producers*, and one soon to be released, *De-Lovely*, a biopic of Cole Porter in which Kevin Kline plays the lead and the songs are performed by pop stars. Each age gets the musicals it deserves (we must all share the blame for *Starlight Express*), and so, despite its great score, *De-Lovely* is a grim exercise in postmodernity. Instead of telling the story straight, it introduces Jonathan Pryce as the 'director', who keeps a tedious running commentary on the 'authenticity' of the action. It combines bad irony with that brand of humourlessness peculiar to middle-range pop stars. Only Kline, who has the weakest voice, understands that you have to act a song in musicals, that it isn't sufficient to sing it – or in the case of Robbie Williams (who cameos in the film), to gurn it, as if fighting the effects of an extreme G-force. This was a problem in *Moulin Rouge*, too, a film in which Ewan McGregor and Nicole Kidman reminded us that people who can't sing shouldn't sing, unless, like Rex Harrison in *My Fair Lady*, they are willing to make up the shortfall with acting.

There is no reason why modern audiences can't be carried by new musicals, but the films have to respect the rules of the game. Eminem's *8 Mile*, one of the most successful of the recent musicals, was also one of the most traditional: it recoursed to the logic of the show within the show, the Busby Berkeley model, in which the songs appear without compromising the film's realism. In the 1930s, Berkeley was choreographing while seemingly under the influence of crack; crazy giant wedding cakes, women popping out of things, orchestras cast in plaster-of-Paris and those mad Esther Williams swimming flicks, in which she would dive from a board above the stage through flaming hoops into a shallow tank – the kind of stuff CGI (computer generated imaging) would take care of today. Berkeley paid no heed to the requirements of the plot; in fact, as he said in an interview in the *New York Times* in 1970, 'I did my numbers and the director did the story. Sometimes I'd even forget who was directing.'

The alternative to the show within a show is the musical in which characters sing at each other in place of dialogue. These are the ones people who don't like musicals complain about; all those freaks in orange make-up bellowing, 'If I loved you la la la', then snapping out of it and behaving as if nothing happened. It is the model for the Rodgers and Hammerstein hits of the 1940s and 1950s and the golden reign of MGM when one-third of all Hollywood films were musicals. These seem, in some ways, more dated than the bitchy, art-deco hits of the 1920s and 1930s. All the talent in them went into the songs and the dialogue was left to stretch unnaturally between show-stoppers.

'I had to leave France,' says Rossano Brazzi, in a typical exchange from *South Pacific*. 'I killed a man. But he was a wicked man. The town bully. Everyone in our village was glad to see him die. It was not to my discredit.'

'You just told me that you killed a man,' replies Mitzi Gaynor, who has met him for the first time five minutes before. 'And [you say] that it's all right. I hardly know you ... and yet I know it's all right.' They embrace over a tureen of soup then she pulls herself together to sing 'I'm Just a Dope Who is Stuck on Hope'.

The politics of these films haven't dated well, either. In *Carousel*, which gave us the classic torch song 'You'll Never Walk Alone' and the less classic song 'Real Nice Clambake', Shirley Jones says wistfully in her role as battered wife, Julie: 'Can it really be that someone hits you, hits you hard, and you don't feel a thing?' The film redeems itself slightly when her evil husband Billy, played by Gordon MacRae, is murdered, but sexual politics is a fraught area in musicals.

In *Funny Face*, Audrey Hepburn abandons her own version of herself to adopt one suggested by a creepy old Fred Astaire – way too ancient in 1957 to be playing opposite Hepburn. And yet at the same time, musicals in the 1940s and 1950s were really the only form of mass entertainment in which women were allowed to have ambitions not only equal to, but exceeding those of the men. They were consistently more talented, more ambitious and more successful in the plot and in life than their male co-stars. In the 1954 version of *A Star is Born* (from a 1937 original co-written by Dorothy Parker), Judy Garland plays the star while her husband, James Mason, plays the washed-up actor, an arrangement that so unhinges him, he walks clean into the sea. 'I hate him for failing,' says Garland's character, miserably. In *Funny Girl*, the biopic of Ziegfeld star Fanny Brice, Streisand tries to comfort husband Omar Sharif for being a loser. 'Everyone has a run of bad luck now and then,' she says.

'How would you know, darling?' he replies bitterly. 'You never lose.'

These women always end up alone at the end of the picture, although they do better than their husbands, who are either dead or, worse, in career Siberia. Even Mary Poppins, God love her, disappears up into the sky, alone despite her excellent powers. This is either an indictment of a culture that fears talented women or an attempt to frighten them into submission; the former, I think, since everything in the furniture of these films encourages one to identify with the women: the men fail as Americans – they give up! – while the women fulfil their destinies. It is important that the heroine in these sorts of musicals isn't beautiful; they have, like Liza Minnelli in *Cabaret*, to be slightly weird-looking. So Gypsy Rose Lee wins out over her pretty sister June, and plain-but-hearty Debbie Reynolds triumphs over the beautiful Jean Hagen in *Singin' in the Rain*. In *High Society*, one of Cole Porter's greatest scores, beautiful Grace Kelly looks vapid beside Celeste Holm, the balance of power leaning firmly towards talent over beauty.

If this is a critique of Hollywood by Hollywood, then it's a patchy but powerful one. There is an irony that stems from the issue of prettiness, which Arthur Miller describes at length in his novella *Plain Girl*: that air of defensive amusement adopted by women who 'should' be better-looking. It isn't camp in the *Rocky Horror* sense of the word, but rather a detachment, an irony so delicate that it doesn't interfere with plausibility. It is what rescues a lot of musicals from oversweetness. You see it in *Meet Me in St Louis*, a potentially saccharine film about the trials of an ordinary Missouri family at the turn of the century. When filming started, Judy Garland played all her scenes tongue-in-cheek, until Vincente Minnelli, her director and later husband, explained that it would really only work if she played it straight. But there remains an edge to her performance, a raised eyebrow that suggests the very concept of 'ordinariness' depicted in films like these is itself an act of some kind.

Musicals of that era, all of which celebrate heterosexual love, didn't have to strive very hard to inject this air of detachment, given that so many of the men who wrote, directed or choreographed them were gay, and so many of the women who starred in them were narcissists. Garland came to epitomize this style of camp. 'Look, sweetie,' she informed the director on the set of *Easter Parade*, 'I'm no June Allyson, you know. Don't get cute with me. None of that batting-the-eyelids bit or the fluffing the hair routine for me, buddy!'

The contrast between the sweet screen versions of these women and their increasingly loopy and bitter personal lives adds, rather unkindly, to the fascination of the films. In the interview she gave to Rex Reed in 1968, Ava Gardner, so mild and winsome in her early movies, screamed bitterly: 'Christ, what did I ever do worth talking about? I've been a movie star for twenty-five years and I've got nothing, NOTHING to show for it. All I've got is three lousy ex-husbands. I can't remember my own family's birthdays. Only reason I know my own is because I was born the same day as Christ. That's Capricorn, which means a lifetime of hell, baby.'

In later films, directors got bolder with their digs at the gap between Hollywood's version of life and its reality. In *A Star is Born*, whenever a particularly tragic scene is taking place, a billboard creeps into the background advertising a sappy musical called *Happiness Ahead*, or the scene cuts to a jolly number with lyrics such as 'Go and get your long face lost'. Musicals are supposed to be 'the apotheosis of romance', as Pauline Kael put it, but they also budget for its failure. 'Love isn't enough,' says Garland tragically at the end of the film. 'I thought it was.'

In the late-1960s, musicals started to lose their appeal. They looked overblown and self-indulgent; they tested the credulity of their audience too severely. The nail in the coffin was *Hello, Dolly!*, a gruesome film directed by

Gene Kelly, with all of the genre's excesses and none of its charms. In the 1970s, the rock musicals gave a brief boost to the genre and then, except for *Fame* and *Grease*, the 1980s were a desert.

It is tempting to read the current revival as a response to all the misery in the world; the other two booms followed the Wall Street Crash and the Second World War. But it is probably just that enough time has passed for the fashion to renew itself. 'I'm as corny as Kansas in August,' trills Mitzi Gaynor in *South Pacific*, with commendable self-awareness. 'I'm as trite and as gay as a daisy in May.' Musicals are pretty silly. But you can't help loving them.

26 July 2004

JOHN TUSA

Coming home to Janáček

As we drove north up the autobahn from Vienna to the Moravian capital of Brno, I wondered what exactly I was looking for. With my BBC Radio 3 colleagues, I had set out to find Leoš Janáček, in his 150th birthday anniversary year. He is the musical puzzle, the composer who came from nowhere, who left no school, yet who strides the international opera scene to this day.

The country north of Brno, central and north Moravia, is utterly Janáček country. He was born in Hukvaldy in the north; he loved and recorded the music of the Lassko villages and people nearby; he frequented the spa town of Luhacovice. He made his name and career in Brno.

These lands are also mine. On the drive from Brno to Janáček's Hukvaldy, you pass Zlin, the Bata shoe town where I was born. The road skirts Bystrice pod Hostynem, where my mother was born. I left Czechoslovakia – as it then was – in 1939. My feelings of being Czech after a lifetime being British are bound to be vestigial. But they do exist. The very sounds of the town and village names, the cadences of the language – to which Janáček was almost unreasonably attuned – are my imprinted sounds and melodies, too. In looking for Janáček, would I also find a part of myself?

On the first evening, the Janáček Opera of the Brno National Theatre were performing *Katya Kabanova*. Part of a fortnight's anniversary festival including all of Janáček's stage works, it was a turbulent evening. Janáček sung in Czech by Czechs has a special impact; this is not surprising, given Janáček's obsession with the way the spoken language sounds and the way in which it influences composed music. But it was the theatrical brutality of the piece that took me aback. The speed with which Janáček disposes of the action, culminating in Katya's suicide, is breathtaking, yet achieved without skimping. The emotional impact is huge, because the economy and concentration of the music are so intense. That is the paradox. That is his genius.

The capacity audience took it respectfully, if not with wild enthusiasm. But as I looked at the almost entirely local crowd, I had a moment of recognition. These were my people – Moravians. I look like them. Had my family not left

Czechoslovakia in 1939 to work in England, one of those people in the audience could have been me. I was closer to this audience than I could ever be to any other.

Two evenings later, we were in Janáček's home village of Hukvaldy, surrounded by the wooded hills he loved so much, the 500-year-old lime trees, the old castle on the hilltop about which he lyricized, clean air and bright sunshine that seemed to give him creative energy. We were in the pub Janáček used, Pod Hradem, below the castle. Then, as now, musicians played folk music, violin and dulcimer, perhaps even the one the composer listened to. They sang while they played. In Janáček's time, the musicians were local farmers and peasants, the music preserved and transmitted through the oral tradition. That evening the two performers were computer programmers by day but had learned folk music at the hands of local musicians.

Lasskian and Walasskian rhythms stirred Janáček deeply. I couldn't establish whether what I heard had that exact origin. But I am sure that the music, enthusiastically accompanied by Pod Hradem's regular Friday-nighters, does not sound like homogenized 'mittel Europaischer' ethnicism. Such checked, off-the-beat rhythms are subtler, unexpectedly displaced. They do not thump obviously, but hold themselves back with an inner instinct. No wonder Janáček, so sensitive to the sounds of nature and speech and music, was captivated.

Standing outside the pub in the cool, spring night, the evening star was up, the young moon lit up the ruins of Janáček's favourite brewery, and owls hooted on the hill. I desperately wanted to hear a fox's bark, distant descendant of Janáček's beloved vixen of his opera. But no amount of imaginative straining could conjure it.

The next day, I got closer to the vixen and to Janáček. Lower down the village is the house where Janáček used to spend many summer holidays. Karel Zak, who lives there today, is the grandson of the forester who entertained the composer. He showed me the rustic seat where Janáček sat to look at the hills, the beehives that he saw, and pressed on us some honey mead from the hives, as the great man would have drunk it.

It was Grandfather Zak who arranged the expedition to show the composer a family of foxes near the castle on the hill. Janáček appeared at nightfall dressed in an immaculate white suit; the Forester sent him packing to dress in something practical. Even when the vixen and her cubs duly emerged, the childlike composer was so thrilled that his yelps of glee finally sent the foxes back to their lair. That sense of pure animal joy permeates the whole opera.

Later, Karel was joined by his friend Joszka, a schoolteacher, to play Janáček's little piece for violin and piano about the castle on the hill. Karel played on a Hammond organ, Joszka rather tentatively on the fiddle. But given the place, the family connection and the music, surely the old man's spirit must have been hovering?

Karel also repairs instruments, the most famous of them being the harmonium that stands in the living room of Janáček's own house higher up the hill. In the last weeks of his life, Janáček persuaded his so-called 'muse', Kamilla Stosslova, to visit, accompanied by her young son, Otto. When the custodian, Karel Dohnal, plays the harmonium it conjures up memories that are both farcical and sad. Farcical, because Janáček made life intolerable for his love and her son by playing the harmonium at night, often hammering the same chord repeatedly. Tragic because he caught a cold days later during a walk in the hills and was dead within days.

On our way to Hukvaldy, my eye was caught by a road sign pointing to a village off the main road – Blahutovice. 'That's where my uncle Joszka lived,' I said to my wife, Ann. 'That's where we went on holiday with him in 1947. I had no idea it was around here.' Driving back to Brno, Ann suggested we turn off and see if I could recognize the farmhouse. Nothing could be more different from the image of the traditional English village. Here are large, free-standing buildings, farmyards and barns, with massive double wooden doors to let in the carts. I could remember all that. I could remember Uncle Joszka's magnificent stallion, and his tame deer. Did we find the actual farm? I doubt it. I just know that it was good to be there and that in 1947 none of my family ever spoke of Janáček.

To the north-east of Brno, we came to Janáček's favourite spa town of Luhacovice. Its fake rustic, half-timbered spa buildings survive to this day. The broad promenade, flanked by hills, has not changed. Here he fell in love with the actress Kamila Urvalkova, about whom he wrote his opera *Osud* (Fate). Here he met Stosslova, whose relationship shaped his creative life and whose correspondence is enshrined in Janáček's Second Quartet, *Intimate Letters*. I stood in front of the house where Janáček once stayed, waiting for Stosslova to appear from the house opposite and then happening to fall in with her in the street.

To look for Janáček is to tussle with contradictions: he was impulsive yet considerate; intuitive yet calculating; a fantasist and a realist; a superb psychologist of women on the stage, yet a disastrous one with the women in his life.

I can't argue with a composer whose understanding is so deep that he makes you feel compassion for Kostelnicka, even though she has drowned Jenufa's baby; who sees the pathos in the Forester, though he has shot the Vixen. There are no easy gestures in his operas, no slick resolutions, only a compelling universality that emerges from the deepest particulars of his Moravian landscapes and sounds.

And myself? Sitting in the spa at Luhacovice, I remembered that my parents gave a Boxing Day party for many years, where the local Czech community gathered for one reason above all. The men needed to sing the old songs of their youth, when they were part of the nationalist, gymnastic movement, Sokol. As they swung instinctively into the old unaccompanied harmonies, I realized that they were singing of their lives and homes. Janáček would have approved.

4 February 2004

NANCY BANKS-SMITH

Change of tack

There were three judges in *Faking It* (Channel 4): Lord Patrick Beresford, silver-haired scion of a noble house; Dr Dallas Burston, trust him, he's a doctor; and Princess Tamara Czartoryski-Borbon, *Carry On* actress and horsey cousin of the King of Spain. Which do you think is the fake? That was my feeling, too. Even with a swig of Pol Roger, I found it hard to swallow Princess Tamara Czartoryski-Borbon. Though admittedly double-barrels often go with blood sports, one way or another.

They were all, however implausible, perfectly authentic. The fake was Malcolm 'Woody' Woodcock, a bicycle courier, who was trying to pass himself off as a polo player.

In some ways, Woody seemed to me a born polo player as he careered through Manchester on his mountain bike, scattering old ladies like litter and giving motorists heart attacks at the traffic lights. Woody could not have burned more rubber if he had been bringing the good news from Ghent to Aix. His job was a daily adrenaline rush: 'There's not many can say they've narrowly missed death.'

In other ways, not. He jangled with ironmongery. He wore eyeliner. You could have whiled away a rainy afternoon reading his tattoos. He painted his own clothes, possibly in woad. His head was shaven but his ponytail could have kept a swarm of flies at bay. The effect was piratical. Prince Harry, catching sight of him, seemed hypnotized. Nevertheless, you liked the lad, a point that is crucial to the success of this series.

He learned to kiss a woman on both cheeks and not to flinch at a pink shirt. He sacrificed his ponytail, his eyeliner and nail varnish. He rehearsed his cover story at a polo party: 'Basically, like, I'm a millionaire.' There was a stunned shush. 'People never talk about money, do they?' said a girl wonderingly.

He had a month to confuse the hell out of the judges. We will throw a horse blanket over his progress and his language. He swore with the monotonous fury of a man who thought the horse wasn't listening. He relaxed with a boozy night with the grooms and, arriving home at 2 a.m., put his fist through the door.

The hangover didn't help in a crucial polo match at the Royal Berkshire. Mark, the captain, explained they simply had to win. Much of the charm of the commentary lay in Michael Kitchen's deadpan delivery: 'Mark's team are out of the tournament and he's not taking it very well.' (Mark was beating the grass to death with his polo mallet.)

Woody, a lad who could not see a sign saying Easy Way Out without taking it, was shocked into action. 'I don't think I did anything right today. I need to pull me finger out and get stuck in.'

His tattoos were blotted out and his piercings plugged to mislead the judges. He was competing against Phil, Sean and Dave, three far more experienced polo players. His tutors watched, suffering, as though they were his parents. Phil played a solid game, Sean lost a stirrup, Dave had an exceptional chukka, but Woody, galvanized, scored a goal.

Sometimes I feel *Faking It* encourages shoddiness. As Woody himself said: 'I don't actually have to know what I'm doing. I just have to look good.' I cannot think of any eventuality where a man who doesn't know what he's doing would be welcome. Then again, a month in the country opened windows for Woody: 'I don't want to go. I've never really been challenged like this before. I ride a bike, I go home, I go to the pub. But if I can do this in a month, I can do almost anything I set my mind to.'

The judges got it all wrong. Judges sometimes do. Look at *Coronation Street* (ITV1), where Rita roundly and rightly denounced the bench as a bunch of numbskulls and is consequently mouldering in a dungeon without her hot water bottle.

So farewell then, Rickee! The most screamed at man in soap. The inspiration for the sign 'Ear-piercing while you wait'. Last night, pursued by his sister's shrieks, Ricky took little Liam and left *EastEnders* (BBC1). Mark my words, one day all these long-lost children – little Courtney, little Liam, little Ben, little Lou and Little Mo's little baby (so small it is barely visible to the naked eye) – will come home to roost. And it will all start all over again.

PASTS

JAMES FENTON

The stamp of history

I met a woman recently who was a medallist by profession: she designed and executed rather large, coin-like objects in many unusual forms and with a range of different finishes – modern variations on ancient techniques. There are two main ways of making a medal – by casting and by striking. When you cast a medal, even using the most sophisticated methods such as silica moulds, the cast that you initially achieve has a rough surface that has to be chased (worked with tools) and polished before it looks good. But when a medal is struck, as a coin is traditionally struck, the object you get looks good straight away.

A struck coin is the result of a piece of hot metal being placed between two dies and hit with great force, so that the metal is forced against the contours of the die, whose shape it takes with utter precision. The more I look at early Greek coins, the more impressed I am by the observation that (with the best of them) we can see an ancient art exactly as the ancients saw it.

Ancient statuary one would expect to show the effects of the weather. Marble gets worn by wind and rain, by frost too in a northern climate. And the marble statues of the ancient world have suffered all kinds of interventions. Once perhaps they were coloured. Now they are clean. Or once their surface had deteriorated and gone sugary, but now they have had their epidermis removed.

Among the freshest of survivors from millennia ago are hard-stone seals, as for instance the cylindrical seals from Mesopotamia, which, when rolled over a piece of clay, still produce an astonishingly sharp image. Classical gems which retained this freshness, producing a perfect image in wax, were objects of wonder in the Renaissance, and still astonish us when we bother to ask of them, for instance, how such a device could have been cut with such precision on such a small scale. What kind of lens, if any, could the gem-cutter have used? What kind of tool? Always, when we look at photographs of such gems and seals and coins, we have to remind ourselves of the scale of the original, for they are routinely reproduced in generous magnifications, and yet they do not lose the decisiveness of their contours. They seem to expect to be enlarged.

The die-cutter's art must have descended from that of the gem-cutter. They thought in the same way, in terms of negative space. They had the same gift for reduction. One worked in the hardest of stones, the other in metal. One – the seal-cutter – worked typically for the individual. The die-cutter generally worked for the state. Uniqueness, in both cases, would have been at a premium, and no doubt the art was usually a rare one.

I used vaguely to imagine that the irregularity of ancient coins, on which images are often only partially present, was a result of wear and tear, that the coins had been clipped or had suffered in the course of commerce. But irregular coins are typically complete. It is the positioning of the die at the moment of striking that has led to the partial image. Beyond the limits of the die, around the edge of the coin, the metal has been pushed out by the force of the blow, exactly like a cushion of sealing-wax. You can feel each blow as you examine or handle each coin. The total shape is dynamic in the way a cast coin never is.

The earlier coins were produced before it had been fully understood that a coin could have two sides. The obverse bears the image. On the reverse it shows the impression of a square punch, the aim of the maker being to force the metal right into the die, to achieve that precise, intended image. Then this punch is elaborated: obverse is complemented by reverse, heads with tails. And leaving aside these heads, this array of portraiture, there are all these tails to consider: bulls, tortoises, lions, hares, tunas, dolphins, cuttlefish, strutting cockerels, eagles, the famous owls, crabs and the all-important horses.

Remember, when you look at these Greek coins, that 'the poor man's purse was generally his mouth'. There is a character in Aristophanes who, during hard times for the Athenian state, has just sold some grapes for a mouthful of bronze, and has gone to the market-place to buy some meal, when the town-crier comes by, shouting, 'Bronze is no longer legal tender; Athens is a silver-using state once more.'

So it was not an odd practice (if we ever thought it was) to place a coin in a dead person's mouth, to ease the passage into the afterworld. The mouth would be the obvious place for keeping money safe. But how the dead managed to pay for their passage before around 700 BC, which is when the first coins are supposed to have been minted – that's just one of those questions that will have to wait for an answer.

4 June 2004

JONATHAN STEELE

Germany moves on

You can hardly blame the Germans for not thinking much about D-day. The economy is barely growing. Young people find it increasingly hard to get jobs. Cuts in the country's generous pension system are never out of the headlines. So, amid the new unease, the fact that Gerhard Schroder will be the first chancellor to attend the commemorations on the Normandy beaches was hardly a talking point as Germans escaped into the countryside at Whitsun.

The fanfare of publicity when he takes his place alongside George Bush and other Western leaders on Sunday will turn it into big news, since hundreds of German reporters are expected among the 3,500 who have signed up. But the significance of Germany's unprecedented participation is still a matter of debate.

Willy Brandt, the only German chancellor with a clear record of anti-Nazi resistance, resigned over a spy scandal just a month before the thirtieth anniversary of D-day. The commemorations had not yet become a bandwagon for politicians, and even if they had, he would probably not have been invited. Impeccable though his own credentials were, 1974 was considered too soon after the war for such an act of reconciliation on so sensitive a day.

A decade later, when the Federal Republic was led by a man who was too young to have fought in the war, similar conditions seemed to apply. François Mitterrand turned that D-day anniversary, as well as the one in 1994, into a massive jamboree, with the US president and the British prime minister on hand. There was no place for Helmut Kohl on either occasion. It was long thought that Western leaders were excluding him. But research by the weekly magazine, *Der Spiegel*, shows that it was Kohl who took the initiative. He told his French counterpart he did not want to be invited. He saw no reason to celebrate 'when others mark a battle in which tens of thousands of Germans met miserable deaths'. His comment encapsulated the complexity of German feelings which still prevailed fifty years after the war. To pretend that 1945 was felt by most Germans as a liberation rather than as a defeat was nonsense. For a German to honour the Allied dead who fell in Normandy and celebrate D-day as a great step to victory would have been perverse.

The mixed feelings which Iraqis have over the fact that outsiders toppled Saddam Hussein show how volatile and uncertain people are in the face of huge changes they have no role in making. Delight at liberation goes hand-in-hand with anger at occupation. For Germans the Nazi collapse was an incomparably greater trauma. Hitler's dictatorship lasted less than half as long as Saddam's, but it commanded much broader and deeper support. Heinrich Mann, the left-wing brother of the better-known writer, Thomas Mann, accurately described Germany in 1945 as 'free but conquered'.

Far more Germans died in the wars that Hitler launched, and the ferocity of the Allied carpet-bombing of German cities, as well as the floods of German civilians who were put to flight on the eastern front, dwarfed the calamity that Iraqis suffered against Iran or in the first Gulf war, let alone the latest one. Hitler's defeat destroyed an empire. Ancient German settlements across central Europe and along the Baltic rim crashed to the ground.

It is only in the last few years that German authors and historians have been able to write about these things without being branded as right-wing revanchists. But in the intimacy of the family they were often discussed, not necessarily under the illusion that Germans as a whole were bigger victims of Hitler than Jews, Poles or Russians, but in the sense that the war brought unrecognized tragedy for millions of Germans, too.

Apart from the Jews, the group of Germans who suffered most from Hitler were the communists, and it was no accident that the East German state was genuinely able, from its beginning, to propagate the notion of Hitler's defeat as liberation. Whatever its internal repression, and its submission to post-war Soviet doctrine, East Germany pursued a firmer policy of de-Nazification than the Federal Republic.

In the West, the process of re-evaluating the past was slow and sometimes grudging. The final taboo only fell in the late 1990s with the Wehrmacht exhibition, which moved from city to city showing how the regular army, and not just the Waffen SS, routinely committed atrocities. But that does not make every German soldier a criminal, for whom surviving family members have to feel shame. Even now, many Germans feel the D-day anniversary is a time primarily to remember their own dead. A poll last week showed 71 per cent of Germans in favour of Schroder's visit to Normandy. This still leaves a sizeable chunk against it. Opposition was especially high among Free Democrats, traditionally the party of the officer corps and the upper-middle-class.

If majority attitudes have changed, it is largely because the generations have moved on. For the young, deciding whether D-day and May 1945 were defeats or the start of liberation is a historical rather than a personal issue. Schroder's visit to Normandy is 'a sign of integration and acceptance', as an engineering student put it in Hanover the other day. She welcomed it as proof that Germany was a normal international player. No doubt Vladimir Putin's attendance in Normandy is a symbol of the same thing. For years, the West played down the Soviet Union's pivotal contribution in defeating Hitler at Stalingrad and Kursk. Moscow criticized D-day and the opening of the 'second front' as at best late, and at worst as the first move in the Cold War, aimed at blocking Russia from liberating the whole of Germany alone. For a Russian president to be invited, and for him to agree to come, are steps forward.

In Britain, the priority should be to have a new look at the way schools approach the study of the world since 1945. The tabloids are incorrigible, and Hitler as an issue will always sell. But it is sad that so few young people are taught the history of Germany's two post-war states, and the complexities of unification and its aftermath. An astonishing 60 per cent of pupils who take history at GCSE level choose Hitler and the Nazis. If they were offered courses on post-war Europe, or if the Hitler material were embedded in a wider course on recent German history, perhaps as adults they would more readily reject the tabloid stereotypes. In France and Poland, young people are well informed about how their neighbour Germany has changed since the war. D-day ought to be an impulse for improvements here too.

7 April 2004

TRISTRAM HUNT

Virtual history

Citing as their inspiration the Gwyneth Paltrow character in the film *Sliding Doors*, a ragged bunch of right-wing historians have clubbed together to issue a new compendium of 'what if' essays. Conrad Black, a man facing a few counter-factuals of his own, asks: what if the Japanese had not attacked Pearl Harbor? David Frum, the former Bush speech-writer, wonders: what if Al Gore had won the 2000 presidential election (I thought he did)? And John Adamson indulges the dream of Cambridge dons down the centuries: what if Charles I had won the English civil war?

E.H. Carr dismissed such whimsical exercises as a red herring worthy not of scholarly pursuit but an idle 'parlour game'. Characteristically E.P. Thompson went one stage further, dismissing 'counter-factual fiction' as 'unhistorical shit'. Both pointed to the futility of pondering multiple variables in the past and the logical problem of assuming all other conditions remained constant. But despite their warnings, the thirst for virtual history remains undimmed. And while Carr was right to dismiss them as an amusing pastime, behind the light-hearted maybes lurk more uncomfortable historical and political agendas.

The conservatives who contribute to this literature portray themselves as battling against the dominant but flawed ideologies of Marxist and Whig history. Such analyses of the past, they say, never allow for the role of accident and serendipity. Instead, the past is presented as a series of milestones in an advance towards communism or liberal democracy. It is the calling of these modern iconoclasts to reintroduce the crooked timber of humanity back into history.

The unfortunate truth is that, rather than constituting a rebel grouping, 'what if' history is eerily close to the mainstream of modern scholarship. The past twenty years has witnessed a brutal collapse in what was once called social history. The rigorous, data-based study of class, inequality, work patterns and gender relations has fallen away in the face of cultural history and postmodern inquiry.

Research into structures and processes, along with a search for explanation, is overshadowed by histories of understanding and meaning. In many cases this has led to a declining emphasis on the limitations that social context – class status, economic prospects, family networks – can place on the historical role of the individual. Instead, what we are offered in the postmodern world of contingency and irony is a series of biographical discourses in which one narrative is as valid as another. One history is as good as another and with it the blurring of factual, counter-factual and fiction. All history is 'what if' history.

No doubt, new-right legionaries such as Andrew Roberts and Simon Heffer would be appalled to be in the distinguished company of those postmodern bogeymen, Michel Foucault and Jacques Derrida. And they have partly atoned for their sins with a traditional Tory emphasis on the role of great men in history. For 'what if' versions of the past posit the powerful individual at the heart of their histories: it is a story of what generals, presidents and revolutionaries did or did not do. The contribution of bureaucracies, ideas or social class is nothing to the personal fickleness of Josef Stalin or the constitution of Franz Ferdinand.

But it is surely the interaction between individual choices and historical context that governs the events of the past. As Karl Marx put it: 'People make their own history, but they do not make it just as they please; they do not make it under circumstances chosen by themselves, but under circumstances directly encountered, given and transmitted from the past.' Moreover, as Professor Richard Evans has noted, in this work there is as much a sense of 'if only' as 'what if'. This is history as wishful thinking, providing little insight into the decision-making processes of the past, but pointing up preferable alternatives and lamenting their failure to come to pass. Hence the focus on Charles I's victory and Britain's decision to sit out the world wars. The late Alan Clark enjoyed charting the consequences of Britain making peace with Hitler in 1940 and managing to retain the empire.

But 'what if' history poses just as insidious a threat to present politics as it does to a fuller understanding of the past. It is no surprise that progressives rarely involve themselves, since implicit in it is the contention that social structures and economic conditions do not matter. Man is, we are told, a creature free of almost all historical constraints, able to make decisions on his own volition. According to Andrew Roberts, we should understand that 'in human affairs anything is possible'. What this means is there is both little to learn from the potentialities of history, and there is no need to address injustices because of their marginal influence on events. And without wishing to be over-determinist, it is not hard to predict the political intention of such a reactionary and historically redundant approach to the past.

6 December 2003

JONATHAN SUMPTION

Occupying England

In the year 1085, William the Conqueror spent Christmas at Gloucester. There, according to the author of the *Anglo-Saxon Chronicle*, he had 'much thought and deep discussion with his council about this country, how it was occupied and with what sort of people'. The outcome of the king's 'deep discussion' was the famous survey of England, which later became known as the Domesday Book. It is the oldest surviving public record of the English state, and one of the oldest of any European state. It is also one of the most remarkable: an early example of the obsessional nosiness of governments, and their perennial urge to number and classify. Despite several attempts, nothing comparable was produced until the nineteenth century. In medieval societies, as in modern ones, the main constraint on the power of the state was its ignorance. William, the most authoritarian ruler this country ever had, was determined to do something about that.

Until it was rebound a few years ago, the book consisted of two stout volumes in the Public Record Office. The first, known as Great Domesday, is a handsome production, 15 inches high and running to nearly eight hundred pages of neat double columns. It was written in the royal treasury at Winchester in a beautiful and distinctive script, probably by a single clerk. It contains a record, county by county, of the whole of England except for the three East Anglian counties of Norfolk, Suffolk and Essex: how much land the king had, how much land was held by the king's tenants, who occupied what, who held the land before the conquest, and how much it was worth then and now.

The survey that produced it was even more intrusive than the final text. 'Not an ox, cow or pig was left out,' one contemporary indignantly recorded. The second volume bears this out. Known as Little Domesday (although it is actually bigger), this covers the three missing counties in much greater detail. It is indeed full of oxen, cows and pigs and a variety of other information, in addition to the facts found in its companion. Little Domesday is a less magnificent affair, scrawled over about nine hundred pages of parchment by a variety of scribes, and peppered with corrections, deletions and insertions. It was probably the actual return sent in by the commissioners from the East Anglian counties. There must once have been equally detailed returns for every other county. They were intended to be incorporated in the final work, leaving out inessential details, and then discarded. Little Domesday survives because the East Anglian material had not yet been incorporated when William died and all further work on the project was abandoned. So the clerks just bound up the returns for these counties as they stood and stored them with the rest.

An example chosen at random will give the flavour. It comes from the Little Domesday entry for Framlingham in Suffolk:

> Aethelmaer, a thegn, held Framlingham. Now Roger Bigod holds it with 9 carucates of land as a manor. Then 24 villeyns, now 32. Then 16 bordars [cottagers], now 28. Then 5 ploughs in demesne, now 3. Then 20 ploughs belonging to the men, now 16. Woodland for 100 pigs. 16 acres of meadow. Then 2 horses, now 3. Then 4 head of cattle, now 7. Then 40 pigs, now 10. Then 20 sheep, now 40. Then as now 60 goats. Now 3 beehives. Then it was worth pounds 16, now pounds 36.

Roger Bigod was one of many young Normans who had flooded into England after the battle of Hastings to join in the fun and grab some land while it was still going. He had done better than most. By the time of the survey, he was the sheriff of Suffolk and one of the largest landowners of East Anglia. He must have been actively involved in the survey for his county. The entry about his estates shows he was a shrewd manager, taking full advantage of the plentiful supply of tied peasants. There are no free men on his manor. But the number of unfree has gone up by 50 per cent, and the number of ploughs has gone down. So Framlingham has become more labour-intensive, and the profits have more than doubled.

Bigod did better than his neighbour, one Manulf, whose affairs are reviewed in the next paragraph. Manulf let most of his land to free men, and made no more out of it than his predecessor. Servility works. But then Manulf obviously went to the wrong business school, like Aethelmaer the thegn.

The whole document fills two massive folios in the only printed edition of the Latin text that has ever been published, in 1783. Its appearance in Penguin Classics, unabridged and translated into serviceable English, is an act of courage that revives one's faith in publishers; and in readers, if the publishers have got their market right. The only complaint one can fairly make is that there is virtually no introduction.

Thanks to the patient detective work of some great medievalists, we know a lot about the Domesday Book. We know more or less how the facts were gathered and how the book was compiled. We know a fair amount about the use actually made of it. We can discover much in it about the economy of early England, its landscapes, the beginnings of its towns, its population, in short, about 'how it was occupied and with what sort of people'. The one-page foreword by Professor Martin hardly does justice to the extraordinary document that follows.

What we still do not really know is what exactly William the Conqueror wanted all these facts for. Nineteenth-century scholars and eleventh-century landowners may not have had much in common, but they did share a profound suspicion of the state and all its doings, especially its financial doings. They were agreed that Domesday was all about maximizing tax revenue. This is not in fact very likely, because the information was extracted and presented in a way that made its use for tax assessment difficult. The book was quite often used as a kind of glorified land register, to resolve disputes about title, but it must very quickly have become useless for that purpose. Land was changing hands even while the survey was being done. Much the most plausible theory is that it was designed to inform the king about his own rights as landowner. It enabled him better to exploit his demesne revenues, and to know roughly what he was doing when he granted and confiscated land. It must have come in useful when Bigod took part in a rebellion in 1088 and temporarily lost Framlingham, together with all his other estates. And serve him right.

Whatever the original plan, the book has in practice been used for many purposes. Three centuries after its creation, at the time of the peasants' revolt, educated serfs started asking for extracts to be made for them to prove that their servile status was a modern invention. They had a good point. Such documents 'should not be allowed to fall into the hands of trouble-makers', as a perceptive landowner observed at the time. In the seventeenth century, Samuel Pepys wrote in to inquire what information it contained 'concerning the sea and the dominion thereof'. He had a less good point, but gets high marks for imagination. The Domesday Book was last cited in court in 1982. Sadly, the judge found it possible to decide the case without reference to it.

One might wonder what the readers of this edition will get out of it. It is certainly not a book to read from cover to cover. It has about as much literary appeal as the annual digest of the Central Statistical Office. Yet they gleam, these fragments of the past, like pressed leaves from long ago found in the pages of childhood books. The Penguin version is a feast for local history enthusiasts. It will give a wider readership glimpses of the places around them as they were 900 years ago. And it will remind the rest of us of the unchanging character of the official mind.

31 August 2004

ZAINAB BAHRANI

Days of plunder

The destruction of the Bamiyan Buddhas by the Taliban was met with an outcry in the United States, Britain and the countries that form the coalition in Iraq. Yet the coalition forces can now claim, among other things, the destruction of the legendary city of Babylon.

Ironically, the bombing campaign of 2003 had not damaged archaeological sites. It was only in the aftermath, during the occupation, that the most extensive cultural destruction took place. At first there was the looting of the museums under the watch of coalition troops, but that was to be followed by more extensive and active destruction.

Active damage of the historical record is ongoing at several archaeological sites occupied as military camps. At Babylon, I have seen, over the past three months, the continuing construction projects, the removal of and digging into the ancient mounds, despite a coalition press release early in June stating that work would halt, and the camp would be removed.

A helicopter landing zone, built in the heart of the ancient city, removed layers of archaeological earth from the site. The daily flights of the helicopters rattle the ancient walls and the winds created by their rotors blast sand against the fragile bricks. When I and my colleague at the site, Maryam Moussa, asked military personnel in charge to shut down the helipad, the response was that it had to remain open for security reasons, for the safety of the troops.

Between May and August, the wall of the Temple of Nabu and the roof of the Temple of Ninmah, both sixth century BC, collapsed as a result of the movement of helicopters. Nearby, heavy machines and vehicles are parked on the remains of a Greek theatre from the era of Alexander of Macedon. The minister of culture has asked for the removal of military bases from all archaeological sites, but none has yet been relocated.

Iraq is ancient Mesopotamia, otherwise called the 'cradle of civilization'. It has more than 10,000 listed archaeological sites, as well as hundreds of medieval and Ottoman Muslim, Christian and Jewish monuments. The coalition did not establish a means of guarding the sites, though they would be protected in any other country rich in antiquities. As a result, archaeological sites are being looted to an extent previously unimagined.

The looting supplies the appetites of an international illicit trade in antiquities, and many objects end up in places like Geneva, London, Tokyo and New York. The lack of border controls has only added to the ease with which the illegal trade in Mesopotamian artefacts functions. The looting leaves the sites bulldozed and pitted with robber holes. Ancient walls, artefacts and scientific data are all destroyed in the process.

But it is not only the stolen artefacts that are lost. The loss of this data is the loss of the ancient history of this land. Many important Sumerian and Babylonian cities have been irreversibly damaged in this way already. Passive destruction of this kind has been widespread under the occupation, but antiquity is not the only area of concern.

In Baghdad, the National Library and State Archives building is a burned-out shell in which the employees work in the most horrendous conditions. The Ottoman archive that records the history of the country, spanning the sixteenth to the early twentieth centuries, is in the gravest danger. Having been soaked by flooding last year, the archive began to mould. Upon the advice of conservators, the entire archive was removed to freezers to stop the mould. Because of the lack of electricity and equipment, the only place that could be found with large freezers, and where power could be maintained, was an abandoned and bombed building that had previously been a Ba'athist officers' club. In Iraq, where it is not unusual for temperatures to soar up to 60°C (140°F) in summer, and where the Coalition Provisional Authority never managed to restore the electrical power to the country, this was no small feat.

The power in Baghdad (outside the US-occupied presidential palace and embassy buildings) is available, sporadically, about nine hours a day. If the archives should thaw, the documents will be destroyed. The conservation process needs to be done in a time- and climate-controlled manner if the archive is to be saved. But the Coalition Provisional Authority reassigned ownership of this building to the Ministry of Justice. There is now still no place to house this archive, the loss of which would be the loss of the modern historical records of Iraq, much of which have not been studied or published.

In the midst of the disasters of Iraq under occupation, the condition of its cultural heritage may seem a trivial matter. But, as a historian of antiquity, I am painfully aware that there is no parallel for the amount of historical destruction that has taken place over the past fifteen months in Iraq. The Geneva and Hague conventions make the protection of heritage the responsibility of the foreign powers during occupation. Instead, what we have seen under the occupation is a general policy of neglect and even an active destruction of the historical and archaeological record of the land.

21 August 2004

JON HENLEY

Almost a party

They were, she says, the most extraordinary days of her life, a kind of 'sacred, patriotic union' that lasted a whole week. 'People of all sorts took part. Everyone who came on to the street got a gun. Kids dug up the roads, people threw down beds, furniture, anything to build the barricades. It was, almost, a party.'

Almost, but not quite. About 1,500 Parisians died in the uprising which preceded the capital's liberation, driving 20,000 occupying Nazi soldiers into a few fortified redoubts and clearing the way for Leclerc's 2nd Armoured and the US army's 4th Infantry divisions to roll into town in the sweltering late summer heat of 25 August 1944.

Madeleine Riffaud might have been among them. She had marked her birthday two days earlier by turning back an armoured German supply train in the nineteenth arrondissement and taking eighty men prisoner. A Resistance veteran at twenty, a lieutenant in the newly formed Forces Françaises de l'Intérieur (FFI), she missed most of the Liberation Day celebration: she was leading a final assault on 1,000 SS troops in their barracks on the Place de la République.

On Monday Ms Riffaud will be eighty. She talks fluently and passionately of the events of sixty years ago but with her eyes closed, the better to summon up what are plainly, at times, images no one would ever wish to see.

In August 1944 Paris had been occupied for fifty months. The five-star Hotel Meurice on the Rue de Rivoli was the German army HQ; savage requisitioning meant food was scarce. Dried and shredded carrot leaf served as tobacco; butter was 1,000 francs a kilo on the black market (the average monthly wage was 2,300 francs); slabs of pine wood soled shoes; bicycles, their tyres stuffed with sawdust, were the only means of transport besides the sporadically functioning Métro, preferably avoided because of the risk of round-ups and reprisals.

Ever since the D-day landings in early June the capital had buzzed with rumours. Since 9 August Parisians had watched with growing excitement as German non-military personnel fled town, followed in increasing numbers by exhausted and defeated troops from the Normandy front. The Allied forces were approaching; release could be only days away.

The steadily mounting fever – Parisian railway and Métro workers began a brave series of wildcat strikes on 11 August, followed by postal workers and finally the police – escaped Ms Riffaud. For the past month she had been in jail, awaiting a firing squad for having shot a German officer in the head on the Rue Solférino.

'In fact, the Paris insurrection started in earnest on 1 July,' she says. 'That was the day the Liberation committee decided to test the temperature of the people. They knew the only chance of avoiding a full-scale military battle for Paris was if everyone came out on to the streets. Our task in the Resistance was to give Parisians confidence, show them we were there. We were each to kill a German, in broad daylight and in a public place.'

She was ready. Ms Riffaud's war had begun in May 1940: her first contact with German forces was when the Luftwaffe strafed the column of refugees in which she was fleeing the Somme for the unoccupied south-west. In early 1941 she took her sick grandfather on a two-day train journey to see her father near Amiens, and a Nazi officer kicked her hard in the backside.

'I landed on my face in the gutter,' she says. 'That moment was the turning point for me. I was seventeen, I was humiliated, my fear turned into anger. I remember saying to myself, "I don't know who they are or where they are, but I'll find the people who are fighting this and I'll join them."'

The problem, she readily admits, was how. 'As many people got caught trying to join the Resistance as did inside it,' she says. In the end, the answer was not of her own making: suffering from the early signs of tuberculosis, she was sent to a sanatorium near Grenoble to recuperate.

It turned out to be a veritable Resistance hub, the contact point for three Maquis networks and home to an underground printing press. By the end of 1941 Ms Riffaud was in Paris, supposedly studying to be a midwife. In reality she was a young Resistance recruit who went by the name of Rainer, a nom-de-guerre she took in stubborn admiration for the German poet Rainer Maria Rilke.

'Hundreds of young women like me were involved. We were the messengers, the intelligence gatherers, the repairers of the web. When men fell or were captured we got the news through, pulled the nets tight again. We carried documents, leaflets, sometimes arms. We walked miles; bikes were too precious and the Métro was too dangerous.'

Many, many people fell, she recalls (up to 5,000 faced the German firing squads at Mont-Valerian alone), but they were always replaced: 'The essential was not to give in. When you resisted, you were already a victor. You had already won. We could be killed at any instant, but we were among the ranks of the combatants.'

By 1943, after the battle of Stalingrad, things had got tougher. Nazi infiltrations, crackdowns and round-ups became increasingly savage and effective. The life expectancy of a three-strong *franc-tireur* partisan cell could be counted in weeks, and getting hold of arms became the movement's greatest challenge.

'I got quite good at it,' says Ms Riffaud. 'I'd walk up to a policeman and sweet-talk him, then show him our requisition bill which said the Resistance needed his revolver. I would say he could do the patriotic thing, or – and I'd gesture towards my two male subordinates who would be behind him. We got a lot of pistols that way.'

It was one of those arms that saved Ms Riffaud's life. In mid-July 1944, on a sunny Sunday afternoon, she cycled up to an SS officer who was standing staring at the Seine opposite the Tuileries gardens, braked, put both feet on the ground and shot him twice in the left temple.

'I remember thinking, "Can he really be such a bastard if he's gazing at the Seine like that? Perhaps he's imagining that soon the war will be over." But I knew I had to do it. I was the leader of a Resistance group, there were crowds of people out walking in the gardens who would see it. It was right. I felt very calm, very pure.'

She was captured by fluke, by French police officers in a rare patrol car, taken to the Gestapo HQ in the notorious Rue des Saussaies, and tortured.

Because she passed out too quickly when they used water or electricity, they strapped her to a chair and deprived her of sleep. They tortured a man to death before her eyes. They captured one of her young recruits, a sixteen-year-old boy, stood him in front of her and broke his arms and legs. 'They said, "Just talk to us, and we'll stop all this. Have you no heart?" I don't know how I didn't talk, but I didn't. I just kept saying I knew nothing, that I had killed to revenge a dead boyfriend, I had no contacts, I was on my own. They had decided to shoot me when finally they identified the gun as one stolen from a policeman by the Resistance. That made me a bigger fish; they had to investigate me again. And by then it was too late.'

She was released in a final exchange of prisoners on 18 August and emerged to find all Paris in uproar. That same day, posters signed by the head of the FFI in Paris, Colonel Henri Rol-Tanguy, appeared everywhere calling on citizens to halt all German movements by erecting barricades throughout the city. More than 600 makeshift barriers of brick, tarmac, vehicles, furniture and lamp-posts were thrown up within hours.

The following day 3,000 determined policemen took over the German HQ and the day after, a group of twenty unarmed Resistance men raised the *tricolore* over Paris town hall. Apart from sporadic tank attacks, the Germans never tried seriously to recapture it. There was to be some fierce fighting to come, but it was the beginning of the end. In all, 3,200 German soldiers were killed during the fighting in Paris.

Next week Madeleine Riffaud will be a guest of honour at many of the dozen or so ceremonies planned to celebrate the anniversary of Paris's liberation, and to commemorate the 900-plus Resistance fighters and 580 civilians who lost their lives in the week-long battle. The main official ceremony, followed by a grand popular ball on the Place de la Bastille, will come on 25 August, sixty years to the day after General von Choltitz, commander of the German forces, signed the formal surrender, and Charles de Gaulle appeared triumphant on the steps of city hall to declare in a historic address that Paris, broken and martyred, was now free. All the church bells rang.

Of that day Ms Riffaud remembers mainly her first experience of real war. 'They were firing proper shells at us on the Place de la République,' she says. 'We were fighting floor by floor, dropping grenades through the windows. It lasted all day and I lost one of my best men, Michel Tagrine, to a bullet fired after the surrender. But you cannot understand how wonderful it was to fight finally as free men and women, to battle in the daylight, under our own names, with our real identities, with everyone out there, all of Paris, to support us, happy, joyful and united. There was never a time like it.'

20 July 2004

JOHN EZARD

The scrivener's tale

After more than 600 years, it was his handwriting that gave him away. A scribe – who until the weekend was known to history only as Adam the scrivener – so infuriated Geoffrey Chaucer with his carelessness that the poet threatened to curse him with an outbreak of scabs.

Now alert academic detective work has unmasked the sloppy copyist of the words of the father of English literature as Adam Pinkhurst, son of a small Surrey landowner during the fourteenth century.

The revelation of his name and some of his background, announced by Cambridge University yesterday, has caused intense excitement and admiration among specialists in the subject. It indirectly helps to authenticate the two most authoritative texts of Chaucer's great work, *The Canterbury Tales*, the first long poem written in an approximation to modern English. And it discloses the scribe as the writer of an elegiac reference in the text of the tales to the fact that Chaucer had died before completing them.

Professor Linne Mooney, a scholar from Maine, who is a visiting fellow at Corpus Christi College, Cambridge, tracked Pinkhurst down by studying his signature to an oath in the earliest records of the Scriveners' company in the city of London, and comparing it with Chaucer manuscripts. His signature is the eighth earliest entry in the company's Common Paper, or members' book of regulations. This indicates that he joined soon after the scriveners began keeping systematic records in the year 1392. The date squares neatly with the period of Chaucer's life and authorship.

'Lots of people have looked at these records before, but they did not happen to be people who were working on scribes,' Professor Mooney told the *Guardian* yesterday. They were not equipped to recognize that Pinkhurst's signature is also the handwriting of *The Canterbury Tales* and of two earlier Chaucer works, *Troilus and Criseyde* and *Boece*, his translation of Boethius's *The Consolations of Philosophy*.

Professor Mooney's formidable immersion in the calligraphic side of the period has resulted in a database of more than 200 scribes working in England between 1375 and 1425, the years immediately before and after the birth of printing. The handwriting of all her scribes is found in more than one surviving manuscript. Until she confided her discovery to the British New Chaucer conference on Saturday, Adam was known only as the butt of a sardonic short poem published with *The Canterbury Tales* after the poet's death.

The poem is titled Chaucer's 'Wordes Unto Adam His Own Scriveyne'. It chides Adam for all his errors in the two earlier manuscript books:

Adam scrivener, if ever thee befall
Boece or Troilus [the earlier books] for to write new [again],
Under thy longe locks thow maist have the scall [scabs],
But [unless] after my makinge thou write mor trew,
So oft a day I mot [must] thy werke renewe
It to correct, and eke [also] to rubbe and scrape,
And all is thorowe thy necligence and rape [haste].

The poem has the primal rage of writers through the ages whose work is sloppily reworded during the editing process. But Pinkhurst, far from being an incompetent, emerges as Chaucer's most favoured scribe in an age where writers worked closely with individual scriveners rather than dealing with scriptoriums (script factories) as they came to do after Chaucer's death in 1400. He can now be recognized as the scrivener of the two most authoritative copies of *The Canterbury Tales*: the Hengwrt manuscript, which is now in the National Library of Wales, and the Ellesmere manuscript, kept in San Marino, California.

Professor Mooney says Pinkhurst is likely to have come from Surrey, where his surname derived from Pinkhurst Farm, near Abinger Common, between Guildford and Dorking. Records exist of property transactions involving an Adam Pinkhurst (probably the scribe's father) and his wife, Johanna, in the 1350s and 1370s over properties in Dorking and surrounding villages. This would have made Adam the scrivener a son of a small landowner, brought up a short distance from London, who went into the City to learn a trade and make his living as a writer of court letters.

Chaucer was already well connected in the city, as the son of a vintner. For twelve years he was controller of the wool custom and had rooms over Aldgate from 1374 to 1386, when he would have been writing *Boece* and *Troilus and Criseyde*.

Pinkhurst also emerges as the closest the poet had to an obituarist. A note in Pinkhurst's handwriting at the end of 'The Cook's Tale', one of the unfinished *Canterbury Tales*, says, 'Of this tale Chaucer wrote no more'.

One academic at the New Chaucer conference said that the discovery had given these seven words the note of an elegy.

BLASTS

The agony you cause
I'm a typical pinko liberal, and I read a typical pinko liberal newspaper. My problem is that my beloved newspaper has just hired a right-wing bigot as an agony aunt. I have no reason to doubt that she is not a perfectly nice person in herself, but her politics make me feel sick (some Tory politicians' views I merely disagree with, but hers really are an emetic for me). My problem is that I don't want to in any way contribute to her loathsome views being promulgated or, in however small a way, contribute to her earnings. Should I switch to another paper altogether, boycott my chosen one on the days she appears or just grin and bear it? Please help.

Joe Morison, Brixton

I suggest you do what I do when confronted with nudity in the newspapers – turn the page quickly and forget what you almost saw. You might prefer to cut out the page and eat it with a pinch of salt or even to turn the house upside down to see where you left your sense of humour. You could ask a pinko liberal friend to lend you his copy, minus the offending page, to avoid contributing to the lady's income or you could read the *Daily Telegraph*. Anyway, who on earth are you talking about? Surely not the nice blonde lady who is always going on about prison reform?

From Ann Widdecombe's G2 Advice Column

7 May 2004

LARRY ELLIOTT

Alcopopalypse

Venture into your town centre at sunset tonight and you will witness a weekly ritual. All over Britain, gaggles of young men in their polo shirts and gangs of young girls tottering on their high heels will be trooping off to a drinking factory, easily identifiable by the couple of heavies on the door. Venture back at midnight and you'll see how the ritual all too often ends. The bonhomie of dusk will have been replaced by something nastier. The shirts will be blood-stained, the girls in high heels will be puking up, the police vans will be full.

The government has had enough of Britain being turned into what looks like a John Wayne movie every weekend, and I can understand why it is concerned. On nine days every fortnight I'm a journalist, on the tenth I'm a magistrate, sitting more often than not in the youth court. And from the bench, it's plain that the crime figures do not lie: more of those appearing in the courts are there for drink-fuelled violent crime. More particularly, the intoxicated offenders are getting younger, more and more of them are girls, and the offences are becoming more serious. When I first became a magistrate twelve years ago, easily the most common offence committed by teenage girls was shoplifting. Now they are likely to be up for affray, serious assaults on police and group attacks where victims are kicked into unconsciousness.

So now we are to have a summer crackdown. There will be spot-checks to make sure the bouncers are not letting in under-age drinkers, there will be 'sting' operations, there will be naming and shaming of bars and off-licences that break the law. And my bet is the impact will be negligible. Why? Because the government has failed to recognize that binge drinking is part of our culture, carefully fostered and manipulated by the drinks industry.

The mayhem on Britain's streets on a Friday or Saturday night is a textbook case of how Labour's kid-gloves approach to business has failed. Take the complete deregulation of licensing laws, which ministers say is based on research that liberalization will lead to a diminution in binge drinking and the criminality that is associated with it. But as one charity, the Institute of Alcohol Studies, notes, this supposedly independent research was based on a report produced for the drinks industry in 1992. In other words, before drinking factories, before drink as much as you can for £15, before Breezers, alcopops and all the other attempts to entice young drinkers. An open-all-hours approach allows more drinks to be sold; the idea that they will be sold to the bloke who fancies a quiet pint and a game of dominoes at 1 a.m. rather than those who have been knocking them back since 8 p.m. seems, to say the least, far-fetched. Certainly the police think so. As the Association of Police Officers puts it: 'Extending hours will not normally stagger hours, and it has the potential to lead to increased anti-social behaviour and costs for the police service and local authorities.'

This message is not getting through. The voice being heard – as with the deregulation of gambling – is that of business, which has convinced the government that it is part of the solution rather than part of the problem. We're doing our best, the industry argues. If there is a crisis, it is a crisis of upbringing, of parenting, of cultural norms, of the tendency for violent crime to increase in economic upswings. All of which is true, up to a point. There is something dysfunctional about a society where the ambition of fifteen- and sixteen-year-olds is to get 'off their face', and where many parents are making no effort to stop them doing so.

But it is risible to argue that the rise in violent crime among teenagers has nothing to do with drinks aimed at young audiences, at the creation of venues meant to deter the more mature drinker and the marketing of drinks designed to make drinking associated with virility or sexual prowess. The industry is quite happy to go along with the idea that there should be a crackdown on the few 'bad apples' in the hope that a show of good citizenship will prevent a more radical conclusion being reached: namely that young people are being cynically targeted and exploited.

Yes, of course, every company worth its salt says it takes corporate social responsibility very seriously, because that's the message ministers want to hear. But what does all the stuff about encouraging sensible drinking mean? There are copious examples of campaigns that suggest having a wild night out makes you cool and sexy; I can't recall one that said you can still be a real man if you stick to a couple of pints of bitter shandy. Stripped of the CSR cant, the industry's modus operandi seems to be to pack 'em in, get 'em drunk and chuck 'em out. Let somebody else pay for what economists call externalities: the noise, the unsafe streets, the ill health, the days off work, the deaths on the roads.

The government believes that Britain could become like those parts of continental Europe where liberal licensing laws are not linked to binge drinking and violence. It may, however, be missing a key point, which is that other countries can cope with deregulation because they already have a more mature approach. The Institute of Alcohol Studies says recent evidence from countries such as Australia, Iceland, Ireland and New Zealand suggests liberalization has led to more violent disorder.

Interestingly, the economic liberalism of the US – the source of many Labour policies – does not extend to the licensing laws, where the legal age for drinking in public is not eighteen but a rigorously enforced twenty-one. When he was at the spring meetings of the IMF two weeks ago, Gordon Brown was complaining that he was being woken every morning at 3 a.m., but it was his jet-lagged baby son who was responsible, not drunken brawlers on Georgetown's M Street. For a UK visitor, it was reassuring to wander around on a Saturday night without fear of being glassed by a total stranger.

The government here has not the slightest intention of going down the American route, and there are good reasons for caution – the risk of pushing the problem underground, the rights of law-abiding eighteen- to twenty-one-year-olds. But if the problem escalates, it will come under pressure to act from other groups who also have rights: the right to feel safe on the streets, to have a decent night's sleep, to go shopping in the morning without encountering lakes of chucked-up chicken tikka masala. For the time being, there will be a slightly harder version of the policy pursued for the past decade or more. The government hopes that deregulation, CSR and sporadic crackdowns by thinly stretched enforcement agencies will work. But in the youth courts, we're not holding our breath.

10 January 2004

ANDREW MARTIN

What's eating me?

About twenty years ago, one of my first journalistic assignments took me to the Edinburgh Literary Festival on a special 'writers' carriage' of a northbound train. Most of the authors on board escape my memory, but certainly Tama Janowitz was there, and so was Douglas Adams.

Sitting in the corner was a grey-haired, cherubic man.

'Who's he?' I asked a press officer for the trip.

'Oh, that's Antonio Carluccio,' she said. 'He's a chef and he writes cookery books.'

'What's he doing going to a literary festival then?' I asked. A very naive question, I admit, and one the press officer didn't stoop to answer. 'What does he actually write about?' I went on.

'Mushrooms,' said the press officer.

'Mushrooms!' I sniggered.

Today, when every vegetable has its laureate, everybody knows about Carluccio. They know about his restaurant empire, his books and his interest in mushrooms. His nickname is 'the mushroom man'. He's been fascinated by mushrooms since the age of seven, and his latest volume is called *The Complete Mushroom Book*. On the face of it, his whole career has been a refutation of Shirley Conran's maxim that 'life is too short to stuff a mushroom'. And the tide is now with him. I'm forty-one, and the food revolution is the biggest single cultural change that's happened in my lifetime – and probably the most disturbing.

It exerts a morbid fascination: I have become addicted to the feeling of queasiness and alienation I experience when scanning the food and drink sections of bookshops. Judging by their photographs on the covers, the authors of food books fall into two categories. They're either morally superior and just incontrovertibly right about everything (Madhur Jaffrey, Delia Smith), or they're jaunty, rakish and humorous (Jamie Oliver, Ainsley Harriott). Most I've never heard of, but I can tell by the confidence of their smiles that they probably preside over a restaurant empire and at least one of the 130 or so cookery programmes broadcast on British terrestrial and digital TV. For example, there's a character somehow implausibly called Brian Turner: he's written a book called *Brian Turner's Favourite British Recipes*, and very pleased about it he seems, too.

The key word in all these works is 'just', as in: 'We just slop about in front of the TV, with great platefuls on our laps.' The tone is casual, modest. The writer knows a vast amount about food, of course, but has retained a certain charming naivety, which you, in your desperate attempts to keep up with the food revolution, have long since lost. Hence Nigel Slater: 'I am a great fan of the frozen pea.' It's as if the writers have furtively concluded: 'Well, what with everybody being obsessed with food, I'm absolutely raking it in ... so I'd better prove I've still got my feet on the ground.'

When I was growing up, our family kitchen boasted one or two cookbooks at most, and they were called things like *The Complete Guide to Cooking*. Mushrooms, Carluccio please note, were dealt with crisply in the course of about half a page, and we used these books for years without noticing who'd written them. In addition, there was a scrapbook into which recipes were pasted. These were cut out of the obscure corners of papers and magazines, which printed them almost as an afterthought, like nature notes or the crossword. The most successful and frequently used of these would eventually disintegrate under the weight of spattered ingredients: it was an example of reverse Darwinism, but it kept things ticking over.

Today, our approach is much more grandiose. We don't cut out and keep individual recipes, we save pullouts or splash out on the book. We want lifestyle, not handy hints. By cooking from the scrapbook, you were not necessarily eating Great British Dinners or 'eating yourself thin' (quite the reverse, probably), or sharing Gordon Ramsay's Secrets.

But, just as the snail goes about on its stomach, so does the modern Briton, moving from one restaurant or eating scheme to another. We have been propelled by late capitalism (because foodie-ism is consumerism in its most unmetaphorical sense) from being an anal culture, costive and shy about food, to an oral one, uninhibitedly enthusiastic. In Freudian terms, this is a regression, the anal stage being associated with the coming of bowel control, the oral stage with the elemental wants of childhood. Some of us are caught uncomfortably between the two, so that all these exuberant food narratives seem unnaturally arrested at the point where the food descends to the gut.

The more that is written and said about food, the more the question demands to be asked: 'What about the thing that comes next?' The transition to the new mindset will be complete only when someone produces a cookbook with follow-through: not only will there be beautifully lit photographs of the food itself, but equally artistic ones of the results.

There is a new excitement every time we sit down in a restaurant. Earlier this year, in a Café Rouge, I heard a man say to his friend, with a repulsive, jittery excitement: 'My fallback position is that I'm going to have the steak, but I really hope they've got the chicken cassoulet on the specials.' He then set off with a predatory lope, searching out the menu blackboard. On another occasion, I was sitting next to four young professionals who were all reading their menus with shining eyes. A waiter neared their table and asked if they were ready to order. 'OK,' said the leader of the group, 'let's go for it!'

Ordering is often preceded by a neurotically intense consultation with the waiter, who sometimes comes worryingly close to sitting down at the table in order to advise. A friend I will call Pete is typical of the modern diner in that he attempts to customize every dish. He wants the experience to be more perfect than it is capable of being, so I must sit, pretending I'm elsewhere, as he asks the waiter: 'That fish pie has cheese in it, right?'

Waiter: 'Just a little Parmesan, sir.'

Long, sceptical silence. 'And it's got anchovies, I suppose?'

The waiter nods.

'Fresh ones?' asks Pete, by which time I'm thinking, why didn't we see that film instead? Because even Pete doesn't send back the popcorn.

Twenty years ago, too great an ardency for food would have been called 'greedy', but greedy is a word that has fallen into disuse. The food critic of *American Vogue*, Jeffrey Steingarten, is a demigod to foodies because of his book *The Man Who Ate Everything*, in which he blithely states that he has always been able to continue eating long after others have finished. The old accusation of greediness – a product of the anal stage – was a check or caution on complacency left over from a less prosperous time; a reminder that the world was not so super-abundant in food as you might foolishly imagine. Arguably, this attitude connects eating with feelings of guilt, and therefore leads in the general direction of bulimia. But are we really so wised up about food today? Do we not have an obesity crisis running alongside our new celebratory attitude?

It's possible that I notice more bad behaviour in restaurants simply because there are so many more restaurants. London is the restaurant capital of the world, and the amazing thing about David Blaine in his Perspex box was not so much 'here is a man going without food' as 'here is a man who is not in a restaurant'. Take London N8, or Crouch End, which is near where I live and typical of certain aspirational hotspots, in that every other business is a restaurant. The question: 'Have you tried the new restaurant in Crouch End?' is completely otiose, since there are so many at any one time. The place is one great mouth, and if you see workmen gutting a building in Crouch End, you don't ask, 'What's this going to be?' You ask, 'What sort of restaurant is this going to be?' Equally redundant is the question: 'What's become of that nice old pub in Crouch End?' It's become a gastro-pub, that's what.

It was the colonization by the greedy people of my own particular province, the nice old pubs of London, that began to make me really angry at them. Up come the carpets; the Hare and Hounds is re-branded the H&H (this depicted in some abstract motif) and dogs are banished not just from the sign, but from the interior. Colour supplements are strewn everywhere to set an intellectual tone. The old pubs that I liked might have had one pickled egg suspended in brown vinegar. It looked like something by Damien Hirst, but eventually someone would become sufficiently hungry that they would actually eat it. But they tended to do so without you noticing. Today, I often find myself in a pub next to somebody who, having stuffed themselves with a braised lamb shank, pushes their plate forwards, then blows upwards in a Billy Bunterish way, so that their fringe flutters. This means: gosh, that was a lot of food, but I managed to stuff it all away. How would these people like it if we ale drinkers set up in Nobu, with our barrels of Adnams, our Hamlet cigars and packets of peanuts? But this is the new generation, and what does it do? It eats.

The food revolution hasn't completely passed me by. I admit that I once asked a taxi driver to follow a bus because I'd left my copy of Delia Smith's *Complete Cookery Course* on it. Whenever people came to dinner, I used to prepare her recipe for sausages in red wine, which, looking back, was not all that good a dish (especially not the way I cooked it), and I wince to think that a fair percentage of those who declared it 'absolutely lovely' must have been lying through their teeth. That was when I was trying to keep up, before I came to the realization that I have no talent for food and no interest in it. My admiration for Delia Smith diminished still further when I saw her on television for the first time about two months ago. 'Er, now I think we'll move on to the carrots,' I seem to remember her saying.

Last Christmas, some kindly but misguided person bought me Jamie Oliver's *The Return of the Naked Chef* and I spent about an hour on Christmas Day riveted and appalled by the acknowledgments in the glutinous finale: 'Respect to Kevin and his mum, for Saturday soup inspiration.' Oliver is rumoured to be the subject of a £12 million film, and has the profile of a rock star. Apparently he actually performs cookery gigs, which to me is like someone walking on stage and, to the accompaniment of screaming fans and strobing lights, beginning to iron their underpants. My generation had the Sex Pistols. Today, the kids have got someone telling them how to make a really good bacon sandwich. A rock star is exotic, takes you out of yourself. Oliver, by contrast, wants to keep us all in the kitchen, and if that was such a good place to be, why have women been fighting to escape it for fifty years?

At the heart of my perplexity is the feeling that, in our well-fed society, the moments of hunger are so fleeting and short-lived ... and yet there's this vast industry pursuing them. Once, fish and chips were wrapped up in newspapers; now, newspapers are wrapped up in fish and chips. If I'd attempted to cook 5 per cent of the recipes with which my newspaper has presented me over the past five years, I'd have had time to do nothing else, and it's reached the point where I actually blanch on seeing the words 'Free 40-page Food & Drink Supplement'. Stone me, I think, it might be free, but I'm going to have to take that magazine, put it directly into the crate in the garage, then cart it off to the Camden recycling centre. I'd pay a little not to have to do that.

Meanwhile, I try to minimize my involvement with the food hype. For what it's worth, I believe that in order to eat less you've sometimes got to eat more, and I find that the full English breakfast at the church-like Simpson's in the Strand (cost £17.95), which is preceded by the serving of what would in itself be an entire continental breakfast, eliminates all further thoughts of food until about 4 p.m.

Among writers, I seek out those not obsessed with food. One is Tony Benn, who has usually had more important things on his mind than Carluccio-esque concerns. In the many volumes of his *Diaries*, he sometimes mentions a meal eaten on the run, in the midst of his frenetic political activity, and it'll always be egg and chips, or gammon, pineapple, peas and chips, except without the gammon because he's a vegetarian.

I also take comfort from my parents' bathroom cabinet in York where, throughout my life, a small bottle of olive oil has been kept for the treatment of certain theoretical ailments that never in practice occur. It reminds me of a time, a quarter of a century ago, when York had approximately one restaurant, and I personally did not crave any more. (The restaurant was in a medieval street called The Shambles, and you went there on your eighteenth birthday, if ever.) I take up that dusty little bottle sometimes, and read the pharmaceutical label that says, not 'Cypressa' or 'Rivano', but 'BP'. It symbolizes a time before Carluccio, when we ambitiously sought to perfect ourselves through politics, religion or art rather than what we ate, and it seems to me to point a very valuable moral.

Stay hungry.

27 November 2003

BENJAMIN ZEPHANIAH

Gong Ho

I woke up on the morning of 13 November wondering how the government could be overthrown and what could replace it, and then I noticed a letter from the prime minister's office. It said: 'The prime minister has asked me to inform you, in strict confidence, that he has in mind, on the occasion of the forthcoming list of New Year's honours to submit your name to the Queen with a recommendation that Her Majesty may be graciously pleased to approve that you be appointed an officer of the Order of the British Empire.'

Me? I thought, OBE, me? Up yours, I thought. I get angry when I hear that word 'empire'; it reminds me of slavery, it reminds me of thousands of years of brutality, it reminds me of how my foremothers were raped and my forefathers brutalized. It is because of this concept of empire that my British education led me to believe that the history of black people started with slavery and that we were born slaves, and should therefore be grateful that we were given freedom by our caring white masters. It is because of this idea of empire that black people like myself don't even know our true names or our true historical culture. I am not one of those who are obsessed with their roots, and I'm certainly not suffering from a crisis of identity; my obsession is about the future and the political rights of all people. Benjamin Zephaniah OBE – no way Mr Blair, no way Mrs Queen. I am profoundly anti-empire.

There's something very strange about receiving a letter from Tony Blair's office asking me if I want to accept this award. In the past couple of months I've been on Blair's doorstep a few times. I have begged him to come out and meet me; I have been longing for a conversation with him, but he won't come out, and now here he is asking me to meet him at the palace! I was there with a million people on 15 February, and the last time I was there was just a couple of weeks ago. My cousin, Michael Powell, was arrested and taken to Thornhill Road police station in Birmingham where he died. Now, I know how he died. The whole of Birmingham knows how he died, but in order to get this article published and to be politically (or journalistically) correct, I have to say that he died in suspicious circumstances. The police will not give us any answers. We have not seen or heard anything of all the reports and investigations we were told were going to take place. Now, all that my family can do is join with all the other families who have lost members while in custody because no one in power is listening to us. Come on, Mr Blair, I'll meet you anytime. Let's talk about your Home Office, let's talk about being tough on crime.

This OBE thing is supposed to be for my services to literature, but there are a whole lot of writers who are better than me, and they're not involved in the things that I'm involved in. All they do is write; I spend most of my time doing other things. If they want to give me one of these empire things, why can't they give me one for my work in animal rights? Why can't they give me one for my struggle against racism? What about giving me one for all the letters I write to innocent people in prisons who have been framed? I may just consider accepting some kind of award for my services on behalf of the millions of people who have stood up against the war in Iraq. It's such hard work – much harder than writing poems.

And hey, if Her Majesty may be graciously pleased to lay all that empire stuff on me, why can't she write to me herself? Let's cut out the middle man – she knows me. The last time we met, it was at a concert I was hosting. She came backstage to meet me. That didn't bother me; lots of people visit my dressing room after performances. Me and the South African performers I was working with that night thought it rather funny that we had a royal groupie. She's a bit stiff but she's a nice old lady. Let me make it clear: I have nothing against her or the royal family. It is the institution of the monarchy that I loathe so very much, the monarchy that still refuses to apologize for sanctioning slavery.

There is a part of me that hopes that after writing this article I shall never be considered as a Poet Laureate or an OBE sucker again. Let this put an end to it. This may lose me some of my writing friends; some people may never want to work with me again, but the truth is I think OBEs compromise writers and poets, and laureates suddenly go soft – in the past I've even written a poem, 'Bought and Sold', saying that.

There are many black writers who love OBEs, it makes them feel like they have made it. When it suits them, they embrace the struggle against the ruling class and the oppression they visit upon us, but then they join the oppressors' club. They are so easily seduced into the great house of Babylon known as the palace. For them, a wonderful time is meeting the Queen and bowing before her presence.

I was shocked to see how many of my fellow writers jumped at the opportunity to go to Buckingham Palace when the Queen had her 'meet the writers day' on 9 July 2002, and I laughed at the pathetic excuses writers gave for going. 'I did it for my mum'; 'I did it for my kids'; 'I did it for the school'; 'I did it for the people', etc. I have even heard black writers who have collected OBEs saying that it is 'symbolic of how far we have come'. Oh yes, I say, we've struggled so hard just to get a minute with the Queen and we are so very grateful – not.

I've never heard of a holder of the OBE openly criticizing the monarchy. They are officially friends, and that's what this cool Britannia project is about. It gives OBEs to cool rock stars, successful businesswomen and blacks who would be militant in order to give the impression that it is inclusive. Then these rock stars, successful women and ex-militants write to me with the OBE after their name as if I should be impressed. I'm not. Quite the opposite – you've been had.

Writers and artists who see themselves as working outside the establishment are constantly being accused of selling out as soon as they have any kind of success. I've been called a sell-out for selling too many books, for writing books for children, for performing at the Royal Albert Hall, for going on *Desert Island Discs* and for appearing on the *Parkinson* show. But I want to reach as many people as possible without compromising the content of my work.

What continues to be my biggest deal with the establishment must be my work with the British Council, of which, ironically, the Queen is patron. I have no problem with this. It has never told me what to say, or what not to say. I have always been free to criticize the government and even the council itself. This is what being a poet is about. Most importantly, through my work with the council, I am able to show the world what Britain is really about in terms of our arts, and I am able to partake in the type of political and cultural intercourse which is not possible in the mainstream political arena. I have no problem representing the reality of our multiculturalism, which may sometimes mean speaking about the way my cousin Michael died in a police station. But then, I am also at ease letting people know that our music scene is more than what they hear in the charts, and that British poetry is more than Wordsworth, or even Motion. I have no problem with all of this because this is about us and what we do. It is about what happens on the streets of our country and not in the palace or at Number 10.

Me, OBE? Whoever is behind this offer can never have read any of my work. Why don't they just give me some of those great African works of art that were taken in the name of the empire and let me return them to their rightful place? You can't fool me, Mr Blair. You want to privatize us all; you want to send us to war. You stay silent when we need you to speak for us, preferring to be the voice of the US. You have lied to us, and you continue to lie to us, and you have poured the working-class dream of a fair, compassionate, caring society down the dirty drain of empire. Stick it, Mr Blair – and Mrs Queen, stop going on about the empire. Let's do something else.

29 October 2003

STUART JEFFRIES

Brideshead regurgitated

It is 100 years since Evelyn Waugh's birth, and to mark the novelist's centenary public schoolboys have been petulantly poring over his posthumous reputation. William Boyd (Gordonstoun) suggests that he was primarily a funny satirist who came unstuck later in his career when he attempted more profound literature. Christopher Hitchens (the Leys School) contends that his late Sword of Honour trilogy about the Second World War was not the masterwork some have supposed it to be. Stephen Fry (Uppingham), who adapted Waugh's novel *Vile Bodies* for the cinema, reckons he was a monster in private life and brands him a 'howling shit', whatever that means. Geoffrey Wheatcroft argues, by contrast, that Waugh was a decent chap, and what's more that his novels are under-appreciated. Wheatcroft has Waugh pegged as a 'notably virtuous man' on account of the ability to raise a large family, be a faithful husband and an 'intermittently doting father'. Love that 'intermittently', Geoffrey.

What none of them considers, for all their supposed left-wing credentials, is the class politics expressed in Waugh's most popular novel, *Brideshead Revisited*. It's a book whose success made Waugh cringe, and yet it's also one that expresses more eloquently, if unwittingly, a nostalgia among the English for a privileged stately home past that by definition only a negligible number of them enjoyed.

It's not enough to disparage *Brideshead* for demonstrating Waugh's inability to depict women convincingly (as Wheatcroft does), nor is it sufficient to highlight its structural inadequacies (as many, Waugh included, have done). Beyond his wit and his ability to construct elegant novels, Waugh is important as an English novelist for expressing a vision of the decline of his nation. On these pages recently, Hywel Williams understood that Waugh, in *Brideshead* and elsewhere, was quite insistent that England was dead; but, sickeningly, Williams went along with the English writer's analysis and his self-flattering corollary – that Waugh was the artist in Philistia.

You'll have to forgive me for feeling more strongly about this and being more sensitive to the slings of flop-locked toffs and the arrows of outrageous Welshmen than perhaps I ought to be. When I read *Brideshead* I was at Oxford and Charles Sturridge's TV adaptation was on Channel 4. Like Glenys and Neil Kinnock, I was the first member of my family to go to tertiary education. How vexing for me and my ilk to read in Waugh's book that thanks to us England had become Philistia.

True, our career opportunities were more promising than those of Jude Fawley (the hero of Hardy's novel *Jude the Obscure*). He repaired the walls to the colleges that kept him out; we could at least sit inside those walls and study as he had dreamed of doing. But for Waugh we had the inverse of the Midas touch: we turned gilded youth to dross, Arcadia to Philistia, aesthetic rapture into commerce. England had gone down the toilet and it was all our fault.

There were working-class people at Oxford in the 1920s and in *Brideshead* Waugh has them bowed stereotypically over their books while his gilded youth throw up through college windows or bawl quotations from Eliot's barely disguised class hatred across the quads. The depiction of working-class experience in Waugh's book would be less irksome if it consisted only of such scenes. Waugh, however, does something else in the wartime sections that bookend the novel. Here, he presents a man called Hooper and it is the age of Hooper that chills Waugh and his fictional self-portrait, the arriviste snob Charles Ryder. 'He was a sallow youth,' says Ryder of Hooper, 'and had a flat, Midland accent.' It's not only that I have a flat, Midland accent that makes me feel protective of this invented champion of Philistia, this butt of Waugh's twisted account of the descent of England towards oblivion in the twentieth century. It's also because my sense of justice baulks at making Hooper symbolically bear responsibility for all that went wrong with England during the novelist's lifetime.

Here's another theory about what went wrong with England. As the British empire was dismantled and as working-class people left their home towns for colleges to lead lives that were trenchantly described by the social commentator Richard Hoggart as 'uprooted and anxious', the attendant intellectual liberation that would have sustained a positive interpretation of the value of these changes never happened, thanks in great measure to books like Waugh's. And it never has happened.

We still look back to an England that either never was or a purported Arcadia in which, really, my ancestors were stuck on the fuzzy end of the lollipop. It's a vision sustained by the popularity of standing behind the velvet ropes of old aristos' pads, of revelling in the televised pomp of Regency bosoms and well-filled britches and forbearing from being harsh on Waugh's class politics. It's one that reveals the self-hatred and inadequacy at the core of our post-war culture and it's one whose persistence shows how distant we are from a truly classless society.

23 October 2003

CATHERINE BENNETT

Snack attack

Daring interviewers occasionally tease Jane Root, the controller of BBC2, by mentioning the things she used to say when she had just got the job. When she wanted things called 'culture snacks' from 'the edges of life'. When she said, 'The lesson of the past might almost be: don't trust the lessons of the past.' And told a programme-maker that arts programmes were 'dead'.

The implication of such reminders – that Root has since performed a cultural U-turn – is to my mind, wholly unfair, a disgraceful slur on her achievement. One wonders if those who doubt her constancy have actually been watching BBC2. Not only has Root worked strenuously to banish the arts from this channel, she has, with her new Big Read, quite brilliantly produced an arts programme which demeans its subject even as its creator – Root – is proclaimed a saviour of the arts.

To ignore books is easy. So is burning them. You just need a match. But to make independent reading sound dull and great books look stupid, to transform literature into a vehicle for celebrities, polls, lists, voting opportunities and confected rivalries, to get books confidently debated by experts who have never read them, to set up a competition between *Winnie the Pooh* and *War and Peace*: that takes a kind of genius.

Even though it is now being promoted on the *Today* programme as well as trailed relentlessly on television, marketed on hoardings and in bookshops, libraries and schools all over the country, some people may still be unaware that the Big Read – a 'search for the nation's favourite book', which was launched in February – has now attracted the votes of 140,000 people and been narrowed down from 100 to twenty-one titles.

This achievement was celebrated last weekend by a special Big Read show, in which Clive Anderson ran through all the titles. Sometimes music and film respectfully matched the book; at other times titles were juxtaposed with deliberately unrelated images, presumably to liven things up. Or to seem anti-establishment and thus more democratic. A book by Roald Dahl – neither alive nor very toothsome – was illustrated with pictures of his granddaughter, the model Sophie. Arundhati Roy, despite being a favourite with many big readers and not unattractive, received no elaboration whatsoever. Why? Why a poll that leads ineluctably to Harry Potter v *Lord of the Rings*? Why *Great Britons*? Why wasn't there a third series of *Happiness*? The answer is Jane Root.

Now and again a novel would be the subject of some light banter among any members of the panel who happened to have read it. Despite having eight months in which to find a suitably bookish, yet not too posh or old or boffiny line-up, the programme-makers had clearly encountered insuperable difficulties in securing the required number of self-loathing book lovers. Instead they managed to create a literary salon where standards were so relaxed that the comments of the well-loved sperm dabbler Robert Winston on Hardy's *Tess of the D'Urbervilles* – 'I think I'm guided by my 21-year-old son, who said it was the worst book he had ever read' – passed for insightful exegesis. In this company, the claims of the alluring poetry promoter, Daisy Goodwin, to have read most of the books under discussion at a very young age began to look dangerously swotty. Does she think she's clever or something?

The whole, quite fabulously patronizing presumption of Root's 'campaign to get the country reading' is that reading is such a painfully lonely and arduous business that we need generous dollops of celebrity, hype and audience participation to force the medicine down. Or as Root describes her mission: 'It's an attempt to turn reading, which can be a very private experience, into something which can be enjoyed together.'

The ramblings of people who actually enjoy this private experience might be as off-putting to the general viewer as the confessions of some sordid onanist. Better a jolly book group, you gather, than a pathetic, solitary exercise in self-flagellation. Better a book festival, with author appearances and signings, than a celebrity-starved book group. And better than any of the above, a full-scale television campaign with lists, votes, music and that Fay Ripley off *Cold Feet*.

Since even favourite books are of themselves lamentably untelegenic objects, usually by dead people, and quite bereft of incidental music and the interventions of effusive IVF clinicians, the Big Read makers are giving the final twenty-one candidates a helping hand with films made by a 'host of celebrity advocates'. Which means, if you can't be doing with books, you can simply vote for your favourite personality. As all the advocates have been on telly recently, it was assumed by the Big Read that, unlike the obscure authors, they would need no introduction. Tolkien had been allocated to Ray Mears, Charlotte

Brontë to Lorraine Kelly of GMTV, and Philip Pullman to a celebrity called Benedict Allen. Daphne du Maurier had even better luck, being awarded the top gardening personality Alan Titchmarsh, while A.A. Milne will be 'championed' by Phill Jupitus. Ronnie Ancona, the gifted Nigella impersonator, will introduce Harry Potter, and her showbusiness partner, Alistair McGowan, will tell us all about *Wuthering Heights*.

Obviously concerned that advocacy could sound a bit close to a lecture, even when delivered by a celebrity, the scriptwriters had laboured to create jaunty literary slogans, which, if they did not have the ring of Wodehouse's 'Little's Liniment – it limbers up the legs' – are certainly catchier than any conventional review. 'Go on,' urged Titchmarsh, 'give yourself a treat.' At that moment I knew I would never read *Rebecca* again.

Next up – as Anderson would put it – are seven weeks during which trios of Titchmarsh-like contributions will constitute the BBC's prime arts coverage, and people who love lists and exchanging insults and enthusiasms on internet message boards will send in their votes for Harry Potter, *Winnie the Pooh* or *The Lord of the Rings*. Eventually, one of these will be proclaimed Britain's favourite book.

Encouraged by the new style of debate being pioneered on the Big Read, where not knowing anything about something is positively smiled on, I feel confident in predicting that this event will ultimately do as much for the printed word as Big Brother does for emotional literacy. The 'best-loved book' will tell us nothing worthwhile about popular taste and less about literature.

No matter: from then on, Root will be acclaimed as the woman who rescued reading. And thereby the licence fee. Thus guaranteeing the future of public-service broadcasting, with its Reithian mission to inform, educate and entertain.

24 June 2004

JONATHAN GLANCEY

Pissing up the wall

This is Architecture Week, a time to consider the wealth and wonder of our built world. In Britain today, our wealth is pumped into and expressed by an ever-increasing number of priapic schemes, real, projected and plain silly, for office towers that shoot their laddish loads high into our city skies uncritically supported by media, mayors and money men. Hey, look, everyone, my tower's 500 feet tall. That's nothing, sonny boy; mine's 1,000. A thousand? Get serious, kiddo, I've got a 1,500-foot tower in my pocket. Know what I mean?

This weeing-up-the-wall architecture – designed and commissioned by those old enough to know better and given the nod by politicians and the wink by journalists – is coming to a city centre near you soon. Should you find such Jack-the-lad design over the top, you will be offered screwball design instead. Presented as what-the-people-want in a 'down-with-the-kids' manner, such playschool architecture – a dolly-mixture of spotty, sugar-candy blobs, whirls and splodges – is designed, we are told, to challenge and redress the mufti of our tedious town and city centres. Both pricks and blobs are supported not only by big business, wannabe streetwise politicians and a sensation-hungry media, but by those nominally charged with looking after architecture and urban design in our name.

Only last week, an independent inquiry reported on the clash of interests at the heart of CABE, the government's Commission for Architecture and the Built Environment. Sir Stuart Lipton, a property developer and CABE's energetic first chairman, resigned in response to the report's findings. It was felt that CABE has been too close to Sir Stuart's property company, Stanhope. In fact, several of CABE's directors are on Stanhope's payroll, while others have business interests that could just possibly encourage lesser professionals than they to favour certain architectural projects over others. Neither CABE nor its trustees are accused of impropriety, yet it has been hard to disassociate this New Labour quango from the concerns of big business and property development.

The truth is that CABE is exactly the right architectural watchdog for New Britain, just as ambitious new offices in the guise of spotty blobs and prickly towers are ideal designs for our cities. Why? Because we are deeply, madly in love with money and fame, and these buildings are, increasingly, media-grabbing machines for making money. And, however hard we find to admit it, this is what most of us want: the kind of money that can offer us greater freedom of choice, ever bigger homes, cars with more gadgets, as-seen-on-TV food, branded goods and just more stuff generally, which has to be a good thing, doesn't it?

Every society, it is said, gets the architecture it deserves, and so, I suppose, we should be cheering from the chilled-out roof-gardens of our zig-zag new apartment blocks as our cities begin to resemble these universal aspirations in three painfully fashionable dimensions. By the same logic, we will get bored with blobs, dissatisfied with towers in the shapes of carrots, cucumbers or prize marrows, just as, one day, we will get bored with the sheer amount of stuff cluttering up our homes. Does this matter? Nah. Just as the Romans might have said, 'Forget the Parthenon, the Pantheon's in', ensuing generations (cooler, richer, hipper and more into popular culture than we can even dream of) will simply build a fresh load of weird, computer-generated money-making stuff. And then get bored with that.

And yet, what if, just for a moment during Architecture Week, we stopped and thought seriously about the world we are making in concrete, glass and steel. What, for example, if we were to get bored with pure sensation and sheer novelty, and crave civility, good manners and intelligence in new architecture instead? What then?

If you look hard enough, you will discover many British architects and those working with them, whether as engineers or clients, including developers and local authorities, working thoughtfully, and sometimes lyrically, on the design of the places we live, love and work in. There is, too, a place for well-designed and even flamboyant towers as there always has been from the ziggurats of Mesopotamia and the spiral minaret at Samarra, to the highly charged temples of Cambodia, their frankly erotic counterparts in India, and on through medieval cathedrals, renaissance domes and Manhattan skyscrapers to Foster's unforgettable, if controversial, 30 St Mary Axe – aka 'the gherkin' – in the City of London today.

The design of buildings and the making of cities are difficult arts and uncertain skills, shot through with political ambition, economic juggling and cultural sensibilities. Neither is the stuff of in-out lists or here today, gone tomorrow chatter. Both require informed debate; an ever-deepening knowledge of history – architecture is a continuum – fewer publicity pranks and less willy-waving.

I have a feeling, though, that the sexed-up neophiliacs among us will disagree and go, all the way, for the blobs and pricks. For this week, anyway.

3 July 2004

JONATHAN JONES

Saatchi all at sea

Charles Saatchi is presumably a Thatcherite – although he reportedly avoided meeting the woman he and his brother helped elect – and Thatcherites don't have much sympathy for losers. But a loser is what, it seems, Saatchi has become. Since the man with more money than critical reservations opened the Saatchi Gallery in London's County Hall fourteen months ago, the myth of him as a silent and mysterious art-world power has disintegrated amid critical attacks on everything from his gallery's architecture to his supposedly catastrophic inflation of prices and reputations. The critic Robert Hughes recently denounced him in a lecture to the Royal Academy, and this week, writing in the *Guardian*, again lambasted a debased art world 'swollen with currency'. No prizes for guessing whose currency he meant.

All of this, however, pales beside the extraordinary national reaction to the fire that destroyed a substantial part of the Saatchi collection six weeks ago. The loss of Jake and Dinos Chapman's *Hell*, Tracey Emin's tent and more than 100 other Saatchi possessions was not, it's fair to say, seen by all as a tragedy. It was celebrated as a hilarious and deserved comeuppance for Saatchi and his bloated, over-praised, over-paid protégés.

I ask Saatchi how he felt about this. He seems the same as usual – shyly avuncular, reeking of cigarettes. He acknowledges that it was terrible, but I get the impression that he avoided the gloating press coverage. After the fire he chose not to brood but move on, he claims, seeking out new art. *Galleon and Other Stories* is the result. This show, opening on Tuesday at the Saatchi Gallery, seems to be Saatchi's attempt to prove to himself and others that he hasn't lost it, whatever it is. Fire or no fire, the Saatchi collection sails on, like Brian Griffiths's Viking ship of bric-a-brac, *Beneath the Stride of Giants*, which gives the exhibition its name.

Unfortunately, almost everything in the show is terrible. I can't see the Saatchi legend being refloated by Tilo Baumgarten's boring painting, or by the posters of Simon Bedwell that invent fictional cultural events of a purportedly surreal nature. There are three problems with Bedwell's posters: they are dismally lacking in contemporary frisson (one features the Spice Girls – who were they again?); they have been done before, and better, by Jeremy Deller; and the wood-panelled corridor in which they are displayed is a dismal exhibition space. Even the best thing in the show, Griffiths's ship, like an Egyptian solar boat made out of old furniture found under a railway arch, is lost in this odd space. It is made of wood and stands in a room with wooden walls and floor. It's just too much wood.

I could go on. Saatchi shows me Conrad Shawcross's wildly revolving armature with its light spinning round in a metal cage. Let it spin for ever for all anyone will ever care – it is ineffectual as art, like the kinetic monstrosities that were fashionable in the 1960s and today are occasionally wheeled out by museums as rusted academic curios. Most of the art being made now won't even have that much of an afterlife, because it doesn't reflect any particular school or idea. But if contemporary art isn't up to much, is this Saatchi's fault? Aren't his critics simply shooting the messenger?

Standing next to a spiralling wall-drawing made from 22,000 wishbones, Saatchi explains that he bought it from the artist's diploma show at the Royal College of Art. I don't see a fraction of the shows by new artists that he does, and I'm supposed to be doing this for a living. How much time does he spend on trips to obscure London dealers and group shows, I ask. A day a week?

That would be an unusually light week. Whatever the quality of the works Saatchi has bought in just these past few months, he has seen some very new and unpublicized things. When I got sent a catalogue for an exhibition a couple of months ago that claimed to tell the life of a child prodigy whose drawings and writings document a strange, sad existence, I thought about reviewing it but decided it looked unoriginal and overwrought. Saatchi not only went to see it, but bought the entire contents of the exhibition, which now fill a room at County Hall. It still seems unoriginal and overwrought, and now, apparently, has been exposed as a hoax. But you can't complain that Saatchi doesn't bring you the very latest thing, direct from the Nowhere Gallery in Nonentity Road.

This is how he has been distracting himself, he says, since the Momart fire. The thing that most upset him was the loss of the Chapmans' *Hell*, which he imagined would always be around, touring to one museum after another, but he finds it hard to talk about this. Instead he insists he's besotted with the newest art generation – they all look like rock stars, and he envies them. 'When I go to these shows I wish I was nineteen,' he says.

It seems hard to square the reality of Saatchi with the image of a cash-laden merchant of reputations whose money distorts our experience of art. The fact is that Saatchi – as the lumpen, childish quality of his new show emphasizes – spends his money diffusely rather than intensely, and his largesse is simply too indiscriminate for him actually to shape taste. He has apparently given up on his attempts to identify a single new mood in art after Britart.

I find it hard to get angry about Saatchi or the Saatchi effect. It's not as if anyone else is prepared to bankroll the British art boom that began in the late 1980s and is still going – despite all the evidence that no one is coming along worthy of comparison with Damien Hirst. Saatchi strikes me not as some manipulative monster, but a British eccentric. Here you have someone who chooses to spend large amounts of money on art that to 'most people' – the *Daily Mail* never tires of reminding us – is fraudulent rubbish. If he's naive, taken in by it, isn't that his problem? Piss-poor the new exhibition at County Hall may be, but personally I would rather give his youngsters a chance than have to pretend to like Sean Scully or Paula Rego or the other respectable artists who never con us or give us any fun.

It is possible he really is on the wane? It may be that his gallery won't last. If so, I suppose we will all feel smug. If Saatchi is a very British phenomenon, so is the loathing for him.

4 June 2004

POLLY TOYNBEE

Voting's too good for 'em

Politics is a curious business. Democracy is sacred and we go to war to bring its beneficence to benighted peoples. We celebrate as every decade it spreads further across a globe where a majority of humans now lives under its benign glow. How odd then that democracy's high priests and priestesses, the politicians, are treated with almost universal contempt. Democracy is holy, politics is lowly. 'The people' are noble, while those they elect are contemptible.

But sometimes when you go out there on the street to watch democracy in action, the nobility of 'the people' is a lot less striking than the patience and tolerance of their servants, the politicians. It is salutary to be reminded how much sheer pig-headed ignorance, nastiness, mean-spiritedness and rudeness politicians encounter every day. Trying to squeeze votes out of people who can't be bothered to inform themselves of the most basic facts is wearying work. 'Don't care, never vote, you're all the same, just in it for yourselves, what's in it for me and when are you going to fix my drainpipe?' Faced with some of that grudge, ordinary mortals might give 'the people' a stinging earful, but of course no politician dare.

Calling Labour HQ to find who (if anyone) was out pressing the flesh for next week's Euro elections, I was offered Jack Straw on a swing around Canterbury, Deal, Broadstairs and Ramsgate. It was not a red-carpet outing – the train offering just one sandwich and no water for him and his hungry entourage.

Out there at one end of Deal high street a flotilla of Labour grandees was waiting; cheering them up is the main success of this otherwise fairly unfruitful expedition. In this constituency with a 5,000 Labour majority, working our way down the main street, what do we find? It's an odd business, approaching total strangers with a jovial handshake, the sort of behaviour that marks out politicians as abnormal beings.

Outside Marks & Spencer, Straw stands on a milk crate to give a rousing hymn of praise for all that Europe has done for Deal. (If only he did more of that and less brandishing red lines and fighting the EU on the beaches – but that's another story.) Today he tells how, since D-day, the EU has brought peace and prosperity to all, how it is the engine of democracy from Spain to Estonia. See how its free trade delivers jobs? Remember how air travel cost an arm and a leg? Thank the EU for cheap fares, freeing up competition. 'Don't let the Tories throw it away!'

So what does he get back from this desultory crowd?

'You stand there talking about all the wonderful things in Europe, but when are you going to do something for us here at home?'

Daft, irrelevant, or what? The man is indignant that he gets less benefit because he's got £16,000 in the bank.

Next up, an angry man: 'Why am I paying £77 a month on council tax, worked all my life and got nothing for it?'

Because it's a Tory council that put it up 9.7 per cent this year, but he's still going to vote Tory anyway.

'Why isn't the police station here open full time?' calls the next man. Not one voice takes up the European theme.

Local MP Gwyn Prosser works the crowd, picking up complaints. 'Why hasn't the council fixed my fence?' says a man who claims he always voted Labour, but now he's going to vote BNP. Why? 'Well, Europe. I don't agree with one big state, not at all. England for the English.'

His MP takes him on: 'Vote for that xenophobic, fascist party?'

Turns out the man's a liar. Labour records show he never voted at all last time and he has never been Labour. But the people are always right, free to lie through their teeth, unlike their leaders.

Next man up tells me, 'They give asylum seekers £160 a week for a single bloke.'

'No, they don't,' says the MP, but no one believes him.

Prod them a bit and most here are anti-European. 'Europe' has become a euphemism for 'asylum', as Michael Howard well knows, bleeding the two together wickedly. In vain, the MP quotes latest asylum figures: a year ago seventy a day claimed asylum in Dover; now it is less than seven. But no one believes figures, they just know. Except they don't. In a haze, many confuse the EU constitution and the euro; many think they're voting on these next week.

But then a group of sixth-form girls bear down on him for the only good debate of the day. Angry about Iraq, voices are raised and fingers prod the air: 'You bombed all those people just to capture one man. Why? If we had bombs falling on us we'd be, like, oh-my-God, as if it was the end of the world. Yet we do it to them!'

On the street you get views never heard on television: 'I was all for Iraq at first, but not any more.' Why not? 'It's the shocking way they behave. Disgusting! They needed Saddam to keep them in order. They deserved him. You don't see Iraqis working to put their country back together, just hanging around the streets.' Her husband adds, 'In their nightgowns, too!'

There follows a long and incomprehensibly meaningless visit to a part-EU-funded business centre, where the foreign secretary listens for half an hour to the marketing plans of a new firm making plastic and cardboard novelty covers, decorated in Scooby Doo or Man United designs, for wall switches for kids' bedrooms. Shortly afterwards, he vanishes briefly, I assume for a comfort break, but it turns out he's taking a call on his mobile from Colin Powell about the progress of the UN resolution on Iraq. But he's back to thank them for a couple of free Blackburn Rovers light-switch covers.

That's a day in the life of democracy, not much sublime and a lot of ridiculous. A busy foreign secretary in the middle of a war goes out to listen to complaints about fences and persuade the wretchedly indifferent to vote pro-European. Politicians are the people who do democracy, day in, day out. And day in, day out they are kicked in the teeth for it. Too often we commentators sit in lofty judgement, saying Labour should do this or that, raise their game, lift their sights, be ambitious, be brave. But we are accountable to no one, just perusing polls, while they have to navigate seas of actual voters who may make scant sense, who vote on whim or through habit with prejudices unmitigated by fact, impervious to evidence.

Politicians are despised partly for their virtues – their willingness to listen and explain anything to anyone, however rude. Their need for votes smacks of a salesman's craven sucking-up, when often voters deserve a good wigging. What about the democratic responsibilities that go with rights? Ask not what your country can do for you ... Stop whingeing, start thinking. Get informed. Make an effort. The country's future is in your hands, not politicians'. At least get out there and goddam vote, which quite a few said they wouldn't. One small step towards making citizens take democracy more seriously would be to oblige them all to vote.

3 August 2004

CHRISTOPHER TWIGG

The Poet Speaks of Mobile Phones

> Foul little plastic implement of deafness and dissociation
> strangler
> with invisible cheesewires
> screwing the air into little balls
> fucker-up of ley lines
> your bleep is the end of poetry
> your buzz is worse than the bite of a dinosaur
> pterodactyl get out of my railway carriage
> Mobile phone you don't know which way is north or south
> your mouth full of rotten teeth smells of 10-day-old oranges
> you are destroying my arteries
> Weeper of toxicity
> Starver of light to underwater plants
> When will you split in half?
> How many heads have you?

You cannot migrate or take part in any rituals
and yet you outnumber the stars in the Milky Way
I was given one once I used it as a trowel
It took two thousand years to disintegrate
I open your lid
and find your head full of maggots
wriggling like the contents of a fisherman's box
You carry on after car crashes
II Angels have been getting tangled in your invisible dragnets
Unfriendly to dolphins you have de-horned the moon
In Wales your masts take up the choicest hilltops
while dead sheep and lambs rot in the farmyards
too heavy to bury –
you separate the head from the body
To use you once is equivalent to a bad LSD trip
The sparrows are departed
leaving no addresses
millions of Vodafones have come in their place –
They loiter evilly by the drinking fountains
Unloveable dildos
Wands incapable of transformations!
You violate the integrity of spaces!
Along with your brother the television
you have destroyed my imagination
made natural telepathy a blessing not for our lifetimes
Children should not know of you
and the time of your existence be perceived
as a shameful period on earth.

6 July 2004

TED WRAGG

Class betrayal

Here's a spelling test. Two tricky words. First word: 'desiccated'. Ah, a catch. One s, two c's. It's d-e-s-i-c-c-a-t-e-d. Correct. Second tricky word: 'Labour', as in Labour education policy. Easy peasy. It's C-o-n-s-e-r-v-a-t-i-v-e. Brilliant. Go to the top of the SATS league.

For years I thought ABA was shorthand for what in music is known as 'sonata form'. The sonata begins with A, an opening melody, 'the statement'; then goes on to B, a fresh melody, 'the fantasia'; before returning to A, the first melody, 'the restatement'. Now I realize ABA is really an acronym for government education policy. Tony Blair makes a statement. It is followed by a right-wing fantasia, invented by him and his adviser Andrew Adonis, a former journalist (though their combined intelligence about education could be distilled on to the back of a postage stamp, leaving enough room for the text of 'Roll Out the Barrel'). Finally it is hammered through parliament, against all opposition – the restatement.

The latest right-wing wheeze to emanate from ABA (the Adonis–Blair Axis), is the proposal of a two-tier schooling system. A few new swish academies will select pupils and glow in the dark, while beneath them festers the morass of bogstandard schools. It seems virtually identical, apart from minor detail, to the grant-maintained school plus city technology college system dreamed up by the Conservatives in 1988. Some of these new super academies will be run by the posher public schools, a hilarious notion if you think about it. A former public school head once told me he was surprised to discover, on his arrival, that the school employed someone to look after the ducks. Another similar school has 'hunting' on the curriculum. Perhaps ABA (Andrew Bloody Adonis) sees these as just the features needed to bring a bit of style to inner-city comprehensives.

Apparently the reason for the blatant rehash of this old Tory dystopia (the utopia of free choice for all, that goes sour when only a lucky minority get it) is to appease middle-class voters. They are believed to want a two-tier system: nice schools for themselves, crapholes for the scruffy peasants of the scumbag class. Yet Labour's greatest success in education has been improving things for the many, not the few – taking children out of poverty, giving money for books and buildings to bogstandard schools, not just to a chosen elite.

So what will happen to this neat Labour–Tory scheme? Ignore heroic talk about backbench revolt and blood on the carpet. It is pure cant. We saw all that malarkey during the top-up fees fiasco. A few brave souls will indeed dissent. Unfortunately, they will be outnumbered by the crawlers, cowards, wimps, chancers and lick-spittles, who threaten rebellion and then fade quietly away at the vote. Whips will threaten to sever vitals, reveal secret sex lives, ruin careers. Some MPs will secure a free ballpoint pen for all their constituents and then capitulate. Don't hold your breath while awaiting a revolution.

Which great work of literature best sums up this sad farce? *Brave New World* or *Nineteen Eighty-Four*, in which the oppressed eventually became fervent supporters of the very regime they once detested? No. The best parallel comes from the end of a story by A. A. Milne, writing about what he called 'that enchanted place on the top of the Forest', but where Christopher Robin and Pooh have been displaced by Tony Blair and ABA (Andrew 'Bear' Adonis).

'Pooh,' said Christopher Robin earnestly, 'if I … if I'm not quite …' He stopped and tried again. 'Pooh, *whatever* happens, you *will* understand, won't you?'

'Understand what?'

'Oh, nothing.' He laughed and jumped to his feet. 'Come on!'

'Where?' said Pooh.

'Anywhere,' said Christopher Robin.

So they went off together. But wherever they go, and whatever happens to them on the way, in that enchanted place on the top of the Forest, a little boy and his Bear will always be playing.

And that, in a nutshell, explains the origination of government education policy in the twenty-first century.